The Soviet Economy
on the
Brink of Reform

The Soviet Economy on the Brink of Reform

Essays in Honor of Alec Nove

Edited by

Peter Wiles

London School of Economics and Political Science

Boston
UNWIN HYMAN
London   Sydney   Wellington

Allen & Unwin, Inc.,
8 Winchester Place, Winchester, Mass. 01890, USA

Published by the
Academic Division of
Unwin Hyman Ltd
15/17 Broadwick Street, London W1V 1FP, UK

Allen & Unwin (Australia) Ltd,
8 Napier Street, North Sydney, NSW 2060, Australia

Allen & Unwin (New Zealand) Ltd in association with the
Port Nicholson Press Ltd,
60 Cambridge Terrace, Wellington, New Zealand

First published in 1988

Library of Congress Cataloging-in-Publication Data
  The Soviet Economy on the Brink of Reform
Includes index.
1. Central planning—Soviet Union. 2. Soviet Union— Economic Policy—
1917– . 3. Saving and investment—Soviet Union. 4. Nove, Alec, I. Nove,
Alec. II. Wiles, Peter John De la Fosse.
HC335.C626 1988   338.947   87–19514
ISBN 0–04–335063–1 (alk. paper)

British Library Cataloguing in Publication Data
  The Soviet Economy on the Brink of Reform
    essays in honor of Alec Nove.
1. Investments————Government policy————Soviet Union————History
————20th century
I. Wiles, P. J. D. II. Nove, Alec
332.6'7252'0947   HG1572
ISBN 0–04–335063–1

Typeset in 10 on 12 point Ehrhardt by Columns of Reading
and printed in Great Britain by Billing and Sons Ltd,
London and Worcester.

Contents

List of Contributors

Richard B. Day   *Professor of Political Science, University of Toronto in Mississauga*

Frank A. Durgin   *Professor of Economics, University of Southern Maine*

Janice Giffen   *Consultant and Trainer in Project Planning Techniques for Developing Countries and Director of Studies (The Gambia) for the Université Cooperative Internationale*

Gregory Grossman   *Professor of Economics, University of California, Berkeley*

Philip Hanson   *Professor of Soviet Economics, University of Birmingham*

Lev Navrozov   *Center for the Survival of Western Democracies*

J. Rostowski and P. Auerbach   *Senior Lecturers of Economics and Politics, Kingston Polytechnic*

Karl-Eugen Wädekin   *Emeritus Professor of International and East European Agrarian Policies, University of Giessen, FRG*

Peter Wiles   *Professor of Economics, London School of Economics and Political Science*

Preface

Among scholars, Alec Nove is the least scholarly and (so?) the most productive and effective. 'Least scholarly'? I do not mean that he is inaccurate, that he gives false references, or reasons sloppily—but rather that 'scholarly' is not necessarily a word of high praise. Alec Nove is able to pick out what is important whether it is a blinding novelty or a simple piece of ancient wisdom; pleased at all times to cut the cackle and delighted to see through whole cloud-capped superstructures of theory as irrelevant, or even wrong in their own terms. He has touched nothing he did not adorn, and he has touched a great deal.

This is meant to be an encomium not a memoir. But there are important personal habits that memoirs may miss. He has no study in his own house, nor any evident need for a vast personal library. On the contrary, this least scholarly of men girdles the earth with the latest copy of *Ekonomika i organizatsia promyshlennogo proizvodstva* in his brief case, and writes his articles and books on the backs of travel agents' itineraries.

The product is, to repeat, not inaccurate or sloppy—merely a witness to what talent and energy can accomplish.

Many Festschriften are collections of 'tributes,' not essays on the subject matter. Such works express the writers' feelings, but are not read. In the end, they do little honor. Personal they may be, but the publisher, who, of necessity, is also a major contributor, bears the consequences. Here then, Alec, are included essays by younger people who know you better than you know them, but have something of importance to say. Though Poland, Chile and British Rail are missing we claim to have adequately covered your range. In following this principle of selection, we intend a greater honor than that conveyed by the 'personal' tribute: that of placing before you, in gratitude and admiration, a work that we hope will actually be read, quoted and used.

Peter Wiles

The Soviet Economy
on the
Brink of Reform

1 *Leon Trotsky on the Dialectics of Democratic Control*

RICHARD B. DAY

1 Introduction

In *The Economics of Feasible Socialism* Alec Nove observes that 'Marx had little to say about the economics of socialism, and . . . the little he did say was either irrelevant or directly misleading.'[1] This hiatus in Marx's writing was a consequence of his methodology. Qualitative change was to involve the intervention of human subjectivity in overcoming the blind forces of the capitalist market, and the results could not be completely predetermined. In *The Critique of the Gotha Program* and brief remarks elsewhere Marx did offer some general thoughts regarding the future society, but beyond that he could not go. To attempt more would be simply to build 'castles in the air' of the type associated in *The Communist Manifesto* with such 'utopians' as St Simon, Fourier and Owen. The result of Marx's reticence was that the Bolsheviks seized power in 1917 with no real theory of the transition period.

In the years prior to the Revolution virtually no thought had been given to questions of economic organization, while the most ambitious theoretical works that did eventually appear were 'liquidationist' in character. Bukharin's *Economics of the Transition Period*, for example, foretold the end of political economy following abolition of the market and commodity production;[2] and Preobrazhensky agreed in his monetary writings that capitalist categories would rapidly become superfluous in a society undertaking conscious planning.[3] In the realm of political theory a similar situation prevailed. In *State and Revolution* Lenin predicted that the dictatorship of the proletariat would 'begin to wither away immediately after its victory': a society free of class antagonisms would have no further need for a state apparatus.[4] Politics would be replaced gradually by authentic public administration, meaning administration *by* the associated producers. 'We ourselves,' Lenin promised, 'the workers, will organize large-scale production . . . we will reduce the role of state officials to that of simply carrying out our instructions as responsible, revocable, modestly paid "foremen and accountants" . . . Such a beginning . . . will of itself lead to the gradual "withering away" of all bureaucracy . . .'[5]

Marx had expected the transcendence of commodity production and the state to result from a condition of economic abundance in which there would no longer be a need for political choice in the social allocation of scarce resources. More recently, Soviet writers have been forced to come to terms

1

with scarcity and to recognize in the division of labor a necessary means for increasing productivity. E. G. Liberman has acknowledged that a continuing social division of labor between state enterprises requires mediation not only through state planning, but also through 'commodity circulation and monetary relations.' Socialist production, according to Liberman, must inevitably be based upon 'a profound social and technological division of labor.'[6] In *The Scientific Management of Society* V. G. Afanasyev describes the human consequences of this new awareness. In his view 'a group of workers is unthinkable . . . without each member being assigned a definite place and function . . . Division of labor and establishment of certain proportions between various spheres of production are necessary in any society . . .'[7] Declaring that administrative relations will also exist 'as long as human society endures,'[8] Afanasyev makes it very clear that in current Soviet thinking public administration means administration *of* the public: 'Direct control is the job of a large group of professional managers.'[9] Socialism means, above all else, a scientifically controlled society; and 'control of society emerges as *control of people*.'[10]

Agreeing that scarcity is, and will remain, a fact of social life, Alec Nove would have no difficulty in accepting the continuing need for a social division of labor. Nove would add, however, that it is not the division of labor which accounts for the bureaucratic authoritarianism of modern Soviet planning; rather the fault lies with Marx's original error in predicting the end of scarcity. To posit the end of the economic problem is not merely utopian; Nove believes it is positively harmful in the sense that it deprives free political and economic choice of any theoretical legitimacy.

> The belief that under socialism there would be unanimity is not just false; the only action it can give rise to is the *eradication of dissent*, the *imposition* of 'unanimity'. Similarly, the utopian view that power would not be abused, or that there would indeed *be* no power (no state, no need for bodies to mediate between individuals, groups and society, no function for specialists in management of any kind), actively prevents consideration of necessary means to prevent the abuse of (necessary) power, or of the institutional arrangements which would enlarge the area of genuine mass participation in decision-making.[11]

In the name of 'feasible socialism,' with real elements of workers' participation, Nove calls for rejection of the utopian aspects of Marxism and recognition of the inescapable need for political and economic choices to be made by all members of society. This type of socialism would entail a planned market together with pluralist political institutions, a model which currently enjoys overwhelming support amongst East European critics of Stalinism. In this essay I shall suggest that it is not a Marxist commitment which stands in the way of 'feasible socialism,' but rather the difficulties of applying Marx's method of analysis. This theme will be developed by analyzing early Soviet debates concerning the economic character of the transitional society and its corresponding political institutions. At the close of *The Economics of Feasible Socialism* Alec Nove expresses his hope to provoke further thought on these matters. My own hope will be to provide a worthy response to a thoughtful challenge.

2 Lenin on the Dialectics of a Transitional Economy

The problem of how best to articulate politics with economics became apparent at the very outset of the Russian Revolution. E. H. Carr describes the 'potential antithesis' which quickly emerged between the majority of Bolsheviks, who favoured *state control* of the economy, and the anarchists and syndicalists, who demanded instead *workers' control*.[12] Use of the term 'antithesis' is suggestive in this context, although not in quite the sense Carr intended. In Lenin's writings of the time, workers' control and state control were not considered to be mutually exclusive; on the contrary, Lenin believed they constituted a dialectical unity of opposites. Referring to the transitional economy as one of 'state capitalism,' Lenin foresaw a combination of the socialist state with capitalist accounting techniques, the beginnings of a plan with continuation of the market, and private ownership of most means of industrial production with close scrutiny on the part of the workers.

The type of system envisaged by Lenin would have required control to be exercised both from above and from below. From above, managerial decisions were to be controlled through the banking system, which the socialist state would take over '*ready-made* from capitalism.' The result would be 'country-wide *book-keeping*, country-wide *accounting* of the production and distribution of goods.' Tracking the movement of commodities throughout the economy, the banks would represent 'something in the nature of the *skeleton* of socialist society.'[13] At the same time, a parallel system of control would operate from below: enterprise owners and bourgeois 'specialists' would continue to make day-to-day production decisions, but their choices would be subject to review by workers and by their elected representatives on factory committees.

When Lenin's critics expressed disapproval of the role given to capitalists and other officials of the old regime, he invariably replied by emphasizing that the most crucial need was to reconcile authority with autonomy. Even in *State and Revolution*, his most anti-authoritarian essay, he insisted that 'authority and autonomy are relative terms,' the one presupposing the other as the state began to wither away.[14] Engels had long ago referred to revolution as 'the most authoritarian thing there is,' and Lenin was perfectly conscious of the fact that modern industry required the 'planned co-operation of many people.'[15] In *The Immediate Tasks of the Soviet Government* he allowed for no misunderstanding of this issue: '*unquestioning subordination* to a single will is absolutely necessary for the success of processes organized on the pattern of large-scale machine industry.'[16] The problem was to render both subordination and power democratic; in other words, to find an economic expression for the organizational principle of democratic centralism.

On the democratic side, Lenin did not doubt for a moment that finance-capitalist accounting techniques would make decision-making accessible to every literate worker. But he also realized that workers' control could not simply be 'introduced'; instead a process was involved, a period of learning on the part of the previously disadvantaged. When Bukharin and the 'Left Communists' disputed this need to combine discipline with self-determination, Lenin replied that 'it is *impossible* to create or introduce socialism *without learning* from the organizers of the trusts. For socialism is . . . the assimilation and application . . . of what has been created by the trusts.'[17] On this basis, Lenin distinguished between 'confiscation' and 'socialization'; the former involved nothing more than the physical seizure of property, the latter implied learning how to administer it, or in Lenin's words, how to 'calculate and distribute properly.'[18] By calling for mere 'confiscation' the 'Left Communists,' according to Lenin, were denying the very need for a transitional, mixed economy. 'But what,' he demanded, 'does the word "transition" mean? Does it not mean . . . that the present system contains elements, particles, pieces of *both* capitalism *and* socialism?'[19]

With respect to centralism, the other element of 'state capitalism,' Lenin's hopes were soon frustrated. The banking system disintegrated with continuing currency inflation; and other forms of organization had to be found, beginning with integration of the factory committees into the more centralized structures of the trade unions. By the end of 1917 the role originally assigned to the banks was assumed by Vesenkha, a new Supreme Council of the National Economy, with its various departments (*glavki*) to supervise the different branches of industry. Even at this stage, however, the principles enunciated by Lenin remained formally intact. The new central organ was accompanied by development of a network of local economic councils, some of which were simply the earlier organs of workers' control functioning under a new name. This balance between central and local authority remained in effect until the civil war began in 1918, causing the Revolution to enter upon its next stage of comprehensive nationalization and centralization, eventually resulting in the system known as War Communism.

Lenin's commitment to diversified economic forms underlies the need for caution in analyzing the connections between Marxist theory and revolutionary practice. Lenin's differences with the Left Communists were rooted not in ultimate theoretical commitments, but in method. Lenin's method was that of a Marxist dialectician: 'Dialectics,' he believed, 'calls for a many-sided investigation into a given social phenomenon in its development and [only then] for the external and seeming to be reduced to the fundamental motive forces, to the development of the class struggle.'[20] Seeing the 'essence of dialectics'[21] in the unity of opposites, Lenin could not for a moment even imagine the possibility of a direct 'leap' into a nonmarket economy. Soviet workers, he pointed out, had inherited a social formation which included a multiplicity of distinct modes of production: among these were the patriarchal mode, small commodity production, private capitalism, state capitalism and socialism.[22] This contradictory unity of backward and advanced features resulted from the law of 'uneven development' and was reflected in class structure. Thus poor peasants coexisted with *kulaks*, backward workers with the proletarian vanguard, and potentially cooperative capitalists with potential counter-revolutionaries. Neither Russian capitalism nor capitalism in general constituted a pure form: internal combinations differed from country to country depending upon unique historical circumstances. Lenin concluded that the specific features of the transitional society would likewise vary:

> All nations will arrive at socialism ... but all will not do so in exactly the same way; each will contribute something of its own to some form of democracy, to some variety of the dictatorship of the proletariat, to the varying rate of socialist transformation in the different aspects of social life.[23]

In *The Economics of Feasible Socialism* Alec Nove quite properly warns against the danger of a more literal interpretation of some of Marx's writings. Discussing Bettleheim's reference to *The Critique of the Gotha Program*, Nove comments that Bettleheim 'is right in ascribing to Marx and Engels the view that, when socialism wins, when the workers take hold of the means of production, "even at the beginning there would be neither commodities, nor value, nor money, nor consequently, prices and wages".'[24] To say that this 'fundamentalist' interpretation of Marx is right, however, is to imply that Lenin was mistaken in his disagreement with the Left Communists and that Bukharin was more orthodox, for Bukharin's approach differed little from Bettleheim's. How might this dilemma be resolved?

The fact is that in several of his works Marx was far more prudent than in certain sections of *The Critique of the Gotha Program*. Frequently, he pointed out that the revolutionary struggle would follow different paths from country to country (in some circumstances even allowing for an electoral victory); and as an economic historian he would scarcely have been so utopian as to expect a direct 'leap' from Russia's combination of semifeudal and modern conditions into a socialist society of comprehensive planning. In volume 3 of *Capital* he drew a clear distinction between the common features of any social formation and the 'infinite variations' of their particular expression:

> It is always the direct relationship of the owners of the conditions of production to the direct producers—a relation always naturally corresponding to a definite stage in the development of the methods of labour and

thereby its social productivity—which reveals the innermost secret, the hidden basis of the entire social structure, and with it the political form of the relation of sovereignty and dependence, in short, the corresponding specific form of the state. This does not prevent the same economic basis—the same from the standpoint of its main conditions—due to innumerable different empirical circumstances, natural environment, racial relations, external historical influences, etc., from showing infinite variations and gradations in appearance, which can be ascertained only by analysis of the empirically given circumstances.[25]

The implications of this remark are clear: a capitalist mode of production determines the existence of some form of capitalist state; a socialist mode of production presupposes a socialist state; but the specific forms of each cannot be universally predetermined in accordance with a single pattern. Lenin simply carried the logic of this argument one step further, inferring that an internally contradictory economic system, one combining several modes of production, could not be artificially compressed into a 'pure' socialist mold. A theoretical commitment to eventual planning did not justify a practical insensitivity to the necessities dictated by Soviet Russia's 'empirically given circumstances.' Lenin considered Bukharin's literal interpretation of Marx to be just as dangerous as Nove considers Bettleheim's to be—and for exactly the same reasons.

3 The Alternative Theory of the NonDialectical 'Leap'

Having traced the origins of Lenin's reasoning, let us now consider more closely the most important rival points of view. In the case of Evgeny Preobrazhensky, the leading party spokesman on monetary theory, it was clear that *The Critique of the Gotha Program* exerted a decisive influence. Marx had predicted the replacement of money by labor certificates, paid out to workers in proportion to their contribution of labor to the social product. The right of the producers was to be 'proportional to the labor they supply.' Equality was to consist in the fact that 'measurement is made with an equal standard, labor.'[26] Marx had demystified the market in theory, showing that commodity relations are actually disguised relations between men and their labor; and Preobrazhensky argued that the collapse of the Soviet currency, together with recourse to rationing in place of money wages, pointed the way towards an immediately impending planned, 'natural' economy.

The 'natural' economy would require norms of pay to be determined in labor values by the state and the trade unions. Consumer goods would be distributed in accordance with the number of hours recorded in each worker's labor book, the latter substituting for Marx's 'certificates.' Representing the major portion of the worker's income, these wages in kind would include a substantial component of universal services, such as the provision of housing, food in factory canteens, education, health services, transport, heating, lighting, and so on. To the extent that the monetary system would continue to function as it withered away, Preobrazhensky relegated it to the status of a hidden taxation mechanism. Those who were foolish enough to accept a depreciating paper currency in exchange for real values, primarily the peasants and private merchants, in reality would promote the final liquidation of capitalism by contributing to 'primitive socialist accumulation.'

One obvious difficulty with this argument was that Marx had expected a 'natural' economy to result from abundance, permitting production for use rather than for sale. It is true that he thought labor accounting might be instituted even in the first phase of communist society, 'just as it *emerges* from capitalist society,'[27] and, in that respect, Preobrazhensky (like Bettelheim) was faithful to the letter of the text. But Preobrazhensky's analogy was also flawed in another respect: Marx had thought that 'united action, of the leading civilized countries at least,' would be 'one of the first conditions for the emancipation of the proletariat.'[28] The Revolution was to come first in mature capitalist societies, where the productive potential for eventually surmounting scarcity would already be coming into existence. Caught up in the euphoria of revolution and civil war, Preobrazhensky rationalized the impoverished content of Russian reality by enveloping it in the economic forms of future abundance. He forgot another passage in Marx's text, one closer in spirit to Lenin's approach, which warned that the new society would inevitably be 'stamped with the birthmarks of the old society from whose womb it emerges.'[29]

Bukharin's interpretation of these issues was inspired by a similar preoccupation with form over content. When Bukharin used the term 'state capitalism' he had in mind not Lenin's concept of a mixed transitional economy, but the wholly 'monistic' and internally integrated system of the imperialist war economies. In Europe he saw capitalism's organizational tendencies reaching their logical limit, or 'the inclusion of absolutely everything within the sphere of state regulation.'[30] A new system of 'collective capitalism' appeared to have arisen, involving subordination of all particular capitalist interests to the universal reason of the imperialist state.[31] This analysis suggested that the proletarian dictatorship must be no less universal in scope. 'Formally,' Bukharin argued, it would be 'similar to that of the epoch of bourgeois dictatorship, meaning that it will be state capitalism *turned inside out*, or state capitalism *dialectically converted into its own opposite.*'[32]

Growing impatient with such abstract analogies, Lenin remarked that Bukharin had in fact failed to 'pose the relation between theory and practice dialectically.'[33] Not only had he overlooked the internal contradictions of Soviet society, but he had done so on the basis of an exaggerated account of imperialism's internal harmony. The theory of 'organized' capitalism forgot the coexistence of monopoly with competition, or the simultaneous process of organization and disorganization, which arose from the law of 'uneven development' and prevented any hope of social 'monism.' Bukharin's entire analysis moved on the level of abstract, pure forms, whereas Lenin believed 'The very concept of purity indicates a certain narrowness, a one-sidedness of human cognition, which cannot embrace an object in all its totality and complexity.'[34] This methodological difference inevitably led to different political conclusions: Lenin thought the Soviet state would be an impure state, 'a workers' and peasants' state,' which by virtue of its dual character would always contain the risk of bureaucratic degeneration.[35] 'Our Party Programme,' Lenin exclaimed in 1920, 'a document which [Bukharin] knows very well, shows that ours is a workers' state *with a bureaucratic twist to it.*'[36]

Throughout the next two decades, Trotsky would develop Lenin's warning against the 'bureaucratic twist' in intricate detail, attributing the triumph of the Stalinist regime to its ability to play off one class against another in conditions of scarcity and backwardness. At the time when Lenin made this remark, however, Trotsky seemed to be as unaware of the danger as Bukharin. In 1920 the Party was divided by an impassioned debate over the role of the trade unions. Lenin insisted upon the need to 'protect the workers from their state';[37] Trotsky and Bukharin thought the trade unions must be 'statified' and subordinated to strict discipline. In the case of Bukharin the rationale for this attitude was not difficult to find. The proletarian state was to aspire to the same organizational universality as its capitalist predecessor:

> The 'statification' of the trade unions and the genuine statification of all proletarian mass organizations results from the innermost logic of the transformation process. Even the smallest cells of the workers' apparatus must be integrated into the general organizational process, which is directed and led according to plan by the collective reason of the working class. The collective reason of the working class, in turn, is materially embodied in its highest and most universal organization—in its state apparatus.[38]

4 Trotsky on the Dialectics of War Communism

Occurring at the height of War Communism, the dispute over the trade unions threatened to eliminate the final vestige of workers' control. In such works as *Terrorism and Communism* Trotsky provided good reason for thinking that he and Bukharin were of one mind. Workers were to be subject to labor conscription, assigned to 'shock work' in the most critical sectors of a disintegrating economy, and severely punished for refusing to obey. A system of labor planning was to be developed, in which the trade unions would 'mobilize' and 'militarize' their members, adopting the same rights 'as have previously been exercised only by a military organization.'[39] Instead of defending the workers they were 'to distribute, to group, to fasten separate groups and separate categories of workers and individual proletarians to the place where they are needed by the state, by socialism.'[40] Plans were to be enforced by 'a planned, systematic, steady and stern struggle with labor desertion, in particular by publishing a list of labor deserters and their internment in concentration camps.'[41]

In view of such extreme language, there can be little wonder that Trotsky alienated most trade union leaders and provoked the antipathy of later historians. In *The Conscience of the Revolution* Robert V. Daniels refers to the War Commissar as 'the most ardent of all centralizers to appear during the first decade of the Soviet regime.'[42] Leszek Kolakowski's judgement in *Main Currents of Marxism* is far less restrained:

> The state of the proletarian dictatorship is depicted by Trotsky as a huge permanent concentration camp in which the government exercises absolute power over every aspect of the citizens' lives and in particular decides how much work they shall do, of what kind and in what places. Individuals are nothing but labour units. Compulsion is universal, and any organization that is not part of the state must be its enemy, thus the enemy of the proletariat. All this, of course, is in the name of an ideal realm of freedom, the advent of which is expected after an indefinite lapse of historical time. Trotsky, we may say, provided a perfect expression of socialist principles as understood by the Bolsheviks.[43]

Had the rhetoric of Trotsky's pronouncements not been mistaken for their substance, his critics might have realized that far more was at issue than appeared on the surface. By using the term 'production union' Trotsky made an important distinction between prerevolutionary unions, whose function was to haggle over wages, and the new Soviet unions, which were at one and the same time both to *implement* and also to help *define* economic policy. Because the traditional class struggle would no longer be waged within Soviet enterprises, Trotsky believed a 'production union' might include all personnel, 'from the most unskilled worker right up to the most skilled engineer.'[44] Going beyond the enterprise level, he foresaw a 'coalescence' (*srashchivanie*) of the new unions with planning and administrative personnel in all state bodies. On several occasions he proposed that from one-third to one-half of the members of Vesenkha and the Supreme Council of Trade Unions should sit on both councils, and that the two councils should sit jointly when resolving all major questions. Through a 'unification of administrative and union organs' workers' representatives were to share responsibility for policy formation in every branch of production.[45]

There is no denying that one purpose of these measures was to eliminate the problem of 'shop narrowness,' or the inclination of some unionists not to see beyond their own enterprise or even their own shop. Nor can there be any doubt that Trotsky was prepared to be forceful in achieving his ends, threatening his opponents with an administrative 'shake-up.' Threats of this sort were issued, however, with a larger purpose in mind. It is no exaggeration to say what Trotsky was in fact dealing with was the same problem Lenin had wrestled with in *State and Revolution*, namely, the need to reconcile authority with autonomy. If working-class representatives shared the responsibility for administrative decisions, then Trotsky reasoned that administration of the workers would become self-administration. According to this argument, the 'statification' of the unions would occur simultaneously with the 'workerization' (*orabochenie*) of the state.[46] The two processes were dialectically interconnected, and their concrete outcome could not be foretold in advance. In Trotsky's words: 'The degree and manner of applying democratic methods must be decided in accordance with objective circumstances.'[47] The most immediate need of the working class was material security. Once that had been ensured 'production democracy' could broaden and assume new forms of expression:

> In those unions where an internal labor upsurge has already occurred on the basis of restoration of the branch of industry in question, we can and must apply more broadly the methods of *workers' democracy*, including a systematic discussion at general mass meetings of all economic-production measures, elections to a whole series of economic-administrative posts, uniting these posts with a definite position within the production organization, and so on and so forth.[48]

A cynical interpretation of Trotsky's motives would find their rationale in co-option. Before indulging such suspicions, however, it is important to compare these comments on the unions with what he was saying at the same time regarding relations between the center and the localities. In this context, too, the principal theme of his writings and speeches in 1920 was that centralization presupposed decentralization, the one being understood as the dialectical counterpart of the other. Indeed, the first signs of disagreement between Lenin and Trotsky were not related to the trade union debate, but to Lenin's fear that Trotsky's excessive emphasis upon local responsibilities might encourage *oblastnichestvo*, or localism, at the expense of the central authorities. This is an aspect of the War Communist period which historians have not previously explored.

In his famous theses on labor conscription, issued in December 1919, Trotsky is generally thought to have embarked upon a ruthless campaign for authoritarian centralism. But a major purpose of the theses was to create a local militia system, in which military and economic officials would closely collaborate in a pattern similar to the relation between unionists and administrators. Attributing the prevailing economic chaos to a contradictory combination of 'fragments' of the past with 'embryos' of the future, the sixth thesis declared that it was impossible even to contemplate 'a fully centralized economy on a nation-wide scale.'[49] In the seventh thesis Trotsky made his intentions still more explicit:

The art of the state power of the proletariat must consist not simply in choking off local initiative in the name of a schematicized state-economic plan, but on the contrary, in giving every possible support to local initiative, in nourishing it in terms of ideas, technically and materially, in providing it with the necessary corrections, and in modifying the general state plan itself in accordance with the tempo and extent of development of the individual economic centers throughout the territory of the country.[50]

The eighth thesis added that labor conscription was not an abstract formula, to be dictated from above, but must be implemented with a strict view to local conditions and requirements:

... the universal labor obligation must not under any circumstances be understood as an abstract labor obligation, whereby certain age groups are entirely mobilized and distributed according to a schematicized economic plan ... On the contrary, the task is one of finding support for labor conscription in regional and community labor bonds, habits and customs, with the basis for labor conscription being located in certain territorial-production districts, defined in terms of natural-historical conditions of life and production.[51]

These comments clearly demonstrate that Trotsky was by no means planning to transform the economy into a 'huge permanent concentration camp' in the name of an ideal realm of freedom—as Kolakowski would have us believe—but was instead carefully addressing present problems on the basis of present needs and possibilities. In all of his proposals the objective was to surmount the superficial incompatibility of state control and workers' control, or of central and local authority, and to do so through the conscious dialectical integration of opposing tendencies.

A trip to the Urals early in 1920 dramatically reinforced Trotsky's sense of urgency. In February he communicated to Lenin his dismay upon finding that everything in the provinces was 'disorganized.' In one Urals *guberniya*, he complained, 'people are being given oats instead of wheat, in a neighboring *guberniya* the horses are being fed wheat ... Greater idiocy in the name of centralism is impossible to imagine.'[52] Lenin responded: 'With reference to the *oblast* centers there is need for more careful thought in order not to fall into *oblastnichestvo*.'[53] In documents prepared for the Ninth Party Congress Trotsky again emphasized the need for local coordination in order to avoid cross-hauls on overburdened railways. On this occasion he made a more specific proposal, recommending enforcement of an earlier decision by the All-Russian Central Executive Committee (VTsIK) to divide industry into three categories: the first would include trustified enterprises, managed from the center and controlled in the localities; the second group would comprise nontrustified enterprises of national significance, managed by local soviets but planned by Vesenkha; and the third category would consist of small-scale local industries, managed by the local authorities with central financial support.[54] Upon reading these suggestions, Lenin once more advised that Trotsky delete, tone down, or formulate his views in more general terms.[55] The Party's Central Committee acted upon Lenin's advice, edited Trotsky's text, and deleted the proposal for the division of industry. The revised text read as follows:

> The organizational task must consist of preserving and developing vertical centralism by way of the *glavki*, while combining this with horizontal co-ordination of enterprises according to the economic regions, wherein the enterprises of different branches of industry and those of different economic significance must be provided for out of the same sources of local material, transportation facilities, labor-power, etc.; together with granting greater independence to local economic organizations, it is also necessary to increase the direct economic interest of the local population in the results of local industrial activity.[56]

Explaining his concerns to the congress delegates, Trotsky indicated that he had less confidence in the *glavki* than other members of the Central Committee. Appealing for 'genuine socialist centralism' in place of the existing regime of '*glavkocracy*,'[57] he repeated the anecdote about the oats and wheat and severely criticized Rykov (the head of Vesenkha) for behaving as if he had some magical 'keyboard' at his disposal for the centralized allocation of scarce supplies.[58] It is worth mentioning that it was at this very same congress that Osinsky, speaking for the Democratic Centralist faction, accused Trotsky and the Party leaders of scheming to replace local soviets with 'red governors.'[59] What Osinsky and other opponents either did not know or else ignored, was the fact that just before the congress Trotsky had submitted to the Central Committee his recommendation for a tax in kind, which he subsequently claimed gave rise to the New Economic Policy (NEP). This issue, too, has been a source of confusion amongst historians. Even Isaac Deutscher, whose excellent biography is considered the authoritative source, accepted Trotsky's claim without qualification and wrote that a year later Lenin took up 'the same proposals and put them into effect as the New Economic Policy.'[60]

The first point to be made in this connection is that Trotsky did not in any sense expect that the proposed tax would, as Deutscher suggested, 'throw the economy back on to the treacherous tides of a free market.'[61] To countenance such a notion at the height of War Communism would have been inconceivable. Indeed, within days of presenting his ideas to the Central

Committee, Trotsky reaffirmed before an audience in Ekaterinburg that the Soviet state was building communism and that communism made no provision for money or markets: 'We are making the transition to a communist system; money in our country is steadily declining in importance. And we hope, as soon as we effect an economic recovery, to guarantee every worker all that he requires in kind from the state granary, and not to pay with monetary notes ...'[62] A month later he remarked that 'the old bourgeois significance of money has been eliminated.' He then continued:

> Previously the money system was based upon gold and was related to a certain volume of commodities circulating within society. How are commodities distributed now? By state orders. So much grain is taken from the peasant, in exchange for which he is given this or that. This is the form of distribution which in developed form will exist under communism ... Have we completely arrived at this point yet? No, we are far from it. Thus the old significance of money has been destroyed, and a new apparatus for proper distribution is not yet in place. That, comrades, is the source of our problems ...[63]

At this point in time, Trotsky was obviously convinced, like Preobrazhensky, of the need to develop a system of 'natural' accounting, expressing the value of every article 'in terms of the quantity of human labor expended upon it.'[64] But if the monetary economy was withering away, one might well wonder just what was the intended significance of the tax in kind. If the peasant would be unable to 'market' his after-tax surplus, what would be his rationale for increasing output? Trotsky's answer was part and parcel of his other suggestions for administrative decentralization: after the peasant had paid his tax *in kind*—the tax itself being another manifestation of a 'natural' economy—he would then exchange his surplus, once again in kind, for the products offered by state, and especially local, industry. In other words, the express purpose of the new tax would be to free up for local enterprises the resources for recovery which could no longer be provided from the center. A second proposal to the Central Committee, submitted along with the one for the tax in kind, was quite explicit on this point: 'Have the local industrial enteprises participate in this task. Pay the peasants for the raw materials, the fuel and food products supplied by them, in part in products of local enterprises.'[65] The first draft of Trotsky's theses for the Ninth Congress—the draft edited by the Central Committee—contained an identical provision. Whereas the revised text ended with the need 'to increase the direct economic interest of the local population in the results of local industrial activity,' Trotsky's own draft made a suggestion as to how this might be achieved: peasants were to be paid 'with the products of local industry for the material and additional labor-power they provide.'[66]

Where do these considerations lead us in our search for the origins of the

NEP? Obviously Trotsky did not foresee the market features of the NEP as they eventually emerged. On the other hand, there is a real sense in which he did anticipate Lenin's views early in 1921. On the matter of the proposed division of industry, for example, the final resolution of the Ninth Party Congress actually reversed the editorial work of the Central Committee and reinstated Trotsky's suggestion—although no subsequent action was taken to put it into effect.[67] A kind of implementation did in fact come a year later, however, when Lenin finally recognized the need for a drastic curtailment of central responsibilities. The NEP provided for the 'commanding heights' of industry and transportation to remain under the supervision of the center, but Lenin now expected, at most, to see 700 of the country's largest enterprises continuing to draw from central supplies. In his *Ideas about a State Economic 'Plan'* he wrote: 'All the rest—lease or give to anybody you please, or close, or "abandon", or forget about, until a *sound improvement* is achieved . . .'[68] In May 1921 Lenin summoned local economic councils to 'help revive and develop small local industry which can do without the procurement and transportation of large stocks of food, raw materials, and fuel.'[69]

On the question of the role of money, during the early months of 1921 Lenin also shared Trotsky's hope that after paying his tax in kind the peasant would enter into exchange on the basis of barter. Not until October did he concede that the monetary system must finally be put back in order. In a speech delivered in Moscow he announced: 'We must admit that we have not retreated far enough, that we must make a further retreat . . . to the money system. Nothing came of commodity exchange [in kind]; the private market proved too strong for us; and instead of the exchange of commodities we got ordinary buying and selling, trade.'[70] Lenin now warned his listeners to adjust to the reviving capitalist market or be 'overwhelmed by the spontaneous wave of buying and selling, by the money system.' In December 1921 instructions were finally issued to the Finance Commissariat to begin replacing the ruinously inflated paper currency with a new one, 'backed by gold.'[71]

Lenin's personal difficulties in accepting the need for these changes were minimal in comparison with those of many other Party members, for he at least could see in them a step-by-step restoration of the mixed economic system he had once described as 'state capitalism.' The real tragedy was that the movement back to the market economy, having originated in trade union protests against excessive centralization, ended with organized workers becoming its principal victims. The dismantling of War Communist planning efforts led to rapidly growing unemployment, making any further discussion of labor conscription superfluous. And most ironic of all, the return to market relationships created the conditions in which the incipient administrative bureaucracy of War Communism gave way to a new party-political bureaucracy on a scale hitherto unimagined.

5   The Origins of the Soviet Bureaucracy

In *The Origin of the Communist Autocracy* Leonard Schapiro pursues a theme
with which we are now familiar: the political degeneration of the Revolution
resulted from the War Communist period, and it occurred because the
Bolsheviks believed they were ultimately serving a noble cause, 'the cause of
justice.'[72] Again I would suggest, however, that it was not a Marxist pursuit of
justice which led to the threat of bureaucratic authoritarianism, but the
requirement for wartime economic centralization, on the one hand, and the
theory of the nondialectical 'leap' on the other. We have seen that Lenin and
Trotsky recognized the need for a *transition*, whereas the notion of a 'leap'
into either a fullly 'naturalized' economy (Preobrazhensky) or one that was
fully 'statified' (Bukharin) implicitly denied that such a need existed. Although
Trotsky agreed with both Preobrazhensky and Bukharin on certain questions,
he also shared with Lenin an awareness of the inevitable transitional
interaction of 'fragments' of the past with 'embryos' of the future. It was this
sensitivity to the dialectics of socialist construction which illustrated both the
impossibility of imposed economic uniformity as well as the need to reconcile
central authorities with the shop floor and the localities. Trotsky was certainly
committed to a system of economic planning, his own proposals for labor
mobilization being intended as a first step in that direction. But more
important that that, he was also committed to a system of democratic control,
a preoccupation which would reappear in his writings throughout the next two
decades.

What really distinguished Trotsky from his critics in the trade unions was
his awareness that while bureaucratic phenomena must be contained, they
could not be eliminated even by the most perfect organizational arrangements.
'Bureaucratism' was 'an epoch in mankind's development, during which he
overcomes the darkness of the middle ages . . . and creates certain habits and
modes of management . . . We must adopt these good aspects of bureaucracy
. . . Precision—this is the greatest lever of economic development.'[73] Trotsky
was concerned to rationalize the content of bureaucracy, believing the workers
might thereby learn precision in management; the Workers' Opposition, in
contrast, concentrated their attacks upon the bureaucratic form, as such.
Arguing that the unions alone should bear responsibility for industry,
Alexandra Kollontai reviled the 'ridiculously naive belief that it is possible to
bring about communism by bureaucratic means.'[74] Creativity could originate
with the masses alone; only a new class could create a new society. The
unions were the only pure class organs; and the slightest compromise with
bourgeois 'specialists' and bureaucracy meant the workers' state was, in fact,
representing a hostile class. Bureaucracy signified 'the growing influence in
the Soviet institutions of elements hostile in spirit not only to communism, but
also to the elementary aspirations of the working masses.'[75] Lenin reacted to

such complaints quite predictably: 'All this syndicalist nonsense . . . must go into the wastepaper basket.' The unions were to continue functioning as a 'school of communism.'[76]

But perhaps the case of the Workers' Opposition should not have been dismissed so peremptorily. The fact is that Alexandra Kollontai saw more clearly than most Bolsheviks the danger that the Party might seek to find a 'middle ground' between rival classes, thereby creating an entirely new basis for bureaucratic politics.[77] There is no more widely held conviction among present-day critics of Stalinism than that which postulates the end of political bureaucracy through reintroduction of the market economy. The more market elements, the less bureaucracy: that is a theme which runs through much of the literature. Yet the historical evidence suggests that this linkage is by no means so direct as is frequently thought. As Robert A. Nisbet has observed: 'One of the most curious conceptions of the nineteenth century in modern writing is that it was the century of the natural economic order, *laissez faire*, and the weak State. In actual fact the State achieved a position of power and direction in human affairs that was unprecedented in European history.'[78] Just as the capitalist market wrought havoc upon premarket communities and required a higher order of social integration, so one might suggest that Stalinism, too, was a product of market relations, the effect of which was to relegate to the background the worry over bureaucracy which was such a prominent theme during War Communism.

War Communist attempts at direct physical planning tended to make relationships of authority and subordination personal, explicit, visible, and therefore subject to political challenge. The market economy has a different effect: it appears to be governed by a 'hidden' rather than a visible hand, with the consequence that power, too, tends to be hidden. If production is unconsciously regulated by impersonal forces, then no one can be held personally accountable for its outcome. The justification for workers' control becomes less evident at the enterprise level—how can workers control what is apparently uncontrollable?—while the central authorities, as Lenin put it, can 'retreat' to the 'commanding heights' and hide from those to whom they profess accountability. This is precisely what occurred with the transition to the NEP.

Marx had seen the capitalist state becoming relatively autonomous in response to the apparently self-regulating character of the market. Likewise the Soviet state, by subordinating its enterprises to the judgement of the market, now relieved itself of direct responsibility to the working class. Bureaucracy became less visible, and for that very reason it continued to flourish. Claiming to be the custodian of working-class interests, in reality the bureaucracy had no alternative but to mediate between workers and peasants through a system of very indirect controls over the market. The further this mediation went, and the greater was the need to pursue the 'social interest' in a society with a fundamental class cleavage, the greater was the possibility of the proletarian state becoming independent of the proletariat.

Marx had argued that transitional societies, those in which no one class can realize an exclusive right to rule, are particularly vulnerable to the condition of state 'independence.' In *The German Ideology* he and Engels wrote:

> The independence of the state is found nowadays in those countries where the estates have not yet completely developed into classes ... and where there exists a mixture; countries, that is to say, in which no one section of the population can achieve dominance over the others. This is the case particularly in Germany.[79]

In *The Eighteenth Brumaire of Louis Bonaparte* Marx similarly maintained that Bonaparte's regime appeared to be 'completely independent' because the bourgeoisie could not yet secure direct dominance over the majority of smallholding peasants.[80] Bonaparte could therefore profess to be above classes, balancing one against the other and behaving 'like an unrecognized genius whom all the world takes for a simpleton.'[81] If Russian workers are substituted for the French bourgeoisie, leaving the majority of smallholding peasants in the formula, then Marx's analysis would apply perfectly to Soviet Russia during the NEP. Trotsky was aware of the similarity throughout the 1920s, and he later expressed it succinctly in *The Revolution Betrayed*. Introduction of the NEP, he reasoned, 'caused an extraordinary flush of hope and confidence in the petty bourgeois strata of town and country ... The young bureaucracy, which had arisen at first as an agent of the proletariat, began now to feel itself a court of arbitration between the classes. Its independence increased from month to month.'[82] In Trotsky's view one of the most important economic instruments promoting the re-separation of state from society was the 'dictatorship of finance.'

6 Bureaucracy and the 'Dictatorship of Finance'

Although Lenin initiated the transition back to the market economy, its details were left to Grigory Sokol'nikov, the Commissar of Finance, to whom Lenin delegated vast authority. In his book *State Capitalism and the New Financial Policy* Sokol'nikov indicated that the major changes associated with the New *Economic* Policy would, in fact, relate to the country's *financial* system. More to the point, he described his intention to control the Soviet market from the heights of the banking system in exactly the same manner as Morgan, Rockefeller, Stinnes, or Rothschild controlled capitalist trusts; that is to say, through allowing differential access to credits. Through their 'clever organizing of finance' the most powerful magnates of finance capital appeared to provide a ready-made model for indirect, but at the same time unlimited, control:

Morgan and Stinnes, the one in America and the other in Germany, are in fact economic dictators. All of the banks, railways, factories and mines are *either directly or indirectly* subordinated to them. But this by no means implies that they have *direct and total* ownership of all this property. Nothing of the kind! In fact they own only a small part of the capital functioning in these spheres . . . [but] they occupy the 'commanding heights'; by way of a clever organizing of finance and so on they secure for themselves full 'control' . . . and what is in fact complete power, and they do so with a strictly minimal expenditure of their *own* capital.[83]

By emulating the practices of capitalist bankers Sokol'nikov proposed to control both nationalized and denationalized enterprises without either guaranteeing their assets or assuming responsibility for their obligations. The system of *khozraschet* (economic accounting) was to be reintroduced; budgetary subsidies to manufacturing were to be systematically curtailed; and the Commissariat of Finance was to focus its attention upon stabilizing the currency (without which neither reliable accounting nor market incentives for the peasantry would be possible).

Trotsky had no quarrel either with the need for proper accounting or with the principle of currency stabilization: at one time he compared the continued printing of paper rubles with 'drinking salt water.'[84] The real issue involved the relation between Gosplan (the new State Planning Commission) and the financial authorities, on the one hand, and the political implications of the 'dictatorship of finance' on the other. When Gosplan began its work by *studying* planning rather than practising it, Trotsky repeatedly insisted that its approach was too 'academic' and that the system of *khozraschet* must be completed by centralized book-keeping.[85] Gosplan's detachment from day-to-day industrial administration left undivided authority with the Finance Commissariat, whose overriding concern with the currency diverted attention from more long-run problems of intersectoral proportionality. A speedy profit became the main criterion for access to financial resources, and sausage factories were being given priority over the most elementary maintenance requirements of heavy industry. Sokol'nikov identified his policies with Lenin's thoughts on 'state capitalism,' but he forgot that Lenin had spoken of both market *and* planned elements. 'Although the market develops spontaneously,' Trotsky complained, 'it does not follow at all that state industry should adapt itself to it spontaneously. On the contrary, our successes . . . will depend in large part upon the degree to which we will succeed . . . in harmonizing state industry with agriculture according to a definite plan.'[86]

During the early period of the NEP most Party leaders were also quick to forget Lenin's other main concern, the problem of bureaucracy, which they treated merely as a 'residue' of War Communism. Late in 1923 Trotsky wrote his articles on the 'New Course' and directly challenged this complacency. As he saw it, the bureaucracy of the civil war period had been 'only child's play in comparison with present-day bureaucratism, which grew up in peacetime.'[87] In particular, he expressed alarm at the apparent indifference of the Finance Commissariat to industrial unemployment. The banking mentality appeared to have infected the entire Party and government apparatus. The state budget was routinely hailed as the only conceivable 'plan' in a market environment; yet this 'plan,' drafted with the assistance of numerous bourgeois 'specialists,' invariably ignored the most urgent needs of the working class. A decline in the number of employed workers was depriving the Party of new cadres and bankrupting its stock of ideas. 'A few thousand cadres' at the top were viewing the masses 'only as an object of action.'[88] If this 'caste spirit' was ever to be overcome, the Party must return to its healthy class roots in the proletariat. 'Democracy' and 'centralism' were the 'two faces' of Party organization, and they must be reconciled through 'organizational self-determination.'[89] Financial control had to be brought into contact with the masses by taking into account 'the experience, the observations, the opinions of all [party] members at the various rungs of the ladder of economic administration.'[90]

Interpreting Trotsky's grumbling in strictly personal terms, his enemies recalled the excesses of the War Commissariat in the earlier struggle over the trade unions and replied that they had not the slightest intention of trading the alleged 'dictatorship of finance' for a 'dictatorship of Trotsky in economic affairs.'[91] In January 1924 Lenin died; and in the very same month Trotsky's supporters were roundly defeated at the Thirteenth Party Conference. Stalin, Zinoviev and Kamenev, forming a caretaker leadership (known as the 'triumvirate'), managed with Sokol'nikov's assistance to preside over a difficult period of economic transition. By the mid-1920s the currency was at last restored, allowing attention to shift gradually to new industrial construction in place of the earlier program of budgetary restraint. The change of priorities brought with it a decline in the influence of the Finance Commissariat, signified by the fact that Gosplan began in 1925 to issue its own 'control figures' as a cautious step toward resumption of planning. Even at this stage, however, control continued to issue from above, workers' concerns being treated as secondary.

In 1926 a 'regime of economy' was proclaimed in industry, the intention being to reduce production costs partly at the expense of wages. Trotsky reacted by declaring that 'vigilant control' by the masses was the only real guarantee of greater efficiency. Until the workers themselves were free to denounce abuses, the struggle to reduce costs would 'inevitably develop along bureaucratic rails.'[92] In reply to a correspondent who advocated 'tightening the screws' in order to reinforce labor discipline, Trotsky maintained that genuine socialist discipline presupposed 'the independent action and growing interest of the workers in the results of their own labor': control from above had to be coordinated with 'collective control' by public opinion.[93] Socialism could not be built by administrative orders, but only by way of 'the greatest initiative, individual activity, persistence and resilience of the opinion and will of the many-millioned masses, who sense and know the affair to be their own business, who never hope that someone will do the job for them.'[94] During the trade union debate of 1920 Trotsky had seen the 'workerization' of the state as the counterpart of the 'statification' of the unions; in 1927 the Platform of the Opposition demanded genuinely self-governing trade unions and 'a firm course towards *workerization* (*orabochenie*) *of the party apparatus as a whole*.'[95]

By breaking with Stalin and Bukharin in 1926 and joining Trotsky in the opposition, Zinoviev and Kamenev appeared to reflect the anxieties of rank-and-file workers in Leningrad and Moscow. But for Trotsky this minor triumph was offset by the fact that Bukharin succeeded in preventing any decisive change of policy. Speaking on behalf of still further concessions to the peasants, Bukharin appeared to be carrying the class cleavage of Soviet society directly into the Party itself. Bukharin thought industrialization might be possible even if it advanced only at a 'snail's pace'; Trotsky thought Bukharin was once again demonstrating his inability either to understand or to apply Marx's approach to social and economic questions.

Bukharin's program for cooperative socialism resembled Sokol'nikov's policies insofar as it continued to rely upon the 'hidden hand' of finance to surmount the anarchy of the market. In capitalist society, he reasoned, the inherent nature of agricultural cooperation was capitalist because the 'commanding heights' were capitalist. When a cooperative saved its revenues and deposited them in a capitalist bank, the unavoidable consequence was a 'coalescence' between the cooperative organization and the bourgeois bank: the peasants became 'subordinated to the economic (and consequently also the political) leadership of the bourgeoisie.' The necessary result was that 'The cooperative organizations *grow into* the overall capitalist mechanism and become one of its constituent elements; they merge with it and are themselves transformed into a type of capitalist enterprise.'[96] Once the commanding heights were socialist, this same rule of social 'monism' would produce a directly parallel but opposite result. As Bukharin explained:

> *Completely different conditions prevail under our system*, i.e., *under the system of proletarian dictatorship.* The general bounds of co-operative development in our country are . . . determined . . . by the fact that the whole of large-scale industry, transport, and the credit system *are under the control of the proletarian state* . . . Peasant co-operation will inevitably *grow into* the system of *proletarian* economic organs in exactly the same way as it grows into the *capitalist* system of economic organs under a bourgeois regime.[97]

Few statements could be more remarkable from one who professed to be a student of Marx. In capitalist societies the cooperatives were readily integrated into the mediating structures of finance capital for the obvious reason that these cooperatives were themselves based upon the organized efforts of small proprietors. For this very reason Marx had criticized early theories of cooperative socialism, pointing out that cooperation among private property owners could never result in transcendence of property as such. Yet, for Bukharin the 'being' of Soviet cooperatives appeared to be determined by the transcendent unifying consciousness—or what he had once called the 'collective reason'—of the state and its financial apparatus. In the quest for an abstract theory of social harmony and uniformity, Bukharin simply failed to recognize that the main interest of the peasant was private property in land. Here was an insuperable barrier to the growth of socialist agriculture, which Lenin had described as presupposing '*social ownership* of the means of production.'[98] The practical implications of Bukharin's views were even more serious. By urging tax concessions in agriculture he intended to subordinate the rate of industrial development to voluntary peasant savings, which would eventually be transferred into industry through the mediation of the banks. In this complacent model for evolutionary socialism—in its thoroughly ideological resolution of dialectical contradictions and its misunderstanding of the potential for class conflict—Trotsky saw a clear threat of still further bureaucratic degeneration.

Trotsky understood the NEP to mean that socialist industry and peasant agriculture constituted a unity of opposites. Within this relationship he saw unity between the proletariat and poor and middle peasants, and opposition between these two groups and the *kulaks*. The policy which resulted from this analysis was one of taxing *kulaks* more heavily than less-prosperous peasants until such time as the industrialization of agriculture through mechanized farming made it possible to surmount the contradiction between town and country. In the meantime, a portion of state resources was to be used for the provision of necessary market incentives. *Kulaks* might be heavily taxed, but they were also to be assured that domestic supplies of consumer goods would be augmented by imports in order to alleviate the 'goods famine' and promote agricultural expansion. Growth of commodity relations with private agriculture might even cause the NEP to expand for a time. This very expansion, however, would be a dialectical process, meaning the NEP would ultimately be overcome through its own successes. Trotsky believed Bukharin had abandoned the theory of the 'leap' only to replace it with an equally one-sided theory of 'Narodnik' socialism. In political terms, Bukharin had become the pre-eminent spokesman of *kulak* interests and the potential architect of a Soviet Thermidor.[99]

The most rigorous theoretical response to Bukharin's program came from Preobrazhensky, now Trotsky's colleague in the opposition. By further developing the concept of 'primitive socialist accumulation,' Preobrazhensky attempted to persuade the Party leaders that socialist construction was governed by objective laws, ignorance of which could only result in economic crises. As a transitional economy, the NEP was said to embody two such laws in the form of a contradictory unity. The law of value expressed the inherent anarchy of the market; the law of primitive socialist accumulation expressed the historical imperative to accelerate industrial investments by tapping nonindustrial savings. Like Bukharin, Preobrazhensky approached these issues through a study of finance capitalism, although he arrived at radically different conclusions. In his view, the state economy of the proletariat, having arisen historically 'on the basis of monopoly capitalism', need only apply the capitalist technique of *monopoly pricing* in order to impose 'another form of taxation' on the private sector.[100] As a trust of trusts, state industry could increase its own tempo of development by dictating whatever terms of trade were necessary with agriculture. A system of planned, nonequivalent exchange would generate the required transfusion of resources without waiting upon the growth of voluntary peasant savings.

In the very rigor of Preobrazhensky's argument, however, Trotsky found an element of the same subjectivism displayed by Bukharin. The fact that Bukharin and Preobrazhensky both reasoned by analogy with modern capitalism meant that they did indeed have a point of theoretical tangency. Bukharin thought the adverse effects of the law of value could be controlled by financial manipulation from above; Preobrazhensky substituted price manipulation and claimed that advanced capitalist forms were already causing the law of value to die out both within nation-states and even 'in the world market as a whole. This is the specific feature of postwar economics.'[101] At this point, Trotsky and Preobrazhensky, however close their political bonds, began to part theoretical company.

For Trotsky, the distinguishing feature of modern capitalism was its tendency to outgrow national boundaries and create a world division of labor, which could not possibly be regulated by any other mechanism than the world law of value.[102] This external pressure from the world law of value suggested that domestic terms of trade could not be manipulated very far without jeopardizing the Soviet monopoly of foreign trade. If prices of manufactured articles ranged too far beyond world prices, then all prospect of Soviet industrialization might be erased by an uncontrollable inflow of inexpensive foreign goods. Whereas Preobrazhensky confronted Bukharin with the law of primitive socialist accumulation, Trotsky worried that Preobrazhensky's own viewpoint overlooked the objective restraints imposed by outside economic forces:

> The interaction of the law of value and the law of socialist accumulation must be put in contact with the world economy. Then it will become clear that the law of value, within the confines of the NEP, is supplemented by a growing pressure from the external law of value, which emerges on the world market.[103]

> We are part of the world economy and find ourselves in the capitalist encirclement. This means that the duel of 'our' law of socialist

accumulation with 'our' law of value is embraced by the world law of value, which . . . seriously alters the relationship of forces between the two laws.[104]

This pressure of external economic forces did not yet exhaust Trotsky's concerns. Still another threat implied by Preobrazhensky's argument was the possibility that its emphasis upon self-contained growth might lend support to Stalin's call for 'socialism in one country.' When Trotsky suggested raising the tempo of socialist accumulation by encouraging foreign trade and seeking capital imports, Stalin announced that such measures would make Soviet Russia too 'dependent' upon the capitalist West. Trotsky replied that it was foolish to debate the question in terms of pure dependence or pure independence: by hastening industrial expansion, dependence would simultaneously create an objective basis for real rather than imagined independence. Having arisen from economic needs and historical circumstances of 'uneven development,' the world division of labor simply could not be willed out of existence or 'disrupted by the fact that a socialist system prevails in one country while a capitalist system prevails in the others.'[105] Stalin's hope to leap out of the world market ignored the unexpected unity of opposites which had come to exist between socialism and capitalism on a world scale. Within this contradictory unity—as in the relationship between Soviet workers and peasants—there were elements of both cooperation and struggle. A European socialist federation would eventually replace the world law of value with planned international trade; but in the interval the dialectics of history allowed for no 'abyss' between present and future. 'On the contrary,' wrote Trotsky, 'a properly regulated growth of export and import with the capitalist countries prepares the elements of the future commodity and product exchange [which will prevail] when the European proletariat assumes power and controls production.'[106]

The real significance of Stalin's call for self-sufficiency and industrial 'independence'—while he continued to work in political league with Bukharin and the Party's right wing—appeared to be an effort by the 'centrists' to secure their own independence from Soviet workers and peasants alike. Lack of decisive action, Trotsky feared, would lead to frenzied overreaction when the 'goods famine' finally stretched the contradictory relations between town and country to their breaking point. When Stalin defeated Bukharin and the right wing in the years 1928–9, the 'centrists' undertook to break the 'grain strike' by adopting the 'Siberian method' of grain collection—in effect, reverting to the requisitioning practices of War Communism. After growing up on the basis of the NEP, the bureaucracy now hoped to obliterate the contradictions of the transitional economy through the thoroughly bureaucratic strategy of forced collectivization and revolution from above. At this stage even Bukharin was struck by the magnitude of the bureaucratic threat and the folly of identifying the state with the 'collective reason' of the working class.

In his early writings Bukharin had compared the imperialist state to a New Leviathan. Now he saw that this title should more appropriately be bestowed upon the Stalinist regime. The problem of leadership, he commented in his essay on *The Theory of 'Organized Economic Disorder'*, must be resolved 'through an organic construction of management.' Quoting approvingly from Western literature on the subject of bureaucracy, he continued as follows:

'In place of the centralized organization, which works through instructions,' we need to build an organization in which the 'living man will take upon himself the task of giving directions.' 'The decision is taken by a system of management that is constructed hierarchically . . . that is, constructed so that each will is guaranteed its own sphere of freedom and deciding wills are so gradually stratified, one upon the other, that they are co-ordinated like a pyramid, into a single higher will.' The result in this case will be the self-management of the whole by its parts: every autonomous centre is free in selecting the forms of its activity and linked to the other centres by the idea of the task that has been posed. 'Co-ordination in the idea prevents anarchic degeneration; freedom of form prevents the regeneration of bureaucracy' . . . this type of organization . . . is an excellent safeguard against bureaucratism: it draws the citizen closer to the apparatus; and it eliminates delays and slowdowns in the course of work as it simultaneously encourages initiative and a sense of responsibility.[107]

Apart from its idealistic overtones, which still suggested that the ultimate focus of rationality was to be found at the apex of the hierarchy, Bukharin's denunciation of Stalinism might just as easily have been written by Trotsky.

7   Stalinist Planning and the Planned Market—Trotsky's Views in Exile

In *The Economics of Feasible Socialism* Alec Nove suggests that Stalinist planning cannot be blamed upon the bureaucracy; rather the commitment to planning logically required growth of the bureaucracy for its realization.[108] In light of the arguments given by two such opposing personalities as Trotsky and Bukharin, I would suggest that the causal connection appears to run in exactly the opposite direction. The NEP created the conditions conducive to bureaucracy; and abolition of the NEP resulted from the bureaucracy freeing itself of all political and class restraints. When Stalin looked back upon the events of the 1930s he unashamedly described them as a 'revolution from above.'[109] With the utmost candor he argued that the proletarian state does not interact with or reflect its economic base, but independently creates it by 'doing everything it can to help the new system finish off and eliminate the old base and the old classes.'[110] This ethos of bureaucratic subjectivism was expressed even more bluntly by Strumilin as early as 1927: 'Our task is not to study economics but to change it. We are bound by no laws. There are no fortresses which Bolsheviks cannot storm. The question of [the] tempo [of economic growth] is subject to decision by human beings.'[111]

In *Economic Problems of Socialism in the USSR*, Stalin's account of economic laws was slightly more discreet but by no means less manipulative. Here one reads that 'the laws of political economy under socialism are objective laws . . . and operate independently of our will.' However, Stalin went on to say that 'man can discover laws, get to know and master them, learn to apply them with full understanding, utilize them in the interests of society, and thus subjugate them, secure mastery over them.'[112] How are such inconsistencies to be explained? For Stalin the answer was clear: economic laws operate 'independently' of the will of *workers*, as the *objects* of planning; they are discovered, mastered and so on by the *bureaucrats*, who fancy themselves the true *subjects* of history. To the extent that laws can be subjugated, they allow for triumph of the bureaucratic will and a bureaucratic 'realm of freedom'; to the extent that they are objective, the bureaucracy cannot be held accountable for its actions, which are undertaken, in any case, 'in the interests of society.' As Marx once commented, 'Each thing has therefore a double meaning . . .'[113]

From his haven in exile, Trotsky mercilessly criticized the excesses of collectivization and the First Five-Year Plan. Historians have also had difficulty with this period of Trotsky's life, wondering how the former Commissar of War, the enthusiast of 'militarized labor' and 'concentration camps,' could possibly be sincere in attacking Stalin's methods. In *The Social and Political Thought of Leon Trotsky*, Baruch Knei-Paz argues that 'Trotsky himself while in power had become committed, if not to the manner and extent, then to the principle of the approach adopted under Stalinism.'[114] I have attempted to demonstrate that Trotsky's approach, in fact, differed profoundly from Stalin's. As a Marxist and a dialectician, Trotsky was both aware of the developmental potential of a transitional society and, at the same time, acutely sensitive to the corresponding limitations. The fact that his commitment to Marxism did not stand in the way of what Alec Nove calls 'feasible socialism' is perhaps no more persuasively illustrated than by Trotsky's defence of political and economic pluralism during the 1930s.

On the issue of forced collectivization Trotsky held to his belief that a higher form of agricultural organization was inconceivable without a higher technology and mechanization. Bukharin had cautioned against attempts to build today's factories with 'bricks of the future'; Trotsky paraphrased the remark and added that 'it is impossible to build *kolkhozy* today with tractors of the future.'[115] After violently disagreeing with Bukharin over rates of peasant taxation and industrial investment, he now called repeatedly for a slower rate of accumulation and greater emphasis upon light industry in the interest of raising mass living standards. Socialist construction was said to be 'a task for decades.' It was possible to see it through successfully 'only by a systematic raising of the material and cultural level of the masses.'[116] For this purpose a 'daring reduction of capital investment' was needed: both the economy and the people required 'a breathing-space from administrative pressure and adventurism.'[117]

Was Trotsky being deceitful in his attack upon Stalinist investments, or had he genuinely repudiated the 'super-industrialist' position once attributed to him by Bukharin? In my view, neither conclusion would be correct. The fact is that Trotsky had always emphasized the importance of material incentives, beginning with his proposals in 1920 for the tax in kind and a new system of relations between the center and the localities. In the early years of the NEP, it is true, he had defended heavy industrial interests against the sausage factories favored by the Commissariat of Finance; by the mid-1920s, however, he became preoccupied with the preservation of intersectoral proportionality, implying, among other things, the need to pay appropriate attention to the 'consumer point of view.' It was this commitment which led to the proposal for 'commodity intervention,' or consumer goods imports to alleviate the 'goods famine'; and it was the same concern which provoked the dispute with Stalin over economic 'independence.'

If there ever was a 'super-industrialist' position, then it had to be Stalin's, for it was the slogan of 'socialism in one country' which pointed the way toward industrial autarky, with its one-sided emphasis upon focusing investments in the capital goods industries. Trotsky was fully aware that it was 'impossible to acquire economic strength without the development of all the basic branches of industry and without electrification.' He was no less aware, however, that it would be courting disaster to invest limited savings along too broad a front in the hope of 'acquiring such a proportionality of all the branches of the economy that we will not need the foreign market.'[118] Arguing the need to import machinery as well as consumer goods, he defined the problem as 'one of preserving the proportion of progress between the main branches of industry and the economy as a whole by means of an opportune inclusion in the proportion of such elements of world economics as will help to speed up development all round.'[119] Historians might well debate the question of whether Trotsky exaggerated Soviet Russia's foreign trade potential or prospects for importing foreign capital, but to suggest that he supported heavy industry without qualification would simply be inconsistent with the evidence. Indeed, it might even be more appropriate to say that Trotsky himself occupied the 'centrist' position he normally attributed to Stalin—'centrist,' that is, in the sense of being midway between Bukharin's snail's pace and the crash industrialization of the First Five-Year Plan.

Related to the issue of industrial investment was the further problem of currency stability. In the early period of the NEP, Trotsky had quarrelled with Sokol'nikov over the 'dictatorship of finance'; yet a decade later he was also condemning Stalin for destroying the product of Sokol'nikov's labors. In this case, too, he appeared to contradict his own previous views, but once again the appearance is deceiving. In 1925 Dzerzhinski had been head of Vesenkha with Pyatakov, one of Trotsky's close supporters, as his deputy. Dzerzhinski and Pyatakov pressed for, and received, party approval for a first round of new investments in metallurgy, financed in part by currency expansion. Trotsky provoked Pyatakov's shocked disbelief when he advised against the investment program, predicted a new speculative fever, and commented that it was 'impossible to push industrialization forward with the aid of unreal credits.'[120] There was no difference between this response and the criticism levelled against Stalin in the 1930s. On both of these occasions, Trotsky saw a need to restrain the planners' ambitions by defending the currency and imposing 'strict financial discipline'—even at the expense of shutting down enterprises.[121]

Although Marxists had long spoken of the eventual withering away of both money and the state, the Stalinists were pursuing these ends in an entirely perverse manner: money was dying out 'by way of inflation, the dictatorship of the proletariat by way of bureaucratization.'[122] Rational planning was now said to require 'control by the ruble' in the same way as a market required a reliable unit of account. A direct logical link appeared to exist between the new wave of inflation and the process of bureaucratic degeneration:

> The parallel between the fate of the currency and that of the state confronts us here in a new and very striking way. Disproportions in the economy lead the bureaucracy onto the path of increasing paper-money inflation. The dissatisfaction of the masses with the material consequences of economic disproportions pushes the bureaucracy along the path of naked force. Economic planning emancipates itself from control in terms of value, just as bureaucratic discretion emancipates itself from political control. A denial of 'objective causes' and material limits to the acceleration of tempos, and a negation of the gold basis of the Soviet currency—these are two 'theoretical' expressions of the delirium of bureaucratic subjectivism.[123]

The Stalinists had launched their industrialization program by abolishing the NEP 'too soon and too definitively,' and now they hoped to eliminate both money and the state 'by decree.'[124] The key issue in both politics and economics, as in the days of War Communism, was who would exercise 'control' and how. Although Trotsky had acknowledged the need in the 1920s for independent trade unions, the Five-Year Plan impressed upon him more urgently than ever before the need for trade union autonomy. On this issue there is no doubt that he really did make a decisive break with his own past. The same man who had once threatened union leaders with an administrative 'shake-up' now traced the root of all Stalin's crimes to the 'statification' of working-class organizations:

> The relative independence of the trade unions is a necessary and important corrective in the Soviet state system, which finds itself under pressure from

the peasantry and the bureaucracy. Until such time as classes are liquidated the workers—even in a workers' state—must defend themselves with the help of their professional organizations. In other words: *the trade unions remain trade unions just as long as the state remains a state, that is, an apparatus of compulsion. The statification of the trade unions can only take place parallel with the de-statification of the state itself.*[125]

A planned market, free trade unions, and the restoration of soviet democracy: these were the three elements without which any talk of socialism was but a mockery of Marxism.

The struggle of vital interests, in the form of a new factor of planning, brings us to the role of politics, which is concentrated economics. The equipment of the social groups of Soviet society is (and must be): the soviets, the trade unions, the cooperatives, and above all the ruling party. Only the interaction of the three elements; of state planning, of the market, and of soviet democracy, can provide the economy with proper leadership in the transitional epoch.[126]

Although he remained faithful to his conviction that ultimately a higher technology might alleviate the technical problems associated with planning, for the foreseeable future Trotsky thought '*a priori* planning hypotheses' must be tested in the market, verified through the interaction of supply and demand, and subjected continuously to mass discussion and criticism:

The innumerable living participants in the economy, state and private, collective and individual, must announce their needs and their respective intensities not only through the statistical calculations of the planning commissions, but also by the direct pressure of supply and demand. The plan . . . [must be] verified, and in an important measure must be achieved through the market.[127]

The Soviet economy might be 'directed by a plan,' but Trotsky was adamant that it must be 'controlled by the market.'[128] Rykov had thought he possessed a magical 'keyboard' during War Communism; Bukharin had ascribed to the state the 'collective reason' of the working class; and now Trotsky thought the planners were behaving as if they were the repository of a 'universal mind.'

If there existed the universal mind described in the scientific fantasy of Laplace—a mind which might simultaneously register all the processes of nature and society, measure the dynamic of their movement and forecast the results of their interactions—then, of course, such a mind could *a priori* draw up a faultless and exhaustive economic plan, beginning with the number of hectares of wheat and ending with buttons on a waistcoat. True, it often appears to the bureaucracy that it possesses just such a mind: and that is why it so easily emancipates itself from control by the market and by soviet democracy. The reality is that the bureaucracy is cruelly mistaken in its appraisal of its own spiritual resources.[129]

In *The Revolution Betrayed*, his most thorough analysis of the political economy of Stalinism, Trotsky returned to the starting point of Marxist economic theory in the problem of scarcity and the division of labor. Every Marxist was aware that class relations grew out of the economic problem and could only be dissolved by abundance, but Stalin had added an entirely novel dimension to the question. Instead of mitigating scarcity, he had intensified it; instead of raising the real incomes of workers and peasants, he had sacrificed them to heavy industry. If poverty created hierarchy in capitalist society, the same truth applied even more forcefully to the Soviet Union. The real basis of the bureaucracy's power had nothing to do with its industrial triumphs, with its conquest of nature, or with any of its other pompous claims so tirelessly repeated in the Soviet press; the horrible truth was that the whole bureaucratic edifice rested upon nothing more profound or despicable than its ability to manufacture poverty. Queues were the foundation of Soviet power and the innermost secret of the police state:

> The basis of bureaucratic rule is the poverty of society in objects of consumption, with the resulting struggle of each against all. When there are enough goods in a store, the purchasers can come whenever they want to. When there are few goods, the purchasers are compelled to stand in line. When the lines are very long, it is necessary to appoint a policeman to keep order. Such is the starting point of the Soviet bureaucracy. It 'knows' who is to get something and who has to wait.[130]

Helplessly witnessing from afar the events leading up to the Great Terror, in *The Revolution Betrayed* Trotsky found himself reluctantly admitting that there was as little hope left of redeeming the old Bolshevik Party as there was of rescuing its former leaders, whom Stalin was busily hunting down and arresting. This final political insight could point in only one direction: a new party had to be created, one having all the attributes of the old Bolshevism. What was even more important, Trotsky added that one of the first duties of such a party would be to restore the freedom of Soviet parties in general. In the official Stalinist view there could not possibly be any justification for more than one political party: a consensus had already been established in favor of socialism and was shared by all but the broken remnants of defeated classes and the agents of foreign intelligence services. Trotsky treated this nonsense with the contempt it deserved. Even if such a consensus did exist, he noted, there remained the equally important issue of deciding what roads to follow toward the agreed destination. 'Who is going to choose the road? If the nourishing soil for political parties has really disappeared, then there is no reason to forbid them. On the contrary, it is time, in accordance with the party program, to abolish "all limitations of freedom whatsoever".'[131]

Comments such as these indicate that Trotsky was finally on his way toward a theory of the socialist state which might reconcile the unstructured direct democracy of Lenin's *State and Revolution* with the organizational features needed to accommodate social diversity. At the very least, it is certain that he now fully understood the legitimacy of political differences even within one and the same social class. In *The Revolution Betrayed* he acknowledged that 'classes are heterogeneous; they are torn by inner antagonisms, and arrive at the solution of their common problems in no other way than through an inner struggle of tendencies, groups and parties.'[132] It seems reasonable to conclude, therefore, that through this repudiation of the bureaucracy's claim to scientific infallibility Trotsky had come to accept structured political pluralism as one of several mechanisms for the realization of democratic control.

The emphasis upon control from below was by no means a new theme: it had been visible in his writings even at the height of War Communism. The difference between the two periods lay in the fact that during War Communism he had thought 'coalescence' between trade unionists and state officials would provide a means for transcending diversity and reaching a social consensus of views. The NEP had shattered this confidence in officialdom, while the First Five-Year Plan repeated the lessons of the NEP a thousand times over. The growth of state 'independence' emphatically underscored the need for genuinely autonomous trade unions and thereby opened the way to a whole new perspective on the relation between politics and economics in the transition to socialism.

The evolution of Trotsky's thought from War Communism, through the NEP to Stalinism, has important implications for the relation between Marxist theory and practice. Alec Nove has suggested that the methods of Marxism can be deduced from its goals, that the objective of overcoming scarcity implies the use of force. It is a fact, however, that far from wishing to eradicate dissent and impose uniformity, Trotsky ended up being committed to protection of diversity and the political mediation of contradictions. That is not to say that Nove's warning against 'fundamentalism' should be taken lightly. One would be a fool, indeed, to ignore the experience of Stalinism, when the bureaucratic suppression of money and the market really were proclaimed to be identical with the Marxist 'realm of freedom.'

But the point is that Stalinist ideology, whatever its proclaimed textual basis in Marx's writings, cannot be identified with Marxism. In *History and Class Consciousness* Georg Lukács wrote that the essence of Marxism is its method: 'Orthodox Marxism, therefore, does not imply the uncritical acceptance of the results of Marx's investigations. It is not the "belief" in this or that thesis, nor the exegesis of a "sacred" book.'[133] Rather method, as Lenin understood so well, has to do with rationally responding to what Marx called the 'empirically given circumstances' of a particular time and place. Alec Nove is absolutely right in saying that 'Marx had little to say about the economics of socialism': for Marx the future belonged not to the critical theorist but to the proletariat, who would emancipate themselves through their own practical-critical activity. Lenin and Trotsky understood the difference between practical-critical activity and a sacred text. The Stalinists did not. And that is why the worth of Marxism cannot be inferred from the experience of the 1930s or from the pronouncements of the scientific Stalinists of our own day.

As far as the Trotskyists of our own day are concerned, the most 'orthodox' among them take a position substantially the same as Trotsky's in the 1930s. In the *Transitional Program* of the Fourth International, written in 1938, Trotsky repeated the need both for the 'legalization of soviet parties' and for workers to control production.[134] It is important to emphasize, however, that Trotsky did see these features as explicitly *transitional*. The 'mixed' economy, as modern writers would describe it, was to provide the internal dynamic required eventually to propel society beyond the plan-market dichotomy. Workers' control was to serve as a 'school for planned economy,'[135] the latter being seen as the necessary consequence of advancing technology and the transcendence of class contradictions rooted in scarcity. As early as the Twelfth Party Congress in 1923 Trotsky had declared that 'We established the New Economic Policy seriously and for a long time, but not forever. We introduced the "new" policy in order to overcome [the market] on its own grounds, and in large measure by its own methods. How? By wisely exploiting the behavior of market laws . . . and systematically expanding the planning principle.'[136] In the 1930s the NEP had clearly been abandoned prematurely, but Trotsky never gave up his Marxist commitment to the eventual transcendence both of scarcity and consequently of the need for the market mechanism.

Modern Trotskyists share this traditional commitment. Ernest Mandel, for example, explicitly acknowledges the need for a multiparty system and for workers' control in an economy with significant market elements. 'The survival of money economy and market economy,' he observes, 'is a consequence . . . of the relative shortage of consumer goods.'[137] Mandel looks forward, however, to the growth of a 'social dividend or social wage,' which will gradually replace individual wages and strictly individual consumption with the expanding collective provision of essential social needs without recourse to market forms of distribution.[138]

The market, in the final analysis, is a means of rationing scarce goods through price. Once one posits, as Mandel does, the overcoming of scarcity, the need for the market simultaneously vanishes. How is this process to occur? For Mandel, as for Marx, human needs are biologically limited, with the result that growing affluence reduces the price and income elasticity of demand for essentials toward zero. To the extent that demand becomes inelastic, production, in turn, is to become more amenable to planning. Consumption of salt, Mandel notes, neither rises nor falls in an advanced economy, regardless of what happens to prices and incomes. The need for individual wages might continue to exist in declining measure, but only as a 'small supplementary bonus' to ration the last 'scarce' goods and services.[139] The end of biological insecurity will erase the acquistive features of capitalist society; productivity gains will increasingly be taken in the form of increased leisure time; and automation, by shortening the working day, will provide growing opportunities for public participation at all levels in the collective management of social and economic affairs.

For Ernest Mandel, as for Trotsky and Marx, economic growth cannot be the eternal goal of human society. And it is this philosophical commitment to the end of scarcity which fuels the conflict between Alec Nove and his Trotskyist critics. Nove believes that market socialism is the only 'feasible' socialism one can imagine in a world of relative scarcities; Marxists reply that such a formation is inherently contradictory and transitional, in the sense that it both promotes and prevents the final emancipation of human subjectivity. For Marx, to be human meant to possess the capacity for 'free, conscious activity.' Trotskyists accept the transitional need for a planned market, but they insist that a market of any kind simultaneously negates this human potential by imposing the alienation of labor-power and the mediation of human relationships by 'things' through the exchange process. Socialist society, in contrast, implies the emancipation of human subjectivity; and the collective exercise of human subjectivity, in turn, requires conscious social planning.

Acknowledging these differences of philosophical commitment, it seems no less important to me to emphasize the important areas of agreement between Alec Nove and modern Trotskyists, particularly their shared respect for the market and democratic politics in opposition to the alternative tradition of Stalinism. Nove's belief that a mixed economy can be indefinitely sustained offends the Trotskyist view that such a formation is inherently contradictory; and the seeming 'naiveté' of the Trotskyists offends Alec's conviction that relative scarcity is inescapable. Such differences are unlikely to be settled by debate. What matters for the immediate future of socialism is that both Alec Nove and Trotskyists like Mandel see both the need for a market and the theoretical obligation to examine its social and political implications. As for the final outcome of the debate, perhaps here the last word should go to Marx. In the second thesis on Feuerbach, Marx wrote: 'In practice man must prove the truth ...'[140] 'Social life,' he added in the eighth thesis, 'is essentially practical. All mysteries ... find their rational solution in human practice and in comprehension of this practice.'[141]

Notes: Chapter 1

1 Alec Nove, *The Economics of Feasible Socialism* (London: Allen & Unwin, 1962), p. 10.
2 N. I. Bukharin, *Selected Writings on the State and the Transition to Socialism*, ed., trans. and intro. Richard B. Day (New York: M. E. Sharpe, 1982), pp. 38–9.
3 See Richard B. Day, 'Preobrazhensky and the theory of the transition period,' *Soviet Studies*, vol. 27, no. 2 (April 1975), pp. 196–201 ff.
4 V. I. Lenin, *Selected Works*, 3 vols (Moscow: Foreign Languages Publishing House, 1960–1), Vol. 2, p. 324.
5 ibid., p. 341.
6 E. G. Liberman, *Economic Methods and the Effectiveness of Production* (New York: International Arts and Sciences Press, 1971), p. 46 *et passim*.
7 V. G. Afanasyev, *The Scientific Management of Society* (Moscow: Progress, 1971), p. 32.
8 ibid., p. 120.
9 ibid., p. 142.
10 ibid., p. 84; original emphasis.
11 Nove, op. cit., p. 239; original emphasis.
12 E. H. Carr, *The Bolshevik Revolution 1917–1923*, 3 vols (Harmondsworth: Penguin, 1966), Vol. 2, p. 65.
13 Lenin, *Selected Works*, Vol. 2, p. 438; original emphasis.
14 ibid., p. 351.
15 ibid., p. 350.
16 ibid., p. 725; original emphasis.
17 ibid., p. 759; original emphasis.
18 ibid., p. 745.
19 ibid., p. 746; original emphasis.
20 V. I. Lenin, *Collected Works*, 45 vols (Moscow: Progress, 1961–74), Vol. 21, p. 218.
21 ibid., Vol. 38, p. 223.
22 Lenin, *Selected Works*, Vol. 2, p. 746.
23 Lenin, *Collected Works*, Vol. 23, pp. 69–70.
24 Nove, op. cit., p. 11.
25 Karl Marx, *Capital*, 3 vols (Moscow: Foreign Languages Publishing House, 1957–62), Vol. 3, p. 772.
26 Karl Marx and Friedrich Engels, *Basic Writings on Politics and Philosophy*, ed. Lewis S. Feuer (Garden City, NY: Doubleday, 1959), p. 118.
27 ibid., p. 117; original emphasis.
28 ibid., p. 26.
29 ibid., p. 117.
30 Bukharin, op. cit., pp. 16–17.
31 ibid., pp. 17–18.
32 ibid., p. 56; original emphasis.
33 V. I. Lenin, *Leninskii Sbornik* (Moscow, 1929), Vol. 11, p. 357.
34 Lenin, *Collected Works*, Vol. 21, p. 236.
35 ibid., Vol. 32, p. 24.
36 ibid.; original emphasis.
37 ibid., p. 25.
38 Bukharin, op. cit., p. 57.
39 Leon Trotsky, *Sochineniya* (Moscow, 1925–7), Vol. 15, p. 133. For a more detailed discussion of this period see Richard B. Day, *Leon Trotsky and the Politics of*

Economic Isolation (Cambridge: Cambridge University Press, 1973), pp. 17–46.
40 Trotsky, *Sochineniya*, Vol. 15, p. 181.
41 ibid., p. 126.
42 Robert Vincent Daniels, *The Conscience of the Revolution* (Cambridge, Mass.: Harvard University Press, 1965), p. 122.
43 Leszek Kolakowski, *Main Currents of Marxism*, 3 vols (Oxford: Oxford University Press, 1981), Vol. 2, p. 512.
44 *Desyatyi s'ezd RKP(B): Stenograficheskii Otchet* (Moscow, 1963), p. 818.
45 Leon Trotsky, *Rol' i zadachi professional'nykh soyuzov* (Moscow, 1920), pp. 25–6.
46 ibid., p. 23.
47 ibid., p. 19.
48 *Desyatyi s'ezd*, p. 818; original emphasis.
49 Leon Trotsky, *Kak vooruzhalas' revolyutsiya* (Moscow, 1924), Vol. 2, pt 2, p. 33.
50 ibid.
51 ibid., p. 34.
52 Trotsky Archives, No. T–448. Harvard College Library.
53 ibid., No. T–475.
54 See Sapronov's comments in *Devyatyi s'ezd RKP(B): Protokoly* (Moscow, 1960), p. 140; also Trotsky, *Sochineniya*, Vol. 15, p. 558, n. 89.
55 *Devyatyi s'ezd*, p. 532.
56 ibid., p. 540.
57 Trotsky, *Sochineniya*, Vol. 15, p. 151.
58 ibid., pp. 147–9.
59 *Devyatyi s'ezd*, p. 123.
60 Isaac Deutscher, *The Prophet Armed* (New York: Vintage, 1965), p. 497.
61 ibid.
62 Trotsky, *Sochineniya*, Vol. 15, p. 298.
63 ibid., Vol. 17, pt 2, p. 369.
64 ibid., Vol. 15, p. 435.
65 Leon Trotsky, *The New Course* (Ann Arbor, Mich.: University of Michigan Press, 1965), p. 70.
66 *Devyatyi s'ezd*, p. 534.
67 ibid., p. 408.
68 Lenin, *Collected Works*, Vol. 32, p. 498; original emphasis.
69 ibid., p. 376; cf. p. 364 *et passim*.
70 ibid., Vol. 33, p. 96.
71 ibid., p. 179.
72 Leonard Schapiro, *The Origin of the Communist Autocracy* (New York: Praeger, 1965), p. x.
73 Trotsky, *Sochineniya*, Vol. 15, p. 420.
74 Alexandra Kollontai, *The Workers' Opposition* (Bromley, Kent: Solidarity, n.d.), p. 9.
75 ibid., pp., 37–8.
76 Lenin, *Collected Works*, Vol. 32, p. 62.
77 Kollontai, op. cit., p. 12.
78 Robert A. Nisbet, *The Quest for Community* (New York: Oxford University Press, 1953), p. 167.
79 Karl Marx and Friedrich Engels, *The German Ideology* (New York: International Publishers, 1963), pp. 59–60.
80 Marx and Engels, *Basic Writings*, p. 337.
81 ibid., p. 330.
82 Leon Trotsky, *The Revolution Betrayed* (New York: Pioneer, 1945), p. 90.
83 G. Ya. Sokol'nikov, *Gosudarstvennyi kapitalizm i novaya finansovaya politika* (Moscow, 1922), p. 4; original emphasis.

84 Leon Trotsky, *Novaya ekonomicheskaya politika* (Moscow, 1921), p. 25.
85 Trotsky Archives, No. T–733. For more detail concerning Trotsky's views on Gosplan and its place in the NEP see Day, *Leon Trotsky*, pp. 70–91.
86 Trotsky, *The New Course*, p. 83.
87 ibid., p. 15.
88 ibid., p. 17.
89 ibid., p. 93.
90 ibid., p. 25.
91 Leon Trotsky, 'Pervoe pis'mo Trotskovo,' in *Sotsialisticheskn vestnik*, Vol. 11, (May 1924), p. 11.
92 Trotsky Archives, No. T–880.
93 ibid., No. T–895.
94 *Izvestiya*, 2 June 1926.
95 Trotsky Archives, No. T–1008, p. 53; original emphasis.
96 Bukharin, op. cit., p. 273; original emphasis.
97 ibid., p. 238; original emphasis.
98 Lenin, *Collected Works*, Vol. 33, p. 471; my emphasis.
99 For greater detail see Richard B. Day, 'Leon Trotsky on the problems of the *smychka* and forced collectivization,' *Critique*, no. 13 (1981), pp. 55–68.
100 E. Preobrazhensky, *The New Economics*, trans. Brian Pearce (London: Oxford University Press, 1965), p. 111; see also Richard B. Day, 'On "primitive" and other forms of socialist accumulation,' *Labour/Le Travailleur*, no. 10 (1982), pp. 165–74.
101 Preobrazhensky, op. cit., p. 156.
102 See Day, *Leon Trotsky*, chs 6–7; also idem, 'Trotsky and Preobrazhensky: the troubled unity of the left opposition,' *Studies in Comparative Communism*, vol. 10, no. 1–2 (1977), pp. 69–86; also idem, 'Socialism in one country—new thoughts on an old question,' in Francesca Gori (ed.), *Pensiero e azione politica di Lev Trockij* (Florence: Leo S. Olschki, 1982), pp. 311–30.
103 Trotsky Archives, No. T–2984.
104 ibid., No. T–291.
105 *Izvestiya*, 1 August 1925.
106 Trotsky Archives, No. T–3034.
107 Bukharin, op. cit., pp. 342–3.
108 Nove, op. cit., p. 77.
109 Joseph Stalin, *Marxism and Linguistics* (New York: International Publishers, 1951), p. 28.
110 ibid., p. 10.
111 Cited in Leonard Schapiro, *The Communist Party of the Soviet Union* (London: Methuen, 1960), p. 364.
112 Joseph Stalin, *Economic Problems of Socialism in the USSR* (New York: International Publishers, 1952), pp. 11–12.
113 Robert C. Tucker (ed.), *The Marx–Engels Reader* (New York: Norton, 1978), p. 24.
114 Baruch Knei-Paz, *The Social and Political Thought of Leon Trotsky* (Oxford: Oxford University Press, 1978), p. 368.
115 *Byulleten' oppozitsii*, vol. 11 (1930), p. 7.
116 ibid., vol. 23 (1931), p. 6.
117 ibid., vol. 32 (1932), p. 12.
118 Trotsky Archives, No. T–3034.
119 Leon Trotsky, *Towards Socialism or Capitalism?* (London: Methuen, 1926), p. 94.
120 Leon Trotsky, *Ecrits 1928–40*, Vol. 1 (Librairie Marcel Rivière et Cie: Paris, 1955), p. 186.

121 Trotsky Archives, No. T–3279.
122 ibid., No. T–3493–4.
123 ibid., No. T–3542.
124 ibid., No. T–3493–4.
125 ibid., No. T–3542; my emphasis.
126 *Byulleten' oppozitsii*, vol. 31 (1932), pp. 8–9.
127 ibid., p. 8.
128 Trotsky Archives, No. T–3485.
129 *Byulleten' oppozitsii*, vol. 31, p. 8.
130 Trotsky, *The Revolution Betrayed*, p. 112.
131 ibid., p. 268.
132 ibid., p. 267.
133 Georg Lukács, *History and Class Consciousness* (London: Merlin, 1971), p. 1.
134 Leon Trotsky, *The Transitional Program for Socialist Revolution* (New York: Pathfinder, 1973), p. 105.
135 ibid., p. 82.
136 *Dvenadtsatyi s'ezd Rossiiskoi Kommunisticheskoi Partii (Bol'shevikov): Stenograficheskii otchet* (Moscow, 1923), p. 313.
137 Ernest Mandel, *Marxist Economic Theory* (New York and London: Monthly Review, 1968), Vol. 2, p. 633.
138 ibid., p. 657.
139 ibid., p. 666.
140 Marx and Engels, *Basic Writings*, p. 243.
141 ibid., p. 245.

2 Soviet Investment Criteria: A Prefatory Note

PETER WILES

1 Introduction

There have been hitherto no general sweeps through the field of investment criteria, yet it is full of interest. The development of these criteria goes in parallel with, but does not at all keep exact periodicity with, the rationalization of wholesale prices or the decentralization of output decisions. Let me try to sum up the remoter past.

In the beginning was the method of balances. One deduced investment projects from the commodity deficits the balances showed up. *This remains the basic criterion.* But a strong contender was, and is, the interest of local Party secretaries in location; this latter of course overrode and overrides almost everything, making nonsense of all calculations. Having emphasized its decisive importance, however, I point out that it affects commodity structure much less: that is still determined by the method of balances. The party regional commitee (*obkom*) secretary wants jobs, and buildings to commemorate him: who cares what they produce?

But almost at once a quite distinct problem was thrown up, at the lowest of micro-levels. The project makers (*proyektirovshchiki*), who were always told what, and for how long, the final output must be, had to choose the appropriate assets, and so also their design and so the whole technology. Whether they were told, as mostly they were until the 1960s, to adopt the most advanced technology, or whether they were instructed—under the prevailing rule of 'cost-effectiveness not cost-benefit'[1]—to plan the cheapest possible assets for the purpose, they always had a great deal of micro-choice. In the celebrated railway case, 'steep gradients plus two locomotives versus tunnels plus one locomotive' is a choice at all levels of technology. This gave, and still gives, the *proyektirovshchik* substantial power, since the method of balances and the *obkom* secretary's desire for a monument give him no guidance. For construction was, and is, the most decentralized sector after agriculture: the passive prices for bricks, cement, and so on, are only half passive, and no one really controls the *proyektirovshchik*, whose every project is unique.

So there is, from the very nature of things, micro-choice as to the commodity-structure of inputs. But there is also micro-choice as to time, for (where K is initial, S current cost, L the project life) the temporal outlay profile of K_1, $\Sigma_O^L S_1$ may be quite different from that of K_2, $\Sigma_O^L S_2$. Time is inescapable, even by Marxists, but the rate of interest has been abolished.

2 An Unknown Soldier of Economics

So some brave unknown genius smuggled back temporal choice, but not, of course, in the forbidden form of the rate of interest. He chose instead a normative period of recoupment (*srok okupaemosti*) of capital cost (T), embodying it in a formula called the coefficient of relative effectiveness (CRE, original form in Giffen, p. 48 below). From about 1932 to 1946 it quietly vegetated,[2] a much disregarded shadow price (probably the first shadow price in world history), used on rare occasions, set by each ministry for itself, alone, and so variously set—as if electricity time were different from railway time, while roads had no time at all.

The CRE comes out of a different world from the coefficient of absolute effectiveness (CAE). The latter is the wave of the future; it betokens an intellectual opening up and a slow marketization; it is easy to understand. But the CRE sheds light upon the past, and probably also on the present, and requires an extra effort of explanation. This work has not been done.

So we now state and examine three propositions. (A) The CRE is not the same thing as the rate of interest, however often this is alleged. (B) Nor is T (that is, the basic concept within the CRE) the same as the length of life of a group of fixed assets (L). For L is, however vague *ex ante*, a technical datum. T is arbitrarily determined as a shadow price, by superior authority; and may have any value so long as it is shorter than L. (C) T is 'paid'—insofar as a shadow price can be paid—over and above all replacement and repair. The latter are indeed explicitly added to ordinary running cost in the CRE formula.

(A) Let us start with interest. It is true, but not at all the same thing, that under capitalism interest is paid over and above depreciation whatever the rate of the latter, for the effects of the two surcharges are very different, as Durgin shows (Chapter 4, Section 4b). Giffen's virtual identification seems much too strong for me.

Interest is not the cost of capital but of using capital over time. The current costs S' also use up capital, and over a long period of time. To add them together year by year without any futurity discount is to exaggerate them, too. But the bias of the CRE is against capital-intensity in comparison with net present value (NPV)—a most surprising state of affairs. (See Durgin, Section 4, for an illustration.)

High interest under capitalism has two effects that concern us. (i) It does not really cut off long-lasting projects or short-lasting projects, but unprofitable ones. In this it acts like the high price of any other input, say bricks. But (ii) where there is a choice of technical lengths of life (for example, shall we transport gold by air or by ship? Shall we use marble or brick?) it does incline us—on cost grounds, always—to the shorter ones, even if other costs are greater. For (i) it is just one cost in many and must be covered like the rest, but for (ii) it is the cost of time in particular.

So, to repeat, $1/T$ in the CRE formula is not the same as r. But while a higher r inclines us to a project with a lower L as in (ii), if technology affords no lower L it acts simply as in (i), pushing up the total cost. Under capitalism this is quite acceptable; if demand cannot meet the high interest cost of such and such a commodity branch with a high L, the commodity ceases to be produced. The CRE, on the other hand, cannot fulfill function (i) at all, since it is only a shadow cost, and contains no revenue term at all. Moreover, in respect of (ii) it must *choose between Ls*, (i.e. techniques), and *not* suppress commodity branches. So 'electricity time' *must* differ from 'railway time,' and *the separate departmental CREs are a rational necessity*. For to choose between a railway tunnel and a long détour concerns two Ls both very much longer than those of, say, a fossil fuel plant and a nuclear generating plant. At all sets of prices, railway Ls will exceed the Ls of electricity generation.

(B) How does T relate to L? Our strong inclination is to say that T must be $<L$, so that after the replacement fund has been built up there must be something left over for the state. In Soviet ideology (the word is not too strong) the replacement fund is envisaged as being the counterpart of the original *gift* of capital by the state; it is not repaid into the treasury, but recovery rates[3] are built into prices and the sums recovered are handed over to the enterprise's trust or commodity-branch ministry, which may switch them around (cross-subsidization). Such a procedure may either be called amortization, because a sum advanced is being written off, or the covering of an asset's physical depreciation, because it is at the rate of such depreciation that the sum is amortized. Hence the near identity of the two words in Russian.

So in a profitable enterprise the due replacement fund can be seen as having been built up out of early amortization payments *plus* early profits; and the asset's survival up to and beyond L is clear profit to the economy as a whole, however divided between the branch ministry and the Ministry of Finance. $T > L$ entails a subsidy when the asset is replaced.

There are, then, all-important distinctions between T and L. T is a shadow price; L is a technological fact, related to the official amortization payments required of every enterprise on *khozraschet*, i.e. bound to balance its expenditures with its revenues from what is sells.

(C) So why does the CRE include depreciation? Its unknown inventor set $r = 0$, as he was politically bound to do, but he included depreciation in his current costs, thus 'recovering' capital in L years as well as 'recouping' it in T years. The most probable answer to this paradox is very simple: it seems as if our unknown genius was considering the very ordinary *break-even point over time*:

year	1	2	3	..	7	...	11
expenditures	K	S	S		S		S
revenues		R	R		R		R

where $T = 6$, $L = 10$, S is current costs including depreciation (*sebestoimost'*); and $6S + K = 6R$, so that year 7 is the intertemporal break-even point; but the project continues until year 11 inclusive, so that the intertemporal profit is $(L-T)(R-S)$; and where $r = 0$ so there is no time discount.

The break-even point over time is a very ordinary thing. It is the 'naive businessman's recoupment period,' which I personally met, as a young Oxford economist interviewing businessmen, in the early 1950s. Doubtless our unknown genius was very familiar with it, even believed in it, from his prerevolutionary youth. He effectively said to himself (I suggest), both amortization and interest would be surcharges over other costs: but *sebestoimost'* includes amortization. So I shall cope with time by setting an arbitrary $T < L$, since interest is forbidden. British businessmen were doing less well twenty years later. For since they had a rate of interest they did not need a period of recoupment.

On top of all this the 'unknown soldier' had no absolute knowledge of R, only that it was an invariant function of output. For the very word 'profit' entails a notion of the prices of outputs: the very thing that the CRE is supposed not to consider, since the preoccupation of *proyektirovshchiki* under Stalin was with 'cost-effectiveness, not cost-benefit' (see above). How can you talk of recoupment, one might ask, if you don't know your revenues, still less your gross profits?—if prices are a *chasse gardée*? But since our hero was only *comparing* technologies, the CRE left him sufficiently informed. Whether he was maximizing a profit or minimizing a loss he did not care.

3   The Period 1943–9

Reverting now to the course of history, in the middle of the war Stalin took a personal interest in the law of value,[4] and gave the go-ahead for the great ambiguous—and anonymous—article in *Pod znamenem Marksizma* (1943): the law of value does operate under socialism, but in a transformed manner. The result was Voznesenski's false dawn (1947–50). What we would recognize as the really basic issues—plan versus market, need versus demand, passive prices for current production, bonus specification, indicators—were not discussed. The CRE, still the sole investment criterion, was the center of attention. But, as we see in Durgin's and Giffen's chapters in the present volume, the CRE raises indirectly every other issue.

There was even a new theory: that of S. G. Strumilin, a loyal Stalinist but a good scholar, who suggested that the real reason for our needing a time discount was that the secular rise in productivity cheapens future production, so activity would be postponed unless some futurity discount like the CRE operated. And precisely the rate of general productivity increase should be the normative value of the CRE. Revisiting Strumilin after thirty-four years[5] I observe that (i) if we could know which outputs would benefit *most* from productivity increases we should postpone investment in *them*; (ii) he has made a good argument for postponing all investment, for why should we sacrifice ourselves to the future if it will be richer anyway? For the rest he was simply wrong—and this is the implicit verdict also of his Soviet successors. But note the extraordinary parallels with the CRE: both inventors—one famous, one unknown—are trying to find a time discounting device that is not the rate of interest.

In 1951–6 economic discussion was forbidden. The fact that the law of value had actually shed blood (Voznesenski's blood) was not easily forgotten. But from then on, the same field that had first flowered was free to bear its second crop: 'investment criteria' had a clear start on 'plan versus market.' The first Standard Methodology (1960) did not wait for Liberman (1962).[6]

Very quickly the CAE was added to the CRE. This is still more threatening to orthodoxy since it does not require a predetermined output, and merely chooses between two ways of achieving it. It sits directly in judgement on what outputs the planner has ordered. This is not quite the same as saying 'cost-benefit, not cost-effectiveness,' because the planner still confines the CAE to comparisons within one commodity-branch, decides on final output *and prices it*. But it does demand from him more rational prices, for both inputs and outputs.

Still more threatening to ideological, if not to administrative, orthodoxy is the flat recognition extended to the cost of time in certain restricted circumstances: the discount coefficient V described in Durgin (Section 4a) is a shadow rate of interest. The remaining history is clear from Giffen's chapter in this volume. The astounding parallelisms with various Western criteria are treated by Durgin.

4   Value Added versus Profit

I conclude quite unhistorically by pointing to a question of extremely general, nay worldwide, interest. Giffen (in her note 13, below) quotes Chernyavski's remarks on a 'need' for the profit criterion at enterprise level, while he is content with value added at the national level. But this distinction, observed in the 1960 and 1969 SMs (cf. Durgin, Section 3a), is abandoned in the 1980 one. For Chernyavski it is not a question of the availability of statistics, as it is for Giffen—and indeed are not value-added figures at enterprise level always easy to work out?

It seems to me that with the dual criterion of the 1960 and 1969 SMs the Russians stumbled on to a very important point indeed, and that they should not have adandoned it. For, in practice, the Western world also recognizes the duality, though naturally it stresses profit; and there *should* be these two criteria.

The basic facts are: (i) in a fully employed economy, investment can reasonably be considered from the point of view of profits, since the workplaces it creates are mostly substitutes for other workplaces, and the changes that it makes in overall employment and overall wage bills are not great. Labor is a cost, even from the highest social point of view, and forms no part of the maximand. But (ii) when there is unemployment, labor, while not quite ceasing to be a cost, enters the maximand. We are directly interested in new workplaces, and the 'yield' of new capital is enormously multiplied, since it is no longer just profit but all value added. In both cases, of course, there must be a market for the product. Moreover, catastrophically labor-saving devices must be tolerated under (i) but not always under (ii), since they always create unemployment.

The value-added criterion is suitable for:

- Foreign-aid projects. For the object of these is to increase the income of the aided, and their yield to lenders is quite secondary matter. If they succeed in their object, their yield to the borrowers in general, though not to capitalists in particular, will be very much higher than their cost to the lenders (opporunity yield considering world capital market conditions). Moreover, 'success,' being measured in value added, is wholly compatible with financial loss, which treats wages as a cost.
- By analogy, investment in backward but inhabited areas of one's own country (uninhabited areas are very different indeed: see under 'profit,' below).
- Judging the general result of a policy on a national level; for the national income *is* value added, and the yield on capital is not an important policy aim but the total investment bill is an important cost.
- Deciding whether a country with unemployment at home should export capital: it will do so, if capitalist, simply because profit is lower at home than abroad, and thus sacrifice many workplaces at home.
- Making technological choices when labor intensity is required to create jobs.

The profit criterion is suitable for:

- All aspects of a project irrelevant to value added. These will no doubt be much the majority.
- Making decisions when there is full employment.
- Investing in the face of severe competition (for most of value added is a cost, and it is a dangerous maximand).
- Investing in uninhabited areas. These areas should be most strictly treated

on a profit-only basis, and the Soviet failure here results in the subsidized hypertrophy of the frozen North. The contrast between the Canadian Arctic or the Australian outback and the Brazilian jungle or the Soviet North is very great, and wholly in favor of the former pair, in which investment has always been according to profit, not value added. Value added is the settler's investment criterion, and these four places ought not be settled.

● One must add that profit is part of value added, so it is by no means neglected when the latter is the criterion.

Note that if at the macro-level there is only the one criterion, this does not mean that at the micro-level there is only the other. If the value-added criterion is to be used for decision-making, as opposed to merely passing judgement *ex post*, it must be applied to individual projects and people: it becomes a micro-criterion and ousts profit. Chernyavski at this point makes a great mistake (see Giffen, note 13, below).

There is here a whole complex of ideas which we can only adumbrate. I conclude only by saying that in very many cases 'value added' is the correct criterion; that neoclassical theory never recognizes this at all, and Western governmental policy too seldom. The French exception[7] only confirms this judgement (see Giffen, note 42, below): France has only briefly been a purely capitalist country, and persists down to this day in a loose form of central planning that must, nevertheless, be called detailed and serious. The Russians, by contrast, put something vaguely resembling dual criteria into official practice for a few years but, in the end, profit was ideologically unacceptable. They have turned back from an extremely promising mixed position.

Notes: Chapter 2

1 My phrase, of course, not theirs. We do not here go further into the imposition of technological-level-constraints of the pure rule of cost-effectiveness.

2 Gregory Grossman, article in *Quarterly Journal of Economics* (1953).

3 In detail these rates are laid down by commodity-branch ministries, according to asset-type. Slightly less than half the payments are used for 'capital repair' (which is distinguished from current repair which is part of Giffen's *S*). It is the 55 to 60 percent of amortization payments reserved for 'replacement' that concerns us. They are often expressed as annual percentage rate on the original cost of the asset. They were published in the Narkhoz, 1962–9), for industry at least. The reciprocals of these rates are the wished-for, or feared, or normal *L*s of the asset-types given. They have no connection with the *T*s of particular projects.

4 Michael Kaser, personally communicated.

5 Peter Wiles, 'Scarcity, Marxism and Gosplan,' *Oxford Economic Papers* (1953).

6 'Plan, profit, bonus,' *Pravda*, 9 September 1962.

7 See M. Cherval, 'The rationale of the effects method,' *Oxford Bulletin of Economics and Statistics*, no. 4 (1977).

3 The Allocation of Investment in the Soviet Union: Criteria for the Efficiency of Investment

JANICE GIFFEN

This chapter is an evaluation of recent developments in the Soviet debate on, and official instructions concerning, the criteria for allocation of investment.

It is reasonable to suppose that a socialist policy may well wish to include objectives other than financial profitability, even objectives which cannot be measured in price terms, in its appraisal and choice of investment projects. Indeed the earliest tentative Soviet discussions were conducted during the period when the law of value officially did not function in the Soviet Union, and hence any suggestions of measuring alternative investment strategies in price terms were anathema to the official doctrine.[1]

1 The Background to the Standard Methodologies

Initially, in the Soviet Union of the 1930s, the question of choice between investment projects was not regarded as a problem. Sectoral allocations were made centrally, and the task within sectors was to fulfill the plan using the most advanced techniques of production available.[2] It was the engineers in the electricity and railway sectors, whose task it was to implement plans, who first began to devise means of measuring alternative ways of fulfilling the plan.[3] The benefits of alternative investment strategies were not enumerated, since the notion of production of benefits for sale (= commodity production) was not central to Soviet thinking. Rather the techniques concentrated on measuring the costs of alternative projects. The classic example is the choice between building a hydroelectric power station (which requires a large capital outlay, but has low annual operating costs) and a thermal power station (with significantly lower capital investment but higher operating costs). The engineers devised norms based on the payback (or recoupment) period which could be used as criteria in decision-making. The formula was that of the CRE (see below).

However, such attempts at measurement in price terms were contrary to the notion that investment decisions in socialist society should not be based on prices. Such measures were seen by the critics as being a return to the use of a rate of interest which, by definition, was a measure associated with the

44

·eproduction of capital in capitalist society. In the late 1940s several articles appeared in which attempts were made to measure the effects of alternative investment strategies in a way more in keeping with socialist objectives. However, these attempts were based on specific examples and were not able to be generalized into a new methodology. Developments were temporarily silenced by an official article 'summing up' the debate on choice of capital investments within socialism, according to which the question should 'be considered within the framework of a higher form of profitability arising from the operation of the basic economic law of socialism, the law of planned proportionate development.'[4]

2   The Standard Methodologies for Allocation of Investment

The first official publication on ways of measuring investment choice appeared in 1958 after a conference on the 'Problems of Definition of Economic Effectiveness of Capital Investment.'[5] It is significant that this conference took place after the recognition that the law of value did function throughout the Soviet economy.[6] The recognition had led to work on the improvement of the price sysem, since it was now felt that prices should reflect value. In turn this facilitated the reopening of the debate on how to measure the effects of alternative investment projects, using prices.[7]

The recommendations arising from the 1958 conference set the scene for the development of future debates and official guidelines:

(i) Given that choice based on profitability alone is insufficient in socialist society, the recommendations state (point 5) that 'Calculation of the effectiveness of capital investment and of new techniques should be based on *value* and *natural* indices, which make it possible to compare expenditures of living labour of different qualities and of different branches of production with past labour' (my emphasis). Throughout the different editions of the Standard Methodology (SM) it continues to be stressed that any measurements of efficiency of investment in value (price) terms must be used alongside the traditional performance indicators—norms in natural (or physical) units.

(ii) As regards calculation in value terms, the 1958 recommendations state (point 10): 'Indices of value alone do not always give a complete picture of the actual effectiveness of capital investment. For example, a variant which would be acceptable on the basis of value indices may require labour and materials which are in short supply. In such cases application of value indices alone may result in a wrong decision. Thus selection of the most advantageous system of alternatives of capital investment requires indices expressed in physical units in addition to value indices—labour productivity, expenditure of fuel, power, raw materials

... utilisation of equipment, factory area etc.' (From the point of view of neoclassical efficiency analysis such problems could, of course, be solved by 'efficiency pricing,' where the prices of resources represent the opportunity cost of using those resources.)[8]

(iii) Point 22 of the same recommendations states that in addition to calculation in value and physical indicators, 'social factors' should also be considered in the estimation of effectiveness of investment. This objective is more difficult to incorporate into one criterion for investment allocation.

Since 1959–60 there have been three editions of the SM for the definition of capital effectiveness.[9] All speak of the need to measure the existing effectiveness of capital investment in both value and physical terms. Thus each sector of the economy (for, as we shall see, the choice between investment projects is found within sectors, not between different sectors), is charged with defining existing norms within the sector. These norms will provide guidelines for new investment projects—in that new investments should result in similar or better norms of effectiveness. Of course, there is a problem that with a multitude of norms there is no one ultimate criterion by which projects can be compared.

The most important 'value' norms (that is, norms measured in units of value) are:

(i) The coefficient of absolute or general effectiveness, which is to be used as a guide for comparing the absolute effectiveness in the sector as a whole or the economy as a whole.

(ii) The coefficient of relative effectiveness (or its inverse, the recoupment period) which is to be used within sectors in the choice between two investment alternatives. This is essentially the same measure that was developed and used in the 1930s by the engineers in the electricity and transport sectors (see above, p. 44).

Other 'value' norms to be calculated include the return on fixed capital stock (*Fondootdacha*), the capital/output ratio (*udel'noe kapital noe vlozhenie*) and the expenditure on materials per ruble of social output.

(a) The Coefficient of Absolute Effectiveness (CAE)

This coefficient is an empirically based norm which can be established for the economy as a whole, for each sector of the economy, and at levels within sectors (for example, enterprise level). The norm expresses the ratio of some measure of annual output to the existing stocks of fixed capital or increase in stocks of fixed capital. Discussion took place at the 1958 conference as to whether the coefficient of absolute effectiveness should be the relationship between net income (= value added) and capital investment, or between accumulated income (= profit) and capital investment. The 1960 SM does not specify how this coefficient is to be measured at the national level—however, it does give instructions on how to measure absolute effectiveness at the enterprise level.[10]

The 1969 SM defines two possible measurements at the national level:

(i) the relationship between national income and capital stock, and
(ii) the relationship between annual increase in national income and capital investment for that year.

The 1980 SM prefers the latter measure (see below).

The 1960 and 1969 SMs state that at sectoral level the CAE can be measured by the ratio of sectoral profits to capital stock or, alternatively, by the ratio of increase in profits to capital investment. At enterprise level the coefficient is again found by the ratio of either total annual profits to captial investment, or of increases in annual profits to capital investments. Thus the CAEs at different levels of the economy were defined in 1969:

(i) at national level D/F or $\Delta D/K$
(ii) at sectoral level Profits$/F$ or ΔProfits$/K$
(iii) at enterprise level $\dfrac{Ts - S}{K}$ (= Profits$/K$)

where D = national income (*national'ni dokhod*), E = fixed capital (*fondy*), K = capital investment, Ts = value of annual output at wholesale prices, and S = cost of annual inputs, including labor costs and amortization (*sebestoimost'*). It should be noted that at subnational levels the measure was based on profitability, whilst at national level it was based on value added.

The 1980 SM recommends using the *same* measure in the numerator at all levels of the economy. At national level the CAE is to be defined by growth in national income ÷ capital investment; and at lower levels in the economy it is to be defined by increases in net product divided by capital investment. For the first time, CAEs at different levels of the economy are directly comparable. This innovation was made possible by the reform of 1979 where a measure of value added at subnational level was introduced.[11]

Greater emphasis is given to the CAE in the 1980 SM where it states that more attention is to be given to the CAE in Five-Year Plans. The National CAE is given as being equal to 15 percent, being based on the average of the actual ratios for the previous five-year period. The CAEs at sectoral levels are calculated in the same way and vary from 5 percent in the transport and communications sector to 25 percent for international trade, material technical supply, and so on.

The pre-1980 discrepancy between the measures of CAE at different levels of the economy seems, therefore, to have arisen because of the statistics available[12] (that is, until 1979 there was no measure of value added at lower levels of the economy). This discrepancy does not seem to have been seen as a problem by most Soviet commentators.[13] This would seem to support my thesis that the CAE should not be seen as the ultimate criterion according to which projects are accepted or rejected. The CAE at national level is not, as claimed by Abouchar,[14] the benchmark for evaluation of all possible investments in the economy and has nothing to do with neoclassical notions of the marginal efficiency of capital.[15] The CAEs at different levels of the economy are only one part of the series of performance indicators; they are empirically derived and are to be used along with other criteria in judgements about investments.[16] The CAEs were originally seen purely as a means of extending decision-makers' knowledge about the existing situation which, it was hoped, would encourage them to give greater consideration to the efficiency of their investment decisions.

The reasons for preferring a value-added measure to that of profitability are not, to my knowledge, specified. In the 1957 debate, Khachaturov stated that in calculating *effect* of a given amount of capital investment, account must be taken not only of the 'product for society' (surplus product or profits), but also of the 'product for self' (wages), since the latter also arise from increased investment and are a means of satisfying people's needs.

(b) The Coefficient of Relative Effectiveness (CRE)

This coefficient (and its inverse, the recoupment period) is to be used within sectors in the choice between two investment alternatives. It measures the relationship between the extra capital investment required by the more costly of the investment projects being compared, and the annual savings in operating costs resulting from the adoption of this alternative. It is much the oldest of these coefficients dating back to the 1930s, but only officially recognized in SM 1960.

The CRE is based on a recoupment period $T = (K_1 - K_2)/(S_2 - S_1)$ where T is the number of years for the cost of extra investment required for project 1 to be recouped, K_1 is the investment cost of project 1; K_2 is the investment cost of project 2; S_1 is the *sebestoimost'* of project 1; S_2 is the *sebestoimost'* of project 2; $K_1 > K_2$; and $S_2 > S_1$. S includes depreciation.

Each sector is to calculate a norm for the recoupment period/coefficient of relative effectiveness which will be a guide to the maximum recoupment time/minimum effectiveness of the investment project over another required in that sector. In the choice between two projects, if T is greater than the norm then the less capital intensive variant should be chosen. The CRE is the inverse of the norm for the recoupment period in a given sector; where this is used the planners are to select that project with the lowest costs defined as $S_i + 1/T\ K_i$.

Suggestions are made about how to cope with measurement of alternative projects where the outputs (benefits) of the different projects are not identical. (That is, it is recognized that, ideally, the coefficient of relative effectiveness should only be used to compare two ways of producing the same output, in terms of both quality and quantity.)[17] Where two alternative projects produce different quantities, the 1964 recommendations suggest that the coefficient of relative effectiveness can be calculated using the increase in profits as the numerator:

$$E = \frac{(Ts_1 - S_1) - (Ts_2 - S_2)}{K_2 - K_1}$$

where E is the coefficient of effectiveness, Ts_1 and Ts_2 are the wholesale prices of annual production of techniques 1 and 2 respectively; S_1 and S_2 are the *sebestoimost'* of annual production of techniques 1 and 2, and K_1 and K_2 are the capital investment of techniques 1 and 2.

Later instructions suggest that projects producing different quantities of output should be made commensurable by calculating unit costs of each technique and multiplying these by the larger of the outputs.[18]

Different methods of getting around the problem that the use of the CRE requires the benefits from alternative projects to be identical continue to be propounded (see below). The quantification of benefits (as is done in Western cost-benefit analysis) is generally not accepted as a solution—even in sectors where goods are produced for sale. This is because the Soviet ideology is committed to producing for need (that is, fulfilling the planned output)—so traditionally there was no room for any measure which implied that the purpose of production was the sale of output or which used retail prices of output to determine the efficiency of production.

3 The Issue of Uniformity throughout the Economy

Different sectoral norms for the CRE are calculated from the existing situation within each sector. At the 1958 conference the view had been expressed by the proponents of 'prices of production' that such a norm should be uniform throughout the economy, but this view has always been, and continues to be, opposed in the official instructions. The official view continues to be as stated by A. N. Chukharov at the 1958 conference, that 'economic calculations should not be used to determine *what* is produced, but rather *by what methods* the planned products should be produced' (my emphasis).

In 1965 Khachaturov stated that the normative coefficients of relative and absolute effectiveness could only be uniform throughout the whole economy if: (i) there were free transfer of capital from one sector to another, (ii) there existed similar conditions of investment (time lags in construction periods, and so on) in every sector and area, (iii) there existed the same rate of technical progress in each sector and (iv) all other criteria by which the effect of investment could be measured were ignored (that is, all were to be subordinate to the criterion of maximum effect in value terms).[19]

Again, in 1977 a publication of the Academy of Sciences justified the fact that there must be different sectoral indicators of effectiveness of investment because of the sectoral differences in productivity of labor, time lags in construction projects, turnover of investment and goals of the investment program.[20]

In 1962 Gosplan, together with the Academy of Sciences, published a list of normative coefficients of relative effectiveness for use in different sectors[21]—these varied from 0.1 in the transport and energy sectors (a recoupment period of about 10 years) to 0.2–0.33 in the wood products and chemical sectors (a recoupment period of between 3 and 5 years).

The 1969 and 1980 editions of the SM estimate the average economy-wide CRE to be 0.12, and both recommend that sectors use coefficients greater than this average. However, lower coefficients are to be allowed where necessary. The 1980 SM states that the lowest sectoral CRE (empirically defined) is equal to 0.08, and the highest is 0.25. As Dyker says, 'so many possible grounds for making an exception are spelled out that one wonders how big a change there may really have been at the policy level.'[22]

Problems which Western observers would attribute to the 'nonparametric nature' of Soviet prices are also mentioned. It is pointed out that in cases where prices do not reflect value, or where changes in price have resulted from administrative changes rather than value changes, prices cannot be used in the calculation of coefficients. *Sebestoimost'*, has to be used in the calculation of the relative coefficient. The 1964 recommendations suggest that in such cases the absolute coefficient can be calculated from the wage fund marked up by the average rate of surplus value.[23] Where two projects use different amounts of a deficit good it is stated that the one using more of the scarce resource should be additionally penalized.[24]

4   Time

Since, in Marxist theory, capital itself is not productive, the use of interest for intertemporal comparisons has been taboo. It is amazing, then, to find scattered applications of compound interest. They mainly refer to that quintessential Soviet nightmare, the overlong gestation period.

The time factor is first mentioned in the 1960 SM where a brief recommendation is made that all investment costs could be compounded through the gestation period to the first year of operation by the relative coefficient of effectiveness for the sector in question (that is, different compound/discount rates for each sector).

The 1964 recommendations add that any future inputs of capital required during the life of the project should be discounted back to the first year of operation. It also talks of discounting operating costs of projects where their operating costs have different time ptterns. (However, the formula given compounds all costs.)[25] The 1964 and 1966 recommendations advocate the use of a uniform discount rate of 10 percent for the whole economy. The uniform rate advocated in 1969 is 8 percent.[26] (These can be compared with the economy average coefficient of relative effectiveness which was said to be 0.1 in 1964,, 0.12 in 1969 and 1980.)

5 Miscellaneous Points

The SM also mention, in varying degrees of detail, the need to include linkages in calculations, the need to determine correctly all costs,[27] and to forecast costs allowing for increases in productivity.

The correct determination of costs continues to occupy a large amount of literature on efficiency of capital investment. Guidelines which seem quite basic to us elaborate, for example, how overhead costs should be attributed to production costs, etc.

Such ill-defined notions of productions costs, etc., seem to me to be a legacy of the idea that production in socialist society can be (and has been) likened to production in one giant enterprise—in that there is no private ownership of the means of production. Thus rigorous definition of costs of production at enterprise level was not seen to be important.

Differences in geographical conditions have to be taken into account in the allocation of investment. Any extra transport costs must be included, proximity to consumers and suppliers must be taken into consideration, as must any regional differences in wages and other costs.

Salvage value is mentioned as an additional cost where the displaced machinery has not been fully amortized (not as a benefit, which is how it is treated in Western cost-benefit analysis).[28]

The 1980 SM includes a new section on the calculation of efficiency of capital investment in the modernization of existing plant, in the nonproductive sphere and in the sphere of circulation (trade).

6 The Absence of Theory

The Soviet criteria of investment effectiveness are all empirically derived norms—derived from the existing situation in the economy.

The committee,[29] set up following the Twenty-second Party Congress in 1961 to examine the need to increase effectiveness of capital investment, had coordinated the empirical work which led to the publication in 1962 of the sectoral norms, and continued to be the central instigator of such empirical and related theoretical work. (It continues in this function today.)

The 1965 report of this committee warns of the *actual declining* efficiency of investment and calls for more empirical work and greater precision in the definition of norms:

> The creation of the material and technical basis of communism requires great capital investment. The task is for this investment to be used in the most judicious and most economical way, with the maximum result and most advantageous timing. The achievement of this task requires significant theoretical work from a wide circle of scientific research, planning and scholarly (*uchebnye*) institutes on the study of the actual effectiveness of capital investment, further work on methodology and normatives and the advancement of concrete propositions on the increase of efficiency of capital investment and new technology.[30]

Dyker cites one of the authors of the 1969 SM as noting, 'much work remains to be done before these principles can be transformed into working instructions for each sector, ministry, department and their subordinate institutions. It is necessary to finish this work quickly, so that instructions for the different sectors can be properly confirmed this year.'[31] But even the 1980 SM states in the preface that its recommendations are provisional pending further study.

Confusion still seems to reign about what precisely is meant by economic effectiveness. For instance, in the 1974 edition of directives to be used in planning,[32] the chapter devoted to planning for increasing economic effectiveness of social production (ch. 2) begins by defining (absolute) economic effectiveness at the national level: 'the estimation of the economic effectiveness of the production plan is carried out on the basis of one single national economic criterion, the maximum growth of national income in relation to production expenditure in conditions of optimal relations between the accumulation fund and the consumption fund.'[33] The measures of effectiveness at sectoral and enterprise levels are then mentioned (being the growth of profits and profitability) but these indicators are subordinate to the absolute criterion at national level. However, the next paragraph of the 1974 directives point out that such indicators are, after all, only one aspect of measurement of economic effectiveness: 'the planning of economic effectiveness of social production is done not by just any one indicator, but by the complete series, since a whole set of factors influence the effectiveness of production and only by employing a system of additional indicators is it possible to make the correct choice of the level of effectiveness.'[34] There then follows a table showing all the relevant indicators to be used at each of four different levels (national, union republic, sectoral and enterprise). There are more than ten indicators, some having further subdivisions. At each level these indicators have to be estimated slightly differently, depending on the

Table 3.1

Norms	Old Technique	New Technique	Savings (−) Expenditure (+)

(A) Physical
(1) Raw materials
(2) Fuel and electricity
(3) Stocks
(4) Labor

(B) Value

(1) *Absolute*
   (a) materials used/value of
      production
      (*materialoemkost'*)
   (b) individual
      (*materialoemkost'*)
   (c) wages/value of production
      (*zarplatoemkost'*)
   (d) fixed + circulating capital/
      value of production
      (*fondoemkost'*)

(2) *Relative*
   (a) wages per ruble of increased
      production
   (b) labor expenditure per ruble of
      increased production
   (c) capital expenditure per ruble
      of increased production

statistical information available and the nature of prices at the level concerned. The recoupment period is mentioned as only one of the indicators and is the last indicator on the list.[35] These instructions are supplemented in later chapters by more detailed instructions for separate sectors of the economy.

Instructions published in 1977 on calculating effectiveness of investment in new technology[36] give examples of the sorts of criteria which ought to be taken into consideration (see Table 3.1). Additional tables are drawn up which may be used in different situations.

Thus the official Soviet guidelines on investment appraisal continue to include a multitude of coefficients/norms. It seems to be left to specific sectors (and subsectoral levels) to adopt those norms (in value and/or physical terms) which they feel appropriate.[37]

There are Soviet critics. For instance, Chernyavski states that the physical indicators of efficiency had a role to play before the development of value coefficients. He points out that the different indicators advocated are contradictory in that they can lead to different decisions. And he advocates the use of profitability as the synthetic measure of effectiveness.[38] There are also those who see the problem as lying in the nature of Soviet prices. Annikin stated (in 1973) that the Standard Methodology would only be useful if the system of fixed prices were replaced by a system of correlative (*korrelyativnye*) prices—where prices would reflect quality of products and substitutability.[39] The problems of efficiency of capital investment are also seen as part of the problem of implementing planned projects. Indeed, a vast proportion of current literature on the effectiveness of capital investment is concerned not with economic efficiency as understood by neoclassical economics but with management and implementation problems. Increasing attention is being given to use of techniques like network analysis (*metod setevogo planirovaniya*). Linked with this, is advocacy of the measurement of the 'integrated effect' of capital investment (that is, it is thought that effectiveness of investment cannot be isolated from the particular type of project concerned). Krasovskii states that the integrated effect must be calculated from empirical experience and careful approximations.[40] Together with the use of networks and graphs the whole pattern of capital investment can be examined. This method is particularly necessary for the planning of large-scale (*krupnomasshtabnye*) economic programs.

7   Conclusion

In neoclassical cost-benefit analysis alternative projects can be compared and ranked in order of preferability on the basis of the synthetic measure of rate of return. This synthetic measure can either be a simple measure of financial profitability or it can be a measure of the total return to the national economy—it can be based on market prices or it can be based on shadow prices where these are thought to represent a more realistic measure of the opportunity cost of use/production of resources. If required, this synthetic measure can also include other policy objectives such as redistribution of income, through appropriate weights attached to the relevant benefits.

Other methods for project selection have been developed in the West, notably the French 'effects method,'[41] which do not attempt to evaluate projects by one single criterion. The argument against the single synthetic measure is that by reducing all the effects of the project to terms which can be incorporated into the 'rate of return,' the specific effects of the project are hidden. Advocates of this method maintain that it is both more realistic and more desirable to specify all the effects of a project—thus permitting decisions which take account of the different effects.[42] The effects method also uses a 'value-added' measure (rather than a measure of profitability), arguing that consumption of wage earners should be regarded as a benefit and not as a cost. The three following effects of each project are calculated:

● the value added arising from the project (at market and shadow prices, domestic and national);
● the foreign exchange effect of the project;
● the employment effect of the project.

The Soviet methodology of investment appraisal resembles this method in that it requires several different measures of effectiveness (unit cost of raw materials, labor, etc.) to be taken into account—and rejects the use of one synthetic measure of efficiency.

Yet the Soviet methodology differs from the effects method in that:

- The choice between projects is at subsectoral level. Allocation of investment to the sectors is a centralized decision.
- The Soviet methodologies suggest the use of several coefficients; each coefficient may be measured in a slightly different way according to the particular circumstances. It is up to the sectoral authorities (and decision-making bodies within the sectors) to select the coefficients to be used and to define their measurement.
- Although the measure of value added is used in the coefficient of absolute effectiveness at national level, the measure at project level has not until recently been a value-added measure but one based on profitability.
- The Soviet criteria are not measures which take account of the life of the project.
- Other specific differences lie in the nature of Soviet prices, which are not suitable tools for choice between alternative uses of resources.

Although the Soviet methodology may seem to be similar to the approach taken by the effects method, the former has arisen from the specific Soviet heritage: that is, the explicit rejection of 'economic' measurement as the basis for decision-making and the original confinement of the notion of efficiency to technical efficiency (rather than economic efficiency). Technical efficiency can be defined and compared by performance indicators (norms). Economic efficiency requires the incorporation of some measure of trade off between uses of resources.

The problem is that in the Soviet methodology, in contradistinction to cost benefit analysis and social cost benefit analysis (SCBA), there is no underlying theory which can produce one synthetic measure of efficiency. This is not to say that the neoclassical basis of cost benefit analysis is any more realistic (in describing the relationships in the real world). The point is that SCBA has been developed by theoreticians from a neoclassical theory of economics. SCBA is therefore theoretically rigorous.

The Soviet methodology, on the other hand, has developed as a result of the immediate and pressing need to make planning decisions.[43] This has resulted in a multitude of norms and instructions precisely because there is no *a priori* theory, acceptable to the Soviet Union, which allows all expenditures and benefits to be measured on one scale. Technical efficiency determines one set of norms; 'economic' efficiency is interpreted as the least cost method of meeting a given need.

Notes: Chapter 3

The research on which this article (first published in *Soviet Studies*, vol. 33, no. 4, October 1981) is based was made possible by a British Council scholarship at Leningrad University in 1980, for which I would like to express my thanks.

1 For a history of these early debates, see J. P. Collette, *Politique des investissements et calcul économique, l'expérience soviétique* (Paris: Editions Cujas, 1964); also Holland Hunter, 'The planning of investments in the Soviet Union,' *Review of Economics and Statistics*, vol. 1 (1949). For examples of Soviet contributions see *Soviet Studies*, vol. 1, no. 2 (October 1949), p. 119; vol. 1, no. 4 (April 1950), p. 356; vol. 2, no. 3 (January 1951), p. 317; vol. 4, no. 3 (January 1953), p. 340.

2 This was bound up with the belief that only in socialism was society freed from the constraints to development which existed in capitalist countries—namely, the contradiction faced by capitalism which was constantly pressurized, on the one hand, to undercut competitors (by increasing capital investment—the organic composition of capital), and yet still had to employ sufficient labor power to extract sufficient surplus value (this was a pressure against increasing the organic composition of capital). I do not intend to evaluate this belief here. See A. Emelyanov, 'O metodakh opredeleniya ekonomicheskoi effektivnosti primeneniya mashin v sovetskom khoziastve,' *Voprosy ekonomiki*, no. 11 (1949); D. T. Chernomordik, 'Effektivnost' kapital 'novo Vlozheniya i Teoriya Vozproizvodstva. K Opredeleniyu Problema,' *Voprosy ekonomiki*, no. 6 (1949); and also Collette, op. cit., p. 217.

3 Hunter, art. cit.; and Collette, op. cit.

4 'Itogi diskusii ob opredelenii ekonomicheskoi effektivnosti kapital'nykh vlozhenii v promyshlennost' SSSR,' *Voprosy ekonomiki*, no. 3 (1954), p. 99. Translation in *Soviet Studies*, vol. 6, no. 2 (October 1954), p. 201.

5 'Rekomendatsii vsesoyuznoi nauchno-tekhnicheskoi konferentsii po problemam opredeleniya ekonomicheskoi effektivnosti kapital'nykh vlozhenii i novoi tekhniki v narodnom khozyaistve SSSR,' *Voprosy ekonomiki*, no. 9 (1958), p. 154. Translation in F. Holzman (ed.), *Readings on the Soviet Economy* (Chicago: Rand McNally, 1962), p. 388.

6 A limited role for the law of value had been recognized in 1943 in an anonymous (and so quasi-official) article in *Pod znamenem Marksizma*; this, however, had no implications for policy. In the late 1940s reaction had set in again with the criticism, dismissal (March 1949), and the ultimate shooting of N. A. Voznesenski, the Politburo member and Gosplan chairman who had attempted to give greater significance to the law of value in the Soviet economy. Four debates on the 'law of value' and its role in the USSR were held in 1956–8 (see *Voprosy ekonomiki*, nos. 2 and 8 [1957]; and no. 2 [1958]), as a result of which it seems to have been generally accepted that the law of value did indeed function in the USSR. This, in turn, led to a spate of work on how prices should better reflect values (a task seen as crucial if 'social labor' were to be rationally planned). Whether rational allocation can, in fact, be based on labor values (labor embodied) does not concern us here, since the intention of this chapter is to understand the Soviet approach to investment choice.

7 'In view of the fact that in socialism we do not yet have the ability directly to calculate expenditures of social labour ... and that commodity production exists and the law of value functions in socialism (in a limited form), it is entirely

expedient to measure different expenditures of labor in value form' (T. S. Khachaturov, *Ekonomichestkaya effektivnost kapital'novo vlozheniya v SSSR* [Moscow, 1958]).

8 Prices based on 'values' are prices based on costs. The Soviet methodologies do recognize that problems will arise where measurements are being made in prices which are *not* based on values. However, the neoclassical critique of Soviet prices is more fundamental than this. It is the problem clarified by Oskar Lange's statement: 'If the price of a scarce productive resource is planned too low, and the price of an abundant resource is planned too high, the cost of production shown in the book-keeping of the plants can be reduced by substituting the scarce resource for an abundant one. Considered from the point of view of the economy as a whole, such a substitution is a waste of resources and the reduction in the book-keeping costs of the plants represents a decrease, not an increase, of their economic efficiency. This discrepancy between the cost accounting of the plants and their true economic efficiency can be avoided only by pricing the productive resources according to their scarcity relative to demand' (*The Working Principles of the Soviet Economy* [New York: Research Bureau for Postwar Economics, 1944] p. 14). Of course, Lange is talking about static efficiency prices. The point is still relevant, however, in that Soviet prices are not 'rational' in a static or dynamic sense. Whilst some Soviet economists do recognize this problem of using nonparametric prices for criteria of choice (the mathematical school), the official guidelines, and indeed the majority of economists, see such critiques as 'bourgeois' in inspiration.

9 (i) 1960 SM. 'Tipovaya metodika opredeleniya ekonomicheskoi effektivnosti kapital'nykh vlozhenii i novoi tekhniki v narodnom khozyaistve SSSR,' *Planovoye khoziaistvo*, no. 3 (1960), p. 56. Translation in *Problems of Economics*, vol. 3, no. 6 (1960).

(ii) 1969 SM. *Tipovaya metodika opredeleniya ekonomicheskoi effektivnosti kapital'nykh vlozhenii* (Moscow, 8 September 1969). Ratified by Gosplan and the Academy of Sciences. Translation in *Matekon*, vol. 8, no. 1 (1970).

(iii) 1980 SM. Ratified by Gosplan, September 1980. See 'Metodika opredeleniya ekonomicheskoi effektivnosti kapital'nykh vlozhenii,' *Ekonomicheskaya gazeta*, nos 2 and 3 (1981).

Two sets of recommendations concerning investment criteria are also cited here:

(i) 1964. *Tipovaya metodika opredeleniya ekonomicheskoi effektivnosti kapital'nykh vlozhenii i novoi tekhniki v narodnom khozyaistve SSSR*, 2nd edn (Moscow, 1964). Issued by the Institute of Economics of the Academy of Sciences with the participation of scientific institutions and Gosplan.

(ii) 1966. *Tipovaya metodika opredeleniya ekonomicheskoi effektivnosti kapital'nykh vlozhenii* (Moscow, 1966). Special report issued by the Nauchnyi sovet po probleme ekonomicheskoi effektivnosti osnovnykh fondov kapital'nogo vlozheniya i novoi tekhnologii of the Academy of Sciences.

10 Alan Abouchar sees this as the main difference between the 1960 SM and the 1969 SM ('The new Soviet Standard Methodology for investment allocation,' *Soviet Studies*, vol. 24, no. 3 [January 1973], p. 402). He interprets the absolute coefficient at national level defined in the 1969 SM as an innovation and, furthermore, he interprets this coefficient as the introduction of a single synthetic criterion by which all investments are to be judged. I shall show that this is not the case.

11 The decree of the Central Committee of the Communist Party and the Soviet Council of Ministers, July 1979, whereby a new measure of net ('normed') output (measure of value added) was introduced to replace global value of sales as the

main indicator for production associations: 'Ob uluchshenii planirovaniya i usilenii vozdeistviya khoziastvennogo mekhanizma na povyshenie effektivnosti proizvodstva i kachestva raboty,' *Planovoye khoziaistvo*, no. 9 (1979), pp. 4–36.

12 The first mention of subnational measures of the CAE is in the 1964 recommendations. Here it states that at 'branch' and 'subbranch' level, 'if net product is not calculated' an approximation of the coefficient can be made by a measure of profitability. Similarly, in the 1966 recommendations, it states that profits can be used in the calculation at *otrasl* level, '*where full net product is not calculated*' (my emphasis).

13 For instance, V. O. Chernyavski simply stated: 'At the level of the national economy the actual size of produced national income ... characterizes the effectiveness of social production. However, at *otrasl* and enterprise level other indicators are *needed*, such as the minimization of total expenditure, profit and profitability' (*Voprosy effektivnosti i optimal'nosti* [Moscow, 1977], p. 10).

14 See note 10. As a result of his interpretation of the meaning of the absolute coefficient, Abouchar is confused by the existence of what he calls the 'enterprise allocation coefficient' (= the absolute coefficient at enterprise level).

15 This is not to say that there are not advocates of such a marginal criterion of efficiency in the USSR. the point being made here is that the official directives do not give support to such views.

16 Point 125 of the 1964 recommendations states that the coefficient of absolute effectiveness should be used along with other measures (the capital/output ratio, profit, etc.). 1969 SM, point 16, states that additional criteria affecting the absolute effectiveness of capital investment are changes in labor intensity (*trudoemkost'*), volume of raw materials used in production (*materialoemkost'*), capital funds involved in production (*fondoemkost'*), and reduction of the construction period and budgeted costs. 1969 SM, point 17 states that in order to coordinate efficiency with other sections of the plan, account must be taken of productivity of labor, return on funds, gross production, capital output ratio, natural indicators, etc. In other words, the plan as determined by material balances continues to be all-important.

17 Point 19 of the 1958 recommendations states that improved quality will not be reflected in the measurement of the coefficient of relative effectiveness, and indeed, that if improved quality involves increases in the costs of production, the alternative in question will be further handicapped. It is suggested that there should be allowance for price changes, but at this stage it is not stated how such price changes would be incorporated. The 1960 SM does state that where the alternatives to be compared do not produce exactly the same output (quantity), then adjustments must be made so that comparisons do involve equal volumes of production. Again, however, it does not specify how to make such adjustments.

18 Gosudarstvennyi komitet soveta ministrov SSSR po nauke i tekhnike, Gosplan SSSR, Akademi Nauk SSSR, and Gosudarstvennyi komitet soveta ministrov SSSR po delam izobretenii i otkrytii, *Metodika (osnovyne polozheniya) opredeleniya ekonomicheskoi effektivnosti ispol'zovaniya v narodnom khozyaistve novoi tekhniki, izobretenii i ratsionalizatorskikh predlozhenii* (Moscow, 14 February 1977, no. 48/16/13/3).

19 T. S. Khachaturov, in his contribution to the international symposium held in Moscow in 1965 on the problem of definition of norms of economic effectiveness of capital investment. Attended by economists from the USSR, Bulgaria, GDR, Poland and Czechoslovakia. Proceedings published in *Voprosy izmereniya effektivnosti kapital'nykh vlozhenii* (Moscow, 1968).

20 V. Krasovski, M. Loiter, *et al.*, *Metodicheskie problemy ekonomicheskoi effektivnosti*

kapital'nykh vlozhenii (Moscow, 1977).

21 *Metodika opredeleniya ekonomicheskoi effektivnosti vnedreniya novoi tekhniki avtomatizatsii proizvodstvennykh protsessov v promyshlennosti* (Moscow, 1962), cited in 1964 SM, point 31. Also reproduced in Michael Ellmann, *Socialist Planning* (Cambridge: Cambridge University Press, 1979), p. 141.

22 David Dyker, *The Process of Investment in the Soviet Union* (Cambridge: Cambridge University Press, 1983), p. 107.

23 Thus $E_H = W(1 + a)/F$, where W = total wage costs, F = fixed capital stock, a = relation of surplus product to wages (average for the whole economy). The 1969 SM suggests that, where prices do not reflect value, this coefficient (at enterprise level) can be calculated using *sebestoimost'* of one time period compared with the previous time period, $(S_1 - S_2)/K$.

24 An arbitrary formula, together with an example, is given in 1964 SM, point 73. This formula is $A = P(S + E_H K)$, where P is the additional amount of the deficit good needed by one variant, S is the *sebestoimost'*, E_H is the norm of comparative effectiveness, K the capital costs and A the amount by which costs have to be increased.

25 Point 72, 1964 recommendations, advocates the use of the formula:

$$K = \sum_{t=1}^{T} [K_t - P_t (Ts_t - S_t)] (1 + E_H)^{T-t}$$

where K is the total commensurable costs, K_t is the capital investment, P_t is the quantity of production in year t, S_t is the *sebestoimost'* in year t, E_H is the 'discount' rate. Thus benefits are being quantified here.

26 The discount rate advocated in a 1977 Gosplan publication is 10 percent. In the same publication the economy-wide coefficient of relative effectiveness is said to be 0.15. *Metodika (osnovnye polozheniya) opredeleniya*, op. cit at note 18. This publication gives a table of discount factors for 10 percent.

27 Instructions on the correct determination of *sebestoimost'* were published by Gosplan in 1955 and revised in 1970. *Osnovnye polozheniya po planirovaniyu, uchetu, i kal'kulirovaniyu sebestoimosti promyshlennoi produktsii*, 18 March 1955; *Osnovnye polozheniya po planirovaniyu, uchetu i kal'kulirovaniyu sebestoimosti produktsii na promyshlennykh predpriyatiyakh* (Moscow, 1970, reprinted 1975).

28 Salvage value was not seen as a benefit since the individual enterprise would not receive any benefit even if the old machinery were put to productive use elsewhere. Unamortized equipment was to be reckoned as a loss, however, since it was increasingly being recognized at this time that there was need for more realistic rules for amortization. See Marie Lavigne, *Le Capital dans l'économie soviétique*, Collection développement économique, no. 7 (Paris: SEDES, 1961).

29 The Nauchnyi sovet po probleme ekonomicheskoi effektivnosti kapital'nykh vlozhenii i novoi tekhnologii, chaired by Khachaturov, publishes annual reports on its research work.

30 *Ekonomicheskaya effektivnost' osnovnykh fondov kapital'nykh vlozhenii i novoi tekhniki, Informatsiya o deyatel'nosti nauchnogo soveta po problem ... v 1965 godu* (Moscow, 1965).

31 Dyker, op. cit., at n. 22, p. 103.

32 The 1974 edition is the most recent; *Metodicheskie ukazaniya k razrabotke gosudarstvennykh planov razvitiya narodnogo khozyaistva SSSR* (Moscow, 1974).

33 It is interesting that the notion of optimality between consumption and investment is mentioned. However, this is a loose use of the word 'optimality,' it has no

rigorous mathematical meaning but is rather a continuation of the notion of the 'law of proportional development of socialist society.'

34 1974 directives, op. cit. at note 32, p. 33.

35 The indicators are subdivided into (i) general indicators (growth of national income, of consumption funds, return on funds, relative savings in the costs of material production—savings of wages, inputs, etc.—general profitability, capital output ratio); (ii) indicators of increasing the effectiveness of labor (rate of growth of productivity of labor, percentage of increase of national income due to increases in productivity of labor, savings in living labor); (iii) indicators of increasing the effectiveness of use of capital funds, circulating funds and capital investment (return on funds, rate of turnover of circulating funds, relationship of growth of annual national income to the capital investment responsible for such growth, the recoupment period); (iv) indicators of increasing the effectiveness of material resources (expenditure on materials—not including amortization—per ruble of social product), ibid., pp. 34–7.

36 *Metodika (osnovnye polozheniya) opredeleniya*, op. cit. at n. 18.

37 This chapter does not attempt to examine the ways in which investment decisions are actually taken. In 1977 Krasovski, Loiter, *et al.* state: 'The most important principle in defining economic effectiveness and the choice of one or other method of calculation (of economic effectiveness, general or comparative) depends on the particular task' (op. cit. at n. 20).

38 Chernyavski (op. cit. at n. 13) comments on the different possible criteria:
(i) Gross product/capital investment. This will, he says, discourage capital investment.
(ii) Net product/number of workers. This measure may increase 'effectiveness in one sector of the economy, at the expense of losses elsewhere in the economy.'
(iii) Minimization of *sebestoimost'*. Chernyavski does not agree that capital expenditure is reflected in *sebestoimost'* through amortization charges (which are included).
(iv) Recoupment period. This can only be used for additional capital investment.
(v) $Z = S + E_H K$, where Z is the value to be minimized, $S = sebestoimost'$, $E_H =$ sectoral CRE, $K =$ capital invested. These measurements can only be used where the output concerned are identical in composition, quality and timing.

39 I. M. Annikin, *Limitnaya tsena: ekonomicheskaya effektivnost' povyshenia kachestva produktsii* (Moscow, 1973). Of course, the mathematical school of Soviet economists has long since advocated a 'rational' price set.

40 V. Krasovski, 'Integralnii effekt i faktor vremenii,' *Voprosy ekonomiki*, no. 8 (1974), p. 3; and in *Ekonomicheskie problemy effektivnosi ispol'zovaniya investitsionnogo potentsiala strany v period razvitogo sotsializma* (Moscow: Academy of Sciences, October 1977), ch. 1.

41 For example, M. Cherval, 'The rationale of the effects method,' *Oxford Bulletin of Economics and Statistics*, no. 4 (1977), p. 333.

42 For a critique of the effects method see Bela Balassa, 'The effects method of project evaluation,' *Oxford Bulletin of Economics and Statistics*, no. 4 (1976), p. 219.

43 For example, discounting of the capital costs of a project, where these costs are spread over several years, was introduced because of the problem of constant overshooting of construction plans.

4 *The Soviet 1969 Standard Methodology for Investment Allocation versus 'Universally Correct' Methods*

FRANK A. DURGIN

1 Introduction

The investment decision is characterized by several salient features which mark it for special attention by economists, corporate directors and central planners. First, perhaps, are the political consequences, for both the corporate director and central planner, stemming from the fact that investment visibly eats into dividends and current consumption. Second is the all-important, but less visible, fact that investment is a prime determinant of the corporation's future position and dividend flow as well as a determinant of the nation's economic growth and the pattern and level of future consumption. A third distinguishing feature is the sobering magnitude of the resources involved. Because the resources committed to the acquisition of a facility or piece of equipment can only be recovered through its operation, the decision to invest involves not only a commitment of the resources necessary to acquire or build, but also a commitment of the resources required for its operation during the next five to twenty-five or more years.

Given this critical nature of the investment decision, control over investment is highly centralized in both the East and West. Although investment projects may be defined in operating units many layers deep down inside the corporate and ministerial bodies, final approval of the bulk of the projects is made at the top, or very near the top, of the managerial hierarchy. The volume of investment which can be decided upon at the plant or divisional level in the West is minuscule,[1] a point to which we shall return at the end of the chapter. The volume of investment decided at the plant level in the East, on the other hand, is now running on the order of some 20 percent of the total—with the very substantial qualification that the central planners must then provide nearly all the physical inputs.

Whether the investment authority is centralized or decentralized, the scale of economic organization, both East and West, gives rise to the need for a standardization of procedures governing the choice of projects. Where the authority is centralized it is necessary that the request for resources coming up the ladder to the center from scores of units diversified by geography, level and function be uniform as to format of presentation, criteria for justification and methods of calculation. This is so whether the request travels the department, plant, division, group, corporate center route in the West, or the plant, firm, association, ministry route in the East. If the decision to invest is decentralized, a set of guidelines is likewise necessary to ensure that the decisions taken are in the interest of the corporate or ministerial body as well as in the interest of the operating unit making the decision.

The 1969 Standard Methodology (1969 SM)[2] is the latest version of the Soviet response to this need for a uniformity of criteria and procedures in defining investment projects. It offers no solution to the vital question of optimizing the share of investment in GNP, only a solution to the question of effecting an optimal allocation of the amounts earmarked for investment. It contains rules governing the calculation of two separate measures of the effectiveness of capital investment and the establishment of norms of project acceptability. Furthermore, it makes the observance of those rules 'obligatory for all branches of the national economy.'[3]

The two measures provided for by 1969 SM are (i) the coefficient of the general (absolute) effectiveness of capital investment, and (ii) the comparative cost of capital investment. As there has been some confusion in both the East and the West regarding the purpose having two measures, it may be helpful to point out that all investment projects fall into one of two broad categories: (i) output expansion projects, and (ii) cost reduction (with output fixed) projects.

The coefficient of general (absolute) effectiveness of capital is used to determine the effectiveness of output (or income) expansion type projects. It is a crude rate of return measure used, as one Soviet writer has put it, to determine 'what to produce.'[4]

The comparative cost is used to determine the effectiveness of cost-reduction type projects. It is simply a measure of the cost of different ways of producing a given output. As the same Soviet writer has put it, it is used to determine 'how to produce.'

It is the object of this chapter to examine the theoretical underpinnings of 1969 SM to see if the use of the measures it prescribes could lead to an optimization of the investment process. To do this we will compare the Soviet measures of effectiveness of capital with measures which can be termed as 'true' or 'universally correct,' in a setting of rational prices, economic certainty and stable interest rates.

Section 2 of this chapter explains some of the 'true' and 'universally correct' measures of the effectiveness of capital investments, that is, internal rate of return, present value and equivalent uniform annual costs. The material covered is very basic[5] and can be omitted by people familiar with the use of interest tables and the equivalency concept. We have included them only because they have not yet made their way into standard economics curricula.

Section 3 compares the Soviet coefficient of the general (absolute)

Table 4.1

End of Year	Net Cash Flow ($)	Present Value[a] Factor	Discounted Present Value of ($)	
			Outflow	Inflow
0	−1,000	1.0000	1,000	
1	+ 500	.8333		416.65
2	+ 500	.6944		347.22
3	+ 500	.5787		289.35
		Total	1,000	1,053.22
		Net Present Value		53.22

[a]$1/(1 + i)^N$. These can be found in any set of standard interest tables.

effectiveness of capital investment with the 'universally correct' net present value and the 'true' internal rate of return method used to evaluate investment proposals in the West.

Section 4 compares the Soviet comparative cost of capital with the present value, equivalent uniform annual cost and rate of return methods used in engineering economy studies in the West.

Section 5 takes a brief peek at some US practices.

2 'True' Measures of the Effectiveness of Capital Investments

(a) True Measures of the Effectiveness of Income (Output) Expansion Investments

(I) NET PRESENT VALUE (NPV)

This is considered by most scholars to be the 'universally correct' method for ranking income (output) expansion type investments.[6] It consists of summing up the discounted present value of the cash inflows and outflows associated with a project. If the net present value of those flows is positive, the project is acceptable—if negative, it is unacceptable. In ranking a number of acceptable projects, the project with the highest positive NPV is the best.[7] The rate of interest used for discounting the cash flows is governed by the opportunity cost of capital and is referred to as the minimum required rate of return. To illustrate: consider a firm whose current cost of capital is 20 percent and which is contemplating investing $1,000 today in a project which will produce a net cash flow of $500 receivable at the end of each of the next three years with no salvage. The NPV solution to the problem is shown in Table 4.1.

Table 4.2

End Year	Net Cash Flow ($)	Present Value Factor	Present Value at 20% ($)	Present Value Factor at 25%	Present Value at 25% ($)
0	−1,000	1.000	−1,000	1.0000	−1,000
1	+ 500	.833	+ 416.65	.8000	+ 400
2	+ 500	.694	+ 347.22	.6400	+ 320
3	+ 500	.579	+ 289.35	.5120	+ 256
		Net Present Value	+ 53.22		− 24

Because the project has a net positive cash flow of $53 it should be accepted. One way of envisaging this is to consider the $1,053 discounted present value of the $500 annual income associated with the project as being the amount one would have to invest at 20 percent in order to receive back $500 a year for three years. This project, however, yields a $500 income for three years at a cost of only $1,000. The rate of return, therefore, is higher than 20 percent (that is, 23.375 percent as we shall see below). We are getting a $1,053 value for only $1,000.

(II) INTERNAL RATE OF RETURN (IRR)

A decision on the project just considered can also be made by determining its IRR, that is, the rate earned on the unrecovered balance of the investment over the course of its life. Mathematically this is the rate at which the discounted present worth of all of the cash inflows and outflows associated with the project are equal. It is found by trial and error as we shall illustrate.

We already have the net present value of the project at 20 percent. Since the rate of return of the project (as we have seen) is higher than 20 percent we shall test it at 25 percent. This rate, as is shown above, is too high. We therefore interpolate between the values of the net present values at 20 percent and 25 percent to find the actual rate, as shown in Table 4.2. Interpolating for a first approximation ($53 + $24 = $77, 53/77 = .688). The IRR is close to .20 + (.688)(.05) or 23–44 percent. Successive interpolations over progressively smaller ranges yield an IRR of 23.375 percent. The project is thus acceptable using either the NPV or IRR method.[8]

The fact that the project's IRR Is 23.375 percent can be seen more clearly if it is compared to placing $1,000 in a bank paying 23.375 percent interest. The arithmetic is shown in Table 4.3.

Table 4.3

	($)
Initial deposit	1,000.00
First year's interest	233.75
Balance at end of year 1	1,233.75
Withdrawal at end of year 1	500.00
Balance at beginning of year 2	733.75
Second year's interest	171.52
Balance at end of year 2	905.27
Withdrawal at end of year 2	500.00
Balance at beginning of year 3	405.27
Third year's interest	94.73
Balance at end of year 3	500.00
Withdrawal at end of year 3	500.00
Salvage	0

(b) 'True' Measures of the Effectiveness of Cost-Reduction Investments

There are three measures, all of which can be considered to be 'true,' which can be used to determine the effectiveness of cost-reduction type projects: (i) present value, (ii) equivalent uniform annual cost, and (iii) rate of return. We shall illustrate the use of these three measures to determine whether a firm whose opportunity cost of capital is 20 percent should purchase machine X which costs $2,000 and requires $100 a year to operate or machine Y which costs $1,000 and requires $500 a year to operate. The operating costs cited are for an identical output, and the economic lives of both machines are three years with no salvage value.

(I) PRESENT VALUE (PV)

This is the same method as that used on income-expansion type projects. The sole difference is that in cost-reduction projects there are usually only costs to be considered. The sum of the discounted present worth of all of the costs associated with the purchase and operation of machine X is compared with the sum of the discounted present work of all of the costs associated with the purchase and operation of machine Y. At 20 percent the present value of

Table 4.4

Year	Present Value 20% Factors	Cost of Machine X ($)	Present Value ($)	Cost of Machine Y ($)	Present Value ($)
0	1.0000	2,000	2,000.00	1,000	1,000.00
1	.83333	100	83.33	500	416.67
2	.69444	100	69.44	500	342.22
3	.57870	100	57.87	500	289.35
			2,210.64		2,053.22

machine Y, as shown in Table 4.4, is the smaller of the two. It, therefore, is the best choice.

These present values can be thought of as equivalents. In the case of machine X, the impact on the balance sheet of buying and operating the machine for three years is equivalent to the impact of an immediate $2,210 expenditure. It can also be thought of as the amount of money a firm earning 20 percent on its capital would have to come up with in one lump sum today in order to pay for the machine and provide for all of its future operating costs. The arithmetic of this explanation for machine X is shown in Table 4.5.

(II) EQUIVALENT UNIFORM ANNUAL COST (EUAC)

Because PV analysis is cumbersome to manipulate in comparisons involving projects with unequal lives, the equivalent EUAC method is more widely used. It produces the same ranking as PV and hence can be considered 'universally valid.' It shows what all of the costs associated with a given project are equivalent to in terms of equal annual end of year payments over the life of the project. The uniform annual equivalent of the $2,000 initial investment in machine X consists of the annualized capital consumption plus annual interest costs on the unrecovered balance. Its exact value can be found by means of the capital recovery factor.[9] Multiplying the $2,000 by the capital recovery factor for three years at 20 percent (.47473) gives an annual equivalent of $949.46. Adding the annual operating cost of $100 gives a total equivalent uniform annual cost of $1,049.46. The equivalent uniform annual cost of machine Y is the $1,000 initial investment multiplied by the capital recovery factor (.47473), plus the $500 operating costs, or a total of $974.73 per year. Machine Y, as we saw using the present value approach, is the more economical.

Stating that the equivalent uniform annual cost of machine X at 20 percent is $1,049.46 means that, for a firm able to earn 20 percent on its capital,

Table 4.5

	($)
Initial fund	2,210.64
Withdrawal for purchase of machine	2,000.00
Balance on deposit after purchase	210.64
First year's interest	42.13
Balance at end of year 1	252.77
Payment of operating costs	100.00
Balance at beginning of year 2	152.77
Second year's interest	30.56
Balance at end of year 2	183.33
Payment of operating costs	100.00
Balance at beginning of year 3	83.33
Third year's interest	16.67
Balance at end of year 3	100.00
Payment of operating costs	100.00
Balance	0

spending $1,049.46 at the end of each year for the next three years has the same impact on the balance sheet as buying machine X and operating it for the three years. The arithmetic of this fact is shown in Table 4.6 for machine X. The 4¢ difference is due to rounding.

(III) RATE OF RETURN

The choice between machines X and Y can also be made by determining the rate of return on the extra investment associated with machine X. Buying machine X is, in effect, investing an extra $1,000 in return for a $400 a year income in the form of savings. Since the cost of capital is 20 percent, if the $400 a year savings on the operating cost represented a more than 20 percent return, then the savings would more than offset the cost of the extra investment, bringing the equivalent uniform annual costs of X below those of Y. But if the savings do not represent at least a 20 percent return, then it is not worthwhile going for the higher-priced machine. Mathematically, the rate of return on the extra investment is the rate of interest which makes the EUAC of the two alternatives equal. It is found by a trial and error process, as was illustrated in the previous section. In this simple example with equal lives, no salvage value and uniform costs, the rate is about 9.68 percent. It would

Table 4.6

	Purchase and Operation of Machine ($)	Spending $1,049.46 a Year ($)
Initial fund	2,210.64	2,210.64
Immediate outlay	2,000.00	0
Balance at beginning of year 1	210.64	2,210.64
Interest during year 1	42.13	442.13
Balance at end of year 1	252.77	2,652.77
Expenditure	100.00	1,049.46
Balance at beginning of year 2	152.77	1,603.31
Interest during year 2	30.56	320.66
Balance at the end of year 2	183.33	1,923.97
Expenditure	100.00	1,049.46
Balance at beginning of year 3	83.33	874.51
Interest during year 3	16.67	174.91
Balance at end of year 3	100.00	1.049.42
Expenditure	100.00	1,049.46
Balance	0	−.04

not, therefore pay to invest funds in machine X on which we can earn (or which cost us) 20 percent merely to earn 9.68 percent. Machine Y, therefore, by all three methods is the more economical.

3   The Soviet Coefficient of General (Absolute) Effectiveness of Capital Investments (CGE)

(a) Description

Section II of 1969 SM contains rules for calculating the coefficient of the general effectiveness of capital investments (CGE) at every possible level of the national economy—that of the nation, republic, region, sector, branch, ministry, department, economic association, enterprise and on down to the individual project. The CGE for proposed aggregate investments at the

Table 4.7 *Identity of Rankings Produced by the IRR and CGE When Project Lives Are Equal*

Investment	$1,000,000	$1,500,000
Life	5 years	5 years
Salvage	0	0
Net cash flow	$300,000	$500,000
Depreciation	$200,000	$300,000
Profit	$100,000	$200,000
CGE	10.00%	13.33%
IRR	15.24%	19.86%
NPV (at 10%)	$137,240	$395,400

national, republican and sectoral levels is simply the marginal output/capital ratio (that is, the ratio of the increase in national income to the investment causing that increase). The CGE for investments at the branch, ministry, economic association, enterprise and individual project level is the ratio of the increase in profit to the capital investment causing the increase. The CGE of existing investments is simply the ratio of total current national income or profit (depending on the level) to the total average annual value of the production assets employed at that level. Given the fact that the aggregate of the investment affected at each level (except project level) embraces a large number of projects of varying lives, no exact measure of their effectiveness is possible. The Soviet CGE, consequently, is as good as any which could be devised and, it might be noted, differs only in name from concepts used by economists and Wall Street analysts in the West.

Exact measures are, however, possible at the project level and it is here that the Soviet measure, on a theoretical plane at least, must be faulted. The CGE for a given project is, as we have seen, the ratio of the annual income to the investment producing it. It is, as we shall note in a subsequent section, identical to the financial statement method used in US industry, and as such, has two major flaws. First, it fails to recognize that the investment is recovered through depreciation allowances over the life of the project. Consequently, it produces a rate of return which is considerably lower than the 'true' rate. Second, it fails to consider the timing of the investment expenditures as well as that of the incomes. As a result of these two flaws, the coefficient can turn up an improper ranking of alternatives.

The fact that the rates computed by means of the CGE are lower than the IRR is, by itself, of little importance. In cases where the projects being compared have equal lives and uniform incomes, the coefficient will produce a ranking identical to that produced by the IRR and NPV methods as shown in Table 4.7.

The amount by which the CGE deviates from the IRR, however, varies with the life of the project, as is shown in Table 4.8. Consequently, in cases

Table 4.8 *Deviation of the CGE from the IRR*

Life in Years	Cash Flow = 30% of Investment			Cash Flow = 25% of Investment			Cash Flow = 20% of Investment		
	IRR (%)	CGE (%)	Error (%)	IRR (%)	CGE (%)	Error (%)	IRR (%)	CGE (%)	Error (%)
4	7.71	5.00	−35.15	—	—	—	—	—	—
5	15.24	10.00	−34.38	7.93	5.00	−36.95	—	—	—
6	19.90	13.33	−33.02	12.98	8.33	−35.82	5.47	3.33	−39.12
7	22.93	15.71	−31.49	16.33	10.71	−34.42	9.19	5.71	−37.87
10	27.32	20.00	−26.79	21.41	15.00	−29.93	15.10	10.00	−33.77
20	29.84	25.00	−16.22	24.70	20.00	−19.03	19.42	15.00	−22.76
50	30.00	28.00	− 6.66	25.00	23.00	− 8.00	20.00	18.00	−10.00

where project lives differ, the coefficient can produce a ranking which differs from that produced on the basis of the IRR, as is shown in Table 4.9.

The second flaw, the failure to reflect the impact of the timing of the cash outflows and inflows, is far more serious. Table 4.10 uses a case involving two projects with differing lives and cash-flow patterns to demonstrate the effects of the CGE's failure to reflect the timing of the cash outflows.

With respect to the examples provided in the tables, we remind the reader that the IRR and NPV are calculated on the basis of a project's net cash flow. They weigh projects on the basis of the timing of the actual flows of cash in and out of the cash register. The Soviet CGE, like the popular financial statement method in the West, however, simply relates net profits (cash flow minus arbitrarily timed depreciation changes) to the original investment.

(b) Assessment

While the crudity of the Soviet CGE might disturb the purist, we must not lose sight of the fact that, in spite of its imperfections, the same instrument under other names (financial statement method or average return on investment) has served US industry reasonably well for a great many years. Furthermore, it is highly doubtful if its replacement by a 'true' measure would have resulted in any change in intersectoral or interbranch rationing of capital during these past seven years. 1969 SM does not mandate that the CGE serve as the criterion for the intersectoral or interbranch distribution of investment funds. It merely states that, in drawing up investment plans, the computed CGE will be compared with the planning norms and analogous indices for a preceding period and with the effectiveness of capital in the more progressive enterprises of the *particular branch or subbranch*. The investments 'can be considered economically effective if the CGEs arrived at are not below the

Table 4.9 *Effect of Unequal Project Lives on the CGE as Compared with the IRR*

	Project A	Project B
Investment	$1,000	$1,000
Life	5 years	25 years
Salvage	0	0
Net cash flow	$334	$183
Depreciation	$200	$ 40
Profit	$134	$143
Soviet CAE	13.40%	14.30%
IRR	20%	18%

planning norms and analogous indices for the preceding planning period."[10]

The continuing primacy of development over rate of return considerations can be seen in the magnitude of the variation in rates of profit among sectors. The CGE for the economy as a whole in 1968 was 11.5 percent, 16.3 percent for industry, 7.5 percent for agriculture and procurements and 7.8 percent for transportation.[11] The industry average for 1971 was 19.8 percent, with rates ranging around this from a high of 40.8 percent in light industry to a low of 7 percent in the coal industry.[12] With differences of that order, it would be difficult to argue that a more sensitive measure is needed to effectively ration capital. If the CGE has any potential to serve as a precipitant in the capital rationing process, it has been largely neutralized through manipulations of the CGEs of project acceptability. These ranged among the branches in 1975 from 0.01 to 0.80.[13]

It might also be quite logically hypothesized that even if rate of return considerations were accorded primacy, a pattern of capital allocation precipitated by the CGE would not be greatly different from one precipitated by the IRR. And in the event it were different, it is unlikely that it would be more efficient. Support for this hypothesis is grounded on the fact that exact measures can infallibly lead to optimality only in a setting of economic certainty and a rational structure of prices.

While the Soviet world is characterized by a larger degree of certainty than the West, it, too, as is attested to by the record of plan nonfulfillment, is plagued by uncertainties. The sources of these uncertainties are virtually infinite—the crops, movements on the international exchanges, forecasts of technical reliability, etc. Consequently, norms of project acceptability are padded with safety factors—a fact which, together with the veil of uncertainty itself, obviates the need for exact measuring techniques.[14]

The imperfections of the price structure need no comment. One particular set of prices, which has a particular bearing on the problem of determining rates of return, however, should be noted, that is, salvage values. Typically, over the course of its physical life, a piece of equipment will have several

Table 4.10   *Effect of the CGE's Failure to Reflect the Timing of the Cash Flow*

	Oil Field	Hydroelectric Plant
Investment	$1,000,000,000	$2,000,000,000
Life	25 years	50 years
Salvage	0	0
Net cash flow	$500,000,000 decreasing by $20,000,000 per year	$600,000,000
Depreciation	$40,000,000	$40,000,000
Profit	$210,000,000 (average)	$560,000,000
Soviet CGE	21.00%	28.00%
IRR	45.61%	30.00%
NPV Index	2.0	1.4

Note: oil is the best but CGE indicates hydroelectric.

economic lives.[15] One of the key determinants of these lives is the equipment's salvage value at different points of time. True salvage value at any point in time is the value of the service the equipment can provide until the end of its last economic life, at which time it will be equal to scrap values. Given the absence in the Soviet setting of an effective mechanism for the pricing and resale of used equipment, the salvage value placed on an asset at the end of any of its economic lives would tend to be equal to scrap value. Such an understatement of salvage values results in understatement of the IRR. The magnitude of the errors stemming from this considerably blunt the advantages to be gained from the use of an 'exact' measure.

But despite its inaccuracy and its virtual nonuse as an active instrument of capital rationing, I would lean toward the hypothesis that the requirement that CGEs be computed on all investment has had beneficial effects. As Academician Khachaturov writes: 'Presently not one project, not one program, not one plan is undertaken without computing its CGE.'[16] Such computations, it would seem, can only foster an awareness of the need for efficiency in the use of capital, and cannot help but to eventually bring into focus the fact that prices are not derivative of the planners' scale of preferences. Already one finds a growing concern about the failure of the CGE to reflect time values,[17] interest has been shown in foreign literature on the subject,[18] and new methodologies are being proposed.[19]

One of the most important provisions of 1969 SM, and one which in my view largely overrides the crudity of the CGE, is that which prescribes what must be counted in the investment base. 1969 SM mandates that the investment base used in the CGE calculation include all of the capital expenditures which the project will require in other sectors, such as transportation, energy, water supply, housing, trade facilities, loss of land through inundation, etc.[20] As the magnitude of these secondary effects can

Table 4.11   *'True' Equivalent Annual Cost per $1,000 at 12% Compared with the Soviet Comparative Cost*

Life	Exact or True EAC ($)	CC ($)	Error
2	591.70	620.00	+4.78
5	277.41	320.00	15.35
8	201.30	245.00	21.71
10	176.98	220.00	24.31
20	133.88	170.00	26.98

often surpass those of the project under immediate consideration, these can have a significant impact on the relative CGEs.[21] Even if the CGE is not the criterion of capital allocation, the very fact that it must be computed brings the 'true' size of the commitment to the planners' attention.

4   The Comparative Cost of Capital Investments (CC)

(a) Description

Part III of 1969 SM contains rules for calculating the coefficient of the comparative cost of capital investments (CC). The CC is used to compare the costs of different ways of obtaining a given output. It is the sum of the annual operating costs and depreciation charges plus 12 percent of the original investment. It is a short-cut version of the Western equivalent uniform annual cost method described in Section 2 of this chapter and has one very serious flaw: like the CGE, it ignores the fact that the investment is recovered over the life of the project.[22] Consequently, it results in an approximate doubling of the interest portion of the capital costs. This artificial inflation of interest costs produces a strong bias against capital-intensive projects. The annual cost per $1,000 of investment at a 12 percent rate of interest as calculated by the Soviet CC as compared with its 'true' equivalent uniform annual cost, is shown in Table 4.11.

In contrast to the instructions for the CGE which contain no provision for the timing of the cash outflows and inflows, the instructions for calculating the CC[23] stipulate that in cases where 'the capital investment in the variants being compared are made at different periods, and the current expenditures change over time, then a comparison of the variants should be made by bringing the expenditures of the later years to the present by applying a discount coefficient calculated by the following formula, $V = 1/(1 + E_{np})^t$ where V is the discount coefficient, t is the period of time of discount, and E_{np} is the normative for discounting expenditures at different times.' The formula, it will be recognized, is the standard 'single payment present worth factor,' the value of which for any i and t can be found in standard interest tables. The normative for discounting is set at 0.08. The effect, however, of discounting at 8 percent when the cost of capital is 12 percent is to further artificially inflate capital costs. The true annual cost over a 20-year period at 12 percent of $1,000 investment made at the end of year 10 is $41.05. The Soviet CC of that expenditure, however, is $74.11.

To illustrate the bias against the introduction of new technology, consider the case of a new pipeline which can be equipped with existing model pumps at a total cost of 30,000,000 rubles. These pumps will require 6,800,000 rubles a year of labor, parts and power to operate. The pipeline can also be equipped with new model pumps costing a total of 60,000,000 rubles which, because of their higher level of engineering efficiency, will require only 2,100,000 rubles a year in labor, parts and power. The lives of both models is twenty-five years with zero salvage. The comparative cost of the older model pumps is 11,600,000 rubles, while that of the new model is 11,700,000 rubles. The ministry would therefore opt for the older model pumps because they appear to be more economical by 100,000 rubles per year.

The use of the 'exact' measures, however, shows that at 12 percent the equivalent uniform annual cost of the older model pumps is 10,625,000 rubles, while that of the new model is 9,750,000 rubles. The costs of rejecting the new model can be seen in the fact that if the new model were purchased and the equivalent 875,000 rubles of savings a year reinvested at 12 percent it would result in an 'effortless' accumulation of 116,663,750 rubles over the course of the twenty-five years, that is, almost enough to buy two of the new model pumps. Other things being equal, that sum at 12 percent would, in its turn, be capable of producing an extra 13,999,650 rubles a year of national income a year to infinity.[24]

(b) Assessment

The CC's overstatement of capital costs and the consequent bias against capital-intensive investments is not, as in the case of the CGE, a mere matter of academic interest which evaporates in the face of uncertainty, irrational prices and development strategy. As compared with the calculation of the CGE which involves a forecast of costs and revenues, the CC involves only a forecast of cost and would hence seem to be more certain.[25] As to the matter of prices, irrespective of their rationality or nonrationality, the method itself is irrational in that it induces actions that run counter to long-standing objectives of economic policy, that is, the mechanization of labor and the introduction of progressive technology ensuring savings in materials and power.

Murray Fesbach,[26] in a 1976 study of the developing shortage of labour, has predicted that it will reach critical proportions by 1983. Yet 1969 SM mandates a method of comparison which protects labor-intensive processes against capital-intensive contenders. Joseph Berliner[27] has recently described the pricing gymnastics resorted to since 1950 to stimulate the development and production of new models of machinery embodying higher levels of technology and engineering efficiency. But while important efforts are made to stimulate the production of such models, 1969 SM mandates a method of evaluation which discourages potential users from acquiring them. The CC similarly produces a bias against the contending new machines in replacement-type decisions and results in extending the service period of capital equipment well beyond its economic life. This, of course, results in higher than necessary production costs and runs counter to the current economic order of the day, that is, 'Economic Efficiency in Social Production,' and counter to the goals of the Tenth Five-Year Plan calling for a technical renovation of Soviet plant and equipment.

5 A Peek at US Practices

While we may disdain the primitive methods prescribed by 1969 SM, it is only recently that 'scientific methods' of project analysis have been used in US industry. In 1947 discussion material at a National Association of Accountants forum was illustrated by a replacement problem in which the accounting costs of operating the present machine (including depreciation) were compared with the accounting costs of the new machine.[28] In the early 1950s Joel Dean, whose work did much to stimulate the use of the internal rate of return, found in a study of 'fifty well managed companies' that 'top management is forced to a distressing degree to rely on intuition and authority. Management lacks the skilled analysis and the scientific control needed for sound judgement on these intricate, vital capital decisions.'[29]

In the mid-1950s, investigations by George Taylor[30] into some 120 to 160 companies revealed that 'not one company ... visited ... employed a mathematical concept of [capital] spending decisions.' The methods he found in use were the 'squeaky wheel,' the 'intuitive' and the 'necessity' techniques. The necessity technique is simply that of making no investment until a company is forced to and, in Taylor's view, it was that technique which set many New England industries on a descending path, and which in Britain caused 'the general decline of industries of an entire nation ... According to British economic teams studying the problem, even the nation's technology dries up: its research and development comes to a halt because nobody replaces equipment except for necessity.'[31]

A 1961 study by Donald F. Istvan[32] of the investment practices of 48 large US companies, accounting between them for almost a third of the plant and equipment expenditures reported by the US Department of Commerce, revealed that only 5 used the Internal Rate of Return method, 2 used a special Machine and Allied Products Institute formula, 24 used a simple rate of return (like the Soviet CGE), 13 used the payback method (a notoriously poor tool),[33] while 4 used subjective judgement.

A 1967 survey by the National Association of Accountants,[34] although based on a rather restricted sample, is suggestive of a trend toward the usage of the 'exact methods.' In a survey of 28 companies it was found that half used the financial statement method as the primary method of analyzing projects, while half used the discounted cash flow method (NPV or IRR), and all used the payback method as a secondary method. The payback method, in case it has escaped the reader's attention, is a close cousin of the Soviet CRE of 1959 SM which was the sole measure in use from 1959 to 1969 and which has received so much attention in the West. Payback is the value of the original investment divided by the net cash inflow. The Soviet CRE was the net income (or savings) divided by the investment.

A comparison of the mathematics of investment analysis would carry little weight in any overall evaluation of the comparative efficiency of the capital allocation processes, East and West. Actions induced by, and the results obtained from, the use of a particular method of analysis are strongly influenced by the institutional setting. While that larger question lies beyond the scope of this paper, parts of it are worthy of mention—uncertainty, barriers to entry, tax policies, fluctuating interest rates and corporate bureaucracy.

As regards the question of uncertainty, one might ask of what value mathematical precision would be in arriving at a 'correct' decision in the following actual, and quite typical, case: 'After months of careful study' it was estimated that the project would require an investment of 'about $40,000,' would produce 'revenues between $30,000 and $60,000 a year,' and would have 'a life of from two or six years.'[35] As Dunn and Bradstreet inform us, half of all new businesses fail within 18 months of their formation, while another 30 percent fail over the course of the next 8½ years.[36]

As to barriers of entry, given the sizable variation in the rate of profit among US industries (from a high of 32.8 percent in mining and quarrying in 1975 to a low of less than 1 percent in transportation,[37] it is clear that the major causes of inefficiencies in the capital-rationing process stem from reasons other than defects in the methods of measuring returns in capital. Again, just as Soviet norms of project acceptability vary by sector, industry and branch, so do norms of project acceptability within any large US corporation vary from division to division.

As regards tax policies, a project's 'true' rate of return to society is a function solely of the magnitude and timing of all of its associated costs and revenues. The manner in which these are apportioned between the public and private sectors is irrelevant. Yet the acceptability of a project in the West is a function, not only of its 'true' rate, but also of the rate and timing of the government's share. Regulations governing tax life, methods of depreciation, the tax rate and the existence of special tax credits are often the pivotal element in project evaluations.

The frequent and wide swings in the level of interest rates which have characterized the money markets of the past few years have made it impossible for firms to maintain present-worth maximizing positions. For example, with a cost of capital at 10 percent, a firm maximizes its present worth by investing $10,000 in a machine which saves $2,638 a year in labor, power and materials costs. With a rise in the cost of capital to 15 percent some two years later that same firm, in order to maximize its present worth, should sell the machine.

Corporate systems of managerial incentives and controls are also a source of inefficiencies in capital budgeting. In corporations where divisional managers are judged on a rate of return basis, a bias exists against the acquisition of new machinery. This is because the fast depreciation allowances granted by the IRS produce a book value for existing equipment which is usually lower than its true value—a fact which inflates the rate of return on the usage of older as compared with new equipment. A further bias against the acquisition of new machinery is produced by extensive corporate controls which lead 'the lower echelons to recommend repair instead of replacement since they know there will be little difficulty in securing repair funds which are expenses. On the other hand, obtaining new capital money is always a time consuming and frustrating task, since the control in terms of paperwork and organizational layers is substantial.'[38]

An example of the administrative hurdles to be overcome by lower-level management in its struggle to channel resources into their most productive uses is provided by Joseph L. Bower, who cites 'a case reported by an assistant controller of a divisionalized company with highly centralized control.'

> Our top management likes to make all the major capital decisioins. They think they do, but I've just seen one case where a division beat them. I received for editing a capital request from the division for a large chimney. I couldn't see what anyone could do with just a chimney, so I flew out for a visit. They've built and equipped a whole plant on plant expense orders. The chimney is the only indivisible item that exceeded the $50,000 limit we put on the expense orders.
>
> Apparently they learned informally that a new plant wouldn't be favorably received, and since they thought the business needed it, and the return would justify it, they built the damn thing. I don't know exactly what I'm going to say.[39]

Notes: Chapter 4

1 Of twenty-four major US corporations sampled in the early 1960s, eight reported that top management made all capital decisions regardless of size. Five reported that it made all capital decisions in excess of $1,000, five reported a cut off of $2,500, three reported $10,000, two reported $25,000, and one reported $50,000. See Frank Schwab Jr, 'How to delegate financial authority to decentralized managers,' *Business Management* (1960), reprinted in Francis J. Corrigan and Howard A. Ward (eds), *Financial Management* (Boston, Mass.: Houghton Mifflin, 1963), pp. 355–60.

2 For an English translation of the 1969 Soviet Standard Methodology for Investment Allocations, see Morris Bornstein and Daniel R. Fusfeld (eds), *The Soviet Economy: a Book of Readings* (Homewood, Ill.: Irwin, 1974), or Michael Melancon (trans.), 'Standard Methodology for determining the economic effectiveness of capital investments,' *ASTE Bulletin*, vol. 13, no. 3 (fall 1971), pp. 26–36. Alan Abouchar, 'The new Soviet Standard Methodology for investment allocation,' *Soviet Studies*, vol. 24, no. 3 (January 1973), pp. 402–10, contains an excellent discussion of the 1969 Methodology and a comparison with the 1959 Methodology.

3 Part I, Section 1 of 1969 SM.

4 T. S. Khachaturov, 'Sovershenstvovanie metodov opredeleniya effektivnosti kapital'nikh vlozhenii,' *Voprosy ekonomiki*, no. 3 (1973), p. 29.

5 Three of the many good texts on the subject are: Norman Barish, *Economic Analysis* (New York: McGraw-Hill, 1962); Gerald A. Fleischer, *Capital Allocation Theory* (New York: Appleton-Century-Crofts, 1969); and George Taylor, *Managerial and Engineering Economy* (Princeton, NJ: van Nostrand, 1964). Current research in the field can be found in occasional articles in such journals as the *Engineering Economist*, *Journal of Finance*, *Journal of Business*, *Managerial Planning* and *Harvard Business Review*.

6 Ezra Solomon, *The Theory of Financial Management* (New York and London: Columbia University Press, 1963), pp, 134–5.

7 In cases where projects with differing lives are being compared a Present Value Index can be used. This is the ratio of the discounted present value of the cash inflows to the discounted present value of the cash outflows.

8 Both of these measures will infallibly indicate whether or not a project is acceptable, that is, return more than the minimum required rate. In ranking a number of competing projects, all of which are acceptable, however, the NPV and IRR methods can turn up a different ranking. This can happen when there are pronounced differences in the pattern of cash flows of the competing projects, and the minimum required rate is less than the Fisher rate (the rate of interest at which the NPVs of the competing projects are equal). As an example, take the case of two competing projects, each involving an initial outlay of $1,000 and the following net cash inflows:

	A	B
Year 0	−$1,000	−$1,000
1	450	0
2	450	225
3	450	450
4	450	1,500

	A		B
Fisher rate		17.89%	
IRR	28.50%		26.40%
NPV at 20%	$1,164.92		$1,140.22
NPV at Fisher rate	1,213.18		1,213.18
NPV at 10%	1,426.42		1,548.56

At a required minimum rate of return in excess of the 17.89 percent Fisher rate (20 percent in our example) the IRR and NPV show that A is the best. At a rate below the 17.89 percent Fisher rate (10 percent in our example) the IRR and NPV give conflicting indications.

To resolve the conflict one can examine the value of the two projects, not at the present, but at some future point in time—in our example at the end of year 4—and make some assumptions regarding the rate at which the funds generated by the two projects will be reinvested. Reinvesting those funds at any rate above the Fisher rate will produce a larger amount at the end of year 4 for project A (the one with the higher IRR). Reinvesting at any rate below the Fisher rate will produce a larger amount at the end of year 4 for project B (the one with the highest NPV).

Those who believe that the IRR is the universally correct criterion are making the implicit assumption that the funds produced by the two projects will be reinvested at a rate in excess of the Fisher rate. Those who believe that the NPV is the universally correct criterion are making the implicit assumption that the funds can be reinvested only at a rate less than the Fisher rate.

I would argue that in a growth situation where investment opportunities abound (as seems to fit the Soviet case) the assumption that the cash flows may be reinvested at a rate of return in excess of the Fisher rate is a reasonable one. Given the infinity of investment opportunities in the USSR, it does not seem reasonable to assume that any two projects could possibly exhaust the number of opportunities for investing at rates in excess of the Fisher rate—a rate which it must be noted is lower than the IRR on either of the competing projects.

In addition, there is the risk factor. A rate of return is a measure of the rate at which (on projects with equal lives) the original investment plus interest is returned. If one goes through the arithmetic of the recovery of capital with interest in the two above projects, he or she will find that in project A, some 73 percent of the original investment with interest has been fully recovered by the end of the second year, whereas in project B, only 11.5 percent has been recovered. By the end of year 3, 100 percent of the original investment plus interest and a surplus of $185 has been recovered on project A, whereas in project B, by the end of year 3, 63 percent of the original investment remains unrecovered.

Finally, it seems to me that the question is largely academic. In twenty years of teaching the techniques of capital budgeting to evening MBA students, all of whom are required to present and criticize an actual capital budgeting decision made by the firm in which they work, I have never seen a case where the conflict arose.

9   $i(1 + i)/(1 + i)^N - 1$ where $N = 3$ and $i = 20$. The values can be found in any standard set of interest tables.

10 Part II, Section 14 of 1969 SM.

11 *Ekonomicheskaya gazeta*, no. 39 (1969). Translated in *Current Digest of the Soviet Press*, vol. 21, no. 40 (1969), p. 9.

12 *Ekonomika i organizatsiya promyshlennogo proizvodstva*, no. 4 (1973), p. 39. Translated in *Current Digest of the Soviet Press*, vol. 25, no. 43 (1973), p. 23.

13 *Izvestiya*, 18 March 1975. Translated in *Current Digest of the Soviet Press*, vol. 27,

no. 11 (1975), p. 23. This is not a misprint. The Soviet writers write: '. . . that is, by a factor of 80! Its size seems to be adjusted to the attained level of effectiveness and rate of return on investments . . .'

14 B. Vainshtein, 'O metodakh opredeleniya ekonomicheskoi effektivnosti kapital'nikh vlozenii,' *Voprosy ekonomiki*, no. 12 (1971), p. 12.

15 Economic life is that period over which a piece of equipment has the lowest equivalent annual cost. A piece of equipment past its economic life on prime service may have a second economic life on a service requiring less intense and reliable service, and then a third economic life on standby or other service.

16 Khachaturov, art. cit. at note 4, p. 28.

17 See V. Krasovski, 'Intergralnii effekt i faktor vremenii,' *Voprosy ekonomiki*, no. 8 (1974), pp. 3–13.

18 Khachaturov, art. cit. at note 4.

19 A. Vitin, 'Opredelyeniye effektivnosti kapital'nikh vlozenii v govorakh zarubeznikh ekonomistov,' *Voprosy ekonomiki*, no. 10 (1971), pp. 115–26.

20 Part I, Sections 8 and 9 of 1969 SM.

21 It is interesting to reflect upon what might have been the pattern of investment in the US transportation sector if amortization of the public expenditures associated with the use of the automobile had to be financed through automobile prices. It has been estimated, for example, that every time a commuter in the Washington DC area puts a car on the road the city spends some \$21,000 in roads, traffic signals, parking space, etc. Another example which comes to mind is the World Trade Center.

22 Formula 8 or 1969 SM for the coefficient of comparative effectiveness is $C_i + E_n K_i$ = minimum, where C_i is current expenditures (i.e., *sebestoimost'*), K_i is the capital investment, and E_n is the normative coefficient of effectiveness of capital investments which is set at a level of less than 12 percent.

23 There is some confusion on this point among Soviet economists. An article in *Pravda*, 4 May, 1972 (translated in *Current Digest of the Soviet Press*, vol. 24, no. 18, 1972, p. 1) states that for calculations of the CGE 'there are no recommendations on the calculation of time outlays' and gives an example of the errors this omission can lead to. L. V. Kantorovich, however, in an article in *Ekonomika i organizatsiya promyshlennogo proizvodstva*, no. 5 (1974), pp. 3–9 (translated in *Current Digest of the Soviet Press*, vol. 27, no. 10, p. 14) states that the methodology calls for the application of a discount factor but, 'this principle is not applied consistently in practice.'

24 The calculation of the Soviet comparative costs of the two models is as follows:

	Old	New
Annual operating disbursements	6,800,000	2,100,000
Interest costs (investment times .12)	3,600,000	7,200,000
Depreciation charges (investment divided by 25)	1,200,000	2,400,000
Total	11,600,000	11,700,000

The 'exact' equivalent uniform annual cost of the old is the 30,000,000 ruble investment times the Capital Recovery Factor for twenty-five years at 12 percent (.12750) plus the 6,800,000 in operating disbursement. For the new, it is the 60,000,000 ruble initial investment times the Capital Recovery Factor for twenty-five years at 12 percent (.12750), plus the 2,100,000 in annual operating disbursements.

25 In a study of fifty projects carried out in one US company, a comparison of the

actual outcomes with the forecasts showed that the mean of the ratio of the actual to the forecasted net present value was only 0.1 in the case of projects involving new products, 0.6 for projects involving sales expansion, but 1.1 for cost-reduction projects. In other words, the results of the cost reduction projects were better on the average than the forecast. See Joseph L. Bower, *Managing the Resource Allocation Process* (Boston, Mass.: Harvard University Graduate School of Business Administration, 1970), p. 13.

26 I have not yet seen this study. It was cited in the Jack Anderson column, *Washington Post*, 11 August 1976.

27 Joseph S. Berliner, 'Flexible pricing and new products in the USSR,' *Soviet Studies*, vol. 27, no. 4 (October 1975), pp. 525-44.

28 Abouchar, art. cit. at note 2; and J. Fred Weston and Donald K. Woods (eds), *Basic Financial Management: Selected Readings* (Belmont, Calif.: Wadsworth, 1967).

29 Corrigan and Ward (eds), op. cit. at note 1; and Joel Dean, 'Measuring the productivity of capital,' *Harvard Business Review* (January–February, 1954), pp. 120–9.

30 George Taylor, 'The analysis of your spending decisions,' *The Controller* (April 1959), pp. 168–88.

31 Corrigan and Ward (eds), op. cit. at note 1, p. 394.

32 Donald F. Istvan, *Capital Expenditure Decisions: How They Are Made in Large Corporations*, Indiana Business Report no. 33 (Bloomington, Ill.: Bureau of Business Research, Graduate School of Business, Indiana University, 1961).

33 All students of the subject are in agreement on the inadequacy of the payback method as a tool of capital budgeting. George Taylor (*Managerial and Engineering Economy*, pp. 380–1) gives an example involving five projects, four of which are unprofitable, and one of which is profitable. Using the payback method resulted in accepting the four unprofitable projects and rejecting the one profitable project.

34 National Association of Accountants, *Financial Analysis to Guide Capital Expenditure Decisions*, Research Report no. 43 (New York: National Association of Accountants, 1967).

35 W. Warren Haynes and Martin B. Solomon Jr, 'A misplaced emphasis in capital budgeting,' *Quarterly of Economics and Business* (February 1962), pp. 39–46.

36 Cited by *Wall Street Journal*, 12 February 1968, p. 1.

37 Conference Board, *Road Maps of Industry*, nos 1783 and 1784 (May 1976).

38 Schwab, art. cit. at note 1, p. 357.

39 Bower, op. cit. at note 25, pp. 15–16.

5 Intra-year Fluctuations in Production and Sales: East and West

J. ROSTOWSKI and P. AUERBACH

1 Introduction

Rewards for plan fulfillment require not only a clearly defined measure of results, but also a time period to which the results must be related. Hence the great importance of the calendar, and the phenomenon of 'storming' (*shturmovschina*), of a mad rush to fulfill the plan in the last few days of the month, quarter or year, followed by a slack and disorganised period in which production falls sharply until the next mad rush. Denunciations of *shturmovschina* were, and are, extremely common, and the prevalence of the disease is a sign that it is, in a sense, built into the structure of the economy.   (Alec Nove, *The Soviet Economy*)[1]

Storming cycles are of intrinsic interest as a characteristic of centrally planned economies which reveals much about their mode of operation.[2] Our present inquiry focuses on two related questions: If it is true, as Nove suggests, that storming is 'built into' the structure of the centrally planned economy, can the extent of storming be taken as an indicator of the type and intensity of the planning regime? If this is the case, can the extent of storming be used to tell us about the extent of market reforms in such economies, for instance in Hungary?

The storming cycle may then be suitable as a characteristic indicator of the presence of a central planning regime, much as the progressive predominance of market relations and as manufacturing mode of production in nineteenth-century Europe was signalled by the emergence of the modern capitalist business cycle. Figure 5.1 is a 'picture' of the storming cycle from an official source.[3]

Output peaks to fulfill quarterly plans, with a steep gradient as the end of the year approaches. It is these forms of storming (end-year and end-quarter storming) upon which we shall be focusing, but an exhaustive list of possibilities would be as follows:

Annual Storming. There are two possible approaches here:

(i) *Analysis of quarterly data.*   The pioneering studies of Hutchings[4] were limited to this type of data. As a result, Hutchings found it impossible to

82

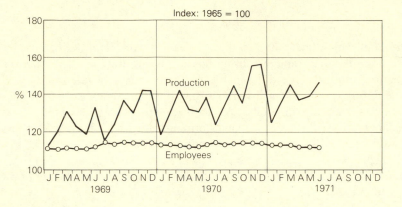

Figure 5.1 *Daily average production in each month and index of number of employees in socialist industry.*

Source: *Statisztikai havi közlemények* (Budapest: Központi Statisztikai Hivatal), a monthly bulletin of statistics.

distinguish climatic and systemic causes of seasonal variations in production.

(ii) *Analysis of monthly data.* The accumulation of a large body of monthly data for centrally planned economies permits the analysis of systemic influences in the generation of short-term fluctuations. Laki[5] studied this question for the Hungarian economy during the years 1975–6, and to our knowledge this work is unique in the literature. We shall be studying global manufacturing data over a broad range of countries, for the years in which they are available. It will be seen that these data are rich enough to yield some interesting and decisive results.

Quarterly Storming. Storming may well exist toward the end of the quarter in order to fulfill quarterly plan targets. We shall be testing for this possibility.

Intra-month Storming. Unfortunately, little but anecdotal information on this interesting topic is available.[6]

What explanations have been offered for the phenomenon of storming in centrally planned economies (CPEs)?

(I) THE WEATHER

The issue can be resolved by a more extensive examination of the data than was undertaken by Hutchings. We shall proceed to investigate a broad range of economies, both market and centrally planned and we shall use monthly, as opposed to quarterly, data. This allows us to examine December/January variations in production, which are less likely to be affected by the weather than are the ratios of output in the fourth quarter to that in the first quarter of the ensuing year, which were the basis of Hutchings's study.

(II) 'COMMONSENSE' EXPLANATIONS

Everybody with a 'plan' storms, that is, puts off work until the last minute. It may even be that capitalist firms storm toward the delivery date on an important contract. The difference is that under capitalism storming is likely to be diffused, different firms storming at different times, so that it will not necessarily show up in production statistics. In CPEs plans (and therefore deadlines) are synchronized, making storming statistically observable. Although enterprises in CPEs have been responding to plans for a long time, so that one might expect a learning process to mitigate the tendency to storm, this could be offset by the tendency for storming to reproduce itself due to points (V) and (VI) below.

(III) DISCONTINUITY OF THE BONUS FUNCTION

Given an incentive system in which bonuses (including the implicit bonus of avoiding the disapproval of superiors) are linked to the achievement of plan targets, 'the marginal value of additional effort rises sharply' toward the end of the plan period.[7] If this is the cause of storming then its amplitude at the end of plan periods of different length will tell us the relative importance of the targets attached to the different plan periods.

(IV) THE RATCHET EFFECT

Substantial revision often takes place in plan targets,[8] and they may not reach their final form until the latter part of the year. Planners and plant managers play a game whereby the latter *purposely* restrict output in the earlier part of the year in order to bargain successfully for a low output target for the year as a whole.[9] It is sometimes argued, however, that since enterprises 'reveal their hand' during the last months of the year, planners learn enterprises' true production possibilities, so that attempts to obtain a reduction in targets by underproduction in the early months of the year will fail, and in consequence such attempts will in time be abandoned by plant managers. If, however, production possibilities vary for a given enterprise from one period to the next due to factors that planners do not know, or whose importance they cannot properly assess during plan construction, then a 'new hand' is dealt to enterprises each year, and the 'ratchet principle' will operate.

(V) PLANNING FROM THE 'ACHIEVED LEVEL'

Targets often take the form of an X percent increase in output or sales over the same period of the previous year. As a result, once a storming pattern comes into existence it tends to be perpetuated.

(VI) SUPPLY CONSTRAINTS

An important proximate but, of course, not ultimate explanation for storming is that once it exists in certain parts of the productive chain it may be forced upon other sections of the economy, since they cannot proceed with production in the absence of the necessary inputs.

As we suggested earlier, many interesting aspects of the storming question will not be discussed in this chapter, but may be noted in passing: storming may take the form of quality deterioration during the storming period;[10] on the other hand, some of the storming which registers statistically *could* be 'paper' storming, as managers lie about the amount of work-in-progress that has been turned into finished production in order to fulfill the plan. However, the substitution of sales targets for output targets which has occurred in CPEs should have reduced the amount of lying about monthly output figures indulged in by managers. The incentive is now to lie about sales. This is probably more difficult, as it involves another organization (the customer) in the deception. More relevant for our purposes, there is no incentive to lie about output, which is our primary 'storming' indicator. Finally, it is worth noting that even if 'storming' were a *purely* paper phenomenon, it could still serve our purpose as an indicator of the existence of central planning, as there is no reason why 'paper storming' should be present in a market economy, be it capitalist or socialist.

In our forthcoming sectoral paper, we shall have more to say about these and other questions, such as the presence or absence of storming in different *kinds* of production processes.

THE QUESTIONS

We wish to answer the following questions related to the existence and pattern of storming:

  (i) Does storming exist in CPEs within plan periods longer than one month?
 (ii) Is it specific to CPEs?
(iii) Has it been reduced as a result of economic reforms?
 (iv) What does the evidence on storming imply about the relative importance of plan periods of different lengths—month versus quarter, quarter versus year?
  (v) Can the data identify the causes of storming, either as a whole or within plan periods of different lengths?
 (vi) Does a different degree and pattern of storming tell us something about the planning procedures in different CPEs? For instance, if East Germany has less storming than other CPEs, does this suggest that planners in that country simply *do not* bargain over the annual plan?

Table 5.1   *Centrally Planned Economies: March/April and September/October Ratios in Manufacturing Output*

Country	Ratios	Average	Standard Deviation	Years
Czechoslovakia	Mar/Apr	1.0251	0.0313	1966–82
	Sept/Oct	0.9917	0.0518	1966–82
GDR	Mar/Apr	0.9982	0.0203	1968–81
	Sept/Oct	0.9939	0.0229	1968–81
Poland	Mar/Apr	1.0305	0.0289	1971–81
	Sept/Oct	1.0156	0.0501	1971–81
Hungary	Mar/Apr	1.0272	0.0134	1963–8
	Sept/Oct	1.0158	0.0241	1963–8

Sources: CZECHOSLOVAKIA—manufacturing output from *Monthly Bulletin of Statistics* (New York: UN); hours/days worked per month from *Hospodarské noviný* (Prague: Central Committee of the Communist Party of Czechoslovakia), work-time calendar published in the first issue of each year. GDR—industrial output (adjusted for number of working days in the month) from UN, *Monthly Bulletin of Statistics*; energy and fuels output (adjusted for number of working days) from *Short-Term Trends* (Geneva: UN Economic Commission for Europe); share of energy and fuels in gross industrial output from *Statistiches Jahrbuch der DDR* (Berlin: Staatlichen Zentralvervaltung für Statistik). POLAND—manufacturing output (obtained by subtracting mining and electricity from industrial output) from *Biuletyn statystyczny* (Warsaw: Glowny Urzad Statystyczny); days worked per month from *Kalendarz robotniczy* (Warsaw: Ksiazka i Wiedza). HUNGARY—*Statisztikai havi közlemények* (Budapest: Központi Statisztikai Hivatal).

Note: All ratios are adjusted for hours/days worked.

2   The Data

We have examined thirteen West European and North American market capitalist economies (including Israel), five CPEs (Czechoslovakia, the GDR, Hungary [before 1968], Poland and the USSR), and two reformed socialist economies (Hungary [post-1968] and Yugoslavia).

Our key indicator of storming is the ratio of production in the last period of the cycle to that in the first period of the following cycle. Thus the ratio of production in December to that in the following January is our indicator for the presence of annual storming, while the March/April ratio measures first quarter storming and the September/October ratio measures third quarter storming. We have not examined the June/July ratio for second quarter storming, because the large number of annual holidays taken in July in both East and West, depress production in that month. Since information on the number of holidays taken in July is not readily available we found it was impossible to adjust accurately for this factor. We also corrected for the number of official workdays (or hours) in various months. This is a necessity for scrupulous measurement, except in really spectacular cases of storming.

Our results suggest that quarterly storming in production was either nonexistent or very slight in centrally planned and reformed socialist economies for either the first or third quarters (Table 5.1). We, therefore, concentrated our research into the differences between centrally planned and market capitalist economies on year-end storming.

We decided, where possible, to examine fluctuations in manufacturing rather than in industrial production, because electricity generation responds to domestic demand (based on the weather) as well as to demand by industry, while mining and fuels also seem to be affected by the weather in some countries. Manufacturing by its nature is less likely to be affected by climate, except perhaps in unusually cold years when the transport of spare parts could be hindered. Within manufacturing, the food-processing sector is likely to be affected by 'seasonality' as opposed to storming, and we intend to examine this in our forthcoming sectoral study.

The data we used for market capitalist economies were manufacturing output adjusted for the offical number of working days in the month, with the exception of Finland and Italy where we adjusted manufacturing output by hours worked per man obtained from national monthly statistical bulletins (Table 5.2).

Data for centrally planned and reformed socialist economies were more heterogeneous. For the USSR it proved impossible to calculate global industrial production fluctuations on the basis of available data.[11] We therefore limited ourselves to the calculation of December/January ratios for fifty-eight manufacturing sectors and subsectors from monthly press reports, which we adjusted for hours worked (Table 5.8).

The GDR data for industrial production, already adjusted for days worked per month, was obtained from UN sources and was adjusted to give manufacturing output by subtracting energy and fuel (Table 5.7). For Czechoslovakia we obtained monthly industrial and manufacturing data from UN sources and hours and days worked from Czech sources (Table 5.4). For Poland unadjusted industrial and manufacturing data was obtained from national sources, as were days worked (Table 5.4). It was the unavailability of monthly manufacturing data or of data on hours or days worked in various months that prevented us from including Bulgaria or Romania in the study.

We proceeded in a similar manner for Hungary, except that for the years 1967–83 we adjusted production by hours actually worked per man—for all other countries we had to adjust for days or hours officially worked (Table 5.10). For the years 1963–8 the Hungarian statistical bulletins provide output adjusted for official days worked. It is encouraging that for the two years of overlap, the two methods of calculation provide almost identical results for the December 1967/January 1968 ratio. For Yugoslavia we used unadjusted manufacturing output from UN sources, which we were able to adjust for the years 1963–7 by hours officially worked per man (Table 5.16).

Table 5.2 *Capitalist Market Economies: December/January Ratios in Manufacturing Output, and March/April Ratios for Countries in which the Financial Year Ends 31 March*

Country	Average	Standard Deviation	Years
Austria	112.6	7.86	1954–82
Canada	100.6	2.13	1954–82
Finland	99.2	9.36	1976–82
France	103.2	2.66	1954–82
West Germany	107.8	4.24	1954–82
Israel—Dec/Jan	100.2	2.01	1958–78
Mar/Apr	102.1	3.49	1958–78
Italy	94.0	5.61	1974–82
Norway—Dec/Jan	95.0	3.41	1954–82
Mar/Apr	109.2	14.71	1954–82
Portugal	101.8	5.66	1968–82
Sweden	103.8	3.03	1965–82
UK—Dec/Jan	100.5	3.61	1954–79
Mar/Apr	104.9	5.18	1955–79
USA	99.8	1.78	1954–81

Sources: AUSTRIA, CANADA, FRANCE, WEST GERMANY, ISRAEL, NORWAY, SWEDEN, UK and USA—manufacturing output (adjusted for the number of working hours/days in the month) from UN, *Monthly Bulletin of Statistics.* FINLAND—manufacturing output from UN, *Monthly Bulletin of Statistics*; hours/days worked per month in mining, manufacturing, electricity, gas and water from *Tilastokatsauksia* (Helsinki: Central Statistical Office of Finland), a monthly bulletin of statistics. ITALY—manufacturing output from UN, *Monthly Bulletin of Statistics*; hours worked per week from *Bolletino mensile di statistica* (Rome: Istituto Centrale di Statistica). PORTUGAL—manufacturing output (adjusted for the number of working days in the month) from *Bulletin mensuel de statistique* (Lisbon: Nacional de Estatistica).

Note: All ratios are adjusted for the number of working days/hours in the month.

3   The Findings

(a) Market Capitalist Economies

We chose our control group of capitalist countries on the basis of whether it were possible to obtain for them monthly manufacturing data adjusted for the official number of working days. We then examined the ratio of manufacturing output in December to that in January in all the countries, the March/April ratio for Israel, Norway and the United Kingdom (where the fiscal year ends on 31 March), and the June/July ratio for Sweden, where the fiscal year ends 30 June. In all the remaining countries the fiscal year ends 31 December. The purpose of these measures was to find out whether seasonal or fiscal factors

Table 5.3 *Norway and the UK: March/April Ratios in Manufacturing Output and the Years in which Easter Fell in March (M), April (A), and Those Years in which it Overlapped Both (A—M)*

Year	Norway	UK	Easter
1955	120.6	95.8	A
1956	97.5	102.6	A—M
1957	114.8	108.0	A
1958	116.7	109.7	A
1959	86.8	95.2	M
1960	115.0	104.6	A
1961	100.0	102.3	A—M
1962	114.2	107.1	A
1963	115.4	107.0	A
1964	89.1	96.2	M
1965	111.3	106.1	A
1966	122.0	109.7	A
1967	85.2	96.6	M
1968	116.8	108.8	A
1969	115.2	105.7	A
1970	84.1	101.6	M
1971	119.3	106.5	A
1972	94.8	102.3	A—M
1973	124.3	112.7	A
1974	108.2	109.4	A
1975	84.0	104.9	M
1976	123.3	109.0	A
1977	127.7	111.9	A
1978	82.4	98.2	M
1979	123.0	111.5	A
1980	118.5	—	A
1981	123.9	—	A
1982	124.1	—	A

Sources: Manufacturing output from UN, *Monthly Bulletin of Statistics*; dates of Easter from *Whitaker's Almanack.*

Note: March/April ratios are adjusted for the number of working days in the month.

caused annual storming-type phenomena to occur in advanced capitalist countries.

As can be seen from Table 5.2 December/January storming is either nonexistent or very small (under 4 percent) in ten of the capitalist countries. This is in spite of the fact that in seven of them the fiscal year corresponds to the calendar year.

In Austria and West Germany the amount by which output in December exceeds that in January is quite large (12.6 and 7.8 percent respectively). The whole of the fall in output occurs in the capital goods producing sector. The

Table   5.4   *Centrally   Planned   Economies: December/January   Ratios   in   Manufacturing Output*

Country	Average	Standard Deviation	Years
Czechoslovakia	116.9	15.45	1968–81
GDR	109.1	3.579	1965–70
	97.7	3.329	1971–81
Hungary	118.8	8.220	1963–7
Poland	114.1	8.400	1970–80

Sources: CZECHOSLOVAKIA—manufacturing output from UN, *Monthly Bulletin of Statistics;* working days/hours per month from *Hospodárské noviný*. GDR—as Table 5.1. HUNGARY— *Statisztikai havi közlemények.* POLAND—manufacturing output (obtained by subtracting mining and electricity from industrial output) from *Biuletyn statystyczny*; days worked per month from *Kalendarz robotniczy.*

Note: Adjusted for the number of working days/hours in the month.

fall in capital goods sales, and also in capital goods exports sales, is even greater than the fall in output, and this suggests that the cause of the phenomenon is the fact that many factories remain closed in both countries between 24 December and 6 January. As a result, capital goods producers, wishing to reduce the amount of 'work in hand' standing idle in the factory during the year-end break, boost production and sales in December. In January capital goods have to be 'built up' from a lower than usual stage of completion. This depresses 'completions' (and thus 'output' in the official statistics), and also reduces sales.

In Israel, Norway and the UK the financial year ends on 31 March. In Israel there is no significant March/April decline in production. In Norway and the UK there is such a decline (109.3 and 104.9 percent respectively on average). This is due, however, to the effect of Easter on production in both countries (Table 5.3). Presumably workers take additional free days off around Easter. It should also be noted that in neither country are companies obliged to make their financial year correspond to the state's fiscal year. Sweden's fiscal year ends on 31 June, and the June/July ratio in that country averages 237.8 percent. This is presumably overwhelmingly due to annual holidays, however, and any 'financial year effect' which might exist cannot be distinguished from the 'holiday effect.'

We can summarize our investigation of annual storming in market capitalist economies quite simply: as expected on theoretical grounds there is no evidence of annual storming, either at the end of calendar years or of fiscal years, with the exception of West Germany and Austria, in all of which special circumstances prevail to boost production in December and/or to depress it in January.

Table 5.5   *Czechoslovakia: Total Exports, and Poland: Total Exports and Exports to Nonsocialist Countries, December/January, March/April, and September/October Ratios*

Country	Ratios	Average	Standard Deviation	Years
Czechoslovakia:	Dec/Jan	2.4744	0.5527	1959–83
Exports	Mar/Apr	1.5129	0.2522	1959–83
	Sept/Oct	1.4263	0.2758	1959–82
Poland:	Dec/Jan	2.6719	0.6445	1960–82
Exports	Mar/Apr	1.5655	0.2254	1960–83
	Sept/Oct	1.4296	0.2782	1959–83
Poland: Exports to	Dec/Jan	2.6084	2.1095–3.0509 (range)	1980–3
Nonsocialist Countries	Mar/Apr	1.4248	1.2143–1.6724 (range)	1980–3
	Sept/Oct	1.2377	1.1119–1.4557 (range)	1980–3

Sources: CZECHOSLOVAKIA—UN, *Monthly Bulletin of Statistics.* POLAND—*Biuletyn statystyczny.*

(b) Centrally Planned Economies (CPEs)

Turning now to CPEs, we can see from Table 5.4 that Czechoslovakia, Poland, Hungary before 1968, and the GDR before 1970 clearly exhibit annual storming in manufacturing, though storming in the GDR for the years 1965–70 is no greater than in West Germany in the same period (109.1 percent in the GDR and 109.3 percent in West Germany.)

Furthermore, there is clear and extremely high annual and quarterly storming in exports in both Poland and Czechoslovakia (Table 5.5) with the December/January ratio averaging 267 percent in Poland and 247 percent in Czechoslovakia, and exports at the end of the first and third quarters being about one and a half times as high as at the beginning of the second and fourth quarters in both countries. Exports to the West in Poland do not behave markedly differently from total exports. The exports of the GDR and the USSR to the West also exhibit annual storming (Table 5.6), although the average amplitude of the fluctuations is much smaller than in Poland and Czechoslovakia (monthly data on Soviet and GDR exports to socialist countries is not available). GDR exports to the West also exhibit a fairly mild degree of first-quarter storming.

After 1971 annual production storming completely disappears in the GDR (Table 5.7), although storming in exports to the West continues. This seems to be linked to the 'counter reforms' of 1971, when the New Economic System (NES) of the 1960s was abolished.[12] The experience of the GDR thus runs counter to what we had expected in two important ways: first, it

Table 5.6   *GDR and the USSR: Exports to the West, December/January, March/April, and September/October Ratios*

Country	Ratios	Average	Standard Deviation	Years
GDR	Dec/Jan	1.1528	0.1714	1975–83
	Mar/Apr	1.1204	0.1577	1975–83
	Sept/Oct	0.9760	0.0816	1974–82
USSR	Dec/Jan	1.1710	0.0458	1975–83
	Mar/Apr	0.9985	0.0868	1974–83
	Sept/Oct	0.9868	0.0818	1974–82

Source: Calculated on the basis of *Direction of Trade Statistics* (Washington, DC: IMF).

shows that a CPE can avoid annual storming; secondly, that moving to a more centralized system can coincide with a reduction, rather than an increase, in storming. There are a number of possible *ad hoc* explanations for these surprising results. There is no doubt that CPEs can avoid annual storming if they desire it sufficiently. To abolish annual storming, it should be enough to penalize managers who consistently allow output to fall in January. One could also make the fulfillment of monthly planned targets more important than the fulfillment of annual targets. It is not, therefore, that annual storming cannot be controlled, but rather that most CPEs have not considered it worth their while to do so. It is maybe not surprising that the GDR, which lays such stress on inspection and control of productive units (enterprises and combines) by the center,[13] should be the CPE to have succeeded in banishing annual storming.

Another reason for the absence of annual storming in the GDR may lie in the degree of vertical integration in GDR industry. With all industrial producers now organized into 150 (generally vertically integrated) combines, the supply side of most centrally planned material balances must be the responsibility of just *one* combine. Now, in general, aggregate output targets in CPEs are rigid, because the national plan must be made to balance. It is the disaggregated plans (of particular enterprises) that are most subject to bargaining between the enterprise and the center. Nove[14] quotes *Pravda* (27 November 1974) on what happened within an industrial ministry: '... the habitual procedure was followed: reduce the plan for the laggards, increase it for the successful. After these arithmetical procedures, not a single enterprise has underfulfilled the plan ...' Yet the ministry's aggregate (national) plan targets probably remained mechanized. In the GDR the combine's target usually *is* the national aggregate target. It cannot, therefore, be tempered without unbalancing the national plan. With the center less likely to validate plan underfulfillment by reducing the combine's target or, possibly more importantly, less likely to try to jack the target up after a successful first half,

Table 5.7   *GDR: December/January Ratios in Manufacturing Output*

Year	Ratios	Year	Ratios
1965	104.7	1974	95.9
1966	106.4	1975	96.1
1967	115.9	1976	93.7
1968	110.6	1977	97.9
1969	109.3	1978	104.2
1970	107.8	1979	99.9
1971	101.6	1980	92.8
1972	—	1981	96.4
1973	98.7		

Sources: Calculated by the authors on the basis of data from UN, *Monthly Bulletin of Statistics* for industrial production (adjusted for the number of working days in the month); from UN Economic Commission for Europe, *Short-Term Trends* for production of energy and fuels (adjusted for the number of working days in the month); and from *Statistiches Jahrbuch der DDR* for share of energy and fuels in gross industrial output.

Note: Adjusted for the number of working days in the month.

of the plan period, there would be less scope for the operation of the 'ratchet principle' than in other CPEs. A separate point is that the vertically integrated nature of most combines may have reduced production storming due to input shortages in the early part of the annual plan period.

The 'combine system,' however, is unlikely to be the sole reason for the absence of annual storming in the GDR. Although all manufacturing occurs at present within some 150 combines, in 1971 when annual storming disappeared there were only 35 combines.

As we have explained,[15] it is impossible to derive conclusions about monthly industrial output in the USSR on the basis of published data. The sectoral evidence in Table 5.8, however, would seem clearly to indicate annual storming (December/January ratios greater than 1.00) for the economy as a whole. Out of 58 sectors and subsectors in manufacturing industry (excluding agriculture-related sectors), 28 exhibit December/January ratios in excess of 104 percent, while only 3 demonstrate 'counter-storming' of the same magnitude (less than 96 percent). Of the remaining 27 sectors, 16 are above 100 percent, while 11 are below. Casual observation appears to suggest higher storming in new sectors of high priority (computers, automation devices, etc.), than in established sectors such as steel and cement. Overall, the data does not disappoint our expectation that the USSR is an 'orthodox' CPE. The data in Table 5.6, indicating substantial storming in exports to the West, would seem to reinforce the sectoral conclusions.

It is interesting to note that planners in the USSR do not seem to take the length of the month in a particular year into account when setting targets. For instance, in January of 1984 industrial labor productivity was 4.9 percent

Table 5.8   *USSR: December/January Ratios in Production in Fifty-Eight Sectors and Subsectors of Soviet Manufacturing, (Excluding Agriculture-related Sectors)*

Name of Sector	Average	Standard Deviation	Years
Reinforced concrete	3.221	0.256	1979/80–1983/4
Turbines	2.534	—	1967/8–1970/1
Generators for turbines	1.877	0.825	1967/8–1970/1
Computers	1.443	0.261	1972/3–1983/4
Smith's and pressing machines	1.191	0.153	1967/8–1982/3
Automation devices	1.172	0.181	1967/8–1983/4
Outerwear	1.159	0.061	1967/8–1975/6
Machines for agriculture	1.151	0.017	1967/8–1977/8
Radio apparatus	1.136	0.090	1967/8–1982/3
Metal cutting machines	1.135	0.134	1967/8–1983/4
Television sets	1.114	0.087	1967/8–1983/4
Including colour TVs	1.123	—	1979/80–1983/4
Furniture	1.114	0.108	1967/8–1982/3
Spare parts for agricultural machines	1.112	0.118	1967/8–1973/4
Heavy goods carriages	1.108	0.089	1967/8–1982/3
Bulldozers	1.092	—	1967/8–1971/2
Trains (electrical)	1.083	0.153	1967/8–1978/9
Light industry equipment	1.081	0.090	1971/2–1977/8
Washing machines	1.079	0.127	1967/8–1982/3
Underwear	1.075	0.042	1967/8–1975/6
Trains (diesel)	1.065	0.110	1967/8–1974/5
Food processing industry equipment	1.058	0.093	1970/1–1977/8
Leather shoes	1.058	0.034	1967/8–1982/3
Refrigerators	1.054	0.108	1967/8–1982/3
Caustic salt	1.048	0.054	1967/8–1976/7
Glass	1.042	0.088	1967/8–1973/4
Grain harvesting combines	1.041	0.115	1967/8–1982/3
Excavators	1.041	0.049	1967/8–1982/3
Cloth—silk	1.036	0.027	1967/8–1975/6
—cotton	1.034	0.019	1967/8–1975/6
—linen	1.034	0.031	1967/8–1975/6
—wool	1.026	0.029	1967/8–1975/6
Tractors	1.034	0.035	1967/8–1977/8
Cement	1.026	0.084	1967/8–1982/3
Electric motors	1.025	0.068	
Synthetic fibres	1.023	0.062	1967/8–1979/80
Chemical equipment	1.021	0.488	1967/8–1982/3
Chemical equipment (spare parts)	1.021	0.095	{ 1967/8–1972/3 { 1974/5–1982/3
Steel pipes	1.011	0.074	1967/8–1982/3
Chemical fertilizer	1.014	0.088	1967/8–1982/3
Clocks. watches	1.014	0.044	1967/8–1982/3
Motor bikes and bicycles	1.007	0.047	1979/80–1982/3
Car bodies and motor bike bodies	{ 1.005 { 1.005	0.046 0.068	1967/8–1982/3 1967/8–1976/7
Sulphuric acid	0.999	0.060	1967/8–1982/3

Name of Sector	Average	Standard Deviation	Years
Rolled iron	0.997	0.040	1967/8–1975/6
Plastics	0.994	0.073	1967/8–1982/3
Cars total	0.991	0.041	1968/9–1982/3
Including Lorries	0.990	0.046	1968/9–1982/3
Steel	0.971	0.063	1967/8–1982/3
Caustic soda	0.988	0.037	1967/8–1975/6
China	0.989	0.037	1970/1–1982/3
Steel pipes (millions of meters)	0.967	0.078	1967/8–1973/4
Chemical means of plant's protection	0.963	0.083	1967/8–1982/3
Rolled iron prepared	0.955	0.069	1967/8–1982/3
Oil equipment	0.950	0.150	1967/8–1982/3
Metallurgical equipment	0.917	0.086	1970/1–1976/7
Addendum:			
Robots	1.746	range 1.626–1.848	1981/2–1983/4

Sources: Production from *Ekonomicheskaya gazeta*; hours worked per month from *Ekongazet* (Moscow: Central Committee of the Communist Party of the Soviet Union), work-time calendar published in the first issue of each year.

Note: Adjusted for hours worked per month.

above the level for January 1983. However, the plan was overfulfilled by 2 percent, so that labor productivity was planned to rise only 2.9 percent. Furthermore, the 'work-time calendar' published at the beginning of each year shows that work time in January 1984 was to be 4 percent greater than in January 1983.[16] This implies that planners planned for a 1.1 *reduction* in labor productivity per hour worked as compared with January 1983. This is highly improbable. Much more likely was that the plan was for a growth rate roughly the same as for the rest of the year (3.4 percent),[17] and ignored the fact that in January 1984 work time was to be 4 percent longer than in January 1983. Much the same situation occurred in 1983 as well.

To summarize the evidence on production storming in CPEs, the following general features may be noted:

(i) There is hardly any quarterly (as opposed to annual) storming in production (Table 5.1—we have seen, however, that a very different picture emerges when we examine exports).

(ii) Annual storming in production seems to be less violent than intramensual storming (reported by Kvasha[18] to be between 280 percent and 400 percent in some sectors in the USSR).

(iii) Quarter on quarter fluctuations within the year, due to the weather, are less important than the December/January decline due to annual storming (Table 5.9, where we compare December/January production

Table 5.9 *Czechoslovakia, GDR, Hungary, Poland and the USSR: Ratios of Manufacturing Output in the Fourth Quarter of One Year to the First Quarter of the Following Year, and December/January Ratios (Excluding USSR)*

Country	Ratios	Average	Standard Deviation	Years
Czechoslovakia	4th Q of Year t 1st Q of Year $t + 1$	1.0632	0.0855	1968–81
	Dec. of Year t Jan. of Year $t + 1$	1.1690	0.1545	1968–81
GDR	4th Q of Year t 1st Q of Year $t + 1$	1.0441	0.0262	1965–71
	Dec. of Year t Jan. of Year $t + 1$	1.0804	0.0423	1965–71
	4th Q of Year t 1st Q of Year $t + 1$	0.9613	0.00190	1973–80
	Dec. of Year t Jan. of Year $t + 1$	0.9729	0.0323	1973–80
Hungary	4th Q of Year t 1st Q of Year $t + 1$	1.1267	0.0408	1968–82
	Dec. of Year t Jan. of Year $t + 1$	1.2299	0.0654	1968–82
Poland	4th Q of Year t 1st Q of Year $t + 1$	1.0035	0.0712	1971–80
	Dec. of Year t Jan. of Year $t + 1$	1.1465	0.0962	1971–80
USSR	4th Q of Year t 1st Q of Year $t + 1$	1.0085	0.0087	1958–66

Sources: CZECHOSLOVAKIA, GDR, HUNGARY, and POLAND—as Table 5.4. USSR—R. Hutchings, *Seasonal Influences in Soviet Industry* (Oxford: Oxford University Press, 1971), statistical appendix IXE.

Notes: All results adjusted for hours/days worked per month or quarter.

ratios with the ratio of output in the last quarter of the year to output in the first quarter of the following year).[19]

(iv) Export storming is more intense than production storming in every CPE for which we have the relevant data, with the possible exception of the USSR (Tables 5.4, 5.5 and 5.6).

(c) Reformed Socialist Economies

HUNGARY

Manufacturing data for Hungary (Table 5.10) shows clearly that December/January storming—far from having declined after the 1968 reform—increased slightly and then doubled in intensity after the 1972 'counter-reform.'

Table 5.10 *Hungary: Manufacturing Output*

Year	Dec/Jan Ratios	Mar/Apr Ratios	Sept/Oct Ratios
1963	122.5	101.6	100.7
1964	114.6	103.7	102.7
1965	108.7	103.1	102.9
1966	115.5	102.1	102.9
1967	132.7	100.9	96.6
1968	123.7	104.9	103.7
1969	120.1	104.4	102.3
1970	124.1	108.5	101.3
1971	124.4	103.2	99.0
1972	142.3	95.5	102.8
1973	144.8	99.8	105.6
1974	147.8	105.8	109.7
1975	142.9	112.2	100.3
1976	134.3	101.2	102.7
1977	137.7	96.9	103.3
1978	142.9	105.9	104.0
1979	161.6	103.4	103.9
1980	137.3	110.8	101.9
1981	128.8	107.9	99.0
1982	147.1	99.4	101.1
$\bar{X}$	118.8	102.3	101.2
σ	8.21	1.01	2.43
n	1963/7	1963/7	1963/7
-	120.7	103.6	101.3
σ	6.58	2.12	2.15
n	1963/71	1963/71	1963/71
$\bar{X}$	142.5	103.5	103.1
σ	8.1	5.25	2.72
n	1972/82	1972/82	1972/82
$\bar{X}$	132.7	103.6	102.3
σ	13.2	4.14	2.63
n	1963/82	1963/82	1963/82

$\bar{X}$ = average, σ = standard deviation, n = years.

Sources: Hours actually worked per month from *Quarterly Bulletin of Statistics* (Geneva: ILO) (these sometimes refer to 'state industry' and sometimes to 'socialized industry,' but the differences are minimal in those years in which we have both); manufacturing output (calculated by substracting indices of mining and electricity output from output of state industry) from *Statisztikai havi közlemények*, weighted by the shares of these sectors from *Statisztikai évkonyv* (Budapest: Központi Statisztikai Hivatal), a statistical yearbook. For 1963–8 *Statisztikai havi közlemények* provides industrial output and the output of industrial branches already adjusted for the number of official days worked. For these years we merely adjusted total industrial output for mining and electricity as above.

Note: Adjusted for the actual number of hours worked per month.

Table 5.11 *Hungary: Sales by Socialized Industry and by Sectors of Socialized Industry; Exports to Socialist and Nonsocialist Countries*

	Dec/Jan Ratios			Mar/Apr Ratios			Sept/Oct Ratios		
	$\bar{X}$	σ	n	$\bar{X}$	σ	n	$\bar{X}$	σ	n
Output by state industry	123.0	6.54	1968–82	112.9	4.09	1968–82	99.5	3.03	1968–82
Sales by socialized industry	164.4	10.41	1967–82	123.4	5.23	1967–82	112.1	3.74	1967–82
Consumer goods	122.3	5.86	1970–82	109.7	5.25	1970–82	103.5	6.11	1970–82
Exports	340.4	33.69	1968–82	146.1	15.88	1968–82	129.2	9.41	1968–82
Investment	829.9	173.5	1968–82	271.8	57.89	1968–82	297.6	54.52	1968–82
Intermediate goods	122.4	8.16	1970–82	117.4	3.93	1970–82	102.8	3.54	1970–82
Consumer and intermediate goods	121.3	6.50	1968–82	113.4	5.37	1968–82	102.2	3.71	1968–82
Export to socialist countries	359.5	78.81	1968–82	142.9	15.19	1968–82	116.6	11.73	1968–82
Export to nonsocialist countries	377.7	69.72	1968–82	136.3	18.76	1968–82	112.0	11.85	1968–82
Export of capital goods to convertible currency markets	1233.1	564.6	1970–82	162.7	39.50	1970–82	141.9	52.90	1970–82
Imports from socialist countries	223.7	35.2	1968–82	111.0	16.25	1968–82	108.9	9.81	1968–82
Imports from nonsocialist countries	246.3	67.8	1968–82	131.3	21.55	1968–82	109.9	16.32	1968–82

$\bar{X}$ = average, σ = standard deviation, *n* = years.

Source: Statisztikai havi közlemények.

March/April and September/October storming is quite small, but even these increase slightly in the postreform period. This was exactly the opposite of what we had expected. We had anticipated a considerable reduction, if not a complete elimination of annual storming, reflecting the abolition of binding annual, quarterly and monthly plan targets and the supposed move to a 'market socialist' economy in Hungary in 1968. How can one account for not only the persistence, but the marked accentuation of annual (and to some extent quarterly) storming in production in Hungary in the post-1968 period?

The data in Table 5.10 would seem to strongly corroborate the view of many Hungarian economists that the 1968 reform was in many important respects more apparent than real. For example, Marton Tardos[20] states that the independence of enterprises, though it exists *pro forma*, is completely lacking in reality. What is particularly interesting in our results is that they show that this dependence of enterprises on the center is not limited to pricing and investment decisions as is often claimed, but extends to production and, as we shall see below, sales (particularly exports).

Mihaly Laki, whose important study examined annual and quarterly storming in sixteen industrial and foreign trade enterprises in Hungary for the years 1975–7, confirm this view.[21] He quotes the head of the business management department at a big precision engineering enterprise: 'the situation is the same as in the old mechanism, the plan is broken down by factory units ... The task of the units is to create stocks of saleable goods.'

The 'plan' referred to is theoretically formulated by the enterprise itself and is supposed to be nonbinding, but in Laki's view '... the supervising authority, usually the sectoral ministry, prescribes for the enterprise—or, which is equivalent, makes the premium of managers dependent on it—by how many percent turnover and other indicators of production ... have to be increased.'

The main difference between the present system in Hungary and classical Soviet-type output targets is that Hungarian plans are formulated in terms of sales rather than production targets although, as already mentioned, at present sales targets are generally the rule in CPEs, including the USSR. In the words of Laki's respondent: 'Recognition and premium can be obtained if sales plans are fulfilled.' This is reflected in the statistical data. As can be seen from Table 5.11, sales storming is much greater than production storming, both at the end of the year (almost three times as high), and at the end of the first and third quarters. Sales targets are the motors that drive the vehicle of production storming.

Turning to the incidence of storming by sectors, we find that both annual and quarterly sales storming is strongest in the sale of industrial goods for investment purposes (Tables 5.11 and 5.12). This is hardly surprising since investments are generally acknowledged to be highly centrally controlled in Hungary.[22] It is the amplitude of the storming fluctuations, both annual and quarterly in the sale of industrial investment goods that it astonishing (830

Table 5.12   *Hungary: Sales by Socialized Industry for Export and for Investment, 1973 and 1974 (In Millions of Forints)*

Year	Month	Export	Investment
1973	Jan	4,115	493
	Feb	6,221	502
	Mar	10,784	1,668
	Apr	6,440	527
	May	8,576	784
	June	11,460	2,103
	July	6,999	542
	Aug	8,758	835
	Sept	11,069	1,817
	Oct	9,071	864
	Nov	9,659	882
	Dec	14,786	3,256
1974	Jan	4,994	341
	Feb	7,026	411
	Mar	11,490	1,763
	Apr	8,208	528
	May	9,891	799
	June	13,781	2,471

Source: Statisztikai havi közlemények.

percent on average for annual storming, 272 percent for the first quarter and 298 percent for the third quarter). Equally surprising is the extremely high level of storming in exports (as in traditional CPEs). Tables 5.11, 5.12 and 5.13 clearly show the presence of extreme planners' pressure on both foreign trade enterprises (Table 5.13) and on industrial enterprises producing for export markets (Tables 5.11 and 5.12), in spite of the failure of analysts such as Marer[23] to note the phenomenon. Sales by industrial enterprises for export purposes are on average 3.4 times higher in December than in January, 1.5 times higher in March than in April, and 1.3 times higher in September than in October (Table 5.11). The fact that annual indusrial export sales storming is in no way due to a Christmas consumer boom in the West is shown by the fact that annual storming in the export of capital goods to the West is very high (12 times), as indeed it is in sales to the East. Quarterly storming in the export of capital goods to the West is also very high (1.6 times at the end of the first quarter and 1.4 times at the end of the third quarter) and again the same pattern repeats itself in sales to socialist countries (Table 5.11). Particularly interesting is the fact that the amplitude of sales storming in Hungarian exports is much the same as that in Czechoslovakia and Poland (Table 5.5), although annual storming is somewhat higher and quarterly storming is somewhat lower in Hungary.

Table 5.13 *Hungary: Exports to Socialist and Nonsocialist Countries, December/January Ratios, All Years*

Year	Exports to Socialist Countries	Exports to Nonsocialist Countries
1968	346.8	434.8
1969	263.8	221.2
1970	329.8	327.0
1971	355.1	368.3
1972	360.9	428.5
1973	250.0	306.7
1974	341.3	441.2
1975	—	—
1976	359.9	407.9
1977	506.0	524.4
1978	229.7	392.8
1979	494.0	394.4
1980	390.4	347.6
1981	443.4	337.0
1982	361.7	355.7

Source: Statisztikai havi közlemények.

Laki's respondents were in no doubt as to the reality of planners' pressure on enterprises producing exportables: 'It is a prescription and guideline of development in the case of exports that the enterprise should raise the plan by 6 per cent . . .' Nor is there any doubt as to the center's ability to influence the enterprise, the same source continues: 'The main point at present is how much wage funds are allocated by the ministry in return for a given result.' The same situation obtains for the foreign trade enterprises: 'Our superior ministry says "you should provide 64 million, but you will be nice boys if you bring 68 million".' The result is the familiar one of plan bargaining: 'Enterprises are asked how much they will contribute, and when they propose an amount, it is said to be not enough and they are asked to contribute 1.2 times as much.'

Nor is there any significant difference between the amount of export storming in sales to socialist and nonsocialist countries (Table 5.11). Annual storming is slightly greater to nonsocialist countries, and quarterly storming is slightly greater to socialist countries. Up to 1978 there was considerably more annual storming in exports to nonsocialist countries, reflecting the priority given by Hungary to trade with the West.[24] More recently, the situation has been reversed (Table 5.13), possibly as a result of the importance of Hungary's hard currency exports of food to the USSR, and of its imports of crude oil.

Table 5.14   *Hungary: Sales by Socialized Industry of Intermediate and Consumer Goods, December/January, March/April and September/October Ratios, All Years*

	Intermediate Goods			Consumer Goods		
Year	Dec/Jan Ratios	Mar/Apr Ratios	Sept/Oct Ratios	Dec/Jan Ratios	Mar/Apr Ratios	Sept/Oct Ratios
1970	135.6	112.3	104.0	122.2	102.7	100.8
1971	131.8	117.6	105.8	116.2	106.5	101.2
1972	123.0	123.8	101.2	116.6	113.4	100.4
1973	124.9	121.0	100.5	113.4	106.4	95.3
1974	119.4	118.2	106.2	115.6	104.7	96.0
1975	129.1	109.9	103.4	126.3	104.0	102.2
1976	127.5	118.7	106.7	129.1	104.2	111.7
1977	112.4	116.2	101.8	129.3	118.1	115.2
1978	119.5	119.4	104.2	116.7	116.5	103.2
1979	104.5	122.2	99.2	129.5	112.6	96.8
1980	119.5	113.7	102.2	122.4	114.9	105.5
1981	115.8	113.7	93.6	122.1	106.8	104.6
1982	128.4	120.0	106.9	130.0	114.9	112.7

Source: Statisztikai havi közlemények.

The process by which planners' pressure for enterprises to fulfill export targets is transformed into production storming is described by the economic director of a medium-sized precision engineering enterprise, who, at the same time, points to the possible existence of a five-yearly cycle in Hungary: '. . . the Ministry of Foreign Trade announced at the end of the Five Year Plan, that those bringing in some more exports will be given an extra premium. The concomitant end-year rush led to the bad start of 1976.'[25]

It is interesting to note that large-scale storming also exists in Hungarian imports both from socialist countries and, more surprisingly, from nonsocialist countries (about 2.5 times in December/January—Table 5.11). In fact, import storming is somewhat higher from nonsocialist than from socialist countries. Import storming may be due as much to the desire of importing productive enterprises to spend their full allocation of scarce foreign currency within the period for which it was budgeted, so as to avoid having the allocation reduced by the authorities in subsequent years, as to the desire of foreign trade enterprises to fulfill their plans.

It needs to be stressed, however, that sales storming exists in industry, both at the end of the year and for the first quarter, in both the consumer goods and intermediate products sectors, and not just in investments and exports (Table 5.11). Nor has sales storming in these sectors been decreasing over time (Table 5.14).

We would not expect the existence of profit targets rather than sales targets in certain parts of the Hungarian economy at certain times to affect the outcome. In an economy in which there is almost universal excess demand for inputs, partly because prices of both inputs and outputs are sticky upward, profit targets are almost equivalent to sales targets. This is particularly so in the short run in which it will be difficult to cut costs significantly, and it is to the short run that profit targets apply. What is more important than the nature of success criterion—sales or profit—is whether it takes the form of a target, and whether it is imposed from above. On this, one of Laki's respondents in an engineering enterprise says: '. . . the enterprise head office adapts itself to the so-called action programme of KGM (Ministry of Metallurgy and Engineering). This contains . . . profit prescriptions that are of obligatory character.' It is also possible that sales storming in Hungary is due, in part, to informal, *ad hoc* 'on the telephone' pressures exerted by planners toward the end of the year to show their superiors that the enterprises for which they are responsible are doing well.

Having concluded that centrally imposed direct or indirect (via profits) sales targets are the main cause of production and sales storming in Hungary and that, as a result, the Hungarian economic system differs less from traditionally centrally planned economies than is commonly supposed, it remains to be explained why production storming is higher in Hungary than in traditional CPEs, and why it has increased over time from levels which, in the pre-reform period were closer in magnitude to those in other CPEs (Table 5.4). The simplest answer is that the increased share of exports in industrial production, combined with somewhat increased 'sales storming' in industrial exports, is responsible. The importance of export share in determining which branches of industry storm most is stressed by Laki. Such an explanation lacks plausibility, however, as the share of total industrial sales fluctuations accounted for by exports has not risen perceptibly in the period after 1972 (Table 5.15). More convincing is the view—also put forward by Laki—that, more recently, sectoral and functional ministries take the avoidance of storming less seriously compared with other goals.[26] Possibly of equal importance, however, was the abolition of monthly plan targets in 1968, which will have given enterprises more scope for quarterly and annual storming. The 'storming cycle' history of Hungary could then be thought of as follows: the introduction of the New Economic Mechanism (NEM) really did lead to the abolition of *monthly* plan targets, giving enterprises more scope for quarterly and annual production storming, both of which rose marginally in the period 1968–71 (Table 5.10); the 'counter-reform' of 1972 increased the pressure on enterprises to fulfil targets, and resulted in a dramatic increase in annual production storming, and a further, though much milder, increase in quarterly production storming.

To test this view properly we would need information on storming *within* the month, both before and after 1968, which is not available. Laki does, however, describe an attempt by the Ministry of Metallurgy and Engineering

Table 5.15 Hungary: Fluctuations in the Sale by Socialized Industry of Goods for the Purpose of Exports and for Investment as a Share of Fluctuations in the Total Sales of Socialized Industry

	A Exports fluctuation as a share of total fluctuation in %			B Investment fluctuation as a share of total fluctuation in %			A + B		
Year	Dec/Jan Ratios	Mar/Apr Ratios	Sept/Oct Ratios	Dec/Jan Ratios	Mar/Apr Ratios	Sept/Oct Ratios	Dec/Jan Ratios	Mar/Apr Ratios	Sept/Oct Ratios
1970	45.5	30.9	38.3	17.8	21.0	37.5	63.3	51.9	75.8
1971	53.6	36.7	44.1	15.0	14.3	34.0	68.6	51.0	78.1
1972	58.5	36.7	55.8	13.3	10.9	37.7	71.8	47.6	93.5
1973	53.5	45.7	77.4	15.9	12.0	36.9	69.4	57.7	114.3
1974	57.2	39.4	32.5	16.9	14.8	43.2	74.1	54.2	75.7
1975	53.0	55.2	48.5	13.5	14.6	32.2	66.5	69.8	80.7
1976	51.4	43.6	43.0	14.4	12.2	21.3	65.5	55.8	64.3
1977	58.2	41.2	47.4	16.9	11.1	24.1	75.1	52.3	71.5
1978	54.8	33.3	55.3	16.9	14.0	24.1	71.7	47.3	79.4
1979	65.0	40.0	76.7	18.7	11.9	33.9	83.7	51.9	110.6
1980	55.8	46.9	56.5	14.0	9.2	24.0	69.8	56.1	80.5
1981	58.6	47.8	90.6	13.6	9.1	49.4	72.2	56.9	140.0
1982	54.9	29.4	51.1	9.8	8.4	16.7	64.7	37.8	67.8
$\bar{X}$	55.4	40.5	55.2	15.1	12.6	31.9	70.5	53.1	87.1
σ	4.4	7.0	16.2	2.3	3.2	9.0	5.2	7.0	21.0
n	1970–82	1970–82	1970–82	1970–82	1970–82	1970–82	1970–82	1970–82	1970–82

$\bar{X}$ = average, σ = standard deviation, n = years.

Source: Statisztikai havi közlemények.

Table 5.16 *Yugoslavia: December/January Ratios for Manufacturing Output (Adjusted and Unadjusted for 'Hours Paid For'), and for the Production of Manufactured Investment Goods*

	Manufacturing Dec/Jan Ratios		Industrial Investment Goods Dec/Jan Ratios
Year	Unadjusted	Adjusted for Working Hours	
1958	140.5	—	—
1959	140.7	—	—
1960	138.9	—	—
1961	125.8	—	—
1962	127.5	—	—
1963	122.2	124.0	—
1964	128.0	122.5	—
1965	134.7	130.1	—
1966	134.2	128.6	174.0
1967	122.7	—	169.9
1968	123.7	—	161.1
1969	115.8	—	146.3
1970	120.8	—	138.3
1971	120.0	—	141.7
1972	112.6	—	140.0
1973	98.4	—	132.9
1974	117.6	—	150.0
1975	116.4	—	144.8
1976	118.0	—	143.0
1977	114.7	—	143.2
1978	107.1	—	140.2
1979	115.6	—	137.8
1980	117.2	—	142.5
1981	118.8	—	141.2
1982	—	—	145.8
$\bar{X}$	132.5	126.3	—
σ	6.47	—	—
n	1958–66	1963–6	—
$\bar{X}$	116.0	—	146.6
σ	6.12	—	10.9
n	1967–81	—	1966–82

$\bar{X}$ = average, σ = standard deviation, n = years.
Sources: Manufacturing output from UN, *Monthly Bulletin of Statistics*; hours paid for per month from ILO, *Quarterly Bulletin of Statistics*; manufactured investment goods (*sredstva rada*) from *Indeks* (Belgrade: Federal Statistical Office), a monthly statistical bulletin.

Table 5.17 *Yugoslavia: Manufacturing Output Unadjusted March/April and September/October Ratios*

Ratios	Average	Standard Deviation	Years
Mar/Apr	1.0257	0.0304	1955–82
Sept/Oct	0.9517	0.0314	1955–82

Source: UN, *Monthly Bulletin of Statistics.*

to control storming in 1976 which seems to corroborate our 'history.' For a while, enterprise managers were given bonuses for meeting *monthly* plan targets. The system broke down fairly rapidly, as one interviewee describes: 'It is merely a pious wish at present. We have immediately torpedoed it, saying we are not a bread-making factory.' The story is instructive in two ways. First, it indicates that the balance of power seems to have shifted somewhat from central planners to enterprises in Hungary, in that the attempt to reimpose monthly targets was successfully torpedoed. Secondly, it suggests that it is indeed the reduction in central control, combined with a maintenance of planners' pressure at levels traditional for CPEs, that has led to the dramatic increase in annual (and to some extent quarterly) production storming which we have observed in Hungary.

It is intriguing that annual and quarterly storming has not fallen after the supposed resumption of the reform process in 1979–80 (Table 5.10). This would seem to confirm the view of Tamás Bauer that the 1979–80 reforms 'have aimed not at strengthening and activating a market regulation system independent of state administration ... but at transforming the control of sales from a semi-legal activity of the ministries into the entirely legal main activity of another authority (the price board).'[27]

To summarize: we do not deny that the number of instruments of central control over enterprises is smaller in Hungary in the post-1968 period than in a traditional CPE. This may even have reduced the degree of central control over enterprises (although we believe many of the instruments of central control in a traditional CPE to be quite superfluous). We do believe, however, that our findings show that sales (and particularly export) plans are binding on enterprises; that since these plans are imposed from above they become the object of plan bargaining. It follows that the Hungarian economy *is* subject to the 'ratchet principle.'[28] In spite of statements by commentators such as Cave and Hare,[29] it seems clear that Hungarian enterprises are judged on their performance in relation to plans, and not on actual performance.

Table 5.18 *Yugoslavia: Exports and Imports (to All Countries and to Capitalist Countries), December/January, March/April and September/October Ratios*

		Ratios	Average	Standard Deviation	Years
Export		Dec/Jan	1.5587	0.4090	1951–83
	Total	Mar/Apr	1.0124	0.1174	1951–83
	Exports	Sept/Oct	0.9326	0.0952	1951–83
	Exports to	Dec/Jan	1.6089	0.4165	1977–83
	Capitalist	Mar/Apr	1.1109	0.1113	1977–83
	Countries	Sept/Oct	0.9182	0.0962	1877–83
Import		Dec/Jan	1.1768	0.3221	1951–83
	Total	Mar/Apr	0.9770	0.1490	1951–83
	Imports	Sept/Oct	0.9604	0.1319	1951–83
	Imports from	Dec/Jan	1.2969	0.6298	1977–83
	Capitalist	Mar/Apr	1.0196	0.1175	1977–83
	Countries	Sept/Oct	0.9639	0.1879	1977–83

Source: Indeks.

YUGOSLAVIA

Turning to Yugoslavia, we can see that, although quarterly storming does not exist (Table 5.17), annual production storming does, and is large (Table 5.16). The fact that we only have data for hours worked in various months for six years (1962–7) is a problem. As we can see, however, adjusting by hours worked does not make that much difference to the December/January ratios for the years 1963–6 for which the information is available (Table 5.16), and we may guess that much the same would be true in later years. It is interesting to note that annual production storming seems to fall into two periods (1958–66 and 1966–81), with storming about twice as large in the first as in the second period. It seems likely that this reduction in production storming is linked to the second wave of marketizing reforms of 1965, when planning ceased to be officially compulsory for enterprises, and the degree of investment planning and of planning within enterprises was reduced.[30] The supposed tightening up of the planning system in 1975–6, did not, however, noticeably affect the amplitude of storming.

If we look at the incidence of storming in investment and foreign trade, we see that production storming in industrial investment goods not only exists but at a 1.5 December/January ratio, is about three times as large as in manufacturing as a whole during the same period (Table 5.16). This reveals a pattern similar to that in Hungary. Unlike in Hungary, however, there is no significant quarterly storming in manufactured investment goods in either the first or third quarters. Much the same picture emerges when we look at total exports (Table 5.18). Exports to the West exhibit the same pattern, except that there is some, fairly irregular, first quarter storming. Imports also exhibit annual storming, although slightly less than exports, and this applies almost equally to total imports and to imports from capitalist countries.

It seems from these results that there is some pressure on enterprises or Organizations of Association Labor (OUR), as they are called in Yugoslavia, to boost sales and/or production toward the end of the year. As in Hungary, this pressure seems particularly strong in foreign trade. The exact mechanisms involved can only be guessed at given the absence, to our knowledge, of Yugoslav studies of the phenomenon. Nevertheless, Yugoslav institutional arrangements allow us to hypothesize as follows:

(i) We know that planning does exist in Yugoslavia, even though plans are formulated 'from below.' Plans are drafted by the OUR themselves and are subsequently made consistent with those of other OUR by local chambers of commerce (consisting of representatives of OUR). Once a plan has been confirmed, failure to fulfill it can lead to 'moral and political' sanctions, which presumably can include the removal of the offending managers.[31]

(ii) The perpetual shortage of foreign currency gives the central authorities (the Ministry of Foreign Trade and the central bank) the ability to pressurize OUR to increase exports at the end of the year, so as to get a good allocation of foreign currency in the following year. Imports from the West, on the other hand, might storm at the end of the year because of the need to spend one's allocation of hard currency during the period for which it has been allocated.

(iii) In the case of industrial investment goods, pressure from customers eager to spend their allocation of investment credits could be a source of annual storming.

To conclude, annual production storming in Yugoslavia since 1970 has been significantly lower than in Hungary (Tables 5.10 and 5.16) as has been export storming. Average annual export storming was 155 percent in Yugoslavia and 370 percent in Hungary in the years for which we have data (Tables 5.11 and 5.18). Furthermore, Yugoslavia, unlike Hungary, exhibits little quarterly storming in exports. All this suggests that in Yugoslavia pressure by supervising authorities on productive units to fulfill plans, or *ad hoc* instructions regarding output, sales or exports, may exist but has been much smaller than in Hungary.

4   Conclusions

We have confirmed the popular notion that annual production storming is usually (though not invariably) present in CPEs, as is annual export storming.

On the other hand, production storming is not found in capitalist market economies either at the end of calendar years or of financial years, except in a few cases in which special circumstances obtain (Austria and West Germany). The presence of statistically observable storming is, therefore, a systemic characteristic, a sufficient (though not necessary) indicator of whether an economy is largely centrally planned. This analysis, together with the evidence of severe annual and quarterly storming in Hungary, allows us to conclude that very large elements of central planning persist in that country, particularly in the investment and export sectors. Indeed, our results support the view of some Hungarian economists that Hungary, particularly after the 'counter-reform' of 1972, is better classified as an 'informally administered centrally planned economy' than as a 'regulated market socialist economy.' The data also suggest the presence of some 'plan pressure' in Yugoslavia, particularly before 1965 and particularly in exports.

The fact that in socialist countries exports storm more than manufacturing or industrial production suggests two possibilities: the first is that exports are given more priority than the rest of production, and therefore more pressure is exerted on exporters, leading to greater storming; the second possibility is that exports being a part of sales, rather than production, are less obliged to occur rhythmically (that is, without storming) than is production, which is constrained by technical considerations. There is some support for both of these views in the Hungarian experience. On the on hand, Laki points out that there is some correlation between the share of exports in sales of branches of industry and the degree of annual sales storming. On the other hand, Hungarian data show clearly that sales storming is much more violent than production storming (Table 5.11). In any event, the cost of export storming, particularly with respect to Western markets where it is likely to manifest itself in a discount on the prices of exports from socialist countries, may be considerable.

The clear predominance of annual over quarterly production storming in all socialist countries suggests that it is not shortage of inputs but rather either 'plan bargaining' during the plan year, or the greater importance to managers of annual plan targets compared with quarterly or monthly ones, which is the cause of storming in plan periods longer than one month. The predominance of sales over production storming in Hungary, and of exports over production storming in other socialist countries, also points to the relative unimportance of supply constraints in annual and quarterly storming. Enterprises do not seem to bother to sell goods they have produced earlier on in the plan period until toward the end of the quarter or year.

Storming, rather than seasonal variations due to the weather, would seem to be the cause of the (in any case minimal) quarterly variations in Soviet output between the last quarter of the year and the first quarter of the following year, which have been described by Hutchings (Table 5.9).

Another very important conclusion can be drawn from the GDR's experience: production (though not necessarily export) storming *can* be successfully eliminated in a CPE, although it is unclear just how this has been achieved.

In a further study, we shall examine sectoral variations in the intensity of storming and their causes. Another issue is that of intramonth storming. A proper comparative study of this question, however, covering all socialist countries, must await the publication of the relevant data.

Notes: Chapter 5

We are heavily indebted to Janusz Kubsik for this effort and skill in assembling and reconciling the data in five languages with great thoroughness and judgement. We are also grateful to Prof. E. Primorac for suggestions as to how annual storming might be generated in Yugoslavia. Any errors, of course, remain exclusively ours.

1 Alec Nove, *The Soviet Economy*, rev. edn (New York: Praeger, 1966), p. 167.
2 In this chapter we limit ourselves (with some exceptions) to global measures of the phenomenon. In a subsequent study, we shall get 'under the skin' of these cycles with a sector-by-sector analysis.
3 Unfortunately, the chart is apparently uncorrected for the number of work days in the month, so it is not really usable for scrupulous estimation of monthly output fluctuation; we shall be discussing aspects of this question again in this chapter.
4 R. Hutchings, *Seasonal Influences in Soviet Industry* (Oxford: Oxford University Press, 1971), and 'Recent trends of seasonality in Soviet industry and foreign trade,' *Jahrbuch der Wirtschaft Osteuropas*, vol. 8 (1976), pp. 247–85.
5 M. Laki, 'End-year rush-work in Hungarian industry and foreign trade,' *Acta oeconomica*, vol. 25, no. 1–2 (1980), pp. 35–65.
6 Ya. Kvasha, 'Mashinostroenie: reservy moshnosti,' *Ekonomika i organizatsiya promyshlennogo proizvodstva*, no. 6 (1975), pp. 97–109.
7 H. Cave and P. Hare, *Alternative Approaches to Economic Planning* (London: Macmillan, 1981), p. 64.
8 For a Soviet analysis see V. Khaikhin, 'An analysis of the state of plan discipline in enterprises,' *Matekon*, vol. 18, no. 2 (winter 1981–2), pp. 53–74. As translated from 'Analiz sostoianiia planovoi discipliny na predpriiakh,' *Ekonomika i matematicheskie metody* (1980), vol. 16, no. 5, pp. 930–43.
9 There is an extensive literature on intertemporal incentive effects. See, for instance, the discussion between M. Weitzman, 'The new Soviet incentive model,' *Bell Journal of Economics*, vol. 7, no. 1 (1976), pp. 251–7, and J. Zielinksi, 'New Polish reform proposals,' *Soviet Studies*, vol. 22, no. 1 (January 1980), pp. 5–27.
10 Alec Nove, *The Soviet Economic System* (London: Allen & Unwin, 1977), p. 102.
11 In principle, the month-on-month data on global industrial production in the *Ekonomicheskaya gazeta* can be used to construct a series of simultaneous equations which can then be solved for the absolute monthly industrial production values. (This is the procedure followed by Hutchings in his calculation of quarterly fluctuations of industrial production for the USSR. See *Seasonal Influences in Soviet Industry*.) The data did not yield consistent results for different sample periods: this is not surprising given the crudeness of the data. Furthermore, as our colleague Neville Cramer has pointed out, since the month-on-month figures are given cumulatively (the growth rate for January over the previous January is given;

February's output must be deduced from a cumulative January–February growth rate compared with the previous January–February), the monthly growth rates cannot be deduced uniquely. We have decided, therefore, to use our sectoral data on the USSR as a source of conclusions about storming cycles in industrial production.

12 See P. Boot, 'Continuity and change in the planning system of the GDR,' *Soviet Studies*, vol. 35, no. 3 (July 1983), pp. 331–42.

13 ibid.

14 Alec Nove, *Soviet Economic System*, p. 106.

15 See note 11.

16 *Ekonomicheskaya gazeta*, no. 1 (1984). *Ekongazet*, no. 8 (1984) implies that the actual difference in work-time between January 1984 and January 1983 was 2.4 percent (production in January 1984 was 5.2 percent higher than in January 1983, but on a daily basis it was only 2.8 percent higher, giving a difference in work-time of 2.4 percent). This is largely irrelevant as what concerns us is *planned* work-time as published in the 'work-time calendar'; but even if we accept the 2.4 percent figure we are still left with a planned increase of labor productivity in January 1984 as compared with January 1983 of 0.5 percent, which seems improbably low.

17 *Ekonomicheskaya gazeta*, no. 2 (1984).

18 Kvasha, art. cit. at note 6.

19 This runs counter to the view expressed by Hutchings in *Seasonal Influences in Soviet Industry*.

20 M. Tardos, *Közgazdásagi szemle* (June 1982).

21 Laki, art. cit. at note 5.

22 P. Hare, 'The investment system in Hungary,' in P. Hare, H. Radice and N. Swain (eds), *Hungary: A Decade of Economic Reform* (London: Allen & Unwin, 1981).

23 P. Marer, 'The mechanism and performance of Hungary's foreign trade, 1968–79,' in Hare, Radice and Swain, op. cit. above.

24 Laki, art. cit. at note 5.

25 ibid. There is evidence for a particularly sharp December/January decline in 1979/80 (Table 5.8), but not, surprisingly enough, in 1975/6.

26 ibid.

27 Quoted by I. Kamený at the Seminar on Soviet and East European Problems, London School of Economics, 21 February 1984.

28 This is not to say that the 'ratchet principle' is necessarily a direct cause of storming. Rather, storming shows the presence in Hungary of binding targets imposed from above, and these lead to the operation of the 'ratchet principle' in the game that is played over the setting of annual targets from one year to the next. Storming within the year can be caused equally by the structure of bonus payments and the discontinuity of the bonus function (cause iii in the text), as by the operation of the 'ratchet principle' within the plan year (cause iv).

29 Cave and Hare, op. cit. at note 7, pp. 63–5.

30 M. Schrenk *et al.* (eds), *Yugoslavia, Self-Management Socialism, Challenges of Development* (Washington DC: World Bank, 1979).

31 ibid., p. 50.

6 *Assessing the CIA's 'Soviet Economic Indices'*

LEV NAVROZOV

1   The Subject-Matter and Its Importance

Under study are the Central Intelligence Agency's (CIA) and the Defense Intelligence Agency's (DIA)[1] testimonies before, and written submissions to, the Joint Economic Committee of the US Congress from 1959 to 1983.[2] For about a quarter of a century (since the late 1950s) the CIA has been calculating for the Soviet economy the indices which are conventionally calculated for market economies (GNP, military expenditures, the share of GNP devoted to defense, etc.).[3] The hearings and submissions under study are, essentially, rather repetitious annual presentations of these alleged Soviet economic indices, which have been basic to American foreign policy and defense spending, or at least have been widely used to justify them.[4]

What is the military-economic reality behind these indices produced annually by the CIA with the help of the entire US 'intelligence community'? My main objections against the CIA's studies in question are as follows:

(i) The CIA's results are derived not from Soviet 'closed data' (which can only be obtained by intelligence-espionage and which the CIA is supposed to obtain),[5] but from generally available Soviet 'open data,' such as 'official statistics,' produced by Soviet 'open sources' for 'concealment and deception' (to use a Soviet military term) or 'agitation and propaganda' (to use a Soviet civilian term) and not for Soviet top decision-making, which is based on 'closed data.' As for mutually allowed outside inspection (such as space satellite observation), it is also misleading owing to Soviet 'concealment and deception' (such as camouflage).

(ii) The methods of calculating national consumption, which were developed for market economies, produce grossly overrated results as the CIA applies them to the Soviet economy.

(iii) Consequently, the CIA's 'Soviet GNP' in dollars and rubles is grossly overestimated (indeed, in dollars it exceeds the Soviet's obviously propagandistic figure). 'Soviet defense spending' in dollars and rubles is, on the other hand, most likely underestimated even in its post-1976 version. Hence the CIA's 'share of Soviet GNP spent on defense' has been doubly underestimated even after 1976.

(iv) Occasionally, the CIA ventures into specific predictions going far below Soviet official claims (for example, the CIA's prediction in 1977 of the 'Soviet oil shortage') and gets it wrong again.

(v) In both cases—its general estimates and its specific predictions—the CIA merely juggles figures without understanding the Soviet economic realities behind them.

There is no doubt that the CIA, which occupies the leading position in the US intelligence community and which absorbs all intelligence data that the entire intelligence community gathers, is a prisoner of its own methodology and a preserver of its bureaucratic 'face.' On the other hand, the DIA, which was established in the 1960s and which has been testifying before the Joint Economic Committee along with the CIA, has a far smaller economic research staff and, with respect to the CIA, plays a subordinate role, concentrating on military matters. The DIA's estimate of the 'share of Soviet GNP devoted to defense' was, as of 1983, 1–2 percent larger than the CIA's (14–16 percent instead of 13–14 percent). But the DIA was unable to defend even this minor difference.

2 Once Again about Soviet 'Closed Data'

Since the CIA is an intelligence agency, which is supposed to have access to Soviet 'closed data,' the problem of such data has to be re-stated even if it is familiar enough.

In the USA, for example, a person who has no institutional 'affiliation' has, nevertheless, access to statistics—a term which originally meant 'state data.' The right to such access is often purely legal rather than socially useful. There has been a trend toward bureaucratization in the USA as well, and an 'unaffiliated person' becomes an increasingly rare bird, often discounted *a priori* in favor of institutions like the CIA, so that whatever knowledge he or she has legal access to may be socially useless. Still, this right to access exists at least legally.

Soviet civilization has eliminated an unaffiliated person's access to 'state data' as harmful or useless. One must be 'affiliated' (and hence 'qualified' and 'authorized') to have access to 'state data,' the number of those 'admitted' decreasing with the level of state importance of these data. The highest levels comprise from several to several hundred top decision-makers who receive the most important, and hence most secret, data. Then follow the intermediate levels, such as Form No. 1 (top secret, special file), Form No. 2 (top secret, SS) and Form No. 3 (secret). Finally, come the lowest levels, such as materials *dlya sluzhebnogo polzovaniya* (DSP, 'for official-professional use'), which the relevant officials and specialists can study, but from which no data can be published or divulged orally to any outsider.

Citizens of Western democracies are familiar with a hierarchic system of classified data: military data are classified in this way in their countries. The Soviet regime extends the concept of military-strategic data to embrace all 'state data,' that is, all data of state importance. It is believed that a (potential) military enemy may benefit from almost any kind of knowledge of the country: the more that is concealed from the enemy and the more the enemy is deceived, the better it is strategically (the relevant military field is, characteristically, called 'concealment and deception' in the West, too). For example, the CIA ('the key center of enemy espionage') has carried out a study entitled 'Consumption in the USSR: An International Comparison.' So the 'key center of enemy espionage' is even interested in Soviet consumption —the latter is also of military-strategic importance to the enemy. What, then, is not?

Along with 'closed data,' 'open statistics' are created in Soviet civilization, for the same reason and for the same purpose that are 'elections,' 'Soviet parliament,' 'demonstrations' and other such institutions or activities. That is, they are intended to show that the Soviet regime is a 'people's democracy,' fundamentally no different from a Western democracy or developing toward it.

The purpose of 'open economic data' is, predictably, 'concealment and deception' aimed at representing the Soviet economy as a 'people's economy,' still behind the US economy owing to the 'backwardness of tsarist Russia,' but already fairly productive, yet peaceful. Thus, while allocating a small share of its resources for defense, the 'people's economy' produces as many weapons as the USA does.

Let us now recall how closed and open economic sources differ in content.

The Soviet hierarchy of state importance, and hence secrecy, of closed data correlates with the hierarchy of control of all economic activities as part of the hierarchy of all power and wealth in the country. Data at the primary level of civilian consumer production or research may be the least important and hence the least secret. As the flow of data goes up the hierarchy, they become increasingly more important and hence secret. The higher the level of importance and secrecy of closed data, the more their content differs from that of 'open statistics.' Without going into the subject of motivational analysis of Soviet decision-makers, which is beyond the scope of this chapter, it can be said, on the basis of general considerations ('A person is inclined to attend to *his* interests rather than someone else's'), that the top decision-makers, the *de facto* owners of the country and its economy, are, naturally, interested above all in their global military power, which is also the most important condition for perpetuating their political power inside the Soviet civilization. Since they have been immensely successful so far (according to the US government, they were, as of the beginning of the 1980s, more militarily powerful than the USA, and they have certainly left West Germany, Japan, Britain and France far behind), their interest in the subject has, naturally, become even more intense. Hence, at their level, the economic data deal, above all, with the maximization of their global military power. They cannot be expected to be interested in myriads of consumer goods and services for their powerless 'rank-and-file population,' except in the general terms of keeping it in an adequte working and fighting condition. Their attitude resembles that of a war cabinet in a democracy at war.

Inversely, Soviet open economic sources imitate Western peacetime consumerism and exaggerate Soviet consumption. For example, as every Western economist-sovietologist knows only too well, the 655-page *The People's Economy of the USSR in 1985* (I have translated *narodnoye khozyaistvo* as 'people's economy,' for this is how the phrase is perceived today) contained only two words (*na oboronu*) and two figures (19.1 billion rubles, 4.9 percent of the State Budget), to indicate that something called 'defense' did exist in that peaceful society in 1985, but the expenses on it were dwarfed by items like 'socio-cultural activities and science' (125.6 billion rubles).

3 The CIA's Sources

An economist-sovietologist outside any 'intelligence community' has no access to Soviet closed economic data. On the other hand, the CIA is supposed to have access to them. If the CIA believes that intelligence-espionage was, and is, possible *vis-à-vis*, say, France (Germany was reported to have 30,000 agents in France in 1870), but that it is humanly impossible, for example, to send an agent into a totalitarian society like that of post-1917 Russia, plant him or her at a point with access to Soviet closed data and retrieve the agent safely, the Agency ought to have declared as much thirty, twenty or at least ten years ago.

The CIA has never made such a statement. Nor has it ever declared that it has studied the problem. On the contrary, for decades it kept creating the impression that intelligence-espionage *vis-à-vis* post-1917 Russia was its flourishing daily trade, and it has never tried to dispel that impression created by the media. Thus, soon after the establishment of the CIA, the US Air Force delivered its 'requirement' to Frank Lindsay, chief of the Eastern European Division: to have one CIA agent at each Soviet airfield, about 2,000 CIA agents in all, by 1 July 1952, and Lindsay responded to the 'requirement' in the CIA's usual 'sure-we-can-do-that' spirit.[6] If all of the CIA's boasts of this kind in the media in the last thirty-odd years can be dismissed as hearsay, it was the CIA Director William Colby himself who described to Congress in 1975, in nonspecific terms befitting the secrecy of his profession, how CIA agents are sent into Soviet territory and retrieved as a matter of course, and how they 'report what kind of Soviet discussion is all about . . . the reality of their [the Soviet rulers] policy-level discussions in private,' etc.[7]

To prove that the CIA has never been able to engage in intelligence-espionage *vis-à-vis* totalitarian societies is beyond the scope of this chapter. However, the CIA's testimonies and submissions under study here do indicate that the CIA has never had access even to the Soviet least secret (DSP) data. The fact that DSP materials are used by Soviet lowest-level specialists and officials, but are not sold at book stores in Moscow or Washington and hence cannot be 'secured' by 'CIA agents' has reliably barred even Soviet DSP materials from the 'intelligence community.'

Senator William Proxmire, who chairs the hearings of the Joint Economic Committee, asked Frank E. Doe Jr of the DIA in 1982 why the Soviet regime should publish information 'from which we can derive judgements of value to us.'

MR DOE. I am sure that they believe that those estimates that we produce based on their estimates are imperfect. We also believe they are imperfect.
SENATOR PROXMIRE. Well, if both agree that they are imperfect, which is another way of saying they are not true or accurate, what good are they?
MR DOE. There are degrees of imperfection. No estimate that we make is perfect, to my knowledge. I am not aware of a 100-percent confidence estimate.[8]

In this naive sophistry there is not a hint at the existence of Soviet closed data. Senator Proxmire continued to press on, and finally DIA Director James A. Williams said: 'But if you will follow that reasoning a little bit further, Senator, then we would just disregard all the data from the Soviet Union and say that those statistics are unworkable, and then we wouldn't do any analysis.'[9]

That is, if it were not for Soviet open data, the intelligence agencies might as well shut down. The general's logic: Soviet open data (otherwise called 'propaganda' by the DIA itself, as we shall see below) cannot be too 'imperfect,' or else the CIA and the DIA would have to go on the unemployment roll, and surely this is *reductio ad absurdum*.

The materials under study do contain occasional wistful references to Soviet closed sources: 'It is known that a detailed "estimate" (*smeta*) of expenditures on items for military use is compiled each year.'[10] The implication is: 'But how can a mere mortal see a Soviet estimate which is so secret?' Even its name is a mystery: the word *smeta* is an ordinary Russian word for any preliminary cost estimate, as for building a chicken pen.

No less wistfully did Edward Proctor, 'in charge of the basic analytic work' of the CIA, say to Senator Proxmire (the chairman):

The chairman asked us to try to project Soviet military expenditures beyond a 2-year period to, say, 5 years. If the Agency had a source with access to this kind of information—in the planning bureau, for example in the Soviet Union—where they obviously do plan for military allocations 5 years or maybe longer, I would be in a much better position to respond to the request for projections with a great deal more confidence. Of course, this would also improve our estimates of current military spending.[11]

But mostly the CIA has avoided mentioning the very existence of Soviet closed sources. Senator Proxmire asked the CIA the following question concerning Soviet 'published sources':

> Do they not tend to exaggerate their growth, exaggerate their reserves, their progress and so forth, so that statistical material is likely to show larger rather than smaller gains than the actual case? . . .Are you able to take the published sources . . . and reconstruct a fairly consistent picture, coherent picture of their whole economy so it does square out roughly at least?[12]

Having made no mention of Soviet closed sources, the CIA assured the Senator that the 'published sources' are sufficient—take, for example, steel production: '. . . if they claim to have produced 125 million tons of steel, the claim is reasonably consistent with the end use of that metal in the economy. Things roughly check out in the context.'[13]

In 1982, according to Soviet open statistics, the Soviet economy produced 147 million tons of steel, as against 66 million tons produced in the USA. Since little Soviet steel goes into cars (few and small), highways (made without steel), and buildings (constructed out of prefab concrete elements, not steel beams), yet over $5 billion worth of rolled steel was imported in 1982, for example, it is obvious that the 'end use of that metal in the economy' is mainly strategic, and hence is recorded only in closed sources and is passed in open sources as civilian end uses.

> CHAIRMAN PROXMIRE. Let me interrupt again to say that is what puzzled me about your statistics. One of the first questions I asked, I wondered what in the dickens that they are doing with all that steel. A lot of it is there, but over there it seems to me they do not have automobiles like we do. They do not have the highway system we have. They do not have the housing construction or anything of that kind.
>
> If they are producing more steel, how can they use it?[14]

Again, the CIA's truthful answer would be that the CIA does not know, since it has no access to closed data on steel. Instead, the CIA (Messrs Proctor, Noren and Burton) offered two vague conjectures, taken from open Soviet sources:

> MR NOREN. They have such an investment program—
>   CHAIRMAN PROXMIRE. More than ours in machine tools, for instance?
>   MR NOREN. In terms of absolute size their fixed investment approaches our[s] now.

CHAIRMAN PROXMIRE. Thank you.

MR BURTON. They are also very inefficient users of steel. Their machines are very heavy compared to ours.

CHAIRMAN PROXMIRE. The military weapons systems are usually heavy too.

MR BURTON. Yes.

MR PROCTOR. One remembers Khrushchev's cursing of the manufacturers as metal-eaters. He had a campaign to reduce the waste of steel, especially in the manufacture of both military and civilian hardware.

CHAIRMAN PROXMIRE. Thank you.[15]

The first conjecture is irrelevant: if 'in terms of absolute size their fixed investment [in machine tools, for instance] approaches ours,' it is still not clear where the Soviet steel goes which is saved by way of cars, buildings and highways. The second conjecture is even more speculative: many examples can be given to show that the Soviet economy uses steel more sparingly than does the US economy. When Mr Proctor gave his waste-of-steel explanation, the Soviet T–72 tank, weighing 41 tons, was declared by the US military to be faster, more powerful and more heavily armed than anything in the US arsenal, while its US rival, the XM–1, with a smaller main gun, which was expected to come off the assembly line in 1979, was to weigh 53 tons (actually, this tank, now known as M–1, weighs 55 tons). Anyway, in 1982 the CIA declared that 'Soviet defense . . . takes about 10 percent of the rolled steel.'[16] So it is Soviet civilian production that allegedly wastes steel— something even more inconceivable, considering how grudgingly steel is doled out for civilian uses and how eagerly it is replaced by prestressed reinforced concrete.[17]

In the 1960s there appeared mutually allowed US–Soviet space satellite inspection. Surely intelligence-espionage means the clandestine acquisition of information against its holder's will. But the Soviet military had launched earth satellites before the USA did and, as we shall see below, they were fully prepared to neutralize US space satellite inspection. Besides, no optical, electronic, or any other outside observation can give the CIA access to Soviet closed economic statistics.

Satellite inspection has enabled the CIA to sustain its pretense at intelligence-espionage and to pepper its texts under study with 'security deletions' or 'deleted' remarks. Thus in 1971 Senator Proxmire said: 'I was asking you (Lt Gen. Samuel V. Wilson, Director of the DIA] awhile ago about the Soviet spending on R.D.T. & E. And you made an estimate that they were spending about [deleted] again as what we were.'[18]

The deleted words are 'half as much,' for Lt Gen. Wilson said earlier: 'My own feeling, subject to checking this out, is that they are spending more in this area, at least 50 percent more in this area than we.'[19] So Lt Gen. Wilson's guess, when Senator Proxmire repeated it, was deleted because Lt

Gen. Wilson could have presumably made his guess not only on the basis of Soviet 'open statistics,' but also from the satellite inspection of (the roofs of) those Soviet buildings which looked like research institutes and design offices. However, in 1983 the CIA stated that 'RDT&E is estimated directly from official Soviet statistics.'[20] Thus, the very possibility of satellite inspection turns guesses made on the basis of 'official Soviet statistics' into mysteries of espionage.

All in all, what the CIA has been doing since 1959 is retelling what had appeared in the Soviet 'open press,' often without acknowledging its sources and thus creating the impression that these are secret. In 1959 Allen Dulles testified before Congress: 'We estimate the growth of Soviet GNP during the present decade or a little short of a decade, 1950–58, to have been at an annual average rate of about 7 percent measured in constant prices.'[21]

Probably not a single member of Congress suspected that the superspy Dulles's espionage data were what Dulles otherwise called Soviet propaganda: 'The fourth 5-year plan (1946–50) was fulfilled ahead of schedule,' he stated as the CIA's own conclusion. Or: 'The goals of the fifth 5-year plan were more than met.'[22] As of November 1959, after six Soviet space vehicles had been launched, including the world's first artificial earth satellite, the first spacecraft on the moon and the first circumnavigator of it, the major danger to the West, according to Dulles, was not the developoment of Soviet military research, production and training, but the Soviet overall 'industrialization':

If the Soviet industrial growth rate persists at 8 or 9 percent per annum over the next decade, as is forecast, the gap between our two economies by 1970 will be dangerously narrowed unless our industrial growth rate is substantially increased from the present pace.[23]

This was another echo of Soviet propaganda ('We shall overtake and outstrip America economically'). An additional danger, according to the CIA, was that those 'gains will also permit the Soviet to further assist in the rapid economic growth of the Kremlin's eastern ally, Communist China.'[24]

The CIA's testimony of 1983 retells what appeared in the Soviet open press, as much as did its testimony of 1959. The Soviet propaganda messages have changed—and so have the messages of the CIA's testimony. When the Soviet armed forces were strategically weak because of US superior strategic aviation, Soviet propaganda projected the image of a Soviet economy which would soon outgrow the economies of all enemies combined and would thus ensure superior Soviet might. In the 1980s Soviet propaganda is arguing, for the first time in its history, that there is parity between Soviet and US strategic forces, that is, the Soviet armed forces are *weaker* than their enemies represent them. Nor do the Soviet rulers mind, for the same reason, if the Soviet open press shows a Soviet 'economic slow-down.' Accordingly, just as the CIA of 1959 brooded on the danger to the West of 'Soviet growth,' the CIA of 1983 ponders Soviet open-press figures of sluggish production, for example, 'declining growth in production of coal.'[25] A well-read Soviet secondary school pupil is likely to know that coal output in the USA in 1970 (555.8 metric tons) was at about the same level as in 1920. Thus it is not clear why the Soviet decision-makers should worry that Soviet coal output in 1981 (704 million tons) increased in 1982 to only 718 million tons, and why they should try to keep it on a steady, not declining, growth path, if the Soviet output of natural gas (so much cheaper and more convenient to produce, carry and use) has been growing apace, and is expected to reach (with Western aid) a figure far exceeding the US output, with a lion's share of Soviet energy saved owing to the small scale of Soviet civilian consumption.

I do not mean to say that there is no Soviet 'economic slow-down,' as reflected in Soviet open statistics. In all 'industrialized' countries there has been a period of rapid transfer of huge masses of rural manpower to industries. That period is over in the Soviet civilization. Hence the Soviet 'economic slow-down,' which Soviet propaganda does not deem it necessary to conceal. What I mean is that in 1983 the CIA exaggerated the importance of the Soviet 'economic slow-down,' just as in 1959 it exaggerated the importance of 'Soviet economic growth.' What was important then, and is important now, is the (mostly 'closed') development of the (mostly 'closed') economy, maximizing Soviet global military might as expressed in weapons and defenses, and strategic personnel, such as strategically oriented scientists and engineers. For example, from the point of view of highest-level, closed Soviet data which deal with economic realities of the utmost importance to the top decision-makers, Soviet science and technology, plus the transfer of Western science and technology and Soviet military-industrial espionage, have reached such a quantitative and qualitative stage that a Soviet breakthrough in weapons may give the Soviet armed forces the kind of 'absolute superiority' which the USA had from 1945 to 1949 owing to its monopoly of nuclear weapons and its strategic aviation to deliver them.

Compared with such prospects, what the CIA sees in Soviet open sources in 1983 is as unimportant and irrelevant as what it saw in 1959. 'Although information for 1983 is sparse . . .'[26] By 'information' the CIA means Soviet open data. 'The new [Andropov's] regime has shown concern for the welfare of the population in a variety of ways.'[27] To 'show concern for the welfare of the population' is a cliché which has been applied to every Soviet ruler since Lenin. 'Production of fruits and vegetables reached record levels and output of potatoes, sugar beets, and sunflower seeds increased substantially over the depressed levels of 1981.'[28] Or: 'In the crucial livestock sector, meat output from state and collective farms–which produce about two-thirds of total Soviet meat—reached a record level during the first seven months of 1983.'[29]

4 Once Again on the Reliability/Unreliability of Soviet Open Data

When in 1982 there appeared a Soviet response, 'From Whence the Threat,' to the DIA's document 'Soviet Military Power,' the DIA drew up a one-page rebuttal,[30] in which the DIA called the Soviet data 'propaganda' three times within one page (for example, 'Moscow's most recent propaganda document'). So the 'intelligence community' assumes that what is propaganda is *a priori* untrue, and it is sufficient to label Soviet data as propaganda three times in order to refute them. But when the sources of the charts were not indicated in the CIA's testimony (they rarely are), and Senator Proxmire asked for them to be named, Douglas Diamond of the CIA answered: 'All of the data in the charts for both economies are official figures from statistical abstracts.'[31]

In other words, when the intelligence community copies Soviet data from Soviet open sources in its 'intelligence work,' these are 'official figures from statistical abstracts,' 'information,' or 'published sources,' but when the Soviet military begin to argue with the intelligence community, they become propaganda, that is, *a priori* false. Such is the contribution to the analysis of the problem of the reliability/unreliability of Soviet open data the CIA and DIA have made since 1959, judging by the materials under study.

The problem of the reliability/unreliability of Soviet open data is, obviously, outside the scope of this chapter, but a few cursory remarks may be necessary.

As has been said earlier, the Soviet regime need not publish any 'open economic statistics.' Inasmuch as it publishes them, they *are* propaganda aimed at creating on paper an imaginary 'people's economy' for strategic concealment and deception.

However, the imaginary Soviet economy must be self-consistent and generally plausible. A way for Soviet propaganda to create on paper such an imaginary economy is to select *some* data from the real economy and to transfer them to the imaginary economy as they are or metamorphosed (for example, weapons can be renamed machinery). If it is found that authentic data in the imaginary economy are used by the West to derive closed data, the publication of these authentic data is discontinued.

On the other hand, the Soviet increase in the volume of 'open economic statistics' since 1956 has, on the whole, been a great success for Soviet strategy: the CIA has since been busy re-hashing the propaganda message of Soviet 'official data from statistical abstracts.'

Soviet 'open economic statistics,' not to mention 'open data' in general, are certainly worth studying. A person who wants to conceal and deceive is also worth listening to. Students of the Soviet economy outside the intelligence community have no choice but to study Soviet 'open economic statistics,' in the same way as an investigator studies a deceiver's testimony, trying to detect discrepancies and evasions, or glean authentic data that the deceiver has used to make his concealment and deception plausible. In this battle of wits, the sharper-witted Western analysts outside the 'intelligence communities' score brilliant victories over Soviet propaganda bureaucracies.[32] Nor is this surprising: while Soviet strategic bureaucracies have enormous advantages over Western centralized government bureaucracies like the CIA, they are also only bureaucracies and hence are no mental match for the best independent Western thinkers or doers.[33]

However, it is not clear why the CIA and DIA are believed to be mentally superior to the relevant Soviet bureaucracies, are able to outwit them, and derive valuable authentic information from Soviet open data. Within the scope of this chapter, only two random quotations can be given from the materials under study to illustrate the mental level of the CIA and the DIA.

The Director of the CIA (William Colby) and that of the DIA (Lt Gen. Samuel V. Wilson) explained in 1975 and 1976, respectively, why the Soviet military buildup had visibly continued from 1963 to 1976, despite the fact that the USA had given up its end of the arms race. Namely, the US defense budget had decreased from 11.2 percent of GNP in 1955 to 5.8 percent in 1974; US biological weapons had been scrapped, and the chemical warfare program virtually abandoned (unilaterally); all civil defense had long been discontinued (unilaterally); and the treasures of US (West European and Japanese) technology had been thrown open for the benefit of the Soviet economy. Finally, the US army—except for doctors—had become all-volunteer, which meant that while the Soviet regime would continue to produce a new army of 2–3 million men every two years in addition to its standing army of 4.4 million, the USA would have the same 2-million-man army all the time.

Why, then, in the face of all this—Senator Proxmire wanted to know—had the Soviet global buildup visibly continued throughout the 1960s and 1970s just as before, if not more intensely? Senator Proxmire, a Democrat, was left of center (certainly not right of it) in the US political spectrum of foreign policy attitudes. In the mid-1970s he was still more 'pro-détente' than 'pro-defense.' Nevertheless, he wanted to know why the Soviet rulers' military activity had been more and more visible all over the globe, when the USA had even deserted its allies in Southeast Asia and had been visibly reverting to a kind of neo-isolationism.

The CIA Director explained in 1975:

The Soviets, of course, have a national historical fixation on the problem of invasion. They have been invaded and put in very dangerous situations at least twice in the last couple of centuries.[34]

The DIA Director elaborated in 1976:

I am sure you realize that the great experience for the Soviets is the great Fatherland War, as they call it. If I may indulge in hyperbole, for a moment, the Soviet citizen gets up every morning, and he has a wide vivisectional scar from his chin to his crotch, and he scratches it until it hurts. That is World War II. Then he goes off to work, and he lives with hurt all day . . .[35]

Lt Gen. Wilson went on in the same vein and concluded his speech by saying that this 'syndrome' is a 'driving force in the Soviet consciousness.'

From these two random samples it is clear that the two directors visualize the Soviet ruling hierarchy (far more rigidly stratified than that of any society known as a 'Western democracy') *and* its 254 million subjects (1976) of about 100 nations as a single exotic stereotype, 'The Russian.'

By the first time the 'Soviets' were invaded, Colby means Napoleon's invasion of Russia in 1812, though the 'Soviets' appeared only a century later. Surely the Negro slaves in the American South would not have felt endangered if France or Britain had taken over the territory? Why should, then, the 'Soviets' (the Russian chattel slaves, called euphemistically serfs) have acquired in 1812 a 'national historical fixation on the problem of invasion'—to last for two centuries?

As for the second invasion, do the two directors know, for example, that *many* 'Soviet citizens' welcomed the Nazi troops, or collaborated with Nazi Germany, or even fought against the Soviet regime? The two directors cannot even conjecture that *most* 'Soviet citizens' were indifferent as to which regime—Stalin's or Hitler's—would be imposed on their country in the 1940s.

It is, likewise, superfluous in the context to ask how Lt Gen. Wilson knows what 'the Soviet citizen' feels as he 'gets up every morning' or 'goes off to work' or lives 'all day,' given the fact that in his capacity as US defense attaché, the only manifestations of 'the Soviet citizen' that would talk with him were carefully rehearsed Soviet agents, or generals, admirals, and the like, with all conversations videotaped and subsequently analyzed by the Soviet secret police.

The two directors reason at the level of market-booth vaudevilles of a hundred years ago, in which the 100-odd nations of the Russian Empire were represented by 'The Russian,' the population of the USA by 'The American,' and that of the British Empire by 'The Briton,' each acting accordingly. 'The Russian' played his balalaika, 'The American' chewed his tobacco, and 'The Briton' sang 'Rule, Britannia.'

It is not suggested that all members of the CIA and DIA reason at the mental level of these two directors. But the US intelligence community led by the CIA is a paramilitary centralized government monopoly. Certainly, the mental level of its two directors may thus become its top mental level, all brilliant exceptions in its midst notwithstanding.

This vast paramilitary centralized government monopoly merely produces mediocre scholarship, at best, and passes it on as unique secret knowledge; stifles dissent, opposition, competition and discussion; perpetuates its bureaucratic sterility and ignorance; and wastes billions of dollars in playing at intelligence-espionage.

5   The CIA's 'Soviet Consumption'

Traditionally, societies like the USA and Britain conceive of the economy as a tool of the growth of wealth, *our* wealth, the wealth of the estates, the electorate, the parliament. *They*—the monarch, the executive, the government—want part of *our* wealth, to spend it on *their* military activities, while *we*—the estates, the electorate, the parliament—are loath to part with it. *Their* military spending is thus sharply distinct from *our* wealth and *our* consumption of it.

Just like many other Western institutions, the CIA fails to conjecture that there may be a civilization different from a Western democracy yet possibly more viable—'fitter for survival,' in Darwin's phrase.

Senator Proxmire told the CIA in 1981 that only 9 percent of US school students take courses in physics, and 'those that do, have one or two years of it,'[36] while in Soviet schools four years of physics are obligatory for all students (Senator Proxmire did not say that mathematics is studied every day by Soviet secondary school pupils for eleven years, including calculus for three years). The CIA's answer to Senator Proxmire is characteristic: 'It is true,' Douglas Diamond of the CIA conceded, 'that they graduate three times as many engineers as we do,' whereupon he explained that a quantitative difference is unimportant.

This provides for a way to dismiss *a priori* all such quantitative differences. If the Soviet economy produced between 1974 and 1984 ten times more pieces of artillery or assault rifles than did the USA, a common US answer is that Soviet artillery *must* then be worse than its US counterpart by a factor of 10, or is not needed in our age of electronics. If the scale of studies of languages is compared in the Soviet civilization and the USA, and it is said, for example, the number of Russians who study English exceeds that of Americans who study Russian 1,000 times, the CIA may readily respond by saying that Soviet studies of languages are less effective by a factor of 1,000 or that Russians should anyway study English as the language of a superior civilization, while it is useless for Americans to study Russian, Arabic, or even French on a mass scale. Thus, the 'CIA spies' in the Shah's Iran had not known Farsi, as was discovered after the fall of the Shah.

In 1984 Soviet engineers accounted for about half of all engineers in the world. The CIA assumes *a priori* their poor quality. However, Soviet émigré engineers have secret and top secret clearances, working for the best US firms (such as Hughes, Lockheed, TRW and Grumman)[37] on a par with the best US engineers despite the linguistic and cultural barriers: there is no qualitative gap between them. Most Soviet engineers are trained in strategic fields, but apart from a strategic profession (like steel-making), every such engineer has a purely military engineering profession (like mine-sweeping).

The point of the above is that Soviet civilization, including its economy, has taken a different road, and is not just at an earlier and backward American 'stage of growth.' In Soviet civilization, everything strategically important—be it strategically oriented engineering, or training of spies, or studies of strategically important languages—acquires a stupendous scale by Western standards, takes priority and often leads to sophistication, while what is strategically unimportant shrinks, for the 'rank-and-file population,' to a bare standard minimum war ration. Yet to the CIA, Soviet civilization is simply underdeveloped. The Western economy provides for the CIA the prototype from which any other economy is a temporary backward deviation. Therefore, the CIA imposes on the Soviet economy all the features of the Western economy, with Soviet propaganda's full agreement: the goal of the CIA's Soviet economy is assumed to be the growth of wealth in order to increase consumption, while 'defense spending' is regarded as a reluctant appropriation of GNP, a sharply distinct share of it and an undesirable burden, reducing consumption. Accordingly, the CIA calculates 'Soviet consumption' as opposed to 'Soviet defense spending' along Western-market-economy lines.

The CIA's first study of 'Soviet consumption' (*A Comparison of Consumption in the USSR and US*) was finished in 1964 and dealt with 'Soviet consumption' in 1955. As of 1983, the study was still secret. There can be hardly anything secret about 'Soviet consumption' thirty years ago and the CIA's twenty-year-old study of it on the basis of Soviet open data (the year of 1955 was evidently chosen as the year on which open Soviet data began to appear in 1956). The fact of secrecy merely demonstrates the CIA's ability and willingness to hide under the cloak of imaginary intelligence-espionage. Nevertheless, we know, courtesy of those admitted into the CIA's holy precincts of secrecy (and in particular, those who did the CIA's second study of Soviet consumption in 1981), the ultimate conclusion of the study of 1964: Soviet per capita consumption in 1955 was 26.2 percent of US per capita consumption.[38]

Actually, following the war devastation, 'Soviet consumption' had barely regained the 1940 level, which was lower than the 1913 level of consumption in 'tsarist Russia' (wild assertions to the contrary by Stalin's propaganda notwithstanding). Some anecdotal existential evidence may be more useful than any Soviet statistics. Even many members of the 'upper 1 percent' lived in Moscow in 'communal apartments' and other such arrangements which would have been defined in the USA in 1955 as superslums. Most 'communal apartments' were in buildings dating from 1913 or earlier and brought to a state of dereliction under the new management. Outside of military-industrial production, the Russia of 1955 was, basically, the pre-1913 Russia in a state of dereliction forty-odd years later. Pre-1913 clothes had been worn for two generations. Over half of the population lived in the countryside, that is, for the most part just as in 1913 or 1613, except that they had less food, such as bread, than in 1913 and were otherwise reduced to the state of starving medieval serfs. About one-tenth of the population was said to be in the corrective labor camps or to have just emerged from them. Yet the CIA concluded in 1964 (in a study still classified!) that 'Soviet per capita consumption' had amounted in 1955 to over one-quarter of per capita consumption in the USA, where the war had merely led to an economic boom.

The CIA's second study of Soviet consumption (in 1976) was published in 1981: certainly there is nothing secret in it, except that many references to Soviet open sources are again omitted, and some nonperishable Soviet goods were bought by the CIA as samples in Soviet stores, which any US tourist or embassy clerk could have done as well. By involving itself in such 'intelligence operations,' the CIA merely adds to the myth (spread by Soviet propaganda) of ubiquitous US espionage.

The 1981 study followed the methodology of the 1964 study, which was patterned after that used by Gilbert and Kravis in 1953 in their comparison of GNPs of Western countries. 'To the extent allowed by Soviet data,' states the CIA study of 1981, 'the US–Soviet comparison was patterned after the [United Nations] ICP [International Comparison Project].'[39] While Gilbert and Kravis applied the methodology to bona fide market economies, which made sense, the United Nations extended it to Hungary. The CIA took another step and applied it to the Soviet economy on the assumption that it is just one of the underdeveloped economies lying somewhere between the economy of the USA and that of India.

Let us see what is taken for granted when the consumptions or GNPs of Western market economies are compared.

The *Statistical Abstract of the United States* indicates four aggregates of goods called 'alcoholic beverages': 'distilled spirits,' 'beer,' 'still wines' and 'effervescent wines,' the production of which is given in bottles or gallons. Other tables indicate the 'total alcoholic beverage sales,' the sales, in billions of dollars, of 'liquor stores' and 'eating and drinking places,' as well as the imports of 'alcoholic beverages.' Still other tables indicate tax revenues and import duties.

This statistical information is sufficient to draw a fair comparison of the production or consumption of these goods in market economies. For behind these statistical symbols are similar economic realities which these symbols assume and quantify. Thus, according to connoisseurs, 'alcoholic beverages' called 'wines' differ from one another, as do paintings or other works of art. In particular, they differ according to grape, soil, locality, vineyard (châteaux), year of vintage, methods of making and seasoning, and age. We may call it a wine culture or connoisseurship. If certain customers, patrons, or clients value certain wines as they do paintings or other works of art, and are willing to pay accordingly, the corresponding monetary values become the world market prices for these 'alcoholic beverages' (with allowances for custom duties). Inversely: while French 'effervescent wines' were expensive luxuries in early-nineteenth-century Moscow or New York in particular because their transportation from France was expensive, today they are put within the reach of the majority of the US population as they are cheaply flown by plane to any point (just as are pineapples, once a symbol of Russian aristocratic luxury, now sold in New York at the price of potatoes, once a symbol of Russian, Irish, or French peasant poverty). These decreases in the prices of luxuries, putting them within the reach of more and more consumers, occur in all market economies more or less simultaneously. Hence, statistical symbols like the 'sales of alcoholic beverages, billions of dollars' can be used for comparing the production and consumption of these goods in market economies.

Let us now assume, contrary to what every economist-sovietologist knows, that Soviet 'open statistics' yield information as complete and accurate as does the US *Statistical Abstract*. But what will be the economic reality behind those statistical symbols, as compared with the economic reality of the USA?

Let us take the 'liquor store' in my middle-class neighborhood in Kingsbridge, New York, as a statistical average sample of the 'liquor stores' the US *Statistical Abstract* aggregates. The 'liquor store,' 'Buy-Rite, Discount Liquor,' is a 100×20 ft room with one average-size show window and one entrance door, and is obviously intended for median- and lower-income customers, since its prices are specifically advertised in the show window as between $1 and $20 a bottle (the average hourly earning of a production worker in manufacturing industries in New York in 1984 is $9.22). Shelved on one (100-ft-long) wall are over 600 wines from all major wine-exporting countries. The CIA's study under discussion says: 'The USSR produces over 600 brands of wine of varying style and quality . . .'[40] The authors had read this in an open Soviet source they do not name. The reality of this Soviet–CIA statement will be discussed below. But, meanwhile, it is noteworthy that just one wall of an average US 'liquor store' contains no fewer wines than are produced by the entire Soviet civilization.

The owner of the 'independently owned and operated' Kingsbridge 'liquor store' keeps changing the brands on all wall shelves and floor stacks, trying new brands and removing those which do not sell, so that over 10,000 wines and hard liquors pass through his one-room establishment annually.[41] I had a criterion of my own: I asked a salesman whether they had 'Asti spumante,' which was considered an acme of aristocratic sophistication in old Russia and was immortalized as such in a well-known poem about aristocratic luxuries of old. He told me that they had *three* brands at the moment.

From my observation of the personal lives of two members of the Politburo, I am certain that they do not have such a magnificent choice of 'alcoholic beverages' unless a member of the Politburo collects them on his own in his wine cellar.

Only the richest early-nineteenth-century Russian aristocrats were privileged to have such a choice. And here we arrive at the essence of US economic development: to put within the reach of all who have money (and even 'social welfare outlays' accounted for more than $600 billion in 1983) at every point of the USA all those luxuries that only the aristocracy, and then the bourgeoisie, once had.

The Soviet average 'liquor store' of this kind does not exist, especially if the word 'average' is referred to the entire territory of the country and not just the areas where foreigners are allowed to travel and where 'CIA agents' bought the samples of Soviet goods for the CIA study in question. Without going into the macro-sociology of Soviet society, let us recall that owing to every inhabitant's 'attachment' to his or her place of residence, the Soviet territory is a hierarchy of socio-economic cascades, each lower cascade being a different country, as it were, with its own worse supply of worse and fewer goods and services, and its own higher prices and lower wages. The Soviet average counterpart of the US 'liquor store' described above will be two establishments. One will be a (plywood) booth (*laryok*, of a kind which was once jerry-built at village fairs) which *may* sell an alcoholic beverage called 'beer.' This 'beer' is neither canned nor bottled[42] because that would be too expensive and would prevent the free mixing of immature beer, old stale beer, and water. Nor does it represent any specific brand of beer—it is just 'beer,' and the question is 'Have you beer?' Besides, it is usually superfluous because when there is 'beer' there is a queue, and when there is no queue, that means there is no 'beer.' The other establishment is a food store (such as, *prodmag*), where there should be an alcoholic beverage called 'vodka.' According to the CIA study itself, 69 percent of Soviet 'alcoholic beverages' consists of 'hard liquor (spirits),'[43] and 96 percent of hard liquor (distilled spirits) is 'vodka.'[44] So 'alcoholic beverages' are mostly one commodity: 'vodka.' Nevertheless, at the store there may be not 'vodka' on sale, but 'Soviet Champagne,' and then those who wish to buy a bottle of 'vodka' buy several bottles of 'Soviet Champagne,' to take in the same amount of alcohol by drinking them one after the other.

The Soviet rulers' approach to 'consumer goods and services' for the 'rank-and-file population' is 'scientific' or physiological. The population needs food to be able to work and fight, clothes to keep warm and look decent, and alcoholic beverages to make merry in leisure time or on various festive occasions. It is ethyl alcohol that makes one merry. Accordingly, the Soviet economy processes ethyl alcohol out of twigs, sawdust and other waste products of the timber and woodworking industries. The chemical is not on sale, since this would make too many too merry, too cheaply, but the addition of 60 percent of water to 40 percent of it produces an alcoholic beverage which is called 'vodka' (that is, named just like the vodka that was made in old Russia out of grain and is now made for export) and which is sold at an average physician's daily pay for 1 liter. The slang for 'vodka' is *suchok* ('twig'), and it is identified as made *iz taburetki* ('out of a foot-stool'). 'Vodka' (which George Orwell described in his *1984* as 'Victory gin') tastes different from vodka, but there is nothing more subjective than taste, of course.[45]

No less scientific was the invention (ascribed to Stalin personally) of 'Soviet Champagne.' On festive occasions in old Russia toasts were said to have been drunk in French champagne. In all cities of Stalin's civilization, city-mains water was aerated by ubiquitous standard street-carts and sold off them (at 5 kopecks a glass). That suggested a way of making *Soviet* champagne, the content of which has been a state secret, except that it certainly includes ethyl alcohol and thus makes one merry, though not as much as does 'vodka,' since the percentage of ethyl alcohol is lower. As of 1975 (the Soviet data for 1976 are absent) 130 million bottles of 'Soviet Champagne' were produced,[46] that is, about one bottle per family per two major festive occasions (the family head's birthday and at New Year's Eve). Any further expansion of the output of the beverage is faced with the problem of the production of bottles rather than that of the beverage.

As for the 'over 600 brands of wine of varying style and quality' that are produced in the Soviet civilization, according to Soviet–CIA data, they are possibly produced, but (i) many or most of them are not wanted by any consumers (and their origin and content are often as obscure as those of 'Soviet Champagne') and (ii) those brands that are in demand are exported or sold in socio-economically higher-cascade areas, such as Moscow. An 'average store' is not likely to get, except by negligence, any 'wines' besides those which are not in demand. They may be bought just as 'wine' because *some* 'wine' has to be bought (many women still cannot stand 'vodka,' nor can one drink 'Soviet Champagne' on all occasions). The occurrence of even these 'wines' at an 'average store' is purely accidental: several random brands may 'appear' at one store, because no one buys those brands, while several other unwanted brands may be found at another store.

Let us now see how the methodology developed for comparisons of market economies works when applied by the CIA to the Soviet economy. For the aggregate 'alcoholic beverages' the authors take four Soviet representative samples': 'vodka,' a brandy, a grape wine ('Soviet Champagne'?), and a bottled beer, since to buy 'beer' at a *laryok* and pour it into a container in order to carry it to the US Embassy, seal it and fly it to the USA by diplomatic pouch was probably thought by the CIA to be an operation too difficult, conspicuous and hence dangerous.

The brandy the CIA chose costs 19.40 rubles per liter. Since the CIA gives elsewhere[47] the ruble–dollar ratio between the pay of a Soviet physician and his US counterpart (0.041), we can say that, even in purely proportionate terms, a bottle of this brandy in 1976 was as expensive for a Soviet physician as a bottle of wine costing $470 would have been for a US physician. That alone makes the brandy unrepresentative. Besides, 'vodka' accounts for 96 percent of hard liquor (spirits). Finally, even in Moscow it is often impossible to buy this brandy for years since it is exported or distributed through 'closed systems of distribution.'

Anyway, the 'CIA agents' bought the four samples at Soviet stores and brought them to the USA to match them, with the help of US experts, against similar US goods and thus to price them, with allowances for differences in quality. The 'vodka' was priced in this way at $6.82 a liter (that is, about three times higher than many excellent Spanish, Italian and French wines in New York in 1976). Possibly, it tasted horrible to an American expert's palate but, after all, this was an old national Russian drink, and perhaps this was how it should taste.[48] The brandy fetched a good US 1976 price ($16.41 per liter), and an unknown grape wine and a bottled beer also did well.

Now, whenever an American buys *any* US vodka, brandy, wine, or beer he pays for diversity, 'culture,' availability at any point, etc. The Americans are not compelled to drink 'mostly vodka' as they are not compelled to subsist 'mostly on potatoes.'[49] A splash of Smirnoff vodka or a potato *au gratin* are for them whims or fancies among myriads of other whims or fancies.

The CIA's result is predictably absurd: in 'alcoholic beverages' the value of Soviet consumption per capita exceeds that of US consumption by 35.5 percent in terms of rubles, by 4.7 percent in terms of dollars, and by 19.1 percent as geometric mean.[50]

In this travesty of economic analysis, it makes no difference, for example, whether an economy produces 4 primitive products in 500 million identical units each, or 500 million different sophisticated products in 4 units each. If the Soviet economy had produced by way of 'alcoholic beverages' only 'vodka' out of wood-waste products, the CIA's result might have been even better for the Soviet economy, since the CIA's 'representative sample'—'vodka'—would 'match,' say, a US Smirnoff vodka and hence be priced in dollars accordingly, possibly above the US median price per liter of 'alcoholic beverages.'

Obviously, the valuation of Soviet consumption may answer two questions: (i) what is the value of Soviet goods and services in the Soviet consumer's evaluation as far as the latter is possible, and (ii) what would be the cost of their production in the USA as compared with that of the production of Soviet weapons, for example?

Accordingly, the two questions that the CIA should have addressed to the US experts with respect to the 'vodka' the CIA brought from Moscow are:

(i) What is the value of this 'vodka' to US consumers? The answer would have been: next to zero. Characteristically, Soviet exporters export vodka, but they *never* export 'vodka.' It is also relevant that the Soviet exports consist mainly of weapons and raw materials, and Soviet consumers always prefer foreign goods. It could be concluded that many or most Soviet consumers buy 'vodka' only because there is no choice.

(ii) What would be the cost of its production in the USA considering its volume? The answer would have been: next to zero.

What has been said about the aggregate 'alcoholic beverages' applies to all aggregates of 'consumer goods and services.' Thus, for the aggregate 'new cars' four representative samples are taken by the CIA to match them with four US cars. But these four Soviet cars were not 'representative samples,' but the only four Soviet mass-produced cars. They were small, by the US average, all with low-power, 4-cylinder engines, but of four different sizes and hence different prices (9,200, 6,100, 5,500, and 3,500 rubles, respectively). According to Soviet open statistics, there were, in 1975, 16 cars per 1,000 Soviet inhabitants. The *de facto* owners of the Soviet economy (at least one of whom is known to have collected the most expensive and luxurious foreign cars) believed that these 16 car-owners per 1,000 Soviet inhabitants had thus everything necessary by way of cars, speaking again in purely physiological or 'scientific' terms. They are right in such terms. However, Americans buy cars as pure 'means of transportation' no more than they drink 'alcoholic beverages' only to supply their bodies with otherwise unavailable ethyl alcohol, go to restaurants merely to obtain enough calories and vitamins, or buy clothes just to protect their nakedness against prying eyes and the elements. Cars are valued by Americans (and by the Soviet 'upper 1 percent') for the same reasons that the aristocracy and bourgeoisie of old valued luxurious carriages of an infinite variety of styles, even in those cases when it would have been cheaper to ride by omnibus. It is more pleasurable to go by car than by 'public transportation' since, just like a carriage of old, a car gives a keen sense of individual will and venture, of privacy, independence, freedom, wealth and importance. A car is less ornate than a carriage, but it gives an additional sense of technological power and speed at the owner's disposal.[51]

It is not clear why the Soviet rulers should indulge aristocratic-bourgeois whims in their rank-and-file population. So as not to waste an engineer's talent, energy and time on something as frivolous as 'private cars,' all Soviet cars have been copies of foreign models, and once they are built they may be produced for decades without any change. At one time Khrushchev decided not to produce any 'personal cars' for private use, since 'public transportation' is certainly more economical. However, in case of war the armed forces will need an additional number of 'personal cars' (for liaison officers, for example). During World War II all 'personal cars' were duly requisitioned, and the same no doubt will happen on the next D-day. It is that additional minimum of small, standard, primitive yet sturdy 'personal cars' that the Soviet rulers allow to be produced and sold for private use pending the requisition.

Again, the questions which the CIA should have addressed to the experts are:

(i) At what prices would American consumers buy these Soviet cars given the Soviet volume of sales? The price thus determined could have turned out to be a fraction of the price assigned by the CIA, for both American and Soviet consumers may prefer to buy in 1976 a used US, European, or Japanese car of the 1974 vintage rather than a new Soviet car of the 1966 model. The prices for used US products at Soviet 'commission stores' are several times higher than those for 'similar' Soviet new products.

(ii) At what cost can those Soviet cars be produced given the Soviet volume of their production and the time within which they do not change? The answer is important since the Soviet copying of foreign models for all 'durable goods,' their reduction to a minimum of the most primitive models, their standardization and unchangeability, and their low quality make it possible to produce all 'durable goods' at the expense of what military production cannot use at the moment, such as rejected or excessive materials, equipment, premises and manpower, idle time, etc.

The CIA analysts are technicians who have learned computational techniques, traceable to a comparative study of Western economies of thirty years ago. Not only do they have no specific knowledge of the realities of the Soviet economy, but they seem to be no more sensitive to economic realities in general than a computer is. Soviet propaganda feeds into them 'statistical data,' allegedly analogous to those for a Western economy, and they go through conventional computational routines with a computer's indifference to the realities behind 'Soviet data.' Thus, they do not notice that apart from direct war rationing by distribution according to rank in the official-territorial hierarchy, indirect war rationing by prices also exists in Soviet civilization. For example, the ruble–dollar ratio for 'chocolate candy' exceeds that for rye bread almost fourteen times. This is not because the Soviet economy knows how to grow and bake rye bread efficiently, but does not know how to make chocolate candy (some of the world's best chocolate factories were in old Russia). It is rather that the Soviet rulers have upped the price of chocolate candy (though its brands for home consumption often contain more soya than cocoa) almost fourteen times compared with rye bread, in order to confine the 'rank-and-file population' to the rations of rye bread (potatoes, etc.), and make it eat as little chocolate as possible, since cocoa beans, in contrast to rye flour, have to be imported, and good unadulterated chocolate can be exported, while rye bread cannot.

The already quoted ruble–dollar ratio between the Soviet and US physician's pay (.041) enables us to conclude that a $2.66–1 ruble chocolate bar was as expensive in 1976 for a Soviet physician (in purely proportionate terms) as were two $33 (in 1984, $39) jars of caviar, described in the *Wall Street Journal* as an expensive delicacy which an Illinois 'businessman ... treats himself to ... every week or two.'[52]

Soviet 'confectioneries' are made with the cheapest ingredients: soya instead of chocolate, waste sugar-refinement products instead of sugar, potato waste products imitating cream (as in Soviet 'ice cream'), flour-mill waste products, and no end of cheap chemical substitutes.

A visit to a US 'average bakery' or 'average pastry shop,' with its practically infinite variety of freshly baked pastries, will show how Soviet standard factory-made combinations of the above ingredients are utterly lacking in diversity, not to mention sophistication, taste, or just freshness. One US 'average ice cream store' (Baskin Robbins) carried, true to its advertisement, '31 varieties' of ice cream. On the other hand, just as 96 percent of 'hard liquor' is one vodka surrogate, practically one ice cream surrogate has been sold all over the country for more than half a century.

Yet in the CIA study the value of Soviet per capita consumption of 'sugar and confectioneries' (including 'chocolate and ice cream') is 3 percent larger (geometric mean) than that of US consumption.[53] This is the same as claiming that in a country at war, where chocolate and any other such valuable confectioneries are rationed off to expensive-delicacy quantities, the value of consumption of confectioneries is larger than in the USA, where chocolate ceased to be an expensive delicacy decades ago and was consumed by soldiers, for example, as ordinary high-calorie food in World War II rations.

On the other hand, the CIA applies totally different, yet equally unwarranted, manipulations to Soviet education or medical care.

It is absurd for the CIA to regard Soviet education as part of consumption merely because the United Nations does so. The bulk of even Soviet 'civilian' education is military-strategic, something that even the CIA could quantify since much information on Soviet 'civilian' education is contained in Soviet open sources. There is no reason to assume that Soviet secondary, higher-school and postgraduate education instills, essentially, military, military-scientific-technological, strategic-linguistic and ideological knowledge because Soviet inhabitants prefer it, while Americans prefer to be educated in arts and humanities, social sciences, business, etc.

The purpose of Soviet medicine for the 'rank-and-file population' is essentially different from that of US medicine. The latter caters to an *individual* as a client or a customer. If an individual has $1 million (for example, on his insurance account) and is willing to pay such a sum in order to save his life, then US medicine will make an effort worth $1 million to save this one life. (Similarly, if the life of a member of the Soviet Politburo is to be saved, the most expensive US and West European physicians are invited and the latest medicines and medical equipment are imported for an all-out medical effort.) Now, the purpose of Soviet medicine for the 'rank-and-file population' is to ensure its working ability (*trudosposobnost*) and its fighting ability (*boyesposobnost*) *in toto* at the lowest cost. Obviously, the cost of medical treatment of an individual rank-and-file working and fighting 'human unit' that can be easily replaced by another such 'human unit' should not exceed the cost of the replacement. To give a brutal yet helpful analogy, a farmer will not spend more than the cost of a sick horse's replacement on its veterinary treatment.

The contention that the distribution of medical services in the USA is socially unequal, unjust and inhuman refers to the problem of social ethics, not to their monetary value. The fact that some Americans can afford $1,000-a-bottle wines, while others only $1-a-bottle brands, does not decrease the overall dollar or ruble value of the consumption of 'alcoholic beverages' in the

USA. Similarly, the inequality of distribution of US medical care does not decrease its growing value. On the other hand, the distribution of Soviet medical services is stratified more rigidly or even absolutely (it would be impossible for a 'rank-and-file person' to obtain the 'closed' medical services reserved for the Politburo even if he had 1 million rubles); but their overall value for the 'rank-and-file population' is made to stay below a certain low limit. In practice, this means that an 'average Soviet hospital or outpatient clinic' may have no medical supplies beyond the cheapest products used for prevention and emergency, such as the simplest disinfectants. Products of this kind do decrease the mortality and sickness rates dramatically by wiping out epidemics as well as deaths and diseases from gross ignorance and negligence, but to decrease these rates further for the 'rank-and-file population' is not worth the additional expense involved.

The CIA's manipulations to evaluate the Soviet consumption of medical services are irrelevant. The CIA's 'comparison is based on inputs (essentially numbers employed and their wages . . .)'.[54] We learn that a Soviet physician (MD) earns 2,160 rubles a year, while his US counterpart earns $52,919.[55] As a result of mathematically possible, but economically meaningless manipulations, the CIA finds that the Soviet consumption of medical services is 33.4 percent of its US counterpart.[56] The fact that Soviet medical services are poor is known to the CIA from the Western press, for even in Moscow, one of the socio-economically highest territorial cascades, it is poor outside the 'closed' hospitals and outpatient clinics. So 33.4 percent must seem to the CIA a plausible figure, obtained though it is through economically meaningless manipulations.

The overall result of its study of consumption must also seem plausible to the CIA, though it was obtained by techniques inapplicable to the Soviet economy. In 1981 the CIA's Soviet per capita consumption for 1976 was 34.4 percent of its US counterpart. In 1975, the CIA had testified in Congress that Soviet per capita consumption for 1973 was 34 percent of its US counterpart, the same figure within 0.4 percent.[57] As we saw above, the CIA's Soviet–US consumption ratio of 1964 for 1955 was 26.2 percent, that is, over one-fourth.

The figure between one-fourth and one-third seems to the CIA to be the most plausible, evidently because it is hard for the CIA to imagine living on less than one-third to one-fourth of the average US income. The US Official 'poverty level' (to which 11.6 percent of the US population belong in 1984) is $204 a week in cash income for a family of four. This is a fabulous cash income by Soviet standards, but in the USA there are only aristocratic-bourgeois consumption patterns, and the poor have long forgotten how to be poor: they cannot sew and darn or repair, live decently, cleanly and peacefully in a 'corner of a room' or in a log cabin, or enjoy their daily bread in the literal sense of the word. Nor are there living conditions for the poor. The poor have to share aristocratic-bourgeois consumption patterns. Thus, there is no 'daily bread' (or 'daily rice'). One cannot subsist on US mass-produced wheat bread as a medieval or ancient man could (and a Soviet inhabitant can) subsist on his 'daily bread.' It has no taste of its own (as the Soviet rye bread still has, despite adulteration by maize and potato waste products). Nor is it cheaper than myriads of other foods. Nor can the poor buy as 'daily bread' one of the specially baked fancy breads (such as delicious 'Russian breads' in New York), for they are *more* expensive than many other foods. Having found themselves in 'substandard' aristocratic-bourgeois conditions, the US poor often behave like *déclassé* noblemen of old: they lose heart, become degraded, or sink into the underworld supported by crime and welfare benefits.

In fact, only a century or two ago some Americans and Europeans could live and be happy on what is, say, 1 percent of today's average US consumption. Modern science and engineering enable a totalitarian society to improve on this result. On the other hand, poverty in the USA is a kind of aristocratic-bourgeois indigence which it is impossible to maintain at less than one-quarter to one-third of the median income.

Like all the CIA's studies of recent years, the study of 1981 is full of jeremiads, taken from both the Western and Soviet press, concerning the 'poor performance' of the Soviet economy, allegedly trying to overtake and surpass the USA in living standards. However, the CIA explains over and over again that these 'negative aspects' have not been taken into account by the CIA. The CIA states that its comparisons

are believed to be biased in favor of the USSR because of the inability to allow fully for the notoriously poor quality and narrow assortment of Soviet goods and services. The comparisons also cannot take into account the erratic, primitive distribution system and random shortages that make shopping difficult for Soviet consumers.[58]

Similarly: 'Shoddy goods and services, queues and shortages ... These negative aspects cannot be captured in quantitative comparisons.'[59]

And again:

... Soviet manufactured goods are sadly deficient in style, design, and attractiveness in appearance when compared with Western models. The comparisons could not take these important aspects of consumer satisfaction into account. Similarly, allowance could not be made for the notoriously poor quality of retail services ...[60]

After a long journalistic litany, again about the 'lack of variety of color, style and design,' about the 'narrowness of the range of choice,' reducing it to a 'few standardized items,' and again about 'shortages' which 'Brezhnev himself referred to,' the CIA study declares once more that these 'perennial features of the consumer milieu in the USSR cannot be captured in any international comparison of prices and quantities, but they are important aspects of utility.[61]

Thus, the CIA's defence of its results can be summed up as follows. No, the CIA's study does not take into account the 'negative aspects' of Soviet consumption; but these cannot be captured in *any* international comparison; therefore, there is no need to ask whether the CIA's neglect of these 'negative aspects' has made nonsense of the CIA's study.

The CIA paper begins with recalling Khrushchev's slogan (which, as we have already seen in Section 3, preoccupied Allen Dulles in 1959) about the Soviet economy providing Soviet people with the 'highest living standard in the world by 1980.' The study concludes in 1981, in a kind of belated journalistic polemic with Khrushchev, that 'the USSR has a long way to travel to catch up even with . . . Italy, the least affluent of the market economies compared.' The consumption of Italy was, as of 1976, 46.3 percent of US consumption, and so, according to the CIA, the Soviet economy still has 12 percent to go to catch up with Italy. 'All the others,' the study continues, 'are far more distant; overtaking and surpassing them in living standards may be an impossible dream.'[62]

But is this the Soviet rulers' 'dream,' or is the CIA polemicizing in 1981 with a long-forgotten Soviet slogan which was intended for sheer propaganda even a quarter of a century ago?

In 1921 the Soviet rulers 'admitted capitalism.' A flourish of their pens was enough for that, and in seven years the Soviet economy became a 'capitalist economy' among other 'capitalist economies,' with all their superior quality of goods and services, diversity, sophistication, etc. Then a flourish of the Soviet rulers' pens was enough to 'liquidate capitalism' along with the 'capitalists.' A flourish of the Soviet rulers' pens in 1959 would have been enough to 'admit capitalism' and thus, possibly, really overtake the USA in consumption by 1980. Why did they not do it if that was, allegedly, their 'dream'?

Here is one of the reasons. Let us glance at the consumption of a Soviet 'average soldier.' As he begins his service he receives his clothes which have been worn by previous generations and which could only be sold in the USA for rags, if rags were salable. These rags are also his hearth and home because he is supposed to sleep on his trenchcoat—on bare ground and in the open in any weather if necessary—and, at the same time, use it as a blanket. His food, both frugal and coarse, could probably not be sold in the USA even as cattle feed. There are no services except medical care which is, for soldiers, the lowest type of medical care as given to the 'rank-and-file population': soldiers do everything for themselves, including the medical treatment of lighter ailments. The Soviet rulers believe that since war takes the 'rank-and-file people' back to what Hobbes called a 'state of nature,' with 'the life of man, solitary, poor, nasty, brutish, and short,' they must get used to living and fighting under any conditions and dying without fuss. It is such a hardy 'rank-and-file population,' in combination with the most effective weapons and defenses, that will ensure world power, and then the comparison of US and

Soviet consumption will not be even of purely academic interest.

Inversely, in the Soviet rulers' view, almost all of US consumption is a waste of resources, since it is not, in their opinion, convertible into military power and is useless for warfare. Moreover, the transformation of Americans into aristocratic-bourgeois consumers makes them, in the Soviet rulers' view, unfit for warfare against populations like the 20-million North Vietnamese, even when these aristocratic-bourgeois consumers have tremendous advantages in weapons and numbers.

The CIA studies under consideration since 1959 have been almost exuding pity for a backward Soviet economy trying in vain to overtake at least Italy in per capita consumption. This is the perception of those in the West who assume that every individual and every civilization is after wealth, and that wealth can be converted into anything, including military power.

The CIA's 'Soviet consumption' is a major component of the CIA's 'Soviet GNP.' It is arbitrary and wrong (grossly overestimated), as is the relevant component of the CIA's 'Soviet GNP in dollars,' since all the incongruities of the Soviet and US economies ignored in the CIA's 'Soviet consumption' are ignored in that component. As for the CIA's 'Soviet GNP in rubles,' it is similarly overestimated if only because the CIA itself sees no more (or not much more) discrepancy between its US and Soviet GNPs in dollars and those in rubles than there would be between such pairs of GNPs calculated in the currencies of two market economies.[63]

A comparison between the CIA's 'Soviet GNP' in dollars and the 'national income' of Soviet 'open statistics' may be illuminating. According to the CIA, its 'Soviet GNP' amounted in 1976 to 73.7 percent of US GNP in dollars.[64] Now, the 'open TsSU,' that Soviet 'central office' of 'open statistics,' contends that the 'Soviet national income' in 1976 amounted in dollars to only 66.5 percent of its US counterpart.[65] So, according to the CIA, the Soviet economy is more productive in dollars than it is according to the 'open TsSU'! Yet, the latter *is* a Soviet propaganda institution (complete with its own censorship department), for while *some* open TsSU's figures of output of consumer goods may not be overestimated, others are, and the TsSU's overall figure of these goods in dollars is overestimated—perhaps enormously, since statistical aggregation, abstraction and calculation give even an unbiased calculator a wide leeway for subjective samplings, assumptions and techniques. It is remarkable that these subjective factors worked in the case of the CIA and Soviet propaganda in the same direction, and the CIA surpassed Soviet propaganda in its Soviet bias.

However, the CIA's lead over Soviet propaganda in this Soviet over-estimation is far larger than 7.2 percent. The Soviet 'national income' disregards services, and Soviet services account per capita for only 28.6 percent of US services even according to the CIA.[66] But this figure (which includes Soviet education and Soviet medicine) is one of the CIA's most glaring overestimations. Making allowances for a broader Western definition than the Soviet definition, it will be recalled that nearly one-third of US GNP originates in services. On the other hand, Soviet economics does not wish to consider services, even in its own definition, as part of 'material production.' To provide the 'rank-and-file population' with its daily bread (and potatoes) is at least necessary to keep it alive, while the very word 'services' derives from the same word as 'servants,' and services do often perform the same aristocratic-bourgeois function.

Hence when the CIA calculates that the Soviet GNP (the Soviet 'national income' plus, mainly, services) is bigger by 7.2 percent than the TsSU's 'national income,' the CIA's actual overestimation compared with Soviet propaganda is, indeed, staggering. On a GNP basis the Soviet estimate would be still lower than the CIA's.[67]

Since the CIA's figure of Soviet consumption is arbitrary and wrong (grossly overestimated), the CIA's Soviet 'share of GNP spent on defense' would also be arbitrary and wrong (grossly underestimated) even if the CIA's estimate of Soviet military expenditures were well-justified and true. But it is neither.

6   The CIA's Estimate of 'Soviet Military Expenditures'

As has been said in the previous section, the CIA does not wish even to conjecture that the entire Soviet economy may be militarily or strategically oriented. The CIA wants to see 'Soviet military expenditures,' and hence 'Soviet military goods and services,' as something financially separate from the rest of the economy, as is the case in Western democracies in peacetime.

The Gilbert and Kravis methodology, which the CIA misapplies to 'Soviet consumption,' could, on the other hand, be successfully applied to the comparisons between Soviet and US 'military goods and services,' since these are comparable in quality, diversity, innovation, sophistication, availability to the client, etc. All that the CIA needs for such comparisons is to know what military goods and services the Soviet economy produces.

But if the CIA has never managed to gain access even to the least secret Soviet economic data (DSP), how can the CIA have a complete and reliable knowledge of Soviet *military* goods and services, which requires access to incomparably higher levels of Soviet secrecy? The CIA's aplomb merely constitutes another example showing to what lengths a US government bureaucracy can go to conceal its helplessness and thus justify its posts and salaries.

Having failed in intelligence-espionage in the sense of clandestine acquisition of data 'denied' by the 'target countries,' the CIA began, instead, happily to rely on mutually allowed space satellite inspection, which the CIA has shrouded in espionage-like secrecy, to conceal from the US public the fact that even without Soviet camouflage, say, visible-light photography from space satellites has a poor resolution, since no matter how 'clear' the day is, objects on earth have to be photographed through the atmosphere.[68]

However, Soviet camouflage does exist and has been developing since World War II. Even a layman could know in the 1960s that already in the 1950s 'methods and materials for effective concealment and deception *throughout* the elecromagnetic spectrums from the ultraviolet through the visual infrared and radar region were developed.'[69] If the Soviet art and science of camouflage (as part of military concealment and deception) were at least at the level of their Western counterpart, then by the time the US 'spy satellites' appeared over Soviet territory, the Soviet regime could, in principle, conceal from them any military goods and services except those which could not be protected by camouflage methods and materials because of their location in open quarters, size, or too-powerful wave emissions.

A survey of Soviet 'open fundamental studies' basic to secret work on camouflage indicates that the Soviet regime is probably far ahead of the West in military concealment and deception. One random sample is a monograph by Leonid Brekhovskikh, *Waves in Layered Media*, which was published by Nauka, the publishing house of the USSR Academy of Sciences, in 1956. The monograph was reprinted in English by Academic Press in the USA in 1980, that is, twenty-four years after the Soviet publication,[70] and in the Preface the translation is said to have been assisted financially by the US Office of Naval Research (since the study seems to be of special relevance to detection and camouflage underwater).

The stages of existence of military goods and services are as follows: (i) Research and Development; (ii) Experimentation and Testing; (iii) Production proper; and (iv) Storage or Deployment. As is clear from the CIA's materials under study, the CIA does not know anything about stage (i) except open Soviet data and the (roofs of the) buildings which *look* like 'research institutes and design offices' on satellite photographs.[71]

When a weapon is too large to test it under shielded conditions, stage (ii) is observable, and sometimes the CIA can at least find out that the Soviet military has prevented it from being observed.

Stage (iii) is unobservable unless a weapon, such as a battleship, is too large to conceal its construction. But even here there have been surprises for the US intelligence community. Lt Gen. Daniel O. Graham, DIA Director, testified: 'As a matter of fact, one of the fundamental surprises to the whole intelligence community in the 16 years that I have been in the business is the strong effort the Soviets have made to get themselves a broad ocean navy.'[72] That is, the community failed to detect the construction of a whole oceanic navy, not just an oceanic battleship.

Can the CIA's examination of Soviet 'open data' and space satellite inspection reveal what military goods and services the Soviet economy is producing?

A former Soviet civilian engineer who had been familiar with hundreds of 'civilian' enterprises, research institutes and design offices described his experiences in an émigré newspaper in 1978.[73] Top secret military enterprises whose names and locations are state secrets (their addresses can only be given as post office box numbers) often occupy whole streets or whole 'closed cities.' But, apart from them, between 15 percent and 95 percent of output of every Soviet 'civilian' enterprise or research institution is military in the direct sense. The author gives many specific examples. The 'civilian' part of output often merely provides a kind of military camouflage. The Novosibirskiy priboro-stroitelny zavod is known to the Soviet public as a producer of children's slide projectors (which were once called 'magic lanterns'). In reality, these far from complex instruments are 'manufactured in an industrially unsuitable workshop (what was formerly a barn-warehouse) on obsolete machine tools and out of waste products.' Now, 95 percent of the output of the enterprise are naval gun sights.

Naturally, the regime can make any 'civilian' enterprise occupy itself with military production at any time and for any duration. What will happen is that its consumer goods will not be found anywhere in stores, another unpredictable shortage among myriads of unpredictable shortages.

It is a Russian textbook story that in World War I the hulls of armored track vehicles were produced in Britain separately and named 'tanks,' that is, water reservoirs, allegedly for Mesopotamia. This is one of the principles of the Soviet 'civilian' sector. Often it produces various elements of military goods and services which can well be passed off as those of civilian goods or services. As for which expenses are paid from which 'military' or 'civilian' accounts, this is immaterial, since all accounts of all institutions belong to the state. Closed accounts register what was paid for what and from what account, but since this flow of closed data has never been accessible to the CIA, the whole varied and varying percentage of Soviet 'military goods and services' as against 'consumer goods and services' cannot be known to the CIA, no matter how much it copies Soviet open sources.

Another former Soviet engineer, who designed and built Soviet 'civilian' enterprises (if he had built military enterprises he would never have been allowed to emigrate), has described how every Soviet 'civilian' enterprise is designed and built to switch, if ordered, to 100 percent direct military production.[74] Moreover, each enterprise has all the necessary civil defense protection (such as the possibility to transfer its work to its underground nuclear-biological-chemical shelter) in case of conventional or unconventional war.

In general, the CIA's assumption that, just as a Western GNP does, the 'Soviet GNP' contains distinct 'military expenditures' and 'military goods and services' leads *per se* to the CIA's gross misperception of the Soviet economy. Materials, semi-finished products, producer goods and services, construction, education, research, etc., may all be strategic, that is, intended to augment military power, and in particular produce directly military goods and services. Thus steel ('civilian production') can be produced in order to make machine tools ('civilian production') specifically intended to produce weapons ('military production'). In this sense, those Soviet standard uniform 'consumer goods and services' which provide the physiological minimum necessary for keeping the 'rank-and-file population' in a fit working and fighting condition are no less military than food, clothes, or medical service in the US armed forces.

The fact that the Soviet economy is a strategic whole is also manifest in that military production picks the best brains, hands, materials, equipment, etc. The best manpower may flow to the military not because they have made the pay rates high, but because all the pay rates in civilian production have been made low. Besides, under the 'Law of 1967,' the military can mobilize any higher-school-educated male under 30.

So much for stage (iii), Production. In stage (iv), Storage or Deployment, storage is even more unobservable, since warehouses are far more obscure, involve fewer employees, and can be more easily protected against observation than enterprises, research institutions and design offices. Yet since the Soviet military reserve amounts to 50 million men (as against 5 million of the active armed forces), it can be supposed (and the amount of Soviet steel output supports the conjecture) that nine-tenths of weapons produced go into storage, not deployment (for weapons, and not only men, will perish by the thousand every day in all-out war and will have to be replaced). As for deployment, this is where the CIA mainly draws its information on 'Soviet military expenditures' from those observably deployed weapons which the Soviet military either cannot conceal or do not want to.[75]

To give an example linking all stages:

One Pentagon briefer dramatized the problem [of verification of arms treaties] at a session on the mobile cruise missile. He entered a walk-in closet and pullled out 15 true-to-size models. 'How do you verify these?' he asked. Silence. Will the Soviets let us go anywhere at any time? Board any sub or bomber? Inspect missile cones?[76]

All that is necessary is to substitute 'learn of' for 'verify' in the above quotation in order to understand that unless weapons, or parts thereof, cannot be camouflaged, the CIA and DIA will not learn of their existence, no matter what their number is. All the CIA and DIA can learn of, in principle, is the testing of the model, but this will not indicate the number of weapons per each model in storage and deployment.

In view of the above, the CIA's 'Soviet military expenditures' are arbitrary and wrong (underestimated). When Soviet military power was far inferior to its US counterpart in the 1950s, the Soviet military induced the CIA to overestimate it grossly, and they succeeded. Now that the Soviet output of even those weapons which are perceivable by the CIA exceeds the entire US output of weapons, the Soviet military tend to conceal the growth of Soviet military might, and hence the CIA's 'Soviet military expenditures' are, obviously, underestimated.

To evaluate the perceivable Soviet weapons in rubles, the CIA has to evaluate most of them first in dollars and then convert these dollar prices into prices in monetary units which may be called 'Soviet machinery rubles.'[77] Predictably, the CIA's estimates of Soviet 'military expenditures' in 'Soviet machinery rubles' are even more arbitrary. Since the CIA's figures of Soviet consumption are arbitrary and wrong (grossly overestimated) and the CIA's figures of Soviet 'military expenditures' in dollars and rubles are also arbitrary (and, most likely, grossly underestimated), the CIA's 'share of Soviet GNP spent on defense' is all the more arbitrary and grotesquely underestimated even in its post-1976 retroactive version (10–12 percent in the early 1960s, 11–13 percent in the 1970s, and 12–14 percent in the 1980s), which was obtained in 1976 by doubling retroactively the pre-1976 figures, such as 5.5 percent for 1970.

It is noteworthy that the CIA's 'share of Soviet GNP spent on defense' overestimates the Soviet war potential—Soviet military might in case of war. The lower the Soviet GNP percentage of military expenditures, the larger the civilian reserve that can be switched into war production in case of war. On the other hand, even if the productivity or efficiency of the Soviet 'military sector' is not lower than that of its US counterpart, the Soviet 'military sector' has to spread all over the economy to be able secretly to build up in peacetime irreversible military supremacy over the West and hence to achieve world domination *de facto*.

Just as on many other issues, the CIA has, in this case, been echoing Soviet propaganda: from the CIA's figure of 'Soviet GNP' (more overestimated than the 'national income' of Soviet propaganda) and the CIA's 'share of Soviet GNP spent on defense' even in its post-1976 version, there emerges the Soviet propaganda image of the Soviet economy, still backward (because of the 'backwardness of tsarist Russia'), but fairly productive or efficient, on the whole, and hence well able to produce militarily no less than does the US economy, at a fairly low GNP rate of military expenditures. If the Soviet military output has been matching its US counterpart at such a low GNP rate of military expenditures as the CIA's estimates show even after 1976, then the Soviet economy *is* a peaceful giant which will, in case of war, increase its military output tremendously, rather like the USA did during World War II.

7   The CIA's 'Great Revision of 1976'

Though the CIA's 'great revision' of 1976 showed the public at large the arbitrariness and absurdity of the CIA's estimates, the CIA reacted, predictably, to the *scandal* in the same way Soviet officials do when finally admitting that for many years they 'have been making a mistake.' The fact that they 'have been making a mistake' does not disprove, in their view, that they have been doing well, but the fact that they have admitted it proves that they are now doing still better. Accordingly, George Bush, the then CIA Director and now Vice-President of the USA, made a jubilant speech on the occasion of the CIA's admission in 1976 that the CIA 'had been making a mistake' (to put it in Sovietese) for sixteen or so years, ever since the CIA began to digest Soviet 'open statistics' as it expanded in 1956:

> I would like to just say, Mr. Chairman, that I have been impressed with the intelligence community's constant reexamining of old judgments in the light of the unceasing flow of new information. And I have made very clear to Mr. Proctor and others that my view of intelligence simply is that it ought to be prepared from the best information possible without partisanship, without fear of bias ['or bias' is obviously meant: the misprint in the original is ironic]. I think in this case this is what was done, although the results are quite different than previous estimates.[78]

DIA Director Wilson's speech on the occasion was also festive, but he regarded the retroactive doubling of the previous estimates as a 'big step' in the direction of 'direct information on Soviet defense spending such as that provided by the statements made by Brezhnev and Kosygin':

> This new estimate is a big step in that direction but more needs to be done. We still do not have a full appreciation of the extent to which the Soviet economy defers to the military. Dissidents keep telling us that the burden is even higher than 13 percent of GNP, but quantifying these visceral notions is a formidable task . . . So the task before us is to ascertain the full burden of defense and to find the full measure of their past commitment. We are certain that at the 55 to 60 billion ruble range our estimate is a far more accurate assessment of the total defense burden than has ever been the case before. Further investigation may show even this to be a conservative range.[79]

The impression Lt Gen. Wilson created is that if the CIA, say, tripled, and not just doubled, retroactively its estimates for 1959 to 1975, it would be an ever bigger step toward the real situation as described by Brezhnev, Kosygin and the dissidents. However, in all the years that have since passed, the CIA has hardly budged from the 13 percent figure Lt Gen. Wilson mentioned in 1976 as a 'big step.'

In his 1983 article in defense of the CIA's estimates, Donald F. Burton, chief of the CIA's Military Economic Analysis Center in the 1970s, devotes much space to his demonstration of how scientific the retroactive doubling was: thus it was the result, in particular, of 'new information on research and development.'[80] Burton's mysterious vagueness, befitting a vast government organization, allegedly engaged in intelligence-espionage, suggests that the 'new information' came from secret intelligence-espionage sources and cannot be specified quantitatively and qualitatively beyond the phrase 'new information on research and development.' Unfortunately for Mr Burton, the CIA's last testimony under study, that of 1983, says bluntly: 'RDT&E is estimated directly from official Soviet statistics. (For this reason, it is the least certain part of our estimates.)'[81]

I do not discuss Burton's other 'new information' that led to the revision of 1976. The fact is that a mistake had been made annually before 1976. The question is what kind of mistake? Let us suppose that an American student of the Soviet population decided by mistake that the average height of Soviet men of a certain social group was 167 *meters* (instead of 167 centimeters, as a Soviet text said). Then he repeated his mistake for years. It would mean that he knows nothing about the Soviet population and simply juggles figures. The CIA's mistake that the Soviet 'share of GNP spent on defense' amounted in 1970, for example, to 5.5 percent corresponds to the mistake that some Soviet inhabitants are 160 meters high. It means that the CIA knows nothing about the Soviet civilization and simply juggles figures. What compelled the CIA to juggle them in 1976 the way it did?

Let us have a look at the CIA's pre-1976 estimates of the 'share of Soviet GNP spent on defense'[82] to see how arbitrary they are:

Selected years	1950	1955	1960	1963	1965	1970
Percentage	10.8	12.3	8.4	11.1	9.1	5.5

For 1950, under Stalin, when the population was squeezed dry for the sake of military development (in particular, global rocketry and thermonuclear weapons), the figure is 10.8 percent, while for 1955, when there was an interregnum and hence military production slowed down, the figure is 12.3 percent, and for 1960, when the all-out production of global rocketry began, the figure is 8.4 percent. For 1963 it is 11.1 percent, for 1965 it is 9.1 percent, and for 1970 it is 5.5 percent—the Soviet march to a peaceful economy.

The pre-1976 estimates were not just annual mistakes *per se*: they suggested a false picture of entire Soviet military-economic development from 1963 to 1975. Thus, when the CIA set the Soviet 'share of GNP spent on defense' for 1970 at 5.5 percent, the figure for the USA for the same year was 8.2 percent. But even according to the CIA, Soviet GNP has always been far smaller than its US counterpart. Hence Soviet military expenditures were as of 1970 a mere fraction of US expenditures, according to the CIA.

Since the CIA's Soviet GNP grew 'at 5 or 6 percent,' and Soviet military expenditures grew 'in the past 10 years' (1964–74) 'at 3 percent,' the 'share of gross national product spent on defense has been falling.'[83]

'Expenditures for [military] investment,' ('equipment and facilities'—'ships, tanks, planes, missiles and all that'), testified CIA Director Colby before Congress in 1974, 'have dropped from about 40 percent of total expenditures in 1960 to around 20 percent in 1972.'[84]

But tested, deployed and hence observed Soviet weapons had been indicating that in the 1960s and the 1970s the Soviet military expenditures, on the contrary, so far exceeded their US counterpart and grew so rapidly that these Soviet weapons began to surpass US weapons in numbers, size, power and often even quality, diversity, innovation and sophistication. That was already *visible* in 1971, and Lt Gen. Daniel O. Graham described to Congress the howling discrepancy between the deployed Soviet weapons one could *observe* by 1971, and the CIA's figures, demanding that Lt Gen. Graham should not believe the evidence of his eyes:

During that time frame, 1960–71, the Soviets had gone from a handful of ICBM launchers to over 1,500 for five different systems, produced over 50 missile-launching submarines, created a highly sophisticated military space program, introduced a new bomber, introduced five new fighters, deployed several thousand SAM launchers, deployed a large force opposite China, activated about 20 more divisions, and so on.[85]

While the Soviet war economy grew in all of its splendors, US weapons were very much at a standstill. Inversely, while US consumption burst into ever new splendors (or prodigal wastes), Soviet consumption stuck to its role of appendage to military production. Yet the CIA still insisted in 1974 that, as of 1970, Soviet military expenditures accounted for 5.5 percent of Soviet GNP (as against 8.2 percent for the USA), that as of 1974 this percentage had been falling ever since 1964 (the advent of Brezhnev to power), and that the Soviet expenditures on military 'equipment and facilities' were in 1972 half of what they were in 1960, namely, 20 percent of total expenditures, which suggested that only about 1 percent of Soviet GNP was spent on military 'equipment and facilities.'

The CIA had been thus presenting annually an entirely deceptive military-economic image of the Soviet economy, an image that was, in a sense, the opposite of the Soviet military-economic reality which had become visible by 1971, since the Soviet military could not and would not conceal certain weapons and, indeed, sometimes displayed them ostentatiously (as in the oceanic naval exercise of 1970). Thus the CIA was compelled to change retroactively its arbitrary and absurd figures of 'share of Soviet GNP spent on defense' for other arbitrary, but less absurd figures, about twice as high as their predecessors.[86]

However, though the absurdity of the CIA's estimates became *visible* in 1971, another five years were to pass before the CIA made these arbitrary alterations toward lesser absurdity. The fact is that by 1976 the public mood had changed compared with what it was in 1970, and the major (liberal–Democrat) media in the USA began to report more willingly the growth of Soviet perceivable weapons (especially following the Soviet second oceanic naval exercise in 1975).

Yet the CIA's six-year delay was of major political importance. It is mainly within these six years that the US government took its unilateral disarmament measures, launched the transfer of US science and technology to the Soviet economy, and arranged for strategic arms limitation treaties—all on the basis of the CIA's false image of Soviet progress since 1963 toward a peaceful economy.[87]

8 The CIA's Attempt at Prediction

One of the few attempts to predict specifically the output of a specific Soviet product (rather than to project the CIA's arbitrary abstractions like its 'Soviet defense spending growth rate') was made by the CIA in 1977, when the CIA declared that the 'most serious [Soviet] problem is a looming oil shortage.'[88] '[Oil] production will begin to fall in the late 1970s or early 1980s.'[89]

The following exchange took place between Senator Proxmire and the CIA Director in 1977:

> SENATOR PROXMIRE. Are you saying that you are sure that they will not be able to produce, say, 12 million barrels a day in 1985?
> ADMIRAL TURNER. Yes, sir. That is our prediction, that they cannot even sustain the 10 million they are doing today.[90]

The 'oil shortage' meant a general 'energy problem'[91] as well as a general economic problem. 'If current trends are projected with no change in present policies, Soviet oil import requirements by 1985 could cost $10 billion at today's prices.'[92]

The prediction created a national furor: President Carter declared a 'moral equivalent of war,' since the world oil market would now be depleted by Soviet oil imports (not to mention the widely discussed possible Soviet intention of seizing the Middle East to obtain the desperately needed oil). In 1978 the *New York Times* reported that 'one [CIA] report estimated that the Soviet Union and Eastern Europe will require a minimum of 3.5 million barrels a day of imported oil by 1985.'[93]

Four years later the CIA continued to explain to Congress the validity of its prediction: 'Oil is the principal problem. As I am sure you will recall, the CIA in 1977 forecast a downturn in Soviet oil production, and the sense of that still appears valid.'[94]

It is only in 1983 that the CIA stated:

The Soviet Union has thus far averted the downturn in oil production that CIA had earlier predicted by virtue of an enormous, brute-force development effort that has tapped a petroleum reserve base larger in size than we previously believed. The cost of doing this has been high, but we think that the Soviets have already allocated enough investment resources to the oil industry to permit them to come close to their production target of 12.6 million b/d by 1985.[95]

Note this 'enormous, brute-force development' described above. Did not the CIA know in 1977 that 'enormous, brute-force developments' do occur in post-1917 Russia? Besides, there is no evidence that this development was more 'brute-force' than any other.

But the groundlessness of the CIA's prediction in 1977 that Soviet oil output would not 'even sustain the 10 million [b/d]' is a minor point. What is absurd is the CIA's entire vision of a 'Soviet oil shortage.' In 1981 the Soviet crude oil output, if we are to believe, as the CIA does, open Soviet sources, was 23.5 percent of world output, while the Soviet output of cars was about one-half of the US production of 1920. As for Soviet stationary (nontrans-portation) uses of oil, they can all be replaced, and are being replaced, by natural gas. As the CIA could see in 1981, the Soviet output of natural gas had been rising precipitously with Western aid (197.9 billion cubic meters in 1970, 435.0 in 1980, estimated 630.0 in 1985).[96] As the CIA modestly admitted in 1981: 'By 1985, gas production of 10 million barrels a day of oil equivalent is expected.'[97]

It was estimated in 1981 that by the year 2000, Soviet gas reserves would be able to support an annual production level of over 1.5 trillion cubic meters,[98] and as the DIA put it in 1981, 'natural gas is being viewed as a key export resource that soon could generate even greater hard-currency earnings than oil'.[99] Indeed, at the pace the West has since been helping the process, this may prove to be so.

Finally, in its dire 'Soviet oil shortage' prediction for 1978 to 1985, the CIA forgot the present and future trading of Soviet and East European arms for oil to Libya, Iraq and other oil-producing countries in the Middle East. In 1983 nearly $2.5 billion of oil was obtained by the Soviet bloc in this way.

In other words, we have the extraordinary case of a country which has been producing almost a quarter of the world's oil, but is able to spend little of it on civilian needs and concentrate almost the entire output on military and strategic needs, including strategic storage. Yet it is Soviet oil that the CIA chose for its jeremiad (based on Soviet open sources) about the alleged 'Soviet oil shortage,' and petulantly insisted for years that its prediction was valid, as though the gravest question for a regime which survived on two ounces of bread a day per rank-and-file person at a certain point of time between 1919 and 1921 were the question as to whether it would produce in 1982 a full quarter of the world's oil output or again 'only' 23.5 percent, as it did in 1981.

The CIA seems to have been convinced by Soviet propaganda from the 1930s to the 1960s that everything Soviet must grow and will grow, so that it perceives even the world's biggest Soviet oil output (with little civilian consumption to spend it on) as almost disastrous unless it keeps growing.

What the CIA displayed in its prediction is an amazing lack of economic knowledge (outside the juggling of figures it sees in Soviet open sources) and, indeed, of economic common sense, in combination with the stubborn blindness of a self-contained bureaucracy. The Soviet press (including Soviet school textbooks) has been repeating ever since the 1920s what Mendeleyev (1834–1907) said about the use of oil for heating: 'You can burn banknotes for heating too.' Oil has been considered a precious limited resource (certainly not to be spent on the 'rank-and-file population'), and it would not be surprising if, in view of its hard-currency earnings from natural gas, the Soviet rulers did decrease their oil output, to keep more oil in the ground and/or maintain world oil prices at a higher level. Nearly a quarter of the world's oil output (as of 1981) is an immense figure. What has the CIA been expecting the Soviet rulers to do? To push it up no matter what to half of the world's oil output? The CIA seems to assume that in contrast to all other natural resources, the Soviet natural resources are infinite, and any slowdown of growth of, say, oil output will lead to an 'oil shortage,' all the more severe since the Soviet 'rank-and-file population' uses little oil.

Nor did it occur to the CIA that the Soviet rulers may conceal the Soviet present and/or prospective growth of oil output to keep up world oil prices. Indeed, it was found later that the discovery of new Soviet oil fields had been concealed. In this sense, the CIA's 'oil panic' brought the Soviet rulers billions of extra oil dollars.

Notes: Chapter 6

The author is grateful to Peter Wiles for his valuable comments.

1 The CIA relies on the work of the entire 'intelligence community' and often speaks on its behalf. The DIA, the intelligence agency of the US Department of Defense, 'also uses the CIA estimates and, indeed, participates in the cost analysis that enters into their preparation' (Donald F. Burton, 'Estimating Soviet defense spending,' *Problems of Communism* [March–April 1983], p. 85).
2 The materials are listed in *Committee Publications and Policies Governing their Distribution* (Washington, DC: US Government Printing Office, 1984). All the sources listed below without indication of a publisher are materials of the CIA and the Joint Economic Committee of the US Congress and are to be found under these headings at the Library of Congress and in the Committee itself.
3 This study was written in 1983; however, as of 1987 practically nothing has changed either in the CIA's Soviet economic indices, or its sources and methods.
4 Thus, they are used by the US Secretary of Defense in his annual 'defense posture statements.' The *Washington Post* called the 'size of the Soviet defense budget,'

allegedly calculated by the CIA, 'the most important political number in the world.' (Stephen S. Rosenfeld, 'Knockdown of a Soviet "buildup",' *Washington Post*, 23 November 1983). A random example nearest at hand will show in what awe these indices are held and what magic spell they cast. According to the US press President Reagan said in his nationally televised speech as this study was being written: 'Over the last 10 years, the Soviets devoted twice as much of their gross national product to military expenditures as the United States ...' (*New York Times*, 17 January 1984, p. A8). The text does not say how large the Soviet and American GNPs are or what the relation between them is. If 'Soviet GNP' is less than half of its US counterpart, then 'Soviet military expenditures' are smaller than US military expenditures. The CIA's magic numbers seem to be so magic that they can even be cited with no real meaning attached to them.

5 From a single extant copy of the destroyed top secret minutes of the top secret hearing of 27 June 1947 before the Committee on Expenditures in the Executive Departments of the US Congress, we know that the CIA was created specially to be engaged in the *clandestine* acquisition of *secret* data in a target country. I call this activity 'intelligence-espionage,' to imply that it should not be connected with 'human' agents only. But in 1947 'human' espionage was meant, of course.

6 Thomas Powers, *The Man Who Kept the Secrets: Richard Helms and the CIA* (New York: Knopf), 1979, pp. 38–9.

7 *Allocation of Resources in the Soviet Union and China—1975*, pp. 60, 62.

8 *Allocation of Resources 1982*, p. 38.

9 ibid., p. 39.

10 ibid., p. 78.

11 *Allocation of Resources 1975*, p. 61.

12 *Allocation of Resources 1974*, p. 12.

13 ibid.

14 *Allocation of Resources 1975*, pp. 49, 50.

15 ibid.

16 *Allocation of Resources 1982*, p. 261.

17 For more detail see my article, 'CIA and the mystery of where does Soviet steel go,' *Congressional Record*, 10 October 1986, S 15915.

18 *Allocation of Resources 1976*, p. 111.

19 ibid., p. 101.

20 'USSR: Economic Trends and Policy Developments,' JEC Briefing paper, 14 September 1983, p. 48.

21 *Comparisons of the United States and Soviet Economies* 1960, p. 6.

22 ibid., p. 7.

23 ibid., p. 11.

24 ibid., p. 11.

25 'USSR: Economic Trends and Policy Developments,' 1983, p. 3.

26 ibid., p. 17.

27 ibid., p. 21.

28 ibid., p. 5.

29 ibid., p. 31.

30 *Allocation of Resources 1982*, p. 41.

31 *Allocation of Resources 1979*, p. 9.

32 Thus, Philip Hanson has deduced from the Gosplan report in *Pravda* of 1984 a cost of living index that entirely contradicts that of the Gosplan's reports published annually: 3.0 percent for retail trade in 1983. Peter Wiles estimated, also exclusively from Soviet open sources, that the GNP deflator for 1977–80 is not 2.4 percent, as derived by the CIA in Table 20 of its *Soviet GNP in Current Prices,*

1960–80 (ref. SOV. 83–10037 of March 1983), but perhaps 4.9 percent.

33 As this study was being written, a *Wall Street Journal* series (23 April 1984, and following issues) described Soviet biochemical warfare research on the basis of Soviet émigrés' testimony and Soviet open publications in fundamental sciences: genetics, genetic engineering, biochemistry, etc.

34 *Allocation of Resources 1975*, p. 34.

35 *Allocation of Resources 1976*, p. 106.

36 *Allocation of Resources 1981*, p. 275.

37 The figures for 1984 are 95, 68, 39 and 36 émigrés respectively.

38 *Consumption in the USSR: An International Comparison*, 1981, p. 15.

39 ibid., p. 3.

40 ibid., p. 35.

41 Author's interview with the owner, April 1984.

42 In 1975 less than half of beer sold was bottled, while canned beer does not exist. Igor Birman, *Ekonomika nedostach* (New York: Chalidze Publications, 1983), p. 424, n. 166.

43 *Consumption in the USSR*, p. 12.

44 Birman, op. cit., p. 284.

45 The process of adulteration in the Soviet economy is inevitable. A Western producer who secretly adulterates his products risks a loss of customers and faces government inspection, the press and courts. The Soviet producer is a state supermonopoly which cannot lose customers and is the government, the press and the courts.

46 Birman, op. cit., p. 283.

47 *Consumption in the USSR*, p. 99.

48 It should also be recalled how psychological a sense of taste is. I was told by a Soviet offical exporting Soviet alcoholic beverages that the Queen of England had said that 'Soviet champagne' tasted better than (any?) French champagne. True, Her Majesty drank the 'export brand' of 'Soviet champagne,' which may little resemble the brand for Soviet home consumption. Still, I was prompted to say: 'When a country is so powerful, even its so-called champagne begins to taste to an English royal palate better than the champagnes of Champagne.'

49 In 1976 the Soviet population consumed more potatoes per capita (119 kg) than it did in 1913 (114 kg) and would have consumed even more if not for shortages of potatoes. Birman, op. cit., p. 281.

50 *Consumption in the USSR*, p. 6.

51 In keeping with US 'horseless carriages' are ubiquitous restaurants (still an aristocratic-bourgeois word in Russian), which are not inferior to aristocratic-bourgeois restaurants of old; or widespread travelling abroad, another aristocratic-bourgeois luxury; or design clothes; or 'one-family homes' which would have been classified in nineteenth-century Europe as mansions or villas, etc.

52 Roger Ricklefs, 'Gourmets owe much to Armenians who knew their sturgeon,' *Wall Street Journal*, 23 April 1984.

53 ibid., p. 6.

54 ibid., p. 12.

55 ibid., p. 99. Peter Wiles reminded me of the fact that a Soviet physician's underhand fees from his patients, as well as bribes to get a 'closed' hospital bed, for example, possibly triple the Soviet official figure.

56 ibid., p. 6.

57 *Allocation of Resources 1975*, p. 14.

58 ibid., p. v.

59 ibid., p. vii.

60 ibid., p. 4.
61 ibid., p. 5.
62 ibid., p. 19.
63 The CIA's calculation of Soviet GNP in rubles based on Abram Bergson's Soviet 'factor-cost prices' (Soviet 'established prices' minus indirect taxes, plus subsidies, etc.) obviously yields the sum total of Soviet costs, which may have nothing to do with Soviet GNP in US market prices. However, the CIA believes that, miraculously, its US and Soviet GNPs in dollars and those in rubles differ no more (or not much more) than do GNPs in, say, dollars and pounds when the US and British economies are compared. If this is the case, then the CIA's 'GNP in rubles' is grossly overestimated if only because its Soviet 'GNP in dollars' is.
64 *Soviet Economy in a Time of Change*, Vol. 1, p. 378.
65 *Narodnoye khozyaistvo SSSR v 1976 g.*, p. 98. See Birman, op. cit., p. 387. Birman indicates (p. 465, fn. 476) that this incredible lead of the CIA over Soviet propaganda in the overestimation of Soviet GNP had already been noticed in 1970 by the Hungarian economist, Zoltan Kenessey.
66 *Consumption in the USSR*, p. 7.
67 It is, of course, possible that the secret Soviet output of strategic goods and services, unknown to the CIA, is so immense that its excess of value over its US counterpart compensates for the excess of value of US consumer goods and services over the Soviet consumer output. Then the Soviet supermonopoly is as productive as US free enterprise except that the former is as good at supergiant or superstandard military projects as the latter at consumer goods and services. Then the Soviet strategic output accounts for the bulk of the Soviet GNP: that is, the military and civilian sectors of GNP are rather neatly reversed in the two civilizations. However, nothing is further than this picture of the Soviet economy from the CIA's picture of it, according to which the 'share of Soviet GNP devoted to defense' was, as of 1983, 13–14 percent, and before 1976, half of the figure.
68 The inadequacy of all means of mutually allowed 'outside' inspection (infrared waves, radar, telemetric interception, etc.) is analyzed in my three Wednesday 'intelligence-espionage columns' under the general heading ' "CIA" really stands for "Central *Inspection* Agency",' *New York City Tribune*, 4, 11 and 18 March 1987. These and other problems raised in this chapter are treated in more detail in the book I am currently writing on Western intelligence agencies.
69 'Camouflage,' *Encyclopaedia Britannica* (1970), Vol. 4, p. 710; my emphasis.
70 L. M. Brekhovskikh, *Waves in Layered Media*, 2nd edn. (New York: Academic Press, 1980).
71 See, for example, *Allocation of Resources 1976*, pp. 54, 66, 69, 111; *Soviet Military Economic Relations*, 1983, p. 145; 'USSR: Economic Trends and Policy Developments,' 1983, p. 48.
72 *Allocation of Resources 1975*, p. 99.
73 N. Vladimirov, 'Mirnyye voyennyye raskhody,' *Novoye russkoye slovo*, 15 December 1978.
74 Robert Kirshenshtein, 'Dual-purpose industrial plants in USSR,' in Radio Liberty/Radio Free Europe, *Science and Technology Today*, no. 167 (1978).
75 See, for example, *Soviet Military Economic Relations*, 1982, p. 134: 'The costs of all Soviet defense activities except RDT&E are developed by identifying and listing Soviet forces and their support apparatuses.' Or: 'USSR: Economic Trends and Policy Developments,' p. 47 '... once the major weapon systems have been produced and deployed, we can measure what is there. Our projection of future [what about current?] weapon production, however, is obviously less certain.'
76 *Wall Street Journal*, 27 March 1984.

77 See, for example, Burton art. cit. at note 1, p. 86: 'Most weapons costs, however, are estimated initially in dollars, and converted by means of ruble-to-dollar ratios.' The CIA deduces its 'ruble-to-dollar ratios' from the prices of Soviet machinery. The CIA also alleges that it knows (from émigrés?) and uses the Soviet ruble prices of some Soviet weapons.

78 *Allocation of Resources 1976*, p. 4.

79 ibid., pp. 79, 80.

80 Burton, art. cit. at note 1, p. 87.

81 'USSR: Economic Trends and Policy Developments,' 1983, p. 48.

82 *Soviet Economic Prospects for the Seventies*, 1973, pp. 150, 151. *Gross National Product Accounts, 1970, 1975*, p. 7.

83 *Allocation of Resources 1974*, p. 22.

84 ibid., p. 27.

85 *Allocation of Resources 1975*, p. 93.

86 Also, the CIA increased retroactively the annual growth rate of the Soviet defense expenditures from 3 to 4–5 percent, while in 1983 it decreased it back to 'about 2 percent,' manipulations that anyway lie within the alleged range of tolerance of the CIA's calculations, not to mention its 100 percent error before 1976.

87 In his Paris television interview in 1978 President Nixon said that the CIA had grossly misled him and his predecessors for eleven years concerning Soviet military growth (Wendell S. Merick, 'Why the CIA is under fire again,' *US News and World Report*, 11 December 1978, p. 42). In my 1978 article, and during my meeting with the then CIA director, I said that if the CIA consisted of Soviet agents only, it would not have misled the government, the Congress and the public so grossly, for Soviet agents would have been afraid to get exposed. The CIA director seemed to have agreed with what I said, and Ronald Reagan (now US President) had the article outlined with approval in his magazine, *Citizens for the Republic Newsletter*, 18 September 1978 (see Lev Navrozov, 'What the CIA knows about Russia,' *Commentary*, November 1978, and the follow-up material in the author's files including the relevant copy of *Citizens for the Republic Newsletter*). There is nothing, however, Mr Reagan would, or could, do when he became president, opposed as he is by the bulk of the media, universities, and bureaucracies such as the CIA.

88 *Soviet Economic Problems and Prospects*, 1977, p. vi. A parallel case to the CIA's oil prediction of 1977 is the CIA's notoriously wrong prediction of Soviet grain harvests, even though the fields are observable from satellites. Cf. Peter Wiles, *ASTE Bulletin* (now *ACES*) (winter 1964).

89 *Soviet Economic Problems and Prospects*, p. xvi.

90 *Allocation of Resources 1977*, p. 48.

91 *Soviet Economic Problems and Prospects*, p. xvi.

92 ibid., p. viii.

93 Nicholas Horrock, 'CIA oil study upheld,' *New York Times*, 22 May 1978.

94 *Allocation of Resources 1981*, p. 206.

95 'USSR: Economic Trends and Policy Developments,' 1983, p. 37.

96 *Allocation of Resources 1981*, p. 85.

97 ibid., p. 207.

98 ibid., p. 86.

99 ibid., p. 87.

7 *Navrozov versus the Agency*

PHILIP HANSON

Lev Navrozov is an intrepid man. To begin with, he insists on telling us that the Soviet regime is a threat to world peace. This is a view which is not popular among educated Westerners. It is a view which is held to be appropriate for red-necks, hard-hats and, of course, Soviet émigrés, but which is embarrassing for the emancipated. Then, just in case we were prepared to make allowances for him, he mounts an onslaught on the *New York Times* for systematically misjudging Soviet developments.[1] Having been rude about one of the arbiters of our taste, he now turns on that *bête noire* of the person of sensibility and refinement, the Central Intelligence Agency—but only to upbraid it for being insufficiently *noire*. The CIA, he argues, has been overestimating Soviet total output while underestimating Soviet defense spending.[2]

The Navrozov critique of the CIA is a critique of the West's appointed Russia-watchers, in general; for if the CIA is too soft on the USSR to see it clearly, God help the rest of us. His arguments have something in common with those of Alexander Solzhenitsyn and Alexander Zinoviev: the exasperation with Westerners who cannot, or will not, grasp how Soviet society really works. Many émigré intellectuals, having been part of that society, believe that they do understand it, and most of them tell us that it is far more threatening than we think. But like the people in Britain during the war whom Arthur Koestler told about the Nazi concentration camps, we find it all rather far-fetched.[3] This combat of émigré truth-tellers against Western specialists is also a combat between personal experience and what is ambitiously called social science, and I shall come back to it later on in this chapter.

Unlike Solzhenitsyn and Zinoviev, Navrozov employs footnotes. Instead of broad generalizations and lofty disdain, he provides us with chapter and verse. This means that we can negotiate; and I believe we should, for his chapter (see above) contains important and penetrating arguments.

CIA estimates of Soviet GNP and defense spending present methodological problems which have been discussed by Western academic specialists and by CIA analysts themselves. The CIA position, if one can put it in very general terms, is that these problems are real but that their practical importance is small: either evidence is produced to show that the margin of error in a particular CIA estimate is small,[4] or the margin of error is not discussed, but the implication is that the Agency is at least providing the best figures we have. ('Best' here means most lavishly documented, and derived by the most elaborate procedures.)

Several of these problems of method have been raised again by Lev Navrozov. For example, the CIA compares consumer-goods prices between the USA and the USSR in order to obtain ruble–dollar, 'purchasing power' conversion rates with which to compare Soviet and US consumption levels. But this exercise is necessarily confined to those Soviet goods which exist and which are comparable with US goods. Yet many US goods exist which have no Soviet counterpart but which are part of the supply available to US consumers. Moreover, a Soviet product which is obtainable in Moscow one day may be unobtainable the next, and may seldom, or never, be obtainable in Voronezh. What is the 'true' Soviet price of an item unobtainable in Voronezh and not reliably obtainable in Moscow? The purchasing-power comparison overvalues the ruble by an unknown amount because it excludes consideration of the range and availability of goods and services; and those considerations are obviously unfavorable (in total) to the USSR.

Being a born polemicist, Navrozov does not just make this point; he stomps all over it. What the CIA analysts cannot cope with, he argues, is the fact that his neighbourhood discount liquor store in the Upper Bronx contains a greater variety of drinks than are available to a Politburo member, let alone to the average Soviet alcoholic. Fair enough, though we should all be careful in assessing the private means of the Politburo. Even that minor figure at the Soviet court, Mr Victor Louis, has quite a lifestyle.[5]

But Lev Navrozov is in good company. Alec Nove and Peter Wiles have both insisted on the importance, in Soviet–Western comparisons, of differences in product quality and availability.[6] In fact it is something of a British speciality, in Sovietological economics, to draw attention to conceptual shortcomings in monumental US studies. We share with Russians a readiness to credit methodological problems with being insoluble; also a readiness to believe that common sense and common observation are not made ineffective either by their commonness or by their being unquantifiable.

There is no doubt that conventional comparisons of Soviet and Western consumption levels exaggerate the Soviet average level. (As Navrozov notes, the CIA analysts themselves do not dispute this; they merely mention it as an afterthought.) But this line of argument can be extended to defense, and that does not assist Navrozov's second complaint about the Agency. For he also seeks to show that the CIA has been underestimating the Soviet defense effort.

Let us suppose, for the moment, that Western intelligence correctly observes the flow of new hardware to the Soviet military in physical units, along with other elements in the Soviet defense effort. The ruble prices and costs of these items are not, apparently, known, and some marvelously devious methods are used to re-invent them. In brief, the main procedure is to get US defense contractors to provide US dollar costings for observed Soviet military devices. (How the defense contractors are prevented from exaggerating these, is a mystery. They have every incentive to do so, since they are in the business of countering the Soviet threat; and their skills in grossly overcharging the US military for their own products have been finely honed.) The dollar sum thus derived can be converted back to rubles—CIA rubles, as Lev Navrozov calls them—by applying an appropriate ruble–dollar conversion rate. That rate is obtained by a comparison of Soviet and US prices on analogous civilian items (whose Soviet ruble prices are known). That sort of price comparison overvalues the ruble relatively to the dollar for precisely the same reasons as apply in the case of consumer goods. But it is only if the 'defense ruble' is overvalued relatively to the 'civilian ruble' that the measure of the defense burden on the Soviet economy will be understated. And it is not clear that that will generally be the case.[7]

This method of estimating Soviet military hardware procurement could, in principle, be checked. The check would be an estimate of that part of Soviet equipment production (less exports, plus imports) that is not accounted for by identifiable production for civilian uses. In practice, this sort of check, advocated by some, does not work. The Soviet censors have seen to it that it doesn't.[8] That leaves the CIA with an embarrassing problem which Navrozov does not mention: its analysts cannot make their estimates of Soviet defense spending fit into their estimates of Soviet national income (GNP).

The two estimates are to a substantial extent independent of one another. The GNP estimate is broken down into broad end-use categories of investment, household consumption, public consumption and 'other.' 'Other' is a residual containing most defense spending, the net trade balance, changes in stocks, changes in strategic reserves, other unidentified expenditures and the statistical discrepancy between GNP estimated from output and GNP estimated from expenditure. Estimates of the various elements in this residual have not been published by the CIA. But the fall in the residual in 1978–80 is hard to explain, and one CIA analyst, John Pitzer, concluded from it that the Agency's estimates of the growth of civilian consumption or investment (or both) in the late 1970s were probably too high.[9] In general, the CIA has been ready to say publicly that there are gaps, puzzles and uncertainties in its estimates of Soviet output and military spending, and it deserves more marks for modesty than Lev Navrozov will give it.

Still, his theme is that the CIA is nowhere near as modest as it ought to be. It offers measurements of Soviet economic and military power which are misleading. It does so very largely on the basis of official Soviet published information, while pretending that it is using secret information obtained by espionage. And published Soviet data are generally and systematically misleading.

First, the argument that published Soviet data are misleading. The received view among Western Russia-watchers is that Soviet published economic data are mostly usable, though with varying degrees of caution for different series of official figures. The grounds for this view were set out by Abram Bergson in his pioneering study of Soviet national income and product.[10] They are the following. First, there is a broad consistency within the published figures which would be hard to maintain if some of them were merely invented. Second, some (rough) consistency with independent observations exists; for instance, worsening food shortages are visible to foreign visitors in the aftermath of officially reported harvest failures. Third, captured secret documents relating to the 1941 Plan were consistent with openly published information. Fourth, the suppression of official economic statistics on anything that is either embarrassing or remotely security-related would hardly make sense if the published figures were freely invented.

This last argument has always seemed to me to be particularly powerful. If all your published figures are invented for propaganda purposes, why would you ever want to hide any of them? In the past few years all sorts of Soviet official figures that were previously published have gone secret: the grain harvest (for 1981–85, but later published), the volumes of oil and gas exported and imported, total lorry production, the index of peasant-market prices, the estimated dollar value of Soviet per capita national income, and many more. The 1974 Soviet annual statistical handbook contains 786 pages of tables, the 1982 handbook 544. If the numbers on the missing 242 pages had been pure decoration in the first place, it would be hard to explain their disappearance.[11]

That does not mean that the Soviet official figures that are available are all splendid. The plan-fulfillment reports on which they are mostly based are likely to be upward-biassed because of the reporting enterprises' interest in obtaining their bonuses.[12] Measures of price changes over time are generally downward-biassed, mainly because of their failure to allow properly for the prices of new and pseudo-new products. Figures on the 'real' growth of large aggregates (industrial output, national income, investment, etc.) are presented in such a way as to make growth look as impressive as possible (by valuation in base-year prices, for example). They also tend to be upward-biassed to the extent that the price indexes are downward-biassed, and so on. But both the CIA and other Western analysts routinely try to allow for these defects. And, in doing so, we are helped by evidence from Soviet scholars published, despite the censor, in Soviet journals.[13]

I would say, therefore, that Soviet published data, if handled with care, should not be misleading. The whole truth they certainly are not. They are not even nothing-but-the-truth. But they are not simply lies and propaganda. Their gravest shortcoming is not that they are untrue but that they are incomplete. It is not naive to use them, though it would be naive to take them all at face value. I cannot, in other words, agree with Lev Navrozov that the CIA is wasting public money by working with Soviet official figures. I consider that the CIA has sometimes been insufficiently critical of particular Soviet statistical series,[14] but that is a milder offense.

The Navrozov critique, however, does not rest simply on the contention that the official Soviet data are misleading. The further arguement is that, in its analysis of the Soviet economy, the CIA presents itself as a repository of secret information obtained by espionage when it is, in fact, working only with what the Soviet censor provides.

On this, Navrozov is rather persuasive. It is true that it would be hard to prove that all CIA assessments of the Soviet civilian economy are based on open Soviet sources. For example, the sample of Soviet engineering products used by the CIA to create an index of Soviet output of producer durables numbers 135 items. The published sources of information of 58 of these items are specified; for the remaining 77 the source is given only as 'estimates.'[15] I imagine that these estimates are, in fact, obtained by going through a great many Soviet monographs and specialist journals with a fine-tooth comb; but it would take several man-years of work to verify or refute that guess.

Still, Lev Navrozov makes a good case for overwhelming CIA reliance on published Soviet data. He notes that satellite photographs are another source, but that they are used mainly on military deployment, and have their limitations anyway. Like Navrozov, I see no sign that CIA economic assessments are benefitting from the services of bold and skillful spies who tell the Agency, say, the price the Soviet military pay for a MiG–27, the size of the Soviet molybdenum stockpile or Soviet spending on chemical warfare research. Somebody in US intelligence seems to know something about Soviet military-production 'floorspace'[16] but I imagine that floorspace is deducible from roofspace, and roofspace appears on satellite photographs.[17]

Navrozov's references to the US intelligence community require a short digression. What somebody somewhere in the intelligence community knows is not necessarily communicated to the CIA's Soviet analysts. Lev Navrozov assumes that it is. The CIA, he says, 'absorbs all intelligence data that the entire intelligence community gathers.' That assertion shows that Navrozov has not studied Washington as closely as he has studied Moscow. The capacity of US government agencies not to cooperate is one of the wonders of the modern world. (British government departments are much the same, but they do not keep telling the press about it.) The US Commerce Department, for instance, refused for two years to share with the Pentagon and the US Customs Service its information on the routing of VAX computers through a South African company to the USSR.[18] To assume that all information is instantly transferred between the CIA, the Defence Intelligence Agency (DIA) and the National Security Agency (NSA) requires the rich imagination of a neoclassical economic theorist. And if anyone knows any really good secrets, would it not be the NSA, who do not even get a mention?

Still, the thrust of Navrozov's argument is not deflected by departmental barriers in Washington. I believe he is right to say that the CIA's pronouncements about the Soviet economy carry a special weight because it is commonly supposed that intelligence agencies know things that must remain hidden from the rest of us. I suspect he is probably right to say that CIA economic assessments of the USSR are, in fact, almost entirely based on information that has been passed by the Soviet censor. What follows?

To begin with, it is the usefulness of the CIA Soviet analysts' output that matters, not the inputs that went into it. The Soviet censors let a number of items of information out which, when pieced together and carefully considered, tell Western observers things that Soviet policy-makers did not want them to know. The use of Soviet input–output tables to reach conclusions about military allocations, which Navrozov mentions, is an example. The Soviet censors are not stupid, but why assume that they are necessarily brighter than we are? The CIA deploys a small army of analysts who are paid to read tons of unspeakably boring material for the slivers of useful information it contains; and to fashion from that information a more reliable picture of what is happening in the Soviet economy than we would otherwise have. The question is, how good a job do they make of it?

Better, I think, than Lev Navrozov allows. For example, he takes the fashionable view that the CIA's 1977 prediction of falling Soviet oil output was simply and laughably wrong. (This is, incidentally, the only example I know of Mr Navrozov taking the fashionable view on anything.) Certainly, the timing and dimension of the fall which the Agency originally predicted have not been observed. In 1983–4, however, Soviet crude-oil production fell (or so the censored Soviet figures tell us). And there is evidence that the CIA's forecast alerted Soviet planners and led them to take action to prevent its coming true.[19] A clearer example of useful CIA analysis and projection is the Agency's 1967 report on the deal which had recently been concluded between the Soviet government and Fiat to set up a Fiat-designed car plant to produce modified Fiat cars at Tolyatti.[20] At that time, other Western observers were talking rubbish about the dawning of an age of mass motoring in the USSR, bringing motorways, petrol stations and civilization generally to the Russians, plus peace on earth. The CIA correctly forecast that the plant would reach full production only in 1974; that the whole exercise would motorize only a very thin layer of the Soviet population, and that pressure for Soviet roads to be improved beyond the World War I condition of US roads would be negligible.

The Agency has also been wrong about some Soviet economic developments. It would be news if it had not; economics is not a very successful science. But published CIA assessments of Soviet growth prospects, and of problems and policy choices in particular Soviet industries, are more thorough and persuasive than the great bulk of what is published in the USSR itself. And if there is a great volume of superior professional work being done in the USSR that is not published, it is hard to imagine where it is coming from. In the mid-1960s a senior Soviet economist observed, in what he thought was an off-the-record talk, that it was humiliating to have to wait for CIA reports in order to learn what was going on in the Soviet economy.[21] And the Soviet leaders themselves seem to have responded to CIA warnings on the oil industry, and perhaps on other matters. If the Agency were simply the dupe of official Soviet disinformation, its reports would only be a rather esoteric Kremlin joke.

Still, I think Lev Navrozov is right about two important things. First, the Agency does not seem to know any really good Soviet economic secrets. Second, some of its Soviet economic analyses show a reverence for technique that defies common sense.

It is undesirable that CIA assessments should be treated as authoritative for reasons that cannot be sustained. But the Agency is unlikely to confirm publicly that it relies entirely, or very largely, in analyzing Soviet economic developments, on published Soviet data. So the only way in which US citizens and taxpayers, and other innocent bystanders, are going to know more about the basis of CIA assessments is through an extensive discussion of these assessments by independent specialists.

The reverence for technique is bound up with a reverence for numbers. The comparisons of consumption levels which Navrozov ridicules are a case of inappropriate number-crunching. It is not that Navrozov can see snags which the CIA analysts are blind to. It is rather that the Agency cannot be deflected by anything so untechnical as a sense of proportion from coming up with a number. CIA reports acknowledge the problems of product quality and availability, but they do so in a few mild, discreet words at the end of a lengthy and elaborate set of calculations. Both the culture which surrounds the Agency's analysts and the machinery of government in which they serve, want numbers. The notion that, though you can generate a number, it might be wiser not to, is un-American and un-governmental.

For the reasons that Lev Navrozov so eloquently states, however, I think it really would be wiser not to put a number (or even two alternative numbers and their geometric mean) on Soviet per capita household consumption as a percentage of US per capita household consumption. It is not clear what a figure of 30 percent tells us (that means anything) which a phrase like 'very much lower' does not. An array of quantitative comparisons of individual products—bread consumption per head, meat consumption per head, cars per 1,000 persons, housing floorspace per person, and so on—does, however, convey something useful. It avoids the seductive, single, magic number of obscure meaning. It is less misleading about availability than a comparison based on prices and money incomes. And it may give just a glimmering of an idea to the reader of what some of the differences in everyday life amount to.

My personal view is that the same is true for comparisons of Soviet and US military spending in dollars or rubles. These particular CIA assessments are obtained chiefly by the building-block method from observed quantities of men, tanks, planes, ships, and so on. In this case, the CIA's comparisons are likely to exaggerate Soviet strength, rather than underestimate it[22]—unless the observations of men and hardware are too low in the first place.

The useful knowledge that Western intelligence has about Soviet military strength is what is known about the Soviet order of battle, the specifications of

Soviet equipment, the training and combat-readiness of Soviet troops, and other practical military matters. Anything that is reliably known about the progress of particular Soviet military research projects must also be worth knowing. What it all costs is much less important. It would be useful for Western propaganda, for foreign policy in general, and for arms negotiations in particular, to know what Soviet civilian production would be if Soviet military activities were halved or eliminated. But we do not know that and cannot even roughly estimate it with any confidence. We can be sure that the USSR allocates to the military a larger share of its resources than any NATO country does. But the figures for total Soviet military spending which the CIA and others put into orbit are too problematic to be useful.

In 1976 the CIA altered its assessment of the current ruble cost of the Soviet defense effort from 6–8 percent of Soviet GNP to 12–13 percent, and its assessment of the 1970–5 growth rate of that defense effort from 3 percent a year to 4–5 percent a year.[23] Then in 1983, as I have already mentioned, the Agency revised downward its measure of the growth of Soviet defense spending in real terms between 1976 and 1982, from 4–5 percent to 2 percent a year.[24] If our trust in the clock was not undermined in 1976 by its striking 13, we should certainly think again now that it has gone on to strike 14.

It is not, however, all CIA estimates which are unreliable—as Lev Navrozov implies. It is those grand-total figures which are too grand in concept and too tortuous and problematic in derivation to mean very much, which should be ruled out of court. It is on two such figures that Navrozov has concentrated: Soviet per capita household consumption as a percentage of US, and Soviet defense spending as a percentage of Soviet GNP. My argument is that these few digits give an air of spurious precision to notions which we cannot reliably quantify, and add nothing useful to our knowledge either of the material welfare of the Soviet people or of the dimensions of Soviet military power. It would be better not to have these numbers at all. To that extent I agree with Navrozov.

That is not the same as saying, however, that no CIA estimates of Soviet economic aggregates can be justified. Figures for total Soviet GNP and its growth are necessary for any appraisal of Soviet economic performance. (The Soviet official, national income figures will not do because they refer to a different definition of national income, and also provide upward-biassed growth rates.) A breakdown of total final domestic expenditure into consumption, investment and defense end-issues is also desirable. It is, moreover, possible—and not merely desirable—to arrive at such figures, even though the numbers may be less reliable than similar numbers for Western countries.

But the proper limits of these calculations should be remembered. Abram Bergson, who first developed the methods for making them, has always maintained that they were to be interpreted as measures of productive capacity and not as measures of material welfare. To say that 50 percent of Soviet GNP (measured at factor cost) is allocated to household consumption is to say that 50 percent of Soviet resources are so allocated. To say that per capita Soviet household consumption is around 30 percent of US is to make a much more ambitious and much less defensible statement about comparative levels of material well-being.

Estimates of the growth over time of Soviet consumption are also defensible on common-sense grounds. It is true that they may not capture all the changes in the availability and quality of consumer goods over time, just as international comparisons may not capture differences in availability and quality between countries. But in Soviet–Western comparisons this failing is large and glaringly obvious; in Soviet–Soviet comparisons (over time) it is reasonable to assume, as a general rule and over periods of less than a decade or so, that it is small. The sort of objections which Navrozov raises to the CIA's Soviet–US comparison of consumption levels would seem grossly exaggerated if applied to the CIA estimates of growth in Soviet consumption levels.[25]

In other words, I believe that independent specialists should be sniping at particular CIA assessments, not spraying them all with buckshot. The aim should be a cull, not a massacre.

It is, nonetheless, the element of attempted massacre in Lev Navrozov's chapter that gives it its drive. The impulse behind that attempt is the same, I think, as the impulse behind many of the onslaughts by Russian third-emigration intellectuals on Western Sovietologists. They are offended by our limitations and our complacency. They can see perfectly well the career-advancement skills which we are so eager to display: the estimation of CES production functions on Soviet data; the erudite comparisons of the 'totalitarian model' and the 'industrial society' approach to Soviet politics; the cautious appraisal of the patronage implications of Solomentsev's 1957 appointment as chairman of the Chelyabinsk *sovnarkhoz*, and so forth. They can also see attributes to which the profession is less inclined to draw attention: the ignorance of many of us about Russian and Soviet literature, art, music or, often, anything outside our own particular discipline; the inability of many of us to string together two sentences of fluent spoken Russian; the preference for evidence which can be footnoted to Soviet publications (that is, has been passed by the Soviet censor); the reverence for numbers even when their (unspecified) margins of error are large or their meaning unclear.

These limitations of the profession (not of all its members, but of many) would not matter if specialist expertise was enabling us to make accurate predictions. But on the whole it is not. One of the best-informed analysts of Soviet politics, Jerry Hough, correctly backed Andropov to succeed Brezhnev but then incorrectly backed Gorbachev to succeed Andropov.[26] I project Soviet real GNP growth from 1984 to 1990, on average, at below 3 percent a year and probably at about 2 percent,[27] but I would not be totally amazed if the outcome were, say, −1 or +4. As for questions that bear directly on Western policy, such as whether economic pressure by the West on the USSR would make Soviet behavior more docile or more aggressive, the only honest answer is that nobody has the foggiest idea.[28]

This does not mean that those who operate by prophecy, like Alexander Zinoviev and Alexander Solzhenitsyn, know better. But it does mean that technique is no guarantee of success. My conclusion is that Western professional Russia-watchers should pay closer and more humble attention than many of us do to what those who have lived in Russia wish to tell us about the USSR. In understanding what is happening in a closed society, it is no small advantage to have lived in it.

The Soviets themselves, as Lev Navrozov points out, train a great many West-watchers; they make sure that they speak fluently the language of the particular country on which they specialize, and study its history and culture as well as its economic and political institutions. That sort of training is probably more useful than a familiarity with advanced economic analysis or political sociology, so far as the formation of policy judgements is concerned.

What our Russia-watching needs, of course, is not the elimination of all sophists, economists and calculators but their assimilation of other sorts of knowledge and their cooperation with people who know about Soviet life in a less formal, less abstract way. As Alec Nove wrote twenty years ago, about the late Naum Jasny and his (mostly victorious) clashes with more conventional analysts: 'There should be room in our subject for men of different methods and different temperaments.'[29] It will take a lot of room to accommodate both Lev Navrozov and the CIA, but the space ought to be found.

Notes: Chapter 7

The discussion in this essay has benefitted from research in progress in Soviet statistics, in which the support of a grant from the Economic Research Council is gratefully acknowledged. I am also grateful to Elizabeth Teague and Peter Wiles for comments on an earlier draft. The responsibility for the errors and infelicities that remain is mine, especially as I have resisted some of the comments.

1 Lev Navrozov, 'An attempt to interest the West in its "survival",' *Russia*, no. 7–8 (1983), pp. 62–94.
2 See his Chapter 6 in this book.
3 Arthur Koestler, 'On disbelieving atrocities,' in *The Yogi and the Commissar* (London: Cape, 1945), pp. 94–9.
4 See, for example, US Congress Joint Economic Committee, *USSR: Measures of Economic Growth and Development, 1950–80*, (Washington DC: US Government Printing Office, 1982, p. 12) for discussion of the impact of new-product-price inflation on estimates of Soviet investment. I have discussed the measurement of Soviet investment growth in detail in 'The CIA, the Ts^{i}SU and the real growth of Soviet Investment,' *Soviet Studies*, vol. 36, no. 4 (October 1984), pp. 571–81.

There I set out the case for believing that both the CIA and the Soviet Central Statistical Administration have recently been overestimating Soviet investment growth.

5 Appalled recollections of a visit to Victor Louis's country house can be found in most of the recent 'my-year-in-Russia' books. Andrea Lee, in her excellent *Russian Journal* (London: Faber, 1981), noted that Victor and Jennifer Louis had five cars, a German stereo, a Japanese video machine that played both British and American video cassettes, 'a magnificent collection of early icons,' a collection of old Russian wood carvings that made 'the assemblages . . . in State museums seem sparse'; also a Bulgarian typist, two Russian maids and the effrontery to say things like: 'We have a man who does the most exquisite woodworking' and 'we have the cleverest cook who makes these things.' I doubt if even the uppermost reaches of the Bronx can match that, though Manhattan and Texas could, comfortably.

6 See, for example, Alec Nove, 'The purchasing power of the Soviet ruble,' *Oxford Institute of Statistics Bulletin* (1958), reprinted in Nove, *Was Stalin Really Necessary?* (London: Allen & Unwin, 1964); and Peter Wiles, 'The theory of international comparisons of economic volume,' in Jane Degras and Alec Nove (eds), *Soviet Planning. Essays in Honour of Naum Jasny* (Oxford: Blackwell, 1964), pp. 77–116.

7 See Alec Nove, 'Soviet defence spending,' *Survival*, vol. 13, no. 10 (October 1971), pp. 328–33. This is also one of the points made by Franklyn Holzman, 'Are the Soviets really outspending the US on defence?' *International Security* (spring 1980), pp. 86–105. Holzman is mainly concerned to show the importance of the index-number effect, which makes the ratio of Soviet to US defense spending look higher when both are measured in US dollar prices than when both are measured in Soviet ruble prices—but that is a separate issue from the present one.

8 William Lee, a former CIA analyst, has put forward estimates of Soviet defense procurement which are derived from a study of Soviet data on engineering production. These come out substantially higher than the CIA's for the period he covers. See William T. Lee, *The Estimation of Soviet Defense Expenditures, 1955–1975. An Unconventional Approach* (New York: Praeger, 1977). But checks on some of his Soviet sources show that he has interpreted them in ways that go beyond reasonable credibility. See Philip Hanson, 'Estimating Soviet defence expenditure,' *Soviet Studies*, vol. 30, no. 3 (July 1978), pp. 403–10. However, Wiles (unpublished) claims that he has reproduced the CIA's figures from a declared net increase in the stock of arms plus a concealed, but discoverable, depreciation and so replacement of the stock. Thus by splitting 'replacement and repairs' into 'civilian and military' Wiles claims that he can reconcile GNP with the CIA's arms figure.

9 US Congress JEC, op. cit. at note 4, pp. 24–6. This assessment came out in 1982. A year later the CIA went public with an assessment that the real growth of Soviet military spending had slowed after 1976 from about 4½ percent a year to about 2 percent a year. CIA, 'USSR: Economic Trends and Policy Developments,' US Congress JEC Briefing Paper, 14 September 1983. Such a slowdown could explain the decline in the residual, but the simplest conclusion is that all these numbers are dodgy.

10 A. Bergson, *Soviet National Income and Product in 1937* (New York: Columbia University Press, 1953), p. 7.

11 Why do Soviet authorities not lie more than they do? Why, in general, do people so often tell the truth when it against their interests to do so? Why, for example, in the Watergate investigation, did so many people tell Bernstein and Woodward the truth? Social science, as usual, provides no answer.

12 Recent interviews by Stephen Shenfield and myself with Soviet émigrés who used

to be engaged in reporting, collecting and processing such data in the USSR tend, however, to support the view that it really is risky to pad your plan-fulfillment reports too much. And the burden of proof is on those who consider that the percentage margin of such report-padding is increasing over time. If it is not, growth rates are not biassed by report-padding. (This is Alec Nove's 'law of equal cheating.')

13 See for example, Alec Nove, 'A note on growth, investment and price indices,' *Soviet Studies*, vol. 33, no. 1 (January 1981), pp. 142–6.

14 On investment growth. See Philip Hanson, 'Soviet economic growth: a look ahead from 1984,' mimeo., 1984.

15 US Congress JEC, op. cit. at note 4, Table A–1.

16 See US Department of Defense, *Soviet Military Power 1984* (Washington DC: US Government Printing Office, 1984), p. 91.

17 What, Lev Navrozov asks, about camouflage? I pass. But I would like to know the answer.

18 Joseph Fitchett, 'Even friends will be watched closely as US guards its high tech,' *International Herald Tribune*, 23 May 1984, p. 6.

19 More precisely, they took action to preclude the circumstances under which the CIA projected (conditionally) that a fall in output would follow. For a balanced and knowledgeable discussion, see Ed A. Hewett, *Energy, Economics and Foreign Policy in the Soviet Union* (Washington DC: Brookings Institution, 1984), pp. 24–6.

20 The CIA report is contained in *The Fiat–Soviet Auto Plant and Communist Economic Reforms*, a report for the Sub-Committee of the Committee on Banking and Currency, US House of Representatives (Washington DC: US Government Printing Office, 1967).

21 See Stephen F. Cohen (ed.), *An End to Silence* (New York: Norton, 1982).

22 For the reasons given in note 7. The argument here is about the impression given by ruble or (especially) dollar total expenditure figures. Navrozov is right to say that a numerical preponderance of Soviet tanks, ships, etc., cannot be waved aside on the grounds that Western tanks, ships, etc., are necessarily and automatically 'more advanced.' My point is that it is what is known about the numbers and the specifications of tanks and ships that matters; not what is unreliably estimated to be their total 'cost.'

23 CIA, *Estimated Soviet Defense Spending in Rubles, 1970–1975*, SR 76–10121 U (May 1976). See also 'The CIA's goof in assessing the Soviets,' *Businessweek*, 28 February 1977, pp. 96–100.

24 See note 9 above.

25 For example, Gertrude E. Schroeder and M. Elizabeth Denton, 'An Index of Consumption in the USSR,' in US Congress JEC, op. cit., at note 4, pp. 317–402.

26 *International Herald Tribune*, 31 May 1983, p. 6; *Problems of Communism* (November–December 1983), p. 61. On the latter occasion, Jerry Hough was brave enough to give quite specific probabilities: Gorbachev 0.8, Grishin 0.1, Romanov 0.08; all the other Politburo members between them 0.02.

27 In 'The Soviet economy: a look ahead from 1984,' a paper presented at a conference at the National Defense University, Washington DC, May 1984.

28 This is one of the points argued in Philip Hanson, 'Western economic sanctions against the USSR; their nature and effectiveness,' in *External Economic Relations of CMEA Countries: Their Significance and Impact in a Global Perspective* (Brussels: Nato Economics Directorate, 1984), pp. 69–93.

29 In Degras and Nove (eds), op. cit. at note 6, p. x. He meant, of course, persons.

8 *A Tonsorial View of the Soviet Second Economy*

GREGORY GROSSMAN

The provincial town of N. contained so many barber shops and funeral establishments that it seemed that its inhabitants came into this world merely to get a shave and a haircut, freshen up the scalp with hair tonic, and to die immediately thereafter. (Opening sentence from Il'ia Il'f and Evgenii Petrov's *The Twelve Chairs*)[1]

How glimpse the invisible? How measure the unmeasurable? The problem of estimating the size and composition of a hidden economy has busied many a statistician and economist in recent years. Since the actors in an underground economy usually conceal their activities and incomes for good and obvious reasons, direct measurement will not do. A variety of indirect methods have been proposed, and some actually used, to pierce the shroud that covers the hidden economy of a *Western* country. These typically measure certain proxy variables that are presumed to be correlated with the size of the hidden economy, or at least with changes in its size over time, such as, currency in circulation (on the premise that those who wish to conceal their activities or income prefer to pay and be paid in currency rather than by monetary instruments which leave detectable tracks), or even more remote correlates such as the overall tax burden and the size of the government bureaucracy. Where possible, resort has also been made to household questionnaire surveys to gauge the shortfalls in official employment or expenditure data. A large literature has arisen along these lines, and much has been learned in the process, but few conversant with the methods would vouch for a consistently high order of accuracy of the results obtained heretofore. Measuring the unmeasurable remains a problem.[2]

Our own concept of the Soviet 'second economy' is broader than that of an underground or hidden economy, for it includes as well some legal—therefore 'above ground,' at first blush unhidden—activities. By our definition, the second economy is the aggregate of productive and rent seeking activities, and of the corresponding personal incomes, which meet at least one of two overlapping tests: being on *private* account (which can be legal in the USSR within a very narrow range of specified activities), and being *illegal* in some significant respect, be the activity on private or socialist account. Closely related to the second economy are two other widespread phenomena: theft of socialist property (in a broader sense, including the misappropriation of labor

165

time and of services of production facilities), and bribery and other forms of corruption.

Needless to say, all illegal activity and theft and corruption are concealed from official view by the actors. But, in fact, even much of the *legal* private activity is hidden, in whole or in part, to evade the heavy direct taxes that impinge on nearly all of the nonagricultural private activities (compare tax evasion in Western countries), to minimize the 'squeeze' collected by innumerable officials, and to escape the ideological odium that attaches to any private economic activity in the USSR. Finally, much legal private activity may escape official recording because of gaps and deficiencies in the statistical system. Thus, even such important and, in principle, legal activity as the sale of privately produced foodstuffs in the so-called *kolkhoz* market seems to be seriously understated in Soviet official statistics.[3] It should also be noted that in the USSR the line between legal and illegal private activity is blurred and uncertain, and it is a rare legal private activity that does not have its appreciable, if not preponderant, illegal side. In a practical sense, therefore, nearly the whole of the Soviet second economy can be thought of as hidden, either in whole or in considerable part.

The Soviet second economy, like a Western underground economy, is a *market* economy. Insofar as it is illegal and produces for exchange, it cannot but be a market economy—though, naturally, one with its own peculiar institutions and limits. Insofar as the second economy is above ground, it may in certain respects be formally subjected to price controls and other regimens that reflect the ambient command economy—such as, occasional ceiling prices at *kolkhoz* markets, rent controls on privately let dwellings—but, in the event, these seem to be widely evaded. In sum, there is a major difference between the Soviet second and the Western underground economy. The former is a (largely) private-enterprise, market economy coexisting and interacting with an ambient socialist, command economy; while its Western counterpart is a private-enterprise, market economy that coexists and interacts with another (largely) private, market economy—the formal economy. Systematically, in the West, the 'other' economy and its formal 'host' are not very far apart; in the USSR, they are.

Another important distinction has already been alluded to here. To a very large extent, the Soviet second economy depends on theft from the socialist sector, mostly the state, for inputs of materials, labor and production capital, which thus are, in the first instance, acquired at near-zero price.[4] Stolen inputs (other than unpaid taxes) seem to play a much smaller role in Western underground economies.

It follows, from both the systemic distinction and the role of theft in providing inputs, that the Soviet second economy may be expected to have a structure of relative economic values (prices, wages, incomes, etc.) much less similar to that of *its* first economy, than would be true of a Western underground economy in relation to its formal environment.

1 Object of the Study

How can the general structure of economic values in the Soviet second economy be observed? To be sure, a wealth of individual prices and incomes can be culled from the Soviet press, from written and oral accounts of emigrants, and from the limited observations and tales of foreign travelers. Some indications of synthetic price levels in the private market in relation to those in the state sphere can even be found in official statistical compendia, for example, for aggregate *kolkhoz* market prices (though the official data are of dubious reliability, as already mentioned). Interesting results regarding relative hourly remuneration in official employment and in private activity, by economic sector, have been obtained by Ofer and Vinokur from their émigré household survey.[5] Similar estimates are underway in the analysis by Professor Treml and the present author of our émigré household survey (hereafter, the Berkeley–Duke survey).

Yet, apparently, no survey can directly provide an answer to such a basic, though not very simple, question as: what is the level of hourly pay for ordinary unskilled labor in the second economy, in rubles and in relation to the corresponding wage in the 'first' economy? One reason is that the answer to our question is not usually formulated in this way in the minds of both the private employer (household) and the hired help. Because private employment in the USSR tends to be occasional, not regular, remuneration is typically by the job, not by the hour. A second reason is that payment for occasional private labor services rendered by a male worker (especially if he is 'northern', that is, not of Caucasian or Moslem nationality) is often not in cash but in what is effectively the second currency of the USSR—vodka.[6] In such a case, the bargain is struck in terms of a number of standard (half-liter) bottles to be paid upon completion of work, and the liquid medium of exchange is frequently consumed by the recipient on the spot. And yet, it would be rash to infer that the second economy completely overlooks the cash value of time in the labor bargain. Being a market, it surely must take labor time into account so that an hourly cash wage ought not to be devoid of meaning.

Of particular interest, then, is the hourly remuneration of unskilled labor, expressed in money. Not only does this remuneration lie, as it were, at the base of the whole scale of labor earnings in the second economy (as elsewhere), but it also refers to a kind of labor that is relatively easy to compare with its counterparts in both the 'first' economy of the USSR and in all other countries. Moreover, this kind of work performed 'on the left' (informally, illegally, uncontrolled) must be ubiquitous throughout the USSR, with numerous buyers and sellers in many localities, competition on both sides of the market, and virtually no effective regulation or control by the authorities. In sum, an almost perfect market in a given locality. (The fact that 'help is hard to find,' as it mostly is in the USSR, does not invalidate the case—it merely calls for a higher wage). But we can expect major interregional and intercity differences in the pay of unskilled labor, because the spatial mobility of both workers and their employers must be quite limited.

In a private communication, Peter Wiles has justifiably pointed out that 'the ratio of black to official unskilled hourly pay is of great importance in all questions of time budgets. It give us, first, the opportunity cost of a worker's time as a multiple of his official wage—perhaps, even if he is a skilled worker. Secondly, it tells us what is a reasonable time budget . . .' True enough. Empirically, however, this approach is fraught with complications: (i) a good deal of private work of many kinds is accomplished *on* the official job, often using the employer's materials, tools, equipment and customers; (ii) there are other, sometimes lucrative, forms of 'left' income to be derived from being present at the official place of employment, such as, collecting bribes; and (iii) the same person often works at quite different levels of skill in the first and second economies, which throws off Wiles's ratio.

What kind of unskilled work is in question here? Loading, hauling, wood-chopping, unskilled help with own construction of a dwelling or a garage, digging up a garden, and various kinds of housework, such as, cleaning, clothes washing, and minding the very young, the infirm and the aged. In regard to housework alone, the Berkeley–Duke survey contains 28 families (all from the European USSR and nearly all from large cities) that reported payment in a given year for such purposes. On an average monthly basis, the amounts ranged from 2.5 to 33 rubles, plus an outlier figure of 160 rubles per month, and with a median of 8 rubles. Unfortunately, the observations do not include information on hours worked or on whether food or other benefits in kind were provided by the employer in addition to cash.

Since direct estimation of the unskilled wage in the second economy is impracticable—and, moreover, the sample of such cases in a household questionnaire survey is likely to be quite small (particularly in view of the regional differences in the wage)—we proceeded to obtain the answer in an indirect fashion. To do so we made use of an empirical regularity between unskilled pay and the price of a man's haircut (on which more presently), asking all respondents in our survey how much each male member of the household typically paid for a haircut in the last normal year before emigration from the USSR. A sample of almost 900 such answers was obtained.

A major object of this chapter, therefore, is to inquire into the levels of haircut prices, and so to infer the levels of unskilled pay in the second economy by city and region. In addition, we shall take a longish look at barbers' incomes, legal and illegal, as perceived by others and by the barbers themselves, and as actually received by them.

For information on both incomes and haircut prices we shall rely primarily on the findings of the Berkeley–Duke questionnaire survey. The sample consists of 1,007 families of recent emigrants, all from urban localities but from a wide range of republics and regions in Soviet Europe and Asia. All interviews were conducted in the USA by interviewers who themselves are recent emigrants, following the 'snowball' technique, with parallel interviewing in several cities.[7]

2 Haircuts: Fourastié's Law

In a book which received much attention in its day, Professor Jean Fourastié of Paris, a historian of French prices and of economic progress, casually made the point that even among very different countries the price of a man's haircut tends to be approximately equal to the hourly wage of labor. To illustrate this finding—let us accord it the title of an empirical 'law'—he compared haircut prices and hourly money wages of maidservants in Cairo, Paris and New York. One would think that in all three cities at the time (the data seem to pertain to 1947 or 1948) the wages of maidservants would be on the level of unskilled pay rather than of average wages of hourly labor, and we interpret the law in this sense. Furthermore, Fourastié argued that the then rapidly rising employer's social insurance taxes ought to be added to wages for the purpose at hand.[8] We accept this suggestion.

Ever since coming across Fourastié's law the present author has made it a point in his travels to check its validity from country to country and over a good number of years, by a method that may be described as highly casual empiricism on the spot. The law seemed to be confirmed nearly every time, at least in market economies. In our experience in Berkeley, California, beginning with the late 1930s, an approximate 1:1 relationship has held up quite well, especially if one adds employer's social security taxes to the unskilled wage. Some thirty years after Fourastié's aforementioned comparison, we tested the law for Paris—again, casually—with the kind assistance of Dr Eugène Zaleski of that city and his wife. We quote from his letter of 8 November 1979 (with some inconsequential abbreviation and a few minor editorial changes):

> I went immediately . . . to a barber shop for a most ordinary haircut. The price (which is taxed in France) was 16.00 francs, and I tipped 2.00 francs, which corresponds to a [normal] tip of 10–15 percent. [i.e., total payment by customer, 18 francs] My wife, who works in the Ministry of Labor, obtained for me the data on the minimum wage. [The current] minimum hourly wage in Paris is 12.42 francs. Fringe benefits (employer's payments) for this minimum wage are as follows:

obligatory medical insurance	14.45%
old-age insurance	8.20%
family allowances	9.00%
accidents at work [insurance], 2–4%, say 3%	3.00%
total addition to the wage	34.65%
total paid by employer: 12.42 × 1.3465 =	16.72 francs

Thus, in Paris in late 1979, the minimum wage *plus* employer's payments, a measure of hourly employment cost of an unskilled worker, was therefore 93 percent (16.72 : 18 × 100) of Zaleski's expense of an ordinary haircut plus tip. Some unskilled workers may, in fact, have been earning more. The 'law' roughly was confirmed in this instance as well.

Fourastié explained the constancy of the haircut-price-to-unskilled-wage ratio[9] by the relative constancy of the barber's productivity over time and space. One might, however, rather surmise that a barber's and an unskilled worker's productivities do vary over time and space, but tend to vary roughly alike. And one would need to add that there is a tendency for skilled barbers' and unskilled workers' real earnings to be, and stay, in rough proportion to one another at different times and in different countries. If the latter statement is more or less correct, it would be yet another instance of Phelps Brown's 'association between status and relative pay being maintained by custom in defiance of the shifting play of market forces' over long time spans.[10]

Now, the second economy in the USSR being a market economy, can haircut prices tell us something about the level of wages of moonlighting unskilled labor? The official, controlled prices—hardly. But the official price is not what the customer in a barber shop actually pays; instead, he pays a much higher total amount that includes, in addition, a very large tip, so large that many Western visitors to the USSR have remarked upon the fact. (And, on the other hand, as we shall see, the state does not even collect the full official price. A good deal of it adheres to sticky fingers in the barbering business.) The total payment is, of course, part of the second economy, hence, a free price. It is, then, this total payment, including tip, which we take as proxy for the hourly wage of unskilled labor in that economy.

3 Haircuts: the Soviet Scene

A noninstitutionalized Soviet male ready for a haircut has a choice of three venues: having it done at home (an alternative we henceforth ignore), going to a socialist barber shop (either 'communal,' that is, municipal or local, or 'departmental,' that is, at the workplace),[11] or resorting to the services of a private barber operating 'on the left' in his/her or the client's home. From the 1,392 males of all ages in the Berkeley–Duke sample we have obtained a total of 894 observations, of which 829 (93 percent) pertain to haircuts at barber shops (hereonout we omit the qualifier 'socialist'), presumably mostly communal rather than departmental, and 64 to haircuts by private barbers working 'on the left.' The figures are, of course, reported not by the barbers but by their customers.

The modern Russian words for barber, *parikmakher*, and for the establishment, *parikmakherskaia*, refer to women's hairdressing and to 'mixed' operations as well as to men's barbering. Soviet official statistics do not distinguish between the genders, either for the occupation or for the establishment. As for private barbers and their services, official statistics omit them altogether.

Prices of barber shop services are administratively fixed, as are wages of barbers and other employees. Prices of *private* barbering services are, naturally, set by the market and are not administratively fixed. However, as we have just seen, the official prices are in large measure fictitious for all three parties—state, customer and barber—owing to generous tipping, on the one hand, and liberal dipping into the state's till by barber shop personnel on the other.

Generous, even lavish, tipping is a not unexpected phenomenon under conditions of chronic repressed inflation; in effect, it is a way of at once circumventing both price and wage controls, of bringing values in the informal market closer to equilibrium levels. As long ago as the early 1950s, an American correspondent noted that in Moscow 'A haircut (for some reason, the biggest bargain in Russia) [is officially] 2 rubles [old money = 0.2 rubles in post-1960 money] but the tip to the barber should be three times as much; and many individual rubles should be added for a shampoo, shave, and finally and inevitably "Eau de Cologne" ...'[12]

The share of the tip in the total amount paid by the customer may no longer have ·been as high in the 1970s as it was in the 1950s, but the Berkeley–Duke survey finds that for Moscow, on the average, the tip still was 39 percent of the total price paid ($N = 39$, standard error of the mean—2.6 percentage points), very close to the average for all northern cities combined, which was 40 percent ($N = 386$).[13]

The tip to the barber breaks down into the basic tip, which is paid for the haircut alone, and supplementary tips for special consideration and additional services. For the individual customer, the basic tip may be essentially parametric; it is what the social situation dictates and the barber expects. But from the social (aggregate) point of view it is the amount that performs one or both of two functions: (i) raising the price of the haircut to some kind of 'realistic' level in relation to other realistic (that is, second economy) prices, and (ii) elevating the barber's living standard above the niggardly wage that the state pays him (more on this below) to reach a kind of traditionally sanctioned level in relation to the structure of real earnings, including second economy incomes. In other words, it corresponds to the public sense of the fitness of things at the time and place, a sense that may have, subconsciously, survived decades of the command economy and of price-income controls. Note, however, that functions (i) and (ii) need not call for the same size of tip.

Supplementary tips, as mentioned, are offered for services additional to the haircut proper and for special considerations given the customer. Most important of the special considerations is being received ahead of the barber shop queue, usually by prearrangement, which rates a generous additional tip.

Table 8.1   *Total Payment per Man's Haircut by Customer (Tip Included), by City*

	N^a (1)	Mean (kopeks) (2)	Standard Error of the Mean (kopeks) (3)	Median (kopeks) (4)	Erevan = 100		1977 Minimum Wage[f] per Hour (42.73 kopeks) = 1.0	
					Mean (5)	Median (6)	Mean (7)	Median (8)
Northern cities	(476)							
Kiev[b]	43	158.1	11.1	150	75	75	3.7	3.5
Kishinev[b]	26	180.8	16.4	170	85	85	4.2	4.0
Leningrad[c]	111	192.9	12.1	150	91	75	4.5	3.5
Moscow[b]	45	227.1	20.7	180	107	90	5.3	4.2
Odessa[b]	28	200.7	17.6	200	95	100	4.7	4.7
Riga[b]	35	171.4	14.2	180	81	90	4.0	4.2
All other northern cities	(188)							
Population:								
0–50,000	25	88.3	8.09	80	42	25	2.1	1.9
51–500,000	96	136.7	11.75	100	65	50	3.2	2.3
501,000+	67	160.3	11.4	145	76	72.5	3.75	3.4
Southern cities[d]	(353)							
Baku[b]	39	213.2	13.9	200	101	100	5.0	4.7
Erevan[c,d]	224	211.9	7.86	200	100	100	5.0	4.7
Tashkent[b]	22	190.5	12.6	200	90	100	4.5	4.7
Tbilisi[b]	23	190.7	7.80	200	90	100	4.5	4.7
All other southern cities[e]	45	183.1	10.5	200	86	100	4.3	4.7

Source: Berkeley–Duke survey.

[a] *N*'s pertain to means. *N*'s for medians are the same except as follows: Kiev—45, Moscow—47, Riga—37, Baku—40, Tashkent—23, Tbilisi—24, all other southern cities—46. Unit of observation—one person's average payment per haircut during his last normal year in the USSR.

[b] Owing to the relatively small samples for these cities (between 23 and 47 observations), the upper and lower extreme values were eliminated for each city before computing the mean value.

[c] Pensioner families (containing pensioners only) are excluded from the Leningrad and Erevan subsamples for comparability with the other cities. (The two cities are the only ones in our sample containing pensioner families.) Pensioners seem to spend considerably less per haircut.

[d] The subsamples for all southern cities except Erevan consist solely of 'northerners,' mostly Jews, who resided in the respective cities prior to emigration from the USSR, and not of persons of local nationalities. In the case of Erevan, 90 percent of the subsample consists of ethnic Armenians and 10 percent of 'northerners,' mostly Jews.

[e] In Armenia, Georgia, Azerbaidzhan, Uzbekistan and southern Kazakhstan.

[f] See text, p. 174.

In fact, the public may be overtipping in the sense that barbers may be doing quite well despite low salaries, with the help of tips and illegal income. If so, one may surmise that the public's sense of relative values, when tipping, applies not so much to the barber's income as to the price of the haircut.

4 Free Prices of Haircuts

The Berkeley–Duke questionnaire asked each male member of the household to state the amount that he usually paid,[14] per haircut alone, (i) into the state's till (*v kassu*), (ii) for eau-de-cologne (which, in Soviet usage, stands for any hair tonic), (iii) as a tip to the barber, and (iv) altogether, which we call the 'total payment.' The last, as already argued, may be thought of as a free price, thanks to the importance of the tip.

As already mentioned, we obtained 829 answers regarding typical payments per man's haircut in a barber shop. We focus on the variable 'total payment.' The results are summarized in Table 8.1, which presents means and medians by cities, grouped into North and South. Ten of the cities are named—eight republic capitals plus Leningrad and Odessa—while two are composite entities, the residual catch-all categories 'all other northern cities' and 'all other southern cities.' Two named cities have a fairly large number of observations (*N*) each: Leningrad—111, and Erevan—224. (Leningrad and Erevan are the two local case studies in the Berkeley–Duke survey.) The other named cities have much smaller *N*s, from 22 to 45. The composite 'all other northern cities' is broken down by population size into three groups.

To begin with the means, visual examination of column 2 reveals a moderate tendency for the northern cities to have lower total payments per man's haircut than southern cities. (The pattern may be easier to grasp in column 5, where the means are expressed as relatives, with the Erevan mean = 100.) Northern cities with the highest total haircut payments are Moscow and Odessa; the former is exceptional for obvious reasons, the latter is almost southern in its putative involvement in the second economy. Removing the two cities from the northern contingent brings out somewhat more strongly the pattern of lower haircut payments in the North than in the South. Especially low is the mean for the category 'all other northern cities,' 0–50,000 population: 88.3 kopeks per haircut, or 42 percent of the Erevan figure; and the median in this case is only 25 percent.

The North–South pattern of haircut payments stands out much more strongly in a comparison of the medians (columns 4 and 6), where all the northern cities have lower, sometimes considerably lower, values than the uniform value for southern cities, 2.00 rubles per total payment per haircut. By Fourastié's law, a tentative conclusion would be that, in the mid- and later 1970s, an hour of unskilled labor in the North (except Moscow and Odessa) was paid in the second economy, say, 10 to 75 percent less than in the major cities of the South.

The last two columns of Table 8.1 express the means and medians of total haircut payments as multiples of the minimum hourly wage (inclusive of the employer's social security payments with reference to that wage). Strictly speaking, the USSR had no minimum *hourly* wage in the mid- and late 1970s, nor has it had one since. Rather, it has had a minimum *monthly* wage/salary for the category of 'workers and employees' (which excludes peasants and military), then and today set at 70 rubles per month. This minimum began to be introduced by sector or region in 1971, and by 1975 was in effect throughout the economy,[15] in both city and country. Some may, in fact, have been earning less than the minimum even in the second half of the 1970s: part-time workers (less per month though not necessarily per hour) and some of those who could not meet production norms.[16] On the other hand, some, perhaps many, working at unskilled jobs were doubtless earning substantially more in their official employment (not to speak here of the second economy), thanks to the whims of the Soviet system of administered wages, dictates of the labor market in the face of pervasive labor shortage, or nepotism, or plain good luck. All in all, it may not be far wrong to equate the level of official unskilled pay with the minimum wage of 70 rubles per month. Adding employer's social insurance payments, about 6.26 percent, we compute the corresponding hourly rate to have been 42.73 kopeks per hour.[17] Let us abbreviate it as MHW.

We can similarly calculate the average official hourly wage (AHW). The 1977 all-Union average monthly wage for both urban and rural workers and employees was 155.2 rubles. Using the same parameters as in the computation of MHW, we obtain an all-Union AHW in the official sector of 94.73 kopeks, inclusive of social insurance contributions by the employer.

Total payments per haircut in Table 8.1 are, of course, much higher than MHW, and with one exception even higher than AHW. The lowest figure for haircut payment in the Table is 100 kopeks, the median value for 'all other northern cities,' 0–50,000 population, and this figure is 1.9 times MHW and 0.84 of AHW. (The multiples of MHW can be found in the last two columns of Table 8.1.) The highest haircut-payment figure in the table is the mean for Baku, 213.2 kopeks, which is just 5 times MHW and 2.25 times AHW.

Following Fourastié's law—without imputing to him responsibility for liberties we take—and regarding the total payment per haircut, tip included, as a free market price for the service, we can very tentatively offer the following conclusions. The level of monetary hourly (monetary, not in vodka!) remuneration of unskilled labor in the Soviet second economy (HRULSE) in the mid- and later 1970s was (mean and median define the range, respectively; multiples are rounded):

- In Moscow, 1.80–2.25 rubles (4.2–5.3 times MHW; 1.9–2.4 times the all-Union AHW).
- In other northern republic capitals and in Leningrad, 1.50–2.00 rubles (3.5–4.7 times MHW, 1.6–2.1 times AHW).
- In other northern cities and towns (north of the Caucasus range and Central Asia):
  in small towns (up to 50,000), 0.8–0.9 rubles (about 2 times MHW and 0.8–0.9 times AHW);
  in medium-sized cities (over 50,000 and up to 500,000), 1.0–1.4 rubles (2.3–3.2 times MHW, 1.0–1.4 times AHW);
  in large cities (over 500,000), 1.4 to 1.6 rubles (3.4–3.8 times MHW, 1.5–1.7 times AHW).
- In the capitals of Transcaucasia, 1.90 to 2.15 rubles (4.5–5.0 times MHW, 2.0–2.25 times AHW).
- In Tashkent, around 2.00 rubles (around 4.5 times MHW, around 2 times AHW).

No great accuracy can be claimed for these estimates of HRULSE. Beginning with the highly casual basis of Fourastié's law, through the vagaries of sampling for the questionnaire survey and the problems of fidelity of respondents' recall, to the appropriateness of the total payment per haircut in socialist barber shops as a reasonable measure of the 'true' second economy value of this particular service, uncertainties and errors abound and cumulate. And yet, we cannot dismiss the estimates entirely either. They are not patently nonsensical, and the intuitively correct signs of the north–south and center–periphery gradients tend to reinforce the slender methodological reed that supports the HRULSE estimates. So, we take the estimates moderately seriously and proceed with a brief commentary.

Are they not too high in absolute terms and in relation to both MHW and AHW? Is it credible that HRULSE is anywhere from 2 to over 5 times the minimum hourly wage in the 'first' economy, depending on location? And this in the mid- or late 1970s, before or just on the eve of the serious aggravation of consumer goods shortages and the substantial rise in free (legal and black) market prices of the latter part of 1979 and the early 1980s.[18] We do not find the estimates of HRULSE unacceptably high, for the following reasons:

(i) Ofer and Vinokur conclude from their survey, which takes in the urban population of the North alone and pertains to the early 1970s, that hourly earnings from work (of all skills) in the private (second) economy yielded on the average 'close to four times' as much as in the first.[19] Our HRULSE estimates for the North alone, expressed as multiples of MHW, range from 2.3 to 5.3, that is, they bracket the Ofer–Vinokur ratio.

Table 8.2　*Hourly Private Earnings and Haircut Payments, by Cities*

	(N)	(A)	(B)	(C)	(D)
Northern cities					
Kiev	20	2.71	1.50	181	339
Kishinev	15	3.57	1.70	210	446
Leningrad	98	2.69	1.50	180	336
Moscow	24	2.89	1.80	160	361
Odessa	12	2.92	2.00	146	365
Riga	11	2.91	1.80	161	364
All other northern cities, population					
0–50,000	14	2.32	0.80	290	290
51–500,000	96	2.94	1.00	294	367
501,000+	32	2.50	1.45	172	313
Southern cities					
Baku	22	3.51	2.00	175	439
Erevan	106	4.97	2.00	248	621
Tbilisi	18	4.43	2.00	221	554
All other southern cities	31	5.88	2.00	294	735

(ii) A certain—unknown—portion of unskilled urban labor was probably earning somewhat more than the bare minimum wage (MHW), as we have noted. This does not affect our absolute estimates of HRULSE, of course; but it does suggest that the ratios of HRULSE to unskilled pay in the first economy—expressed as ratios to MHW—may in fact have been somewhat lower.

(iii) A good part of urban unskilled employment in the private sector must be occasional, seasonal and otherwise irregular, and is often performed outside regular work hours. This alone suggests a certain premium for HRULSE over corresponding pay in the socialist sector.

(iv) Another and probably more substantial premium of this kind is dictated by the reputedly much higher productivity of labor of all kinds, and surely unskilled labor as well, in private employment than on an official job. The fact is so widely reported and so well known, and the reasons are so obvious, that there is no need to expand on them here. (On the other hand, the risk premium—due to illegality or tax evasion—is probably not an important component of HRULSE, because low-skill private work is generally ignored by the authorities.)

(v) Last but not least, the HRULSE estimates make some sense when confronted with *average* hourly earning from work for private persons, as derived (without re-weighting) from the Berkeley–Duke survey data on both second economy earnings and hours of work. In Table 8.2 we present by city, (N) number of observations, (A) median hourly private

Table 8.3 *Payment per 'Left Haircut,' Leningrad and Erevan (In Kopeks per Haircut)*

	N	Mean	Standard Error of the Mean	Median	Maximum
Leningrad	9	333.3	44.1	300	500
Erevan	21	271.4	27.7	300	500

earnings in rubles, (*B*) median total payment per man's haircut in rubles (from Table 8.1) a proxy measure for HRULSE, (*C*) ratio of (*A*) to (*B*) in percent, and (*D*) ratio, in percent, of (*A*) to our estimate of the mean, official, all-Union wage or salary, net after tax, in 1977, namely, 0.80 rubles per hour.[20]

The reader will note the considerable convergence of median hourly earnings from private work among northern cities (Kishinev excepted), and relative closeness of the figures for Erevan and Tbilisi. Unfortunately, some of the city samples are not as large as we would have them. At this point, we cannot explain the very high figures for Kishinev and for 'all other southern cities.'

The figures for northern cities in column (*D*) tend to agree quite well, though for somewhat later period in the 1970s, with the Ofer–Vinokur finding, cited in (i) above, that hourly pay in the private sector is 'close to four times' (actually, 3.7 times; see their Table 2) as high as the average rate of pay (of their sample population) in the official sector. The Ofer–Vinokur survey did not include southern cities.

In sum, the absolute values of our estimates of HRULSE, and their ratios to the official minimum and average wages, do not strike us as being clearly implausible.

5 Prices of 'Left Haircuts'

Let us now take a quick look at the level of haircut prices in the other institutional arrangement, the 'left haircuts' of privately working barbers. As mentioned, we have only 64 observations of this kind: 30 for Armenia (of which 21 are for Erevan), 17 for the whole North (of which 9 are for Leningrad), and 17 for the South other than Armenia. Those who patronize such private barbers do so either because a 'socialist' barber shop is not within easy reach, which is unlikely in the larger cities, or because they desire better or different service, or a shorter waiting period. The last seems to be an important consideration. Prices so paid are, of course, uncontrolled, 'free.'

Our findings for the two cities are shown in Table 8.3.

Comparing Table 8.3 with Table 8.1, we find that the prices paid to private barbers tend to be considerably higher than the total payment given in the barber shop—a conclusion that would not surprise anyone with firsthand experience. One goes to a private barber for better service with less waiting. For Leningrad: the 'left haircut' mean is 73 percent higher than the barber shop total-payment mean (Table 8.1), and the difference between the two is significant at the 0.01 level; the median is twice as large. For Erevan: 28 percent and 0.05, respectively, and the median is 50 percent larger. Why are private haircuts *relatively*—as well as absolutely—cheaper in Erevan than in Leningrad? Is it because the *supply* is greater in the South, in line with the greater development of the second economy there? This much is suggested by data on barbers' private earnings in Table 8.6.

Should we take the prices of 'left haircuts' as the closest expression of free haircut prices in the USSR, the resultant measures of hourly pay of unskilled labor in the second economy would be considerably higher than those derived in the preceding section. For the two cities in Table 8.3 (bearing in mind the very small samples and, again, rounding): Leningrad—3.00–3.75 rubles per hour of unskilled labor, or 7–9 times MHW; Erevan—2.70–3.00 rubles per hour, or 6–7 times MHW. However, our sample of 'left haircuts' is limited for practical purposes to only these two cities, and for both it is small. Hence, we put it aside and proceed to our next topic, barbers' incomes as a micro-case of second economy incomes.

6 Barbers' Incomes

In the USSR, the income of a barber or hairdresser employed in a barber shop consists of not two but three or four elements: (i) a modest official salary, (ii) the tips, (iii)—apparently for many barbers—a part of the state's rightful revenue misappropriated by him/her, and (iv) side income from moonlighting as a private barber. So far as (iii) is concerned, there is both ample opportunity for such misappropriation and considerable evidence of its occurrence in the tales of émigrés. To wit: 'A woman hairdresser from Minsk explained that she worked in "her" little hairdressing shop . . . as if it were her own: . . . she paid into the official cash register the necessary sum and the rest was her own ("two rubles to the state, three rubles for me").'[21]

But perhaps the most vivid account in print is to be found in a work of fiction by the well-known émigré writer, Efraim Savela. The locale is Melitopol', a medium-sized Ukrainian town, the time—apparently the 1970s, the place—a barber shop in the Soviet sense (including ladies' hairdressing), and the hero is a ladies' hairdresser, one of three barbers and hairdressers in the establishment. The three jointly pay a bribe of 500 rubles a month to the local police chief. Why?

Even an infant would understand ... Every Soviet barber or hairdresser, when collecting the [official] price from a customer, once in every three instances puts it into the state's till (*kassa*), and twice into his own pocket. To keep this fact quiet one must grease someone's palm. We were not pikers and paid the bribe at the very top, to the militia chief. This provides complete security, like being in God's own lap. And to scrape together 500 rubles a month was a cinch for the three barbers in our shop. They were responsible people; withheld the amount from themselves as though it were a tax.[22]

Savela's barber, like his famous counterpart from Seville, did not restrict his attention to the narrow bounds of the venerable trade, but an account of his ribald adventures has no place in this scholarly chapter.

Next, we hear from one of the interviewees in the Berkeley–Duke survey, a hairdresser who volunteered the following explanation of his private income: 'I dyed, cut, and set hair. By agreement with the client I billed her [formally] for only a part of the procedure. The rest I took in cash, directly, by-passing the till. I did this only with regular clients, those who would give me no trouble' (G4–81–0521).

Finally, an authoritative confirmation (referring to an unstated date but, judging from the context, pertaining to Tallin or the Estonian republic): '... during [on the spot] barber shop inspections, cash receipts *at times* (*byvaet*) are double [the usual level].'[23] Service establishments in general, and barber shops in particular, are easy targets for dipping into the till by their personnel, for they have neither output inventories nor significant recorded supplies against which their production can be audited. Consequently, we are not surprised to hear of barbers' and hairdressers' jobs being purchased for bribes. For example, in Kiev in the late 1970s, a barber's job could be bought for about 200 rubles (private information). One is tempted to ask: why not more? Oversupply of jobs for sale in this and other trades? Large bribes and kickbacks to be paid later from barbers' current earnings?

To see how the Soviet public at large perceives barbers' informal and illegal earnings and incomes ('left incomes' in Soviet parlance) we turn again to the Berkeley–Duke survey. Our questionnaire asked respondents to give their opinion of 'left' incomes for three dozen named occupations, professions and jobs, but barbers were not on that list. We also invited respondents to write-in other occupations of their choice, up to a maximum of five, and (as with the three dozen listed ones) to check the range in which, in the respondents' perception, the average monthly 'left' income of the written-in occupations fell. Almost without exception (and not surprisingly) respondents wrote-in occupations which, in their everyday experience, brought high 'left' incomes, though we did not expressly invite them to do so. Of the total of 6,187 individual write-ins by 1,970 respondents, 322 mentioned barbers (in Russian, therefore including hairdressers), cosmeticians and other barber shop trades. In the Soviet occupational classification these fall into the category 'barbers, hairdresssers, make up and cosmetic specialists, and manicurists' (occupation 382). On the assumption that essentially all specialties within this category receive approximately the same official salaries and most likely also very similar 'left' incomes, and to garner the benefits both of a larger sample and of better comparability with Soviet statistics, we shall deal hereonout with occupation 382 as a unit, rather than with barbers alone (though we may occasionally refer to it as 'barbers, etc.').

As it happens, occupation 382 was cited by our respondents more often than any other. The 322 mentions of 382 are 5.2 percent of the total of 6,187 individual write-ins.[24] Respondents from northern republics as a group (all republics except those in Central Asia and Transcaucasia), $N = 1,236$, cited it 247 times (5.7 percent of all write-ins), while those in the southern republics did so as follows (in this order: number of respondents, times 382 was cited, percentage of all write-ins for the given republic):

Armenia	507	40	3.3
Azerbaidzhan	73	13	5.5
Georgia	79	12	4.4
Uzbekistan	75	10	7.0

It should be noted in this connection that while the respondents from Armenia are largely ethnic Armenians,[25] those from the other three southern republics are all 'northerners,' mostly Jewish, who resided in the South.

In the case of 318 of the 322 mentions of occupation 382, we have respondents' estimates (perceptions) of the average monthly 'left' incomes (which they did by checking one of eight columns representing income class intervals, ranging from 'practically none' to 'over 300 rubles per month'). By taking mid-points of intervals to stand for the intervals (and 500 rubles per month to stand arbitrarily for the open-ended uppermost interval) we computed mean and median values of these perceptions for three 'zones' of the USSR: the North (as just defined), Armenia, and the South other than Armenia. The reasons for distinguishing Armenia from the rest of the South are that our subsample for Armenia (i) is relatively large[26] and (ii) is different in that it consists mostly of ethnic southerners while that for the rest of the South does not, as just noted. Further, the respondents from the North were asked to state their perceptions with reference to the USSR as a whole (which practically meant the North, given that this is what they knew best and that the urban population of the North accounts for 88.1 percent of the total Soviet urban population).[27] Respondents in the South were asked to give their perceptions with reference to the respective republic.

Table 8.4 summarizes the findings. The reader will notice the contrast between Armenia and the other two zones. The mean for Armenia is more than double that for the 'North,' 381.8 *v.* 172.1 rubles per month. The

Table 8.4   *Average Monthly 'Left' Incomes*[a] *of Barbers, etc. (Occupation no. 382), as Perceived by Respondents who Wrote-In this Occupation*[b], *by Zone*[c]

	N	Mean (rubles)	Standard Error of the Mean (rubles)	Median (rubles)
	(1)	(2)	(3)	(4)
North	244	172.1	10.2	75
Armenia[d]	40	381.8	26.8	500
South other than Armenia[e]	34	177.1	20.8	150
Total	318			

Source: Berkeley–Duke survey.

[a] Mean value of 'over 300 rubles per month' class arbitrarily assumed to be 500 rubles per month.

[b] Occupation no. 382 comprises 'barbers, hairdressers, make-up and cosmetic specialists, and manicurists.'

[c] Respondents in the North (USSR other than South, which is defined as Central Asia, including southern Kazakhstan, and Transcaucasia) were asked to indicate the income perception for the USSR as a whole. Those in the South were asked to indicate their perceptions for the respective southern republics.

[d] Predominantly ethnic Armenians.

[e] This 'zone' consists entirely of 'northerners' who resided in the South (specifically, in Georgia, Azerbaidzhan, Uzbekistan and southern Kazakhstan) previous to emigration from the USSR.

difference between them is significant at the 0.01 level; in other words, the two means most likely come from two distinct statistical 'universes.' This sharp contrast between the level of values, perceived or actual, in and for Armenia and in and for the North will be a leitmotiv for the remainder of this chapter.

Bearing in mind that the net (after tax) official salary of a barber at the time (middle and second half of the 1970s) was just about 100 rubles per month in all three zones,[28] our northern respondents, in effect, were perceiving a total net income (official + 'left') of about 280 rubles per month, a figure that is almost double the all-Union net official average wage/salary of about 145 rubles per month in 1977. But our respondents from Armenia were, in effect, perceiving a barber's total net income of about 480 rubles per month, or 3.3 times the 145 ruble figure.

Table 8.4 shows that the mean perception by respondents from 'South other than Armenia,' all of whom were in fact migrants from the North, is almost identical with the mean for respondents from the North: 177.1 as compared with 172.1 rubles per month (even though the same respondents from the South or their male relatives were spending for haircuts and tips at the (higher) southern level, as shown in Table 8.6). We surmise that the northerners living in the South brought their perceptions of the levels of 'left' incomes with them, and were insufficiently clued into the southern second economy to change them.[29]

As mentioned, the figures in Table 8.4 derive from perceptions volunteered (written-in) by the respondents themselves. Since, in this context, respondents may have a tendency to write in occupations with relatively high perceived 'left incomes,' there may be some upward bias in the figures. Those who failed to mention occupation 382 may have done so because their perception of the 'left' incomes of barbers, etc., may have been less impressive; or, being limited to only five occupations in the open-ended part of the question, chose other, equally impressive, examples; or for some different reason, such as absence of any perception. At any rate, the figures in Table 8.4 are, at best, upper bounds of the respective means.

Our questionnaire also asked every respondent who had, or had had, an occupation to attempt an estimate of the average monthly 'left' incomes of persons in his/her *own* occupation. This was a fixed question, not an open-ended one. (As in the previous case, however, respondents in the North were asked to give their perceptions with references to the USSR as a whole; those in the South, with reference to the republic of respondent's residence.) In the case of occupation 382, 44 individuals have answered the question (Table 8.5). Thirty-one of these are northerners, 7 from Armenia, and 6 from a number of other southern republics. Thus, all three subsamples are small, particularly the last two, and only a moderate amount of confidence can be placed in the figures. The expected pattern is maintained: Armenian respondents indicated much larger 'left' incomes for their fellow barbers, etc., in the republic than did both the northerners for the USSR as a whole and the other southerners for their respective republics. For all three zones, members of occupation 382 generate lower estimates of mean 'left' incomes of their own trade (Table 8.5) than does the public at large (Table 8.4).

For Armenia, the mean value in Table 8.5 comes within only 15 percent of that in Table 8.4, and the difference is not statistically significant (though we cannot overlook the arbitrary setting of the mean value of the uppermost income class at 500 rubles per month). Thus, for Armenia, the trade's perception does not clearly disagree with the public's. The same is true of 'South other than Armenia.'

In regard to the North, the difference of means in Table 8.4 and Table 8.5, 172.1 *v.* 68.7, *is* significant at the 0.01 level. In this case, it appears that the trade's opinion of its own 'left' incomes is significantly lower than that of the public at large, and the public can be said to considerably overestimate the 'left' incomes of barbers, etc.—and to continue to tip generously nonetheless. (Interestingly, the medians for North in the two tables coincide, suggesting that the public estimation of barbers' 'left' income is highly skewed upward, and it is the upper tail of this distribution, rather than the bulk of public opinion, that is responsible for the just-mentioned overestimation.)

Table 8.5 *Average Monthly 'Left' Incomes of People 'in the Same Occupation' as Perceived by Respondents in Occupation no. 382[a], by Zone*

Respondents by Zone	N (1)	Mean (rubles) (2)	Standard Error of the Mean (rubles) (3)	Median (rubles) (4)	Percentage giving over 300 rubles[b] (5)
Respondents in northern republics answering with reference to all USSR	31	68.7	9.14	75	0
Respondents in Armenia answering with reference to Armenia	7	327.1[d]	67.4[d]	250	43
Respondents in southern republics other than Armenia answering with reference to the respective republic[c]	6	119.3	20.3	150	0
Total	44				

Source: Berkeley–Duke survey.

[a] Occupation no. 382 comprises 'barbers, hairdressers, make-up and cosmetic specialists, and manicurists.' Of the 44 respondents in this category, 26 were barbers or hairdressers.

[b] Percent of respondents in the given zone who gave 'over 300 rubles per month' as their perception of average 'left' income of people in their own occupation.

[c] 1 from Azerbaidzhan, 3 from Georgia, 1 from Uzbekistan—all 'northerners' who were residents of these republics before emigration.

[d] These values are computed by arbitrarily assuming that the mean value for the 'over 300 rubles per month' class is 500 rubles per month.

7 Barbers' Actual Incomes

So much for perceptions. How much did barbers, etc., actually earn in the mid- and late 1970s? The findings of the Berkeley–Duke survey on this score are summarized in Table 8.6. Of a total of 1,824 individuals in the sample who indicated their occupations, 45 (2.5 percent) identified themselves as occupation 382 (barbers, etc.). Of these 45, 30 are from the North, 7 from Armenia, and 8 from southern republics other than Armenia. For the present purpose we distinguish three kinds of income: (i) official salary (including premia, etc.) net after tax; (ii) private earnings from work for private persons, much of it as a kind of professional moonlighting;[30] and (iii) 'other income,' declared by the respondent on the questionnaire but not further identified. The last income category, if sizable, is almost certainly of the 'left' kind and, *inter alia*, presumably contains both tipping and dipping. Thus, both (ii) and (iii) are forms of 'left' income in Soviet parlance, and the two together constitute 'total "left" income,' which, when added to the official salary (i),

Table 8.6 *Average Monthly Official and 'Left' Income of Occupation no. 382[a] by Zone, and Corresponding Figures from Tables 8.4 and 8.5*

| | N | Mean | Standard Error of the Mean | Median (rubles) | Corresponding Figure in Table 8.4 | | Table 8.5 | |
| | | | | | Mean | Median | Mean (rubles) | Median |
	(1)	(2)	(3)	(4)	(5)	(6)	(7)	(8)
I North								
A Official salary, net[b]	30	105.2	6.84	100				
A' (Official salary, net)[d]	(29)	(108.8)	(6.00)	(100)				
B Private earnings[c]	30	71.3	24.6	23				
C (Private earnings)[d]	(17)	(125.9)	(38.7)	(65)				
D Other income[e]	30	34.4	8.9	13				
E (Other income)[d]	(16)	(64.6)	(12.6)	(43)				
F Total 'left' income, B+D	30	105.8	25.3	70	172.1	75	68.7	75
G (Total 'left' income)[d]	(24)	(132.2)	(29.2)	(96)				
H Total income, A+B+D	30	200.0	27.3	167				
II Armenia								
A Official salary, net[b]	7	97.6	4.95	90				
B Private earnings[c]	7	192.9	53.9	200				
C (Private earnings)[d]	(5)	(270.0)	(30.0)	(300)				
D Other income[e]	7	128.6	53.3	100				
E (Other income)[d]	(5)	(180.0)	(60.4)	(150)				
F Total 'left' income, B+D	7	321.4	53.3	300	381.8	500	327.1	250
G (Total 'left' income)[d]	(7)	(321.4)	(53.3)	(300)				
H Total income, A+B+D	7	419.0	52.7	420				

III *South other than Armenia*[f]

A	Official salary, net[b]	8	106.9	14.2	100		
B	Private earnings[c]	8	12.5	12.5	0		
C	(Private earnings)[d]	(1)	(100.0)	—	(100)		
D	Other income[e]	8	144.7	57.9	100		
E	(Other income)[d]	(7)	(165.4)	(62.4)	(150)		
F	Total 'left' income, B+D	8	157.2	54.9	125	117.1	150
G	(Total 'left' income)[d]	(7)	(179.6)	(57.8)	(150)		
H	Total income, A+B+D	8	264.1	58.0	277	119.3	150
	Total	45					

Source: Berkeley–Duke survey.

[a] 'Occupation no. 382' comprises 'barbers, hairdressers, make-up and cosmetic specialists, and manicurists.' Of the 45 respondents in this category, 27 were barbers or hairdressers.

[b] Salaries net of taxes withheld at work.

[c] Earnings from private work for private persons, presumably mostly moonlighting as barbers, hairdressers, etc.

[d] Entries in parentheses refer only to those persons who had positive earnings or incomes of the designated type.

[e] Unspecified. Presumably includes tips and misappropriation of state's money and property. May also include some unrelated to barbering.

[f] Of the 8 respondents in this group, 3 are from Azerbaidzhan, 3 from Georgia, and 2 from Uzbekistan.

constitute a barber's 'total income' in our table. Transfer receipts from the state, such as pensions, are not included.

It should be noted, however, that some or even all of the 'left' income reported by a barber, etc., on our questionnaire could have obtained from nonbarbering activities. We have no way of knowing this as a rule, and so we assume that all 'left' income declared by members of occupation 382 was in fact obtained in connection with barbering or closely related activities in informal or illegal ways. On the other hand, persons identifying themselves in occupations other than 382, and therefore falling outside of our purview in this investigation, could also have received 'left' incomes of a barbering kind, such as moonlighting as hairdressers or men's barbers.

In Table 8.6, statistics not in parentheses refer to the N of the whole subsample of each zone (panel of the table), that is, taking into account zeros and missing values as well as positive values. Those in parentheses refer to positive values only. Thus, for example, in the panel marked 'North,' line C indicates that 13 persons in this zone had positive income from 'private earnings,'[31] and that the mean amount for the 13 was 139.6 rubles per month. But there are altogether 30 persons in Zone North, meaning that 17 had no private earnings, or at least declared none; hence, line B shows that, spread over all 30 persons, the mean value of private earnings was 60.5 rubles per month.

Two things immediately strike the eye as it falls on Table 8.6. First, the official net salary is approximately the same in all three zones, several rubles above or below 100 rubles per month. Now, in the mid- or late 1970s, a monthly net salary of about 100 rubles per month, though substantially above the minimum wage of 70 rubles per month, was also considerably below the nationwide average net wage/salary of 145 rubles per month. Most émigrés would doubtless characterize it as not a living wage, especially with dependants in the family, one that would force its recipient to look for supplementary sources of income. Second, the supplementary sources of income reported by our respondents in each zone are large in relation to the official salary, and vary greatly in total amount between zones. They are all of the 'left' (informal, illegal) kind; none of our 45 barbers, etc., reports any earnings whatsoever from additional lawful employment. We proceed to discuss the three panels separately.

North

One of the 30 northern respondents had no official income, but we leave him in because he may not be unrepresentative of a certain fraction of barbers, etc. Total 'left' income per each of the 30 equalled their average official net salary, 105.8 *v.* 105.2 rubles per month, thereby doubling the average take-home pay. The mean total income from all sources, 211.0 rubles per month, some 45 percent higher than the average official after-tax wage/salary of 145 rubles in the USSR in 1977 (*supra*). This is not a low average income per earner, if not a notably high one. However, we suspect it to be underreported by the respondents—specifically, in regard to 'other income.'

It will be recalled that tips belong in 'other income.' Yet almost half the barbers in the first panel of Table 8.6—14 out of 30—report no 'other income,' implying no tipping (and no dipping) at all in an average month of the given year. This is hard to believe in view of the Soviet custom to tip generously in barber shops. One is led to suspect that either our subsample of 30 is unrepresentative in this respect, or the 14 respondents were deliberately reticent on this point. If, by way of mental experiment, we assume that the 14 did, in fact, have 'other income' and set it at an average of 32.3 rubles per month,[32]—that is, half the mean level for the 16 who did report it (line *I*.E)—the means for the whole subsample of 30 go up as follows (rubles per month): 'other income'—from 34.4 to 49.5, total 'left' income—from 105.8 to 125.2; total income—from 211.0 to 226.1.

Armenia

Keeping in mind that our Armenian subsample in Table 8.6 (like that for the rest of the South) is very small, we may note certain interesting aspects of the level and structure of this group's income. While the *official* salary of Armenian barbers was close to—even 10 percent smaller than—that of northern barbers (lines A), their total 'left' income was three times as high (lines F) and their total income, twice as high (lines H). (The differences of the means for both total 'left' incomes and total incomes are significant at the 0.01 level.) On the average, Armenian barbers, etc., earned *privately* 121.6 rubles per month more, and 94.2 rubles per month more as 'other income' than their northern counterparts (lines B and D), and altogether 216 rubles per month more in total 'left' income (lines F). For the Armenians, 'left' income more than quadrupled their official salary, bringing their total income to double that of the northerners. Perhaps Armenia can, with some reason, serve as proxy for all of Transcaucasia.

Were (are) Transcaucasian barbers twice as well off as those in the North in terms of current income and earnings (lines H)? This is difficult to say. Such factors as traditional local consumption patterns, demographic structures and climatic conditions apart, both the structure of effective consumer prices and the availability of consumer goods have differed, and continue to differ, between the portions of the USSR north and south of the Caucasus range. By all indications, there is little doubt that consumer goods have been more readily available in Transcaucasia than in the North as a whole, owing in part to natural conditions (for example, food) and, in part, to a more developed second economy. Some consumer-goods' prices doubtless have been lower in Transcaucasia, thanks to a more bountiful nature and ample black production. Some prices, on the other hand, must have been higher there, owing to the greater pressure of purchasing power (for example, services; cf. haircuts *infra*) or to their being imported *via* black channels from the rest of the USSR. A full accounting of price levels and ratios, and of relative availabilities, remains to be done. But our data on total incomes of one, not unrepresentative, occupation, that of barbers, etc., and on the spending of their customers, do not seem to refute the prevalent impression of Soviet emigrants and outside observers that Armenians (and other Transcaucasians) 'live much better' than the people of the northern republics, official data on official earnings notwithstanding.[33]

South Other than Armenia

Let us recall again that the barbers, etc., in this group are all transplanted northerners who happened to live and work in the South before emigration. Their official net salary was approximately the same as for the other two groups. In regard to total 'left' income[34] and total income they fall between Armenia and North, which is perhaps not surprising. We may surmise that, on the one hand, these transplanted northerners benefitted from higher tips (*infra*) and a putatively greater development of the second economy in the South; on the other hand, being northerners, they may have found it difficult to fully partake of the local informal economy.

In regard to 'total income,' the difference between the mean for the North and that for 'South minus Armenia' (211.0 and 264.1, respectively) is not significant ($t = 1.07$); the difference between Armenia and 'South minus Armenia' (419.0 and 264.1, respectively) *is* significant at the 0.05 level.

8   Concluding Summary

This chapter has sought to estimate the remuneration of an hour's unskilled labor in the Soviet second economy in the mid- and late 1970s. Since this could not be done directly, resort was made to (what we have called) Fourastié's law, an empirical regularity between such remuneration and men's haircut prices in market economies. In addition, barbers' earnings and incomes—official, 'left' (informal and/or illegal), and total—as actually earned and as perceived by the public, have been estimated. The data come largely from the Berkeley–Duke questionnaire survey of over 1,000 émigré urban families. Some of our subsamples are fairly large; others are perforce quite small. (How many Armenian barbers *can* there be even in a thousand-family sample drawn from all walks of life and the whole USSR? We are glad to have the seven.)

If our results are rough, so surely is the reality of prices and incomes in the ubiquitous and protean second economy of that vast land. We can say, with Adam Smith, that the reality we aim to gauge is 'adjusted . . . not by any accurate measure, but by the haggling and bargaining of the market, according to that sort of rough equality which, though not exact, is sufficient for carrying on the business of common life.'[35]

Identifying the official hourly wage of unskilled labor in the first economy with the minimum hourly wage (MHW), augmented by employer's social insurance contributions, we take it to have been about 0.43 rubles. Following Fourastié's law, we then obtain the following estimates of hourly remuneration of unskilled labor in the *second economy* (HRULSE) in the mid- and late 1970s, by location, (Table 8.1):

- In Moscow, 1.80–2.25 rubles (4–5.3 times MHW).
- In other northern republic capitals and in Leningrad, 1.50–2.00 rubles (3.5–4.7 times MHW).
- In other cities and towns in the North, 0.80–1.60 rubles (2.30–3.80 times MHW), depending on population size.
- In the capitals of Transcaucasia, 1.90–2.15 rubles (4.5–5.0 times MHW).

By comparison, the *average official* wage or salary in 1977, net after taxes, was about 0.80 rubles per hour, while the median hourly remuneration from private work (Berkeley–Duke survey, not re-weighted) was about 2.30–3.00 rubles in northern cities, and almost 5 rubles in Erevan.

We find that barbers (and similar specialists) earned on the average the low official salary, net after taxes, of about 100 rubles per month throughout the USSR; but, with the addition of 'left' income, this was doubled for those in the North (that is, north of the Caucasus range and Central Asia), and as much as quadrupled for those in Armenia (proxy for all of Transcaucasia).

The public at large, that is, our total sample, generally perceived these incomes to have been higher (Table 8.6). Nonetheless, it tipped generously, possibly thanks to a conventional notion of what total payment per haircut ought to be in relation to other market values in the second economy. The total payment per haircut, tip included, ranged from 1 to over 2 rubles, depending on location and whether one looks at means or medians.

Notes: Chapter 8

We are pleased to express appreciation to the following persons: Dmitry Bosky and David J. Sedik for research assistance, Davida J. Weinberg for computer work, and Bent Hansen, Leonid Khotin, Gur Ofer, Vladimir G. Treml, Peter Wiles and Dr and Mrs Eugène Zaleski for advice and comments. All responsibility rests with us. We also take this opportunity to express gratitude for financial and material support of this research to the Ford Foundation, Wharton Econometric Forecasting Associates (Planned Economics Unit), and the Department of Economics and the Center for Slavic and East European Studies, both of the University of California, Berkeley.

1 This is my translation of the opening sentence of this superb satire on the second economy, as it were, of the NEP, published in Moscow, 1927.

2 A fine summary survey of methods used in, or proposed for, measuring Western hidden economies and their critique will be found in Bruno S. Frey and Werner W. Pommerehne, 'The hidden economy: state and prospects for measurements,' *Review of Income and Wealth*, vol. 30 (1984), pp. 1–23. Some of these methods are not suitable in the Soviet case for lack of data, and because of specific Soviet circumstances, such as, repressed inflation, universal price and wage control, and the crucial importance of theft from the state to fuel the second economy. For a stimulating discussion of measurement problems in regard to the Soviet second economy, see Peter Wiles, 'What we still do not know about the Soviet economy,' in NATO Economics and Information Directorates, *The CMEA Five-Year Plans (1981–85) in a New Perspective: Planned and Non-Planned Economies* (Brussels: NATO, 1982).

3 Stephen Shenfield arrived at this conclusion after a close study of the statistical methodology underlying Soviet *kolkhoz*-market sales statistics ('How reliable are Soviet statistics on the kolkhoz markets?' *Journal of Official Statistics*, vol. 2, no. 2 (1986), pp. 181–91. Ofer and Vinokur, and Treml arrived at the same conclusion empirically from their respective questionnaire surveys of consumer spending conducted among Soviet emigrants. See Gur Ofer and Aron Vinokur, 'The private sector in urban USSR' (Santa Monica, Calif.: The Rand Corporation, 1980), R–2359–NA, processed; and Vladimir G. Treml, *Purchases of Food from Private Sources in Soviet Urban Areas*, Berkeley–Duke Occasional Papers on the Second Economy in the USSR, no. 3 (Durham, NC, 1985).

4 One is reminded of the quip that in the transition to full communism 'the state will not wither away, it will be pilfered away.' With a sarcasm uncommon even in a Soviet feuilleton, a recent piece in *Pravda* (19 July 1985) characterized the Soviet state as *beskhoznoe vymia*, a 'masterless udder,' there to be milked by anyone and everyone. The lack of respect for socialist property in the USSR (and other communist countries) does not seem to extend in nearly the same measure to personal property.

5 Ofer and Vinokur, 'The private sector in urban USSR,' cit. at note 3.

6 Cf. Vladimir G. Treml, *Alcohol in the Soviet Underground*, Berkeley–Duke Occasional Papers on the Second Economy in the USSR, no. 5 (Durham NC, 1985). The wage bargain is struck and payment taken in vodka in part so that the acquisition of vodka will circumvent the family purse and the wife's scorn, in part to shorten the lag of gratification behind the effort, and in part possibly to protect the worker against a 'devaluation' of the ruble in relation to vodka. It may be fairly said that in the worker's mind the ruble is on a vodka standard.

7 A fuller, though still concise, description of the questionnaire survey can be found in the introduction to issue no. 1 of the Berkeley–Duke Occasional Papers on the Second Economy in the USSR (1985), available on request from the present author.

8 Jean Fourastié, *Le grand espoir du XXe siècle* (Paris: Presses Universitaires de France, 1949), pp. 110–13. This observation of Fourastié's regarding haircut prices was first brought to our attention by the late Alexander Gerschenkron of Harvard many years ago. In later publications, Fourastié expressly uses *average* industrial wages to deflate current prices to obtain 'real prices' of French goods and services over long periods. See *Pourquoi nous travaillons* (Paris, 1961), p. 62; and *Documents pour l'histoire et la théorie des prix*, Vol. 2 (Paris: Colin, 1961).

9 The striking numerical value of the ratio 1:1 is, of course a curiosum and of little significance compared with the ratio's supposed approximate constancy over time and space.

10 Henry Phelps Brown, *The Inequality of Pay* (Berkeley, Calif.: University of California Press, 1977), pp. 134 ff.

11 Soviet statistical sources rarely give the breakdown between communal and departmental barber shops. Those for Erevan, fortunately, do ('Statisticheskoe upravlenie goroda Erevana,' *Ekonomika i kul'tura goroda Erevana: Statisticheskii sbornik* [Erevan, 1980] pp. 111–12). At the end of 1977, that city had 133 barber shops (including, as we have already noted, ladies' and mixed establishments); of these, communal ones numbered 124, or 93 percent.

12 Frank Rounds, *A Window on Red Square* (New York: Houghton Mifflin, 1953), p. 14. The official price of 2 rubles for a haircut alone (Moscow, 1953) was, in fact, not much of a bargain relative to the then minimum gross wage of 220 (old) rubles per month. Cf. Alastair McAuley, *Economic Welfare in the Soviet Union: Poverty, Living Standards, and Inequality* (Madison, Wis.: University of Wisconsin Press, 1979), p. 203, citing Kunelskii. Comments in square brackets are by the present author.

13 'North' is the USSR less Transcaucasia and Central Asia.

14 Once again, the respondents' answers refer to the last normal year before the family's emigration from the USSR.

15 Cf. McAuley, op. cit., at note 12, pp. 200–1, 210 ff.

16 ibid., p. 260, n. 9.

17 The minimum wage augmented by employer's social insurance payments, per work hour, in 1977 is computed as follows. In that year, the official minimum wage proper was 70 rubles per month. To this we add the proportional share of social insurance payments, computed as the ratio of the total of such payments into the state budget (12.4 billion rubles) to the aggregate national wage bill. The latter is obtained by multiplying the average monthly gross wage/salary (155.2 rubles) by the average monthly number of workers and employees (106,393,000), and further by 12 to obtain the year's wage bill of 198.146 billion rubles. 12.4 billion rubles ÷ 198.146 billion rubles = 6.258 percent; 70 rubles × 1.06258 × 12 = 892.567 rubles. (All data from *Narodnoye khozyaistvo SSSR v 1977 g.*) The last is, then, the annual equivalent of the minimum wage augmented by social insurance contributions from the employer. In 1977 the officially determined number of work hours was 2,089 (*Ekonomicheskaya gazeta*, no. 1 [1977], p. 24), which, divided into 892.567 rubles, gives us the minimum wage per work hour, 42.73 kopeks.

18 The increasing shortages and the rising free prices after 1979 may have been occasioned not only by production slowdowns and bottlenecks, but also by the related acceleration in currency issue. The case is argued in Gregory Grossman, 'Inflationary, political, and social implications of the current slowdown,' in H.–H. Hoehmann, A. Nove and H. Vogel (eds), *Economics and Politics in the USSR: Problems of Interdependence* (Boulder, Colo: Westview Press, 1986), pp. 172–97.

19 Ofer and Vinokur, 'The private sector in urban USSR,' cit. at note 3, p. 14.

20 The figure 0.80 is computed as follows. In 1977 personal income tax revenue was 19.3217 billion rubles, 'bachelor tax' revenue was 1.1611 billion rubles, and the two together were 20.4842 billion rubles (Ministerstvo finansov SSSR. biudzhetnoe upravlenie, *Gosurdarstvennyi biudzhet SSSR i biudzhety soiuznykh respublik, 1976–1980 gg.* [Moscow, 1982], p. 11), which was 10.337 percent of the wage bill of 198.146 billion rubles in that year (see note 30, below). The mean after-tax hourly wage thus was (again see note 30): 155.2 × 12 × (1–0.10337) ÷ 2,089 = 0.7994 rubles per hour, rounded to 0.80. A very small part of the just-mentioned taxes may apply to persons other than the 'workers and employees' to whom the wage bill refers, which means that the 0.80 figure may be slightly understated.

21 Zev Katz, 'Insights from émigrés and sociological studies on the Soviet economy,' in US Congress, Joint Economic Committee, *Soviet Economic Prospects for the*

Seventies (Washington DC: Government Printing Office, 1973), p. 91.

22　Efraim Savela, *Ostanovite samolet—ia slezu!* (Stop the airplane—I'm getting off!) (Jerusalem: STAV, 1977), pp. 135–6.

23　*Izvestiya*, 19 August 1985, p. 3; my emphasis.

24　'Tailors and seamstresses' are a close second with 320 mentions.

25　Because of Soviet emigration policy, nearly every Armenian emigrant family in our sample contains at least one so-called repatriant, an ethnic Armenian who immigrated into Soviet Armenia from some foreign country in the second half of the 1940s. Many of them repatriated at a young age and reached maturity in the USSR.

26　20.9 percent of the households and 22.1 percent of the individuals comprised in the Grossman–Treml sample are from Armenia. Of course, the Armenian share of all Berkeley–Duke respondents answering a particular question may be quite different. At the end of 1977, only 1.2 percent of the Soviet urban population lived in Armenia.

27　The percentage refers to the end of 1977; it omits all Kazakhstan from 'North.'

28　Cf. Table 8.5, infra. In areas of hardship or frontier settlement the salary was significantly higher, but these are of minor significance nationally.

29　This broadly agrees with Nancy Lubin's finding that the European population in Soviet Central Asia is less involved, or less successful, in becoming involved in the second economy (*Labour and Nationality in Soviet Central Asia* [Princeton, NJ: Princeton University Press, 1984], ch. 6). The difference between the means for Armenia and 'South other than Armenia' is significant at the 0.01 level.

30　The moonlighting can actually take place right in the socialist barber shop.

31　Incomes refer to the last normal year before emigration from the USSR.

32　It is possible that some of those who reported no 'other income' were in fact concealing rather high income of this sort, and that those who reported were understating.

33　Higher actual living standards in Armenia and Georgia than in most of the North in contrast to official figures, were computed and published by Peter Wiles (art. op. cit. at note 2, Appendix II), as part of an imaginative adjustment of the official per capita consumption figures for all republics.

34　The reader will notice that 'left' income received by the 'South-minus-Armenia' barbers, etc., consists almost entirely of 'other income' and only to a small extent of 'private earnings.' The subsample is small and the meaning of the fact is not clear.

35　Adam Smith, *An Inquiry into the Nature and Causes of the Wealth of Nations* (1776), bk 1, ch. 5, para. 4.

9 Soviet Agriculture: A Brighter Prospect?

KARL-EUGEN WÄDEKIN

1 Introduction

Soviet agriculture after collectivization has never been able to meet domestic consumer demand. This often meant hunger or latent malnutrition for large segments of the population, but in recent times basic physiological requirements have been satisfied, at the now prevailing overall nutrition level. Shortages of certain foods have become rather a matter of rising incomes and the resulting purchasing power, which exceed food availabilities. The situation of such excess demand turned increasingly acute during the 1970s. For the most part it originated from the combination of income rises and a change in eating habits, which made demand turn to animal products, fruit and the finer vegetable foods. More, not less, crop produce is needed when livestock feed replaces part of the direct human consumption, and the finer vegetable foods require more inputs at lower tonnage yield per land unit (for example, green beans instead of cabbage, or apricots instead of water melons). In both cases, higher demands are also put on storage, processing and retailing, that is, on the forward linkages of agriculture.

Total global output of Soviet agriculture, although growing over the long term at a respectable annual average rate of 2.3 percent (five-year average 1976–80 over 1956–60 according to the official statistics), began to lag more and more behind consumer demand, and by 1984 it exceeded the population growth of the preceding seven years by a mere 0.5 percent per year.[1] This development was exacerbated by the industrialization and urbanization process throughout the USSR, which in a growing total population made the numbers of rural, largely self-sufficient inhabitants decline and that of urban wage earners—that is, food buyers—increase rapidly. Even assuming no higher than the officially implied inflation rate for nominal wage incomes, the growth of the demand for food clearly exceeded that of agricultural global output (see Table 9.1). In addition, consumer goods produced industrially in the socialist sector also did not meet the rising and changing demand, neither in quantity nor in quality or assortment. The latest food supply crisis was only temporarily attenuated by the record harvests of 1976 and 1978, with the resulting rise of animal production up to 1979.

The 1978 record was followed by a series of disappointing harvests, which are mirrored in the statistics not only of aggregate global production, but also

193

Table 9.1   Development Factors of Consumer Demand and Supply in the USSR,
1960–1984

Year	Population (million, 1 Jan.)	Of Which Urban (million)	Overall Wage Sum (billion rubles)[a]	Index for Real Demand for Food (estimate, 1970 = 100)[b]		Index of Gross Agricultural Production (1970 = 100)
				I	II	
1960	212.3	103.8	60.0 −	63 −	60.1/68.0	73
1970	241.7	136.0	132.0	100	100	100
1980	264.5[c]	166.2[c]	228.0 +	133 +	137 +	113
1982	268.8	171.7	245.0 +	134 +	138 +	116
1984	273.8	177.5	259.1 +	138 +	138 +	123

Sources: Narodnoe khozyaistvo SSSR v 1961 g., p. 8; and Narodnoe khozyaistvo SSSR v 1984 g., pp. 5, 224, 409 and 417.

Note: I owe much to Peter Wiles for suggestions and improvements to this table.

[a] The wage sum is derived from nominal average wages and the number of wage earners. Thus it is implicitly assumed that the increase of the monetary labor remuneration of collective farm members (which the statistics do not register as wages) is not spent on food purchases. This, of course, is only partially the case; therefore the wage sum and the food demand is understated to that extent, and a plus sign is added to the index figures for the wage sum and the food demand after 1970, and a minus sign to those of 1960.

[b] Column I is derived from the nominal wage sum by assuming the consumer price index estimated in Handbook of Economic Statistics 1985 (CIA: Washington, DC, 1985), p. 53, to be realistic: 1 percent per annum in 1960–70, 2 percent per annum in 1970–80, 3 percent per annum in 1980–2, 1 percent per annum in 1982–4; and setting the marginal propensity to spend on food at 0.6 throughout the period. In column II we first show (1960–70) sensitivity to coefficients of 0.7/0.5. Next we use the more plausible deflators in 1970–84 or 2 percent per annum in 1970–3 and 3 percent per annum in 1978–84, and an elasticity coefficient of 0.6 since 1970. This appears to show that the excess demand for food has hardly varied since 1980.

[c] No figure was given in Soviet statistics for 1980, therefore this is the median of the 1979 and 1981 figures.

of the physical volume of the main crops and livestock products—the two major exceptions being cotton and eggs. The Soviet leaders did not want, or did not dare, to suppress consumer demand to the corresponding extent and resorted to huge imports of grain (including soya beans and meal), sugar, meat and butter. Obviously, they expected agricultural output soon to regain or even exceed its previous growth rates, so that imports of such a volume would remain only a temporary stopgap measure. This did not come true, although grain shipments to the USSR declined in 1982 and 1983 (see Table 9.2).

The imported grain was essentially for animal feed, even though much of it consisted of hard wheat, which substituted for a portion of domestic low-quality wheat, which thus could be used for feed. It was due to these imports that the overall availability and consumption of concentrate (basically grain) feed could be kept on practically an equal level during 1980–4, while, with a

Table 9.2 *Feed Availability and Livestock Production, 1965–1984*

Year	Grain Availability (in million tons) output 'bunker weight'	balance of import/ export	Feed Consumption (million ton oats units)[a]	Of Which Concentrate[a] (million tons)	(% of total consumption)	Cattle Unit Numbers (annual average)[b]	Animal Output (in million rubles, prices of 1973)	Meat Output (million tons slaughter weight)
1965	121.1	+ 0.8	278.5	65.3	23.4	123.8	—	10.0
1969–71	176.8	+ 5.5	344.3[c]	109.65	31.8	139.4	—	13.9
1974–6	186.6	−12.7	373.5	121.4	32.5	145.9	62.5[d]	14.3
1977–9	204.1	−17.1	405.3	145.2	35.8	151.4	68.4	15.2
1980	189.1	−28.9	398.1	143.9	36.1	154.9	67.4	15.7
1981	158.2	−41.0	397.5	141.2	35.5	155.9	67.5	15.2
1982	186.8	−37.9	402.6	141.3	35.1	157.3	69.2	15.4
1983	192.2	−29.9	424.0	142.8	33.6	160.6	73.6	16.4
1984	172.6	−41.1	431.1	143.5	33.3	162.7	74.6	17.0

[a] An oats unit roughly equals 0.85 barley units (without feed additives), and Soviet concentrate feed is assumed to contain about 85 percent grain matter (including bran, etc.).

[b] Soviet cattle unit numbers, derived from feed consumption figures, total and per cattle unit.

[c] Two-year average 1970–1.

[d] In 1976 only.

Sources: Grain cereals (SITC 041 through 045.2 and 045.9, 046) imports and exports from FAO, *Trade Yearbook*, various volumes; all other data from *Narodnoe Khozyaistvo SSSR*, various volumes. The three-year averages and percentages of concentrate feed are derived from the absolute data in *Narodnoe khozyaistvo*; animal output before 1970 was omitted because of a different price basis, while the later ruble figures are in comparable prices.

slowly improving feed conversion ratio, livestock production began to expand again after the setback of 1980 and 1981 (Table 9.2).

Will and can a satisfactory growth rate of global output be resumed? For an answer one has to look at the reasons why Soviet agriculture has gone through a six-year period of near-stagnation, thus deviating from the trend, which had been possible under the generally known long-term conditions of the Soviet agrarian system. After all, the system impeded growth but did not prevent it. Unfavorable weather in recent years surely played a certain role, but neither the Soviet leaders in their public statements, nor most Western observers consider weather to be the main cause for the stagnation after 1978–9.

The indisputable disadvantages of climate and soil in large parts of the USSR explain its agriculture's low productivity to a considerable extent. However, they are a constant factor and therefore cannot be held responsible for the recent curbing of the trend. Although a change of climate to the worse cannot be excluded, it seems impossible to make a convincing statement to that effect before many more years have passed. It has to be mentioned, however, that the expansions of agricultural production into marginal areas (for example, the Virgin Lands Campaign of the 1950s and, quite recently, the setting up of supply farms in East Siberia for the Baikal–Amur railway) has a negative impact on overall statistical data for yields. (The question of man-made soil depletion and erosion will be dealt with below.)

In the author's opinion the following factors depress Soviet agricultural productivity, in general, and also have influenced the most recent trends.

2 Weaknesses of the Soviet Economy

(a) Shortcomings of the Overall Administrative and Economic Environment

The rigidities and unwieldiness of the centralistic Soviet planning and management system in the economy at large, as well as specifically in agriculture, have been dealt with in the relevant literature so extensively[2] that a few sketchy strokes will suffice here. On principle, farms are not told—as they were in Stalin's time—what to produce but only what to sell to the state; even the sales plans are to be elaborated with the farms themselves participating, on the basis of national and derived territorial 'control figures.' In practice, however, those plans are still very much imposed from above. Equally, the investment and current input buying of farms very much depends on what is assigned to them, with only limited regard to local conditions and without due coordination among the administrations of the branches that produce and distribute these inputs. In addition to central planning and directives, the regional and local authorities impose management and reporting demands on the farms. In spite of numerous decrees to the contrary, most state and Party functionaries, until very recently, have told the farms what to sow, how many animals to raise, where to sell their produce, etc., and have sent down emissaries for controlling the fulfillment of such orders. The specialized Soviet press is replete with the corresponding complaints about extremely restricted possibilities for decision-making on the farm level.[3] As a consequence, most farm managers are not accustomed to apply their own judgement on how to allocate resources and increase output in a way best suited to their farms' conditions. Moreover, the industrially produced inputs for agriculture are inadequate in quantity, quality, assortment and timing of delivery.

For these shortcomings, the Soviet economic and administrative system, at large, is responsible rather than agriculture. The fact, as such, is not new, but to the degree that the technological level of food production is being raised, the shortcomings on the inputs side make themselves felt increasingly.

The same is true for inputs into the forward and backward linkages of agriculture and also for the socio-economic infrastructure on the countryside, which is not up to the requirements of a modern market-oriented and large-scale agriculture. Within the overall 'agro-industrial complex' (which is equivalent to the Western term: food and agriculture sector) 54.4 percent of total final output in 1984 was produced in the forward and backward linkages. Although badly underdeveloped, they received only 27 percent of total investment in the 'complex' and even less (24 percent) on the 1981–4 average.[4]

Things look even poorer for the infrastructural investment within agriculture, in the stricter meaning of the word. Here the economy, at large, and the state administration, whether national or local, provide little help. Soviet collective farms (and, in part, also state farms) have to finance and carry out on their own:

- building and maintenance of most local roads (or else they often have to pay for using them);
- building and maintenance of schools and village retail stores (but not paying their employees);
- building and running of canteens;
- building of farm-owned housing for those among their workers and managers who do not live in their own houses; etc.

Expenses for such 'nonproductive' investment, although a heavy burden on farms, have been very small per head of the agricultural population: during almost a quarter century the annual average was just under 20 rubles, or 60–65 per household, with a rising trend, it is true, but still amounting to only 147 rubles per year during 1981–4.[5]

(b) Soil Erosion and Depletion

It has long been known, and indeed been dealt with in the specialized Soviet press, that processes of heavy wind, as well as water erosion, plague vast areas of agricultural land in the USSR; they date back to tsarist times but were intensified under Soviet-type, large-scale farming. They enhance the low level of productivity of the land and thereby indirectly also that of animals, but have not intensified markedly during the most recent years.

However, a related but different process seems to have recently made itself felt more than before—that of soil degradation and depletion as a consequence of the application of heavy machinery (combined with deep ploughing on dry land), of ecologically questionable crop rotation (often imposed from 'above'), and of insufficient application of organic and/or green manure (due to concentration of livestock herds, lack of labor and machinery for loading, transporting and spreading). The result is often soil compaction with reduced water and air permeability and decline of micro-life. Although such phenomena are not unknown in Western capital-intensive crop farming either, Soviet centralistic schematism contributed to their aggravation: 'The use of such a technique in a manner unjustified by regional systems of tillage, the saturation of farms with it and the application of it without checking the results cause great losses and seriously reduce fertility by strong soil compaction.'[6] Under such conditions, growing quantities of fertilizer and plant-protection chemicals might just suffice to maintain the achieved yields instead of raising them. This would, of course, not apply to all Soviet regions equally.

The great irrigation construction in the southern parts of the European and Asian Soviet territory presents similar problems. Executed frequently without adequate preparation and care, particularly in the drainage part of the irrigation system, these works often suffer from setbacks caused by salinization and also water-logging of the soil after an initial period of seeming production success.

(c) Specifics of Animal Production

With increasing concentration of livestock herds, a few ingrained deficiencies of animal farming in the USSR exerted growing impact in recent years, such as, fluctuations in feed availability (by years and seasons), long haulage of feed as well as of produce, and shortcomings of capital inputs (buildings, machinery). At the same time, the necessarily rising degree of mechanization of work has put specially high demands on regular feed supplies of constant quality, on sanitation, management, labor organization and skill, not to mention storage, marketing and processing facilities. It is worldwide experience that the livestock sector lends itself to mechanization less easily than does crop production. In Soviet animal farming, the low quality of the supplied machinery and frequent breaks in electricity supply are an ever-recurrent subject in the specialized Soviet press and add to the low efficiency of the machinery.

Under the given circumstances, the premature introduction of a highly mechanized, large-scale organization—not necesarily large-scale organization in itself—has done more harm in this sector than in most of Soviet crop farming. And yet it is in animal production that, during the 1970s, huge 'agro-industrial complexes' were propagated most, and average unit sizes increased greatly.

The process caused, and was parallelled by, an increase of the share of concentrate mixed feed (about 85 percent of which is estimated to consist of grain, including bran and other grain by-products) during the 1970s (see Table 9.2). In itself, feeding concentrates can be very efficient with high-breed animals, as is shown in the West where they are given more of such products than their Soviet counterparts, and also yield more produce. Yet in the USSR the concentrates lack protein additives and are overexpended on animals of low productivity and long fattening periods. At least for cattle—which account for more than two-thirds of total Soviet livestock (re-calculated in cattle units)—the relative smallness of the share of roughages and pasture feed also impaired the protein balance and increased the feed consumption per output unit.

(d) Slowing Growth Rates of Investment in the Food Economy

Agriculture's share in total gross investment in the Soviet economy began to increase, after an interruption in 1959–61, still under Khrushchev and not only in 1965, as a Brezhnev myth tended to present the case. By the end of the 1970s, the share of agriculture (in a strict meaning of the term, as well as in that of a more comprehensive food sector) reached a maximum. However, much of that investment seemed to be misdirected. As it was spelled out at the October 1984 plenary session of the Central Committee, one-sixth of total investment for agriculture since 1965 has gone into land improvement of low quality and returns (cf. section (b) on soil erosion, above). Total output in the non-black-earth zone has practically stagnated since 1974,[7] when the development works there began and were assigned almost one-fifth of Soviet agriculture's total investment. A great, though not quantifiable, share of agricultural investment went to the 'agro-industrial complexes' (that is, individual enterprises so named, not the sector as a whole), where statistics show the capital-output ratio to be low.[8]

The high, 64.11 percent (1984) share of buildings and comparable stationary assets in total fixed assets of socialized agriculture is significant, and contrasts with only 16.7 percent for machinery and their implements.[9] Overall, one gets the impression that the ordinary farms, which produce the bulk of Soviet agricultural output, received much less than the totals seem to imply.

Another questionable outcome of the investment policy is the fact that by 1984 the 'productive' assets (excluding livestock herds) achieved a value index (in 'comparable' prices of 1973) of 334 (if 1970 is taken at 100), whereas including material turnover capital (*material'nye oborotnye fondy*) that growth was much slower, reaching only an index of 284.[10] Thus the share of the latter has obviously declined.

It is planned for the current decade to keep the share of the macroeconomic 'agro-industrial complex' in the total investment of the Soviet economy at the high level achieved by the end of the 1970s, but to let that of agriculture (in the strict meaning of the word) decline slightly. In absolute terms, however, even the constant share of the early 1980s implied decreasing growth rates because in the economy, at large, they have been slowing. Moreover, with the greater amount of capital fixed in agriculture, replacements tend to take a growing share of gross investment, which the statistics do not disclose.[11]

It has to be added that with rapidly rising wages in agriculture and an only moderate outflow of labour, capital does not sufficiently substitute for labor and the latter's cost still takes an excessive share of the farms' financial means instead of making these available for investment.

(e) Greater Demands on Management and Labor at a Higher Technological Level

The risk of production shortfalls in Soviet agriculture increases as a consequence of the combined effects of the investment slowdown, of the raised technological level of farming and, in contrast, of the rigid, quantity-oriented, bureaucratic planning and administration in and above the farm management. Although a really high technological level throughout the sector is not achieved yet, it is being aimed at and in parts approached. This rise is characterized by more application of chemicals, a need for high-quality seeds (of which Soviet farms permanently are short),[12] increasing specialization by farms and by regions, expanding irrigation, growing numbers of machines (not only tractors), and a shortage of personnel trained for handling and maintaining such technical inputs. The demands on managers' and workers' skill and on their attitude toward their occupation are greatly raised by all this.

It is true that the process has been accompanied by the numerical growth of skilled labor and specialized managers. However, the number of agricultural laborers of no or low technical skills is still greater than one should expect of Soviet-type farms, which are not only extremely large-scale but, in addition, have to perform more nonagricultural production and service activities on their own than comparable Western farms. As to the managers, a reduction of the high degree of fluctuation among them would be a precondition for

Table 9.3 *Mechanization of Agricultural Work on Public Farms, 1970–1982*
(Percentage of Machinery Work in Total Work of the Indicated Kind)

Year	Ricking/ Stacking of Hay	Combine Harvesting/ Mechanical Loading of Sugar Beet	Potatoes	Milking of Cows	Feeding of Cattle/Pigs/ Poultry	Stable Cleaning of Cattle/Pigs/ Poultry
1970	69/70	78/74	24/24	56	55/71/90	82/89/90
1975	71/79	86/86	42/46	83	29/60/73	56/80/78
1980	77/86	88/91	36/55	90	45/66/85	75/86/86
1982	85/87	95/94	45/61	92	50/68/88	79/88/88
1984	80/87	94/94	45/63	93	55/71/90	82/89/90

Source: Narodnoe khozyaistvo SSSR v 1984 g., p. 123.

Note: These official figures probably reflect the machinery and installations potential of mechanized work, not its actual performance; because of changes of categories comparable data for years before 1970 are not available.

making their numbers and professional education come to bear on the farms.

Some important field work is now said to be fully mechanized, such as, ploughing, drilling of grain, cotton and sugar beet, harvesting of grain and silage. But much manual work is still used in cotton and flax harvesting, on potatoes, feed roots, vegetables, fruit and wine (cf. Table 9.3). In addition, manual labor is still widely employed in animal farming, including haymaking, and much of such farming is located in areas with an above-average rural-urban outflow of population and overaged remaining labor. Low quality of machinery, together with its inefficient use, cause overmanning and explain most of the exorbitant labor inputs per unit of output in the livestock sector, which are greater than in the rest of Soviet agriculture. In large-scale fattening—with herds of predominantly 1,000–3,000 heads of cattle and 300–500 pigs per *kolkhoz* (even greater numbers on intrafarm enterprises)— 59 hours of directly attributed labor are spent on producing one centner (100 kg) of gain in weight of cattle, and 36 hours for pigs. For one centner of milk, direct labor expenditure amounts to 9 hours.[13] These figures do not include overhead and other indirect labor inputs.

Outflow of labor, particularly cf the skilled and young, is known in most agrarian systems of the world, but has a greater impact under conditions of extremely large-scale farming. The ratio of those trained for agricultural occupations of technical or managerial functions to the annual increments of their on-farm numbers is very high (see Table 9.4), obviously because much of such newly skilled labor does not go to the farms or soon leaves them again. It reveals the particularly low attractiveness of work on Soviet-type, large-scale farms.

The discrepancies between capital intensity and labor skill and effort

Table 9.4   *Training and Staff of Cadres in Socialized Agriculture, 1960–1984*
(thousands)

Year	Staff Working on Public Farms Specialists with professional or university-level training for agricultural occupations (as of mid-November)	'Mechanizers' (machine operators, including truck drivers, as of 1 April of following year)	Graduates or Technical School Leavers Trained for Agriculture During Time Period or (for 1984) Preceding Year Professional or university-level training for agricultural occupations[a]	Special schools or courses for 'mechanizers'
1960	294 (1 Dec.)	2,589		
1961–70	+ 434 (43 p.a.)	+ 854 (85 p.a.)	1,203 (120 p.a.)	7,621 (762 p.a.)
1970	728	3,503		
1971–5	+ 293 (59 p.a.)	+ 631 (126 p.a.)	959 (192 p.a.)	4,928 (986 p.a.)
1975	1,021	4,074		
1976–80	+ 262 (52 p.a.)	+ 420 (84 p.a.)	1,078 (216 p.a.)	6,692 (1,338 p.a.)
1980	1,283	4,494		
1981–3	+ 188 (63 p.a.)	+ 98 (33 p.a.)	691 (230 p.a.)	4,407 (1,469 p.a.)
1983	1,471	4,592		
1984		4,608 + 16	226	1,451

Sources: Sel'skoe khozyaistvo SSSR (Moscow, 1971), pp., 464–5; *Narodnoe khozyaistvo SSSR v 1962 g.*, pp. 476, 570–1; *Narodnoe khozyaistvo SSSR v 1964 g.*, pp. 570, 687–8; *Narodnoe khozyaistvo SSSR v 1975 g.*, pp. 559, 685–6; *Narodnoe khozyaistvo SSSR v 1976 g.*, pp. 646–7; *Narodnoe khozyaistvo SSSR v 1980 g.*, pp. 289, 470–1; *Narodnoe khozyaistvo SSSR v 1982 g.*, p. 289; *Narodnoe khozyaistvo SSSR v 1983 g.*, p. 306; and *Narodnoe khozyaistvo SSSR v 1984 g.*, pp. 333, 422, 527–8.

[a] At university level including forestry.

become all the more serious when a pre-industrial level of land productivity is surpassed. In Soviet crop farming such a level has been achieved, on the whole (the vast semi-arid areas of dry-farming are a case in point); the animal sector is only approaching it. Both urgently need an efficiency level corresponding to a more or less industrialized urban society because of the demand pressure the latter exerts on agriculture.

(f) Organization and Remuneration of Labor

The bureaucratic administration of farming imposed by an industry-oriented communist government; the low general esteem for farm work; and the gross rural-urban disparity of the socio-cultural, retail trade and communications infrastructure (which exceeds the disparity in nonsocialist industralized countries) make work in Soviet agriculture unattractive in spite of a level of wages only moderately lower than those in urban areas. Moreover, the organization of the oversized—at least in relation to their low capital-intensity—farms, combined with almost complete job security, discourages individual initiative. Not surprisingly, managers as well as the majority of workers apply little effort or attention and are little interested in the results of their activities.

In opposition to a capitalist 'exploitative' organization, which remunerates work individually, it has been the intent of Soviet agrarian policies to relate work done to the performance of a collective in terms of final product. Yet, in large-scale agriculture this is particularly difficult to achieve, as the results of a production cycle depend on variegated work processes during the whole year (many of which are performed by other workers), and also on external factors. Only to a small degree does the final result depend on the effort of the group who is remunerated. The greater the number of those employed on the huge socialized farm, the less such a relationship is felt. Therefore, it was already the intent in Stalin's time to make smaller collectives within the farms (brigades or links) the locus of measurement of performance and remuneration.

Up to the mid-1960s remuneration of labor on most Soviet farms was so low in absolute amount that incentives connecting the productive performance of individuals or groups with work done had little meaning for those concerned, notwithstanding other merits or demerits of the incentive system, as such. At a very low level, efforts are directed at other sources of income, whether legal or illegal, social (work in formal employment outside the *kolkhoz*: *otkhodnichestvo*) or private.

In 1961–2 a wage reform was introduced on state farms under the name of a 'piecework-and-premium' (*akkordno-premial'naya*) system and subsequently 'recommended' for the *kolkhozy*.[14] Its purpose was to connect remuneration closely with the achieved final output of labor subunits within the large farms. Not accidentally, the 'normless link' and 'contract brigade' came up at that time and remained under discussion for a number of years. It was a form of remuneration as well as of organization of labor and fitted in with the reformed wage system. In combination with 'internal self-accounting' (*vnutrenniy khozraschet*), as was advocated soon after, it was a logical corollary of the wage reform and was implemented for longer or shorter periods on many farms or farm sections. Yet it did not gain general approval at the time[15] whereas the 'piecework-and-premium' system has been basically valid up to the present.

There remained two essential improvements, which emerged by the end of the 1960s as a continuation of the wage reform: the general rise in the agricultural wage level and the implementation of the old aim of a guaranteed minimum remuneration on the *kolkhozy*, paralleled by a stronger premium element in state farm wages. The latter had always—at least in principle—been independent of a farm's production achievements.[16] But the effect of these changes leveled off. Only recently, beginning in 1982, were the 'normless link' and 'contract brigade' resurrected in nonnegligible numbers. (Their possible effects will be discussed below.)

3   Recent Developments in the Soviet Economy

In view of the factors and weaknesses outlined so far, the question arises: what has changed very recently, or is changing, and may result in present or future improvement of productive performance?

(a) *In the Administrative and Economic Environment*

(i) An old objective of Soviet economic administration is the combination of central macroeconomic management and technically modern, efficient microeconomic initiative on the local level. Combined with the Marxist idea of the 'industrialization' of agriculture, it was put forward in the Party Program of 1961 in the proclaimed form of 'agro-industrial associations,' but remained a dead letter during the 1960s. Beginning around 1970, the integration of agriculture with its forward and backward linkages in the form of 'agro-industrial complexes' was propagated and a number of such complexes were established. While similar processes went on more or less intensively in all East European countries at that time, the USSR differed from most of them in that it did not reorganize the central and local administration into an integrated national system of management system for the whole food sector. Integration, often through amalgamating farms, was restricted to the enterprise level.

The most recent effort at integration aims more at the cooperation of existing farms and other food-sector enterprises along territorial-administrative lines. Gorbachev identified himself with that concept even before he became First Party Secretary. The administrative restructuring started experimentally in 1974 on the lowest—the county—level, through the Rayon Agro-Industrial Associations (in Russian: RAPO). During 1978–81 numerous decrees and instructions were issued on the forming of RAPOs throughout the country. By 1982, the process was basically completed, by mid-1983 the system comprised 3,105 RAPOs, consisting of 52,020 farms and 47,712 other enterprises in the forward and backward linkages of agriculture, including forestry.[17]

The final step was the formation of a central State Committee of the Agro-Industry of the USSR (Gosagroprom) in November 1985. Six related ministries, one state committee, those parts of the Ministry of Light Industry which are forward linkages of agriculture, and the state procurement organization were incorporated into it and thereby ceased to be top agencies on their own. Only the Ministry for Grain Products remained outside and was reorganized. The new super-agency with its corollaries on union republic and provincial levels is meant to provide an integrated management of the whole Soviet food economy, freed from the competing and mutually interfering competences of the various former ministries. At the same time, the administrative and directive functions of the former ministries and top agencies are to be reduced and their staff diminished by a full 47 percent at the all-Union level.

Whether the expected economic effect, as distinct from that of merely a bureaucratic reshuffling, will be attained, is an open question. It can be answered only after several years of actual implementation, that is, not in the short term. For the time being, skepticism is in order. If the envisaged diminution of staff can really be achieved, this will be an important symptom of true success.

(ii) The efficiency of the Soviet economy, as a whole, might improve. This, however, needs special analysis beyond the scope of the present chapter. More particularly, the decrees of 23 June and 7 July 1983[18] sought to tie in the profit interest of the farm service organizations of the state more closely with that of the farms themselves by making their success indicators dependent on the latters' performance. At any rate, the positive impact of such improvements is impossible to assess in quantitative terms, as it also depends on allocation policies outside the food sector. On past experience, the effects are not likely to exceed the increase of demands imposed on agriculture by the greater sophistication of inputs and linkages. Moreover, they would make themselves felt only over a longer term.

A similar delay of a possible effect may be assumed for infrastructural improvements, although investment in these fields might continue growing not only in absolute terms but also as a percentage of total investment in agriculture.

(b) The Soil

Soil erosion is not likely to have accelerated during the last one or two decades, after farming in the regions of the former Virgin Lands was more or less consolidated during the 1960s. Things look different for other forms of soil degradation, although it is too early to make a firm or even quantifying statement on that account. Mainly in the drier areas, where most of the fertile black earth is located, the consequences of large-size machinery application seem to have come to bear during the last few years more than before, after an incubation period of twenty years or so. The average weight of Soviet agricultural machines has doubled since the late 1960s,[19] and many kinds of machinery became available to farms in great numbers only during the 1960s. The soil degradation may have similarly accelerated with the great expansion of the irrigated areas during the past twenty years, where hasty, 'grandiose' accomplishments seem to have enhanced problems long known.

The expansion of fallowing and the resulting decrease in the area sown to grain, as it has gone on since the mid-1970s, will be beneficial to the soil in many, but not all, places and will help to raise the yields per hectare and to reduce the costs of grain production. But it is not a way to increase the absolute volume of grain output.

(c) Animal Production

In the livestock sector, procurement prices were raised, beginning in 1983, by one-third for meat and one-quarter for milk. As to other policy changes, it is too early to decide whether they are more than accidental and will continue. At any rate, a lower-key in concentration of livestock in 'agro-industrial complexes' can be sensed in the Soviet media and authoritative statements since the beginning of the 1980s. Another change may be the reversal of the expansion of the share of grain in feed, in spite of a slightly increasing share of pigs in total herds, back to a composition which is more adequate at the Soviet level of animal productivity. Global livestock production of 1984 exceeded that of 1981 by 10.6 percent (value in 1973 prices), whereas the annual average number of cattle units had risen by only 4.4 percent, total feed consumption by 8.5 (but consumption of concentrate feed by only 1.6) percent (see Table 9.2). In other words, the overall composition of feed and the feed conversion ratio improved as output per animal and even per feed unit increased and more nongrain feed was available per animal. This seems to herald continuing improvement. Unmistakable is the steady increase of synthetic protein additives for concentrates and perhaps also for silage feed. Their output was 261,000 tons (physical weight) in 1970, and 1,420,000 tons in 1984.[20]

(d) Investment

The rising demands on the Soviet food economy make quantitative output increase the first priority. A change to a low cost/low yield farming system is precluded, although under the given conditions that would hold the promise of fewer losses and/or higher profits and also smaller fluctuations in yields. This perpetuates the tendency of heavily rising capital requirements.

The published data on investment in most recent and in coming years do not reveal a growth comparable to that of the 1970s. Yet its composition has been changing, a growing share of 'production' investment is spent for machinery and comparable implements;[21] in addition, more fertilizer (that is, circulating capital) is being supplied after a near stagnation in 1979–81. An important change has become discernible in the official emphasis on investing more in the linkages of agriculture and in rural infrastructure. Resulting positive effects may become sizable only over the longer run, as the overall growth of planned investment remains slow, and much of it will be assigned to ongoing projects, which do not represent a new element. Moreover, the outlined changes depend not just on agriculture or the 'agro-industrial complex' but also on the overall development of the Soviet economy.

(e) Management and Labor

With continuing modernization, intensification and specialization of agricultural production, the demands on technological sophistication, on management and work performance are bound to rise, particularly in view of the outflow of labor. Although the numerical development of the trained personnel has remained, and is likely to remain, disappointing (see Table 9.4), its share among the farm labor will continue to increase, and some qualitative improvement of its professional education and corresponding skill is likely. Its age-sex composition may also improve, as the historically and demographically conditioned excess of old and female workforce has somewhat diminished by now. As far as labor is concerned, the demands of modernization might be met at least in part, while the material-technical aspects look less promising because of the slowed investment growth in agriculture in the strict meaning of the word (see above). The progress in mechanizing the labor-intensive kinds of work on public farms—not to speak of private plots—has not accelerated in recent years (see Table 9.3); with potato harvesting and cattle feeding it is still rather low (and very likely also with cotton harvesting and vegetable and fruit growing, for which statistics are not available).

The improvement of farm management basically depends on the changes at the administrative level above the farms, and on the organization and remuneration of labor within them, and therefore, this is dealt with under sections (a) and (f).

(f) Organization and Remuneration of Labor

The intention to make wages in agriculture directly dependent (above a certain minimum level) on quantity and quality of output, and to make this relationship perceptible to each worker, is the gist of the 'normless links' and 'contract brigades,' which have been insistently propagated since 1982 and still more during 1983–4. In essence, there is nothing new about them in comparison with the abortive attempts of the 1960s, except that this time they are approved in the highest quarters and unanimously in the press. As on the earlier occasion, the procurement value of output minus the cost of inputs (including an estimate of labor, based on work norms, to be expended), both calculated in advance and, on this basis, contracted between the small group and the socialist farm, is then recalculated at the end of the production cycle. This is done on the basis of the actual peformance, and a price is paid according to the contract for distribution in amounts decided by the link or brigade among its members according to the quantity and quality of work each has contributed. Such an arrangement makes sense, provided that:

(i) The contract is concluded on equal bargaining terms and neither its conclusion enforced, nor its execution infringed upon by the stronger partner.

(ii) The group has a choice of the inputs it considers adequate.

(iii) The group is small enough for mutual social control (preventing free riders from benefitting from the work of others) and is a permanent one, at least for the mid-term.

(iv) The group enjoys genuine autonomy in its decisions on time, kind and execution of work, etc.

It is fulfillment of these conditions which will decide the success or failure of the system in terms of labor productivity and cost. At last up to 1984 the parameters of Soviet farming, including the intragroup command system and social differences, were such that one could hardly imagine these conditions would be met. Too much in practice was set from above and/or between unequal partners, too much fixed by the overall procurement plan, the prices, the planned and actual supply of inputs, and so on. Even if the improvements of individual links and brigades achieved and reported during 1982–4 were genuine, they applied only to a minority of the agricultural workforce—5 percent in 1982, and 19 percent by 1984.[22] Nor were the overall achievements of Soviet agriculture on the 1983–4 average particularly convincing.

In fact, the underlying principles of labor remuneration in the 'contract brigade' and 'normless link' are the same as those of Stalin's *kolkhoz* and its labor unit. As in the old *kolkhoz* it is the group's remuneration, which depends on the production performance. In practice, though not in theory, the share of each member in the overall receipts of the group continues to be calculated on the basis of work norms and the worker's qualification. (The term 'normless'—*beznaryadnoe*—is mentioned much less than 'contract'—*podryadnoe*.) Significantly, the 'piecework-and-premium' system of labor remuneration (see above) is considered valid also for, and within, the 'contract brigades' and 'normless links.'

One thing is different, however: with technical modernization and decreasing labor numbers in agriculture, the numbers of workers in those farm subunits have become smaller. Soviet statistics for 1982 showed them, on the average, to comprise 27 members per brigade and 9 per link,[23] to which an unknown number of seasonal workers, perhaps 20–30 percent, have to be added. All the same, such a brigade is still too big to meet the above condition under (iii), while the smaller unit—the link—has very little autonomy in its relationship with the brigade, to which it belongs, as many Soviet press reports show. Yet those sizes have slowly been decreasing: By 1984 the average brigade had 24 full members, and the average link 6. No less important is the fact that the share of workers organized in links under 'contract' as compared with those in brigades has been increasing, and in

Table 9.5   *Private Subsidiary Production, USSR Totals, 1965–84*

Year	Index (1970 = 100)	Aggregate Global Output % share in overall production[b]	Potatoes	Other Vegetables	Meat	Milk	Eggs (billion)
1965	100	32.5	56	7.2	4.0	28.3	19.5
1970	111	30	63	8.1	4.3	29.9	21.6
1976–7 average	109	25 (1976–7)	—	—	—	—	—
1978	110	25	52.5	8.1	4.65	27.4	22.6
1980	107	26	43.0	9.0	4.7	27.0	21.7
1982	114	26	49.0	9.6	4.6	27.3	22.4
1984	118	25	50.0	9.5	4.8	28.4	22.2

Physical Volume of Products (million tons)[a]

Sources: Index 1975–7 recalculated from the individual years' indices in *Narodnoe khozyaistvo SSSR v 1979 g.*, p. 223. Physical volumes derived from the data in *Narodnoe khozyaistvo SSSR v 1980 g.*, p. 202, and *Narodnoe khozyaistvo SSSR v 1984 g.*, pp. 227, 252–3, 284–5.

[a] Derived from overall output and the percentage residuals in the Soviet statistics.

[b] Estimates based on the official growth indices and various Soviet publications as indicated in detail in 'The private agricultural sector in the 1980s', *Radio Liberty Research*, 251/85, p. 7.

1984 made up 22 percent of both together, whereas in 1982 that percentage was only 17. Still, the 'family link' (*semeynoe zveno*), although increasingly encouraged after 1984, was mentioned mainly for special production conditions.

(g) Growth Contribution of the Private Sector?

The above text does not refer to the roughly 25 percent of Soviet agriculture's gross output, which is produced by the private subsidiary mini-farming and gardening. Such production is pursued not only by the great majority of *kolkhoz* members, by state farm workers and other segments of the rural population, but also by a sizable minority of urban dwellers.[24] In its quantitative development—as far as it is revealed in Soviet statistics, which are only informed estimates in large part—this sector regained its overall output value of the 1971–5 average as late as 1982, and exceeded it by only 5 percent in 1983–4.[25] As a percentage share its production declined against the early 1970s (cf. Table 9.5).

In the past, Soviet leaders at alternating intervals restricted the private sector or appealed to it as a supplementary supplier of food for the nation. The most recent, and still valid, such appeal was manifested not only in speeches but also in two decrees of 14 September 1977 and of 8 January 1981; they need not specifically be dealt with here.[26] The essence of the decrees, as well as of subsequent policy statements and press coverage, consists in easing the legal restrictions on the sizes of private plots and animal holdings and even in requesting public farms, rural and urban communes, and other administration bodies to support such production, mainly by supplying feed. That such support so far has remained insufficient in practice is a different question.

On the other hand, great emphasis is put on keeping the expected additional produce away from the so-called *kolkhoz* markets and other free-selling outlets. Some of the lifting of legal limits on private plots and animal holdings is explicitly conditional on contracted sales to the public sector. The officially desired marketing alternative consists of two main outlets: the state procurement and semi-state consumer cooperatives network, and the public farms. The latter are now permitted and encouraged to have the produce they buy from farm members accounted toward fulfillment of their procurement plan. Such intrafarm transfers have been possible previously, but either illegally or under certain restrictive conditions. As a rule, the prices paid in these transactions are lower than those of the free market.

For the most part, the intrafarm purchases concern meat and milk, and the quantities involved formally are not counted as private production and therefore would, if they were known, have to be added to the data of Table 9.5. So far, they have been indicated only for Latvia and Lithuania in the recent statistical annuals of these two small union republics.[27] Equally little is known about the purchases by consumer cooperatives, where potatoes, other vegetables and fruit are important. As to the intrafarm transactions, the farm managers are in a position to offer nonmonetary inducements not only in the form of feed supplies but also of grazing and haymaking rights, low-priced piglets and other young animals, and also of nonfood goods in short supply, such as, building materials, heating fuel, transport service, etc. The real volume and the prices actually paid are unlikely to be known to the authorities in precise terms and, to that extent, any published data slightly understate the performance of the private sector in addition to the reservation stated above.

A continuation of the modest growth trend of recent years in the private sector of Soviet food production will largely depend on the attractiveness of the conditions the public farms and the consumer cooperatives are able to offer. However, even a more rapid growth of private production of, say, 4 percent per year would raise overall Soviet food supplies by only 1 percent because it is the public sector which accounts for three-quarters of the total. The contribution that can actually be expected from the private sector is more one of not continuing its decline of 1975–81, and thereby of not disrupting the food supply of the nonmetropolitan areas.

4 Growth Prospects and the Aspect of Future Grain Imports

Having reviewed the weaknesses of Soviet agriculture and their recent development, we arrive at the following conclusions.
(i) Some improvements seem to be in progress

● with the overall administrative and economic environment;
● with the composition of investment;
● with the rise in procurement prices and the improvement of the feed conversion ratio;
● with the composition, organization and remuneration of the labor force;
● with a modest growth contribution by the private sector.

(ii) Other factors may rather put more strain on agriculture, such as:

● the soil deterioration in vast areas;
● the labor situation in animal farming;
● the declining quantitative growth of investment in agriculture in the narrower meaning of the word;
● the generally greater demands on farm management.

With not unusually unfavorable weather, the positive impulses are likely to predominate and to effect modest growth, probably slower than that of the mid-1970s and exceeding the annual rise in population numbers by about 1 percent. At any rate, stagnation at the present level is unlikely to continue. It has to be remembered, after all, that in the past some progress was made over the longer term in spite of the weaknesses reviewed above. On the other hand, it may be assumed that in the absence of new or greatly augmented production factors and of genuine reform of the overall economic setup, marginal returns to greater resource use and the growth rate will continue declining. This is not to say that organizational changes will have no effect at all, simply that their effect will not be up to what is needed.

Whatever growth will be achieved during the current decade, it will fall short of what is needed to meet the demand for food. It remains a question for an uncertain future, when this disparity between supply and demand will be overcome, the more so, as it existed already at the beginning of the period considered here. Mitigating factors will be the slowdown of population growth and a decline of the income elasticity of demand for food because of increasing supplies of nonfood consumer commodities. Perhaps a more restrictive income and price policy will also play a role.

Does all this imply that for the foreseeable future Soviet imports of food and feed will continue on a level roughly comparable to that of 1980–4? The answer is, not necessarily. It is true, that stagnation in the Soviet livestock sector and thus, in view of its great weight, also in the whole food economy during 1979–82, would have been yet more severe without those imports. Renouncing them at once might have grave consequences for the Soviet consumer.

We might well ask at this point whether it is necessary, or even at all desirable, for the USSR to regain near-autarky in food supplies, as it was spelled out by Brezhnev at the May 1982 Plenum of the Central Committee in connection with the Food Program. This is not so much a question of economic rationality and resource allocation as one of Moscow's political priorities. Moreover, it is one of the real value of the ruble spent on domestic production *v.* the dollar spent on imports. Obviously, the shortage value of the latter for Moscow is much higher than the official exchange rate indicates.

The Soviet leaders surely want to do without the great expenses of hard currency which have increasingly been caused by the food and feed imports. Very likely, they would also prefer to supply their allies with grain and other foods and get 'hard commodities' in exchange, instead of Poland, Czechoslovakia and East Germany (less so the other countries) spending their hard-currency earnings on food imports from the West.

The USSR disposes of as much arable land per head of the population as the USA. That land is of worse quality, it is true, but then the USA is the world's biggest food exporter and could be self-sufficient on 70–80 percent of its present arable area. Thus, the potential for self-sufficiency clearly exists also for the USSR, at least on balance (that is, with some imports to its outlying regions, such as, the Far East, and exports toward Western or developing countries).

Finally, a leadership like that in Moscow, with its security aspirations, can hardly bear the idea of being dependent for food deliveries on the presumed ideological, political and strategic adversaries.

Soviet self-sufficiency in food will, of course, not be achievable in the short run. Yet a gradual increase of the grain and other feed production, combined with some improvement of the feed composition and, most important, of the utilization coefficient (not to mention the reduction of grain losses, in general), could strongly affect that residual part of grain which at present has to be imported. Those annual 30–40 million metric tons during 1980–4, although representing one-quarter to one-third of present Soviet feed grain consumption, account for only about 10 percent of total feed consumption (including nongrain fodder, both assessed in barley instead of in oats units). If, as is not impossible, total domestic feed production further increases and, simultaneously, conversion ratios improve, net availability of grain could increase by 15 percent or so within the next few years. Half of this might be used for increasing animal production, and half for saving on imports, so that the absolute volume of those imports could be reduced to an inconspicuous 10–15 million tons per year by the beginning of the next decade. Thus, while the prospects for the Soviet food economy permit only very guarded optimism, those for Moscow's foreign trade balance in grain look brighter.

5   Postscript

When the present chapter was being written, Mikhail S. Gorbachev was in the ascendant in the Kremlin, but did not yet hold the supreme office in the Communist part of the USSR. He had, however, been the Party Secretary responsible for agricultural affairs since late summer 1978, and policy in this field from then on tended to follow what has become the official new line during 1985 and at the Twenty-seventh Party Congress.[28] A number of issues and aspects have now emerged more distinctly, but the basic argument of the present chapter did not have to be changed. However, a postscript seems to be necessary, to point out what has become the most salient feature of the new Soviet agrarian policy and before had been discernible in less distinct relief.

From Soviet press comments and reports during the fall–winter, 1985/6 and, in particular, from the speeches—less so from the final resolution—of the Twenty-seventh Party Congress, it emerges that Gorbachev and those collaborating with him are determined to restructure the Soviet economy, and its agricultural sector in the first place, to the maximum degree that is possible without fundamentally changing the system of centralized economic management and planning. However, neither are the limits of such system-preserving restructuring clearly defined as yet, nor has it fully become clear to what degree even moderate changes can be put into Soviet reality against the existing ideological, political, bureaucratic and social inertia. Apart from the administrative change above the farm level of November 1985, which has been dealt with in the present chapter, intrafarm organization and the relative decision-making power (*samostoyatel'nost* = independence, in the exaggerated Soviet wording) of farm managers may become the crucial issue of the ongoing 'radical restructuring' (*radikal'naya perestroyka*) and deserve a few additional lines.

During the Party Congress Gorbachev's explicit mention of the family in socialist labor organization was extremely striking. It was preceded by a remark by V. S. Murakhovskii, the head of the new Gosagroprom, in his interview with *Literaturnaya gazeta* of 22 January 1986, where he advocated production contracts not only with families but even with individual workers—for certain crops and/or under special circumstances, as he added.

In a way, such contract production has existed before. The household raising or keeping of livestock beyond the legal upper limits on the basis of production contracts, as was advocated by the decree of 7 January 1981 and has been experimentally practiced since 1979, in essence is a kind of 'family link' animal husbandry. What is new is its generalizing endorsement from highest quarters.

The drive for 'contract' subunits of farms has acquired a 'new quality' by the emphasis on the small unit. In itself, the family team or individual contract is not a panacea; in both animal and crop farming the conditions granted by the public sector decide on success or failure. Yet, particularly with labor-intensive products of a low degree of mechanization, it may also help, under less than fully satisfactory conditions, to alleviate some of the evils of negligent work which beset Soviet agriculture.

The economic autonomy of the *kolkhoz* or *sovkhoz* is an essential corollary of the autonomy of its subunits; the autonomy of the former is conditional on the autonomy of the latter, and vice versa. The recent emphasis on the 'independence' of the overall farm is, therefore, significant. The farm needs a certain autonomy of management and planning, if it is also to make its subunits function autonomously. Otherwise it has no choice but to redistribute in a mandatory way the tasks assigned from above among its workers' groups. This also refers to the monetary evaluation of those groups' production performance, which basically depends on the absolute as well as the differential prices as fixed from above. The same tolds true for the whole hierarchical chain upward to Gosplan. In addition, the number of workers to be employed is also a given for the *kolkhoz*, which cannot legally dismiss its 'members'; in that respect, the *sovkhoz* has always been in a better position.

These necessities have been recognized by the new leadership in Moscow, although the installed system of the comprehensive 'agro-industrial complex' on all administrative levels holds no special promise of farm autonomy. Elements of both are contained in a comprehensive decree published on 29 March 1986, which, at the same time, demonstrated that the envisaged changes so far were not sweeping.

Notes: Chapter 9

1 These indices are on a Laspeyres, or initial-year price basis. Our discussion is, of course, about the availability of food and not, in any case, about the cost and profitability of its production. However, Soviet statistics are also global (*valovoi*); they contain double-counting of farm-produced intermediate inputs, such as feed, seed and others. The growth rate, though, is little distorted by this double-counting which, moreover, tends rather to decrease than to increase in importance because of more feed, seed, etc., being processed industrially and therefore statistically deducted as inputs from outside.

2 Such assertions are two-a-penny in the Western literature. But they are seldom backed up by actual instances. For an exhaustive description of the actual recent changes in industrial planning cf. Morris Bornstein, in *Soviet Studies* (1985); for statements on the general resistance to change cf. the quotations from Nove and Zaslavskaya in Peter Wiles's contribution to this book, Chapter 10, p. 223.

3 For a recent example, see the complaint by a Lithuanian *kolkhoz* chairman in *Sel'skaya zhizn'*, 6 December 1985, p. 3.

4 Soviet statistics began to use the term of, and give data on, the 'agro-industrial complex' only recently, including a definition. See *Narodnoye khozyaistvo SSSR v 1984 g.* (Moscow, 1985), pp. 213–14 and, for investment, p. 382. The backward linkages are called 'Ist sphere,' the forward linkages 'IIIrd sphere,' and agriculture, including forestry, represents the 'IInd sphere.'

5 For 'non-productive' investment see ibid., p. 383. A figure for the agricultural

population, that is, labor in agriculture, including the private sector, and their dependants, is given ibid., p. 1, fn.; however, it greatly understates the labor inputs in the private sector. See T. Kuznetsova in *Voprosy ekonomiki*, no. 11 (1984), pp. 101–2.

6 V. Gotlover and N. Davidyuk, 'O nekotorykh aspektakh ekonomicheskogo plodorodiya pochvy,' a conference report in *Ekonomika sel'skogo khozyaistva*, no. 11 (1984), p. 61.

7 See *Narodnoye khozyaistvo RSFSR v 1984 g.*, pp. 181–4.

8 A telling, though only partial example, is that of the interfarm enterprises, of which the great majority specialize in animal production. From 1970 to 1984 their fixed production assets (*osnovnye proizvodstvennye fondy*), excluding those with a nonagricultural function, increased 23-fold, their labor numbers 10-fold, but their pork and beef output (gain in weight of animals) and their 'profits' only 5-fold. See *Narodnoye khozyaistvo SSSR v 1984 g.* p. 312.

9 ibid., p. 238.

10 The indices are those of ibid., pp. 60–1.

11 The difference between the figures for fixed assets added in one year and for those written off during the same year is indicated in ibid., p. 62. However, such data have been published only for the most recent years, so that a picture of the development over a certain period does not emerge.

12 The shortcomings of Soviet plant breeding were commented upon by Philip Hanson (on the basis of an article in *Pravda*, 26 and 27 June 1984) in *Radio Liberty Research*, 269/84.

13 *Narodnoye khozyaistvo SSSR v 1984 g.*, pp. 324–5; for herd sizes, ibid., pp. 296–7.

14 I dealt with the subject extensively in my book *Die Bezahlung der Arbeit in der sowjetischen Landwirtschaft* (Berlin: Duncker and Humblot, 1972).

15 On the fate of that vitiated organizational reform, see Alexander Yanov, *The Drama of the Soviet 1960s. A Lost Reform* (Bekeley, Calif.: University of California, Institute of International Studies, 1984).

16 They gained in importance simply by the fact that by 1968 *sovkhozy* and other state-owned farms already employed one-third of the total annual average labor of the public farm sector, and that this share further increased to almost one-half by 1984, see *Narodnoye khozyaistvo SSSR v 1969 g.*, p. 420, and *Narodnoye khozyaistvo SSSR v 1984 g.*, p. 326.

17 *Narodnoye khozyaistvo SSSR v 1983 g.*, pp. 204–5.

18 *Prodovol'stvennaya programma. Normativnye akty* (Moscow, 1984), pp. 100, 116. Cf. the 'methodical recommendations' of December 1983 and the letter from various ministries of 30 December 1983, ibid., pp. 227 and 248.

19 Gotlover and Davidyuk, art. cit. at note 6.

20 *Narodnoye khozyaistvo SSSR v 1984 g.*, p. 174.

21 Disregarding 'non-production', it was 32.7 percent on the 1981–4 average (and 33.9 percent in 1984 alone), as against 29.2 percent on the 1976–80 average. See ibid., p. 384.

22 ibid., pp. 326–7. The 23.0 percent for 1984, as given ibid., fn. on p. 327, seems not to take into account certain categories of workers outside 'collective contract' units.

23 ibid.

24 On the latter, see my 'Private gardeners in the USSR,' *Radio Liberty Research*, 174/85, pp. 1–5.

25 *Narodnoye khozyaistvo SSSR v 1984 g.*, pp. 228–9.

26 On those measures, see K.-E. Wädekin, 'Die sowjetische Landwirtschaft zu Beginn der achtziger Jahre,' *Osteuropa*, no. 5 (1981), pp. 384–91, and idem,

'Wieviel "Hilfe" vom landwirtschaftlichen Privatsektor,' *Sowjetlandwirtschaft 1981*, ed. by G. Jaehne (West Berlin, 1981), pp. 77–84.

27 It has remained an exception that the statistical annuals of Latvia and Lithuania, at least in footnotes, recently indicated the origin and volume of the purchased quantities of meat and milk. See *Narodnoye khozyaistvo Litovskoy SSR v 1983 g.* (Vil'nius, 1984), p. 88, and *Narodnoye khozyaistvo Latviyskoy SSR v 1983 g.* (Riga, 1984), pp. 135 and 139, and *Narodnoye khozyaistvo Latviyskoy SSR v 1984 g.* (Riga, 1985), pp. 154 and 157.

28 For an account and analysis of Gorbachev's agrarian policy since 1978, up to and including the Twenty-seventh Party Congress, see K.-E. Wädekin, 'Landwirtschaft und Nahrungsgütersektor,' *Osteuropa*, no. 8–9 (1986), and also idem, 'Agriculture,' in Martin McCauley (ed.), *The Soviet Union under Gorbachev* (London: Macmillan, 1987), pp. 118–34.

10 *Economic Policies under Andropov and Chernenko (November 1982–February 1984–March 1985)*

PETER WILES

Omnium consensu capax imperii, nisi imperasset
—Tacitus on the emperor Galba

He hath ... exalted them of low degree
—'The Magnificat,' Luke 1:53

1 Introduction

This chapter is on the Kremlinology of economic policies. It was written mainly in late 1984. Most, but not all, of the information coming to light since Chernenko's death is in the appendices. The Gorbachev period is covered as little as humanly possible.

It stands much to the discredit of economists that they have done this work so little and so ill. Partly this is due to their absurd *déformation professionnelle*, of banishing power, ideology, history, custom, tradition, religion, national character and group solidarity from the study of any particular country's economy. A shining exception to this, all his academic life, has been the honorand of this book. But, even he has been weak on the first two items. It is to these specifically Kremlinological matters that I now draw attention. Another reason for our neglect is that Soviet economics has always been a more open subject than Soviet politics. It *has*, after all, also its technical side; mere rationality does count, even in the eyes of the most purblind. And these rational matters are quite freely handled in the Soviet technical press. It needs no Kremlinological wizard to tell us that the Novosibirsk branch of the Academy of Sciences and its journal *EKO*[1] favor 'reform,' that Krasnaya Zvezda wants more money for defence, that Ukrainian statisticians are flat out to prove the exploitation of their country by the USSR, or that the *Tyumen'* obkom secretary opposes exploratory drilling for oil and gas in the Caspian.

But it is Politburo members that make the decisions. Political experts will ask what Kremlinological *model* I am using. Alas for that much-abused

217

word!—but they are right. It is that of monolithic totalitarianism outside certain limits, but within it the fairly free defence of local, professional, commodity-branch of purely clientelistic *interests*; while beneath the Politburo consultants and experts are permitted to speak their minds on the competing *ideas* that fall within the pale of orthodoxy. However, such people must also observe the totalitarian limits.

This is what Jiri Valenta[2] calls the 'bureaucratic politics paradigm,' which he opposes to the 'rational actor paradigm.' The latter, of course, accommodates itself well to Friedrich and Brzezinski's old concept of a monolithic totalitarian state. Indeed while, in fact, such a state *need* not act rationally at all, another kind of state *could* not. The former paradigm implies, as I do, a much less monolithic state, but is compatible with my own concept of 'bounded totalitarianism,' within the prescribed limits of which by no means just bureaucracies—is the army or the Ukraine a 'bureaucracy'?—but interest groups of all sorts jostle and argue, even publicly.

There follow several rather dull and moderate propositions:

(i) Power struggles in the Kremlin, like virtually all other human power struggles, arise partly from individual ambition and personality clashes, and partly from genuine policy differences. The latter can be relied on to generate the former if they are not already there, but we must not be too cynical: the policy differences are genuine, and personal ambition seldom wholly determines a power-seeker's policy stance. Again, just as the clash of persons and cliques leads to shifting coalitions and even to splits and 'floor-crossers,' so also the clash of policies is extremely complicated.

Above all, we must not think of the Politburo as a cowed rubber stamp for the General Secretary. Neither Andropov nor Chernenko were able to run it like that, nor in all probability did they wish to. Moreover, we must eschew the Western parliamentary paradigm of a left and a right and a uni-dimensional spectrum between them (indeed, that is a false account of a Western parliament too).

(ii) Since individuals shift their viewpoint and their allegiances at least a little, and since large movements in policy are impossible in so conservative a regime, small movements to the (?) right in agriculture—like the spread of the normless link, demanded by Gorbachev—are quite compatible with simultaneous small movements to the (?) left in foreign policy—like withdrawing from the Olympic Games, demanded by Gromyko.

(iii) But this does not mean that thinking in clichés and syndromes is not habitual among individuals. I summarize the probable attitudes of senior Politburo members to the issues here discussed in Table 10.1. 2 scores high and 0 scores low; question marks indicate unusual doubt on my part (*all* figures are doubtful). In the last column, high marks indicate Stalinist tendencies and low marks indicate revisionist ones. Column (2) stands out as something different: everyone reacts according to age, except Andropov. Column (4) identifies the modernizing centralizer Romanov, and cuts across

Table 10.1   *Probable Attitudes of Senior Politburo Members*

	(1) Isolationism in trade and culture	*(2)* No early retirement	*(3)* Hawkish foreign and defence policy	*(4)* Modernize planning but keep it central	*(5)* Do not decentralize, or admit more	*(6)* Tighten labour discipline, fight corruption	*(7)* (1+3+5)
Ustinov	?2	2	2	?0	2	?1	6
Gromyko	2	2	2	?1	?2	?2	6
Andropov	1	0	?2	?1	?1	2	4
Romanov	2	?0	2	2	?1	?1	5
Gorbachev	0	0	?0	?0	0	2	0
Chernenko	?1	2	0	?1	1	1	2

the others much as (2) does. It fails to distinguish the stand-pat old men from the decentralizers, *one* of whom is young, since both rank low. The table tells us that we do not know if Gorbachev is a dove, or rather a 'dawk' (for there are no doves), though it is likely. We simply do not know Gromyko's views on how to grow carrots at all, but we can in all probability surmise them (see Appendix IV). To each his area of specialization, and between them there is often live-and-let-live. Moreover, responsibility within the area does not predict what kind of policy one has for it—except more money. Thus the withdrawal from the Olympic Games (July 1984) was not, to our knowledge, a defeat for Gorbachev: rather he had his *féodalité*, agriculture, and Gromyko, of course, had his.

We have used decentralization in agriculture and détente in foreign policy as paradigmatic illustrations of our position: while other issues come and go, these 'we have always with us.' People have set positions on them. But other issues blow up and go away, like 'what shall we do about Ogarkov?' (the chief of staff, fired in September 1984). Evidently, he offended Ustinov, demanding a subtly different defence-economic policy. It is not possible to predict the positions the others took, except that presumably they all backed Ustinov in the end (but Romanov was away: what did he think?).

Next, why is that presumption so strong? The answer is precisely the doctrine of 'bounded totalitarianism' enunciated above: everybody is dedicated to the fundamental principles of Marxism–Leninism: Full Communism, a communist world, perpetual Party rule, no personal freedom, etc., and, in this case, no Bonapartism. Things like links in agriculture,[3] on the other hand, are, of course, mere *reculer pour mieux sauter*: they will certainly disappear under Full Communism and the betting is very high that Gorbachev agrees.

Reform, we have already insisted, is not coextensive with decentralization. There most certainly exists reforming centralization: rational prices and no subsidies, but continued central command, which could be in physical or in detailed monetary terms. Romanov, see below, belongs to this school, while Gorbachev is a moderate decentralizer. Let it be added that reform is *our* word: they all say 'perfection (*sovershenstvovanie*) of the system.'[4]

2 Andropov and Decentralization

What do we now know of the individual Politburo members' economic policies? What was the general economic-political-ideological-personal scene in which our two protagonists had, or developed, these policies? Andropov himself is acknowledged on all sides to have been an intelligent and comparatively free spirit—like the very good security policeman that he was. There is, of course, no reason at all to expect a top security policeman to be hidebound. Fouché was not. Himmler, who learned Hebrew and flirted with Moral Rearmament, was not. Loris-Melikov (in 1880) was given the job just because he was not. Zubatov (in 1904) founded trade unions. Dzerzhinski wanted (in 1919) legal controls over his own Cheka. Yagoda (in 1930) opposed collectivization. Beria favored the Jews—and opposed collectivization in the newly annexed territories. It is, then, no surprise that, following a long Russian tradition, Andropov was closely associated with some of the best and most 'progressive' Party intellectuals,[5] and signed his name to philosophically Marxist pieces which he may, for all I know, have written without help.[6]

It is, in any case, a commonplace that not much can fairly be expected of a new general secretary, at first. Unlike Napoleon, or indeed a Western prime minister, a Soviet general secretary has no 'hundred days.' No general elections sweep away his obstacles. He is *appointed* by his grudging rivals, who all retain their posts. He must master them gradually, by the appointment process. So, in so short a reign, little was to be expected that was not generally agreed. Indeed, since Andropov was old and sick no one was about to defy the Brezhnev leftovers since he could not be sure that they had lost for good. Moreover, Andropov was, in fact, openly agnostic about the economy, a field within which he had never worked. Nothing much, then, was expected in any case.

But there were more specific reasons than that. There are, perhaps, KGB liberals, the concept is not self-contradictory. But Andropov was not one of them. Two warnings on this could have been given before he took power. First, the most liberal of Andropov's intellectual Party friends, Fyodor Burlatski, (as enumerated by Archie Brown)[7] was dropped long ago from the coterie.[8] The second argument is economic, and we must present it here at proper length, since it is also our first policy issue: the reform of industrial planning and management. It is that Andropov, as ambassador in Budapest, was present during the Hungarian Revolution and its suppression by Soviet troops. This indicates nothing, but subsequently he presided over the installation of Janos Kadar, and here he must have had influence. Moreover, he remained very friendly with Kadar, so he must have been a 'closet Hungarian.' But Andropov left Hungary in 1957 and it was eleven years after (1 January 1968) that Kadar introduced the New Economic Mechanism (NEM)—an event that even a future KGB chief could hardly have foreseen. So what sort of Kadar did he install?

Looking backwards, we forget those eleven years. In 1958 collectivization was completed in a very brutal way: might not this have been more consonant with the ex-ambassador's wishes? Moreover, when the NEM came it was not on Kadar's initiative: he merely permitted it. The initiator was another Hungarian Politburo member, Rezsö Nyers, who joined it in 1962, long after Andropov had left Budapest. However, the ultimate decisions must have been taken in Moscow in 1967, the year in which Andropov left the Central Committee's Socialist Countries Department for the KGB chairmanship; so he must have been indirectly responsible. But he surely played the role of Moscow's Kadar: the permissive figure at the top, not the initiator.

His benevolence toward Hungary remains indisputable. Thus he was pretty clearly responsible for the articles in the Soviet press in early 1982 praising the Hungarian experiment, since he, now a politburo member, had just come back from a visit to Budapest. Moreover, it sticks out that when, in December 1982, the new General Secretary met privately with the East European general secretaries at Brezhnev's funeral, Kadar was the only one to be interviewed 'fraternally.'[9]

No wonder that Hungary is the source of so many pro-Andropov stories, leaked, of course, to Western visitors, especially economists. For Sovietological economists Hungary plays the role of Burlatski and Shakhnazarov in the minds of Sovietological politicians: signs of an Andropovian liberalism that no actual event confirms.

Besides why should Andropov have imitated Hungary? Would a competent Soviet economist without ideological blinkers, or indeed a similar Sovietologist, have advised him to do so? The point is that the Hungarian reform has not succeeded in industry, where growth is no greater than before; but in agriculture and in the service trades—at the price of a relapse into near-capitalism. Sheer agricultural output has been impressive, on the one hand, while there are, on the other, no queues, and the shops of Budapest are the wonder of the communist world. The most we can say for Hungarian industry is that it is much more responsive to consumer demand[10] than it used to be. This means that there was a hidden jump in 'wanted output' in 1968, after which the overall growth figures, which can never at all reflect this factor of the degree of 'wantedness,' mean again just what they say. That is, individual outputs were presumably about as much wanted in 1970 as in 1969, and about as little wanted in 1966 as in 1967; so official measures of growth were equally reliable between these pairs of years.

The once-for-all leap in this hidden factor is not likely to be common coin in Politburo or even Gosplan circles. More evident there is the sheer fact that Hungarian industry does not show exciting growth rates. More centralizing reform, or no reform, must seem serious competitors. And the creeping capitalism that genuinely infects Hungary is exactly the kind of thing that those circles really will be talking about.

There are other good anti-Hungarian arguments than mere poor performance. An important feature of Hungary is the absence of autonomous ethnic regions (the gypsies are numerous but live everywhere). Economic decentralization in the USSR cannot but mean what it has in Yugoslavia: the strengthening of those ethnicities that possess formal territorial status, and the weakening of the center's political power. After all, the Yugoslavs also thought (in 1950–2) that they were decentralizing *managerial tasks* from the federal government toward the enterprise, but they found that they had shifted *political power* to each republic.[11] This is a most serious warning to the Kremlin.

Moreover, the USSR is basically a raw-material exporter. Amply endowed with the gifts of nature, it has no urgent need to develop manufactured exports in the flexible way necessary to sell them to non-communist foreigners. Therefore, its balance of payments does not constrain it to reform.[12] Hungary is in the opposite position. Then, again, there is the huge weight of the military in the Soviet economy. Surely Ustinov liked things the way they are, for reasons set out below, and whatever Romanov wanted it was not decentralization (also see below). Finally, a bad reason: the close links between centralization and corruption are set out below.

3   Andropov's Real Economic Policies

Adnropov did, however, take two issues to heart which in their own way constituted an economic reform as radical as any decentralization: *early* (or at least not very late) *retirement* and *labor discipline*. These are just the essentially human, nontechnical issues that a good KGB man might be expected to understand and initiate. It is wrong, then, to say that Andropov had no concept of economic policy; he had a boy-scout concept—we must all pull up our socks and behave better. The first 'sock' is early retirement. The rules are flexible in the state machine and literally nonexistent in the Party apparat.

Bureaucratic and gerontocratic inertia, not visible at the very top in the days of Stalin, Malenkov and Khrushchev, has now reached the very top.[13] Stalin killed old bureaucrats, so he left a fairly fluid situation. Khrushchev stirred the pot as it had not been stirred since 1938, and even Kosygin made—in 1965 when he had real power—a big impact. But Brezhnev was naturally inert. Ousting Kosygin from all but his actual post, he grew old in power and left a thoroughly ossified, elderly apparatus. Let us note that Shvernik, Mikoyan and Kosygin are the only Politburo members known to have retired since 1917.

Thus in the USSR *early retirement is reform*. Besides, these old men had become *corrupt*, and early retirement, or insecure tenure, at the top is a *sine qua non* in any serious anti-corruption drive.

Corruption at the top leads to conservatism, so in the Soviet case to continued centralization. This needs to be explained before we pass on to labor discipline. Corrupt old people have build up a delicate secret network within the existing system that they know: a great investment in connections and knowledge of people, offices and laws. A new system, even one like a market economy with little bits of private capitalism that promises much to a corrupt young man, threatens *me*. All change is bad.

A further reason for continued centralization is the legal consumption privileges of the *Nomenklatura*. These very considerable privileges, which easily double real income, are based on the detailed, centrally commanded allocation of certain luxury goods. These are allocated according to plan, much as if they were locomotives or steel. The shops' very name is significant: not 'special shops' but 'closed distribution points' (*zakrytiye raspredeliteli*). No doubt in a market with money the *Nomenklatura* could openly buy all that, or get someone to buy it for them; but with how much money? And then the scandal of the higher salaries ...

Khrushchev dared to attack these privileges. He even threw many of the *Nomenklatura* out of Moscow, to govern the *sovnarkhozy* in the provinces. Brezhnev won certain African countries to communism and should be remembered for that. But, at home, he only re-established the privileges and tenure of the *Nomenklatura*: nothing else in eighteen years. The connection with their respective attitudes to central planning is evident.

Zaslavskaya puts this point thus: 'The existing system can only be changed by the social groups which occupy comparatively high positions and so are bound to it by personal interest.'[14] Alec Nove, less authoritative only than she, says:

> However, this kind of radical critic (sc. Sweezy and Bettelheim) is usually unable to see clearly enough the *advantages* to the ruling stratum, or privileged group, that the unreformed system gives. They not only have power and function in relation to resource allocation. They also have privileged access to scarce goods and services unavailable to the masses. *This* privilege is conditional upon their being frequently unobtainable, at the low prices (low, that is, in relation to supplies available). Furthermore, it gives them access to these goods at *low* prices! In terms of crude self-interest, what motive have they to change an arrangement which suits them very well?[15]

Let me add that the 'privileges' of the *Nomenklatura* concern only consumer goods, which *they* want. Their 'power and function in relation to resource allocation' concern mainly producer goods, which subordinate state officials want *from them*. When Trotsky said 'Queues are the basis of Soviet power' he must have meant the latter, the queues caused by planner's tension. Queues for consumer goods are caused by suboptimal plans and by suppressed inflation: although the *Nomenklatura* benefit in the way Alec shows, by heading these queues—they must *spend* power to get there.

Yanov[16] makes the further point that high among these privileges is travel to the West. You can shop in Oxford Street and make a black market killing when you get back; yet simultaneously you wear the Hajji's green turban—you made the voyage, you are distinguished. Therefore, he says, the privileges are linked with détente: not too little, or you'll never get there, and not too much, or everyone will and it's no privilege any more. He should have added that the defense establishment journeys but rarely in the West, probably on security grounds, so is *pro tanto* less interested in détente.

Yet again, the increase of the *Nomenklatura's* privileges is not necessarily the same as late retirement. Indeed, the latter delays the access of many bright and powerful 50-year-olds to privileges they reckon they have deserved.

We turn to the peccadillos of *hoi polloi*: to labor discipline and general social morale. God knows this issue had been kicking around for a long time. Ever since Khrushchev, corruption, absenteeism and the second economy have been a hot issue. There was a vast, threatening, unenforceable and evidently unenforced decree on 20 January 1980, when Andropov had already been seven years in the Politburo. The general discontent with Brezhnev had very much to do with his lackadaisical attitude in this matter. But Andropov took very strong measures. He fired top people, as we have seen. He executed Georgians—Khrushchev's death penalty for corruption had never been applied in that republic. In January 1983 he posted militia outside shops and cinemas in the middle of the day to scare absenteeists back to work.[17] He even went to the proletariat and talked about it (see below).

Personal efficiency, then (that is, discipline and early retirement) and not Hungarian-type decentralization, were Andropov's overt taste. Indeed, in his public pronouncements as General Secretary he gave no hint of an intention radically to decentralize, or indeed to do anything else with the institutions of detailed command planning. Here are a long and a short quotation from Andropov's first economic pronouncement after becoming General Secretary, to the Central Committee on 22 November 1982. The speech devotes about fifty orthodox and anodyne paragraphs to economics. One paragraph only concerns decentralization:

> Recently there has been much talk of the necessity to increase the independence of associations and enterprises, *kolkhozy* and state farms. Clearly the time has come for a practical approach to the solution of this question. On this account orders have been given to the Council of Ministers and Gosplan. We must act carefully in this field, experiment if necessary, weigh and analyse the experience of fraternal countries.

Increased independence must in all cases be considered along with the growth of responsibility and with care for the interests of the whole people.[18]

This is a very moderate passage indeed. The last sentence shows a strongly non-Hungarian suspicion of enterprise freedom. He rubs in his distance from Hungary with this phrase: 'I have no ready recipes for the solution' (of the economy's problems).

4 Discipline versus Decentralization?

Could one be, then, could he have been, a supporter of *both* discipline *and* decentralization?[19] Let us see what history teaches.

(i) The transition from War Communism to New Economic Policy (NEP) (March 1921) *was* a radical decentralization, and it brought with it a substantial relaxation of discipline, even within the Party. Members developed close and corrupting links with NEP men. But labor discipline improved— after all, you can't have much of that under actual communism.

(ii) The transition from Stalinism to Titoism in Yugoslavia (1949–52) was again a radical decentralization. At first no one bothered about discipline, since the *de facto* change was gradual and the country was virtually at war with internal and external Stalinists; nor *was* there much change in this respect. But in the end a NEP-like corruption has become endemic on a grand scale, and discipline is as low as anywhere in Eastern or Western Europe. This, however, may be due to self-management which, of course, is added to decentralization in Yugoslavia.

(iii) The Hungarian NEM (1968) was introduced into an already demoralized, corrupted and indeed foreign-occupied country. Among its objects was, and with the *relance* of 1982 still is, to recapture the second economy by legalizing it. A second economy of that size is, of course, very bad for discipline, while a small acknowledged petty capitalist sector would have less effect. Moreover, since in the usual way too much centralization had destroyed discipline, direct incentives at all levels might, it was thought, bring back *some* of it. This hope has not yet been fulfilled.

(iv) China is a large and amorphous subject. But I lean toward interpreting the events since the fall of the Gang of Four (1976) in a Hungarian manner. Deng is a disciplinarian and a decentralizer. The Cultural Revolution, however, had been exceptionally bad for discipline, and any new system could not but strengthen it.

(v) Jaruzelski has very precisely combined discipline with decentralization, and this parallel is recent and near.

These are the five great instances of communist economic decentralization in history. In each one of them either the revolution was still young or the bureaucracy had recently been destablilized by some traumatic event. The USSR today is in neither condition. Our account of these instances is necessarily amateurish, since there is no genuine measure of labor discipline calculated or published in the whole world.[20] I am, nevertheless, unwilling to believe that discipline at submanagerial level has any tight technical connection with centralization at managerial level, positive or negative. If it is what mainly agitated Andropov he could still, logically, have posted policemen in shops while he decontrolled wholesale prices; or, in a slogan, he could have 'done a Jaruzelski.'

Logic is one thing, psychology another. Let us look at what Andropov actually said to the workers in the Moscow factory in the name of Sergo Ordzhonikidze in January 1983. When the divisional general visits a bad battalion, he does not only speak to the massed other ranks. He takes the officers aside privately and 'tears a strip off' them—and he lets it be known that he has done so. It is of this that Andropov's visit reminds me:

> . . . we must now do everything so that each, I repeat each, of us fulfills his norm, his productive duty . . .
> . . .Without due discipline—working, *planning* and governmental—we cannot go quickly ahead . . .

V. V. Grishin (secretary of Moscow *obkom*, Politburo member) was with Andropov. He said:

> . . . An important component part of the strengthening of discipline is the assurance of good conditions for production: it should be *clearly and cleanly planned, material technical supply must be made certain*, machinery in good repair. We must strengthen both discipline in production and *discipline in planning* . . .

Andropov:

> A few words on what Comrade Grishin was saying . . . discipline concerns not only workers, engineers and technicians. *It concerns everyone, beginning with Ministers* [and on that word he said thank you and left].[21]

The quotations appear decisive. Andropov reacted like neither a Polish general, nor yet an economist, to his country's problems. For discipline meant also plan fulfillment, and this can hardly mean the fulfillment of a less detailed plan. He almost unconsciously diverged from the Hungarian path—which, in any case, he, sitting in Moscow, had merely permitted Hungary to take.

5   Andropov, Chernenko and Planning Reform

We turn to the mini-reform of industrial planning and management (*Pravda*, 26 July 1983). First, it was not a big event. It affected few branches of the economy (two central machine-building ministries and three republican ones responsible for consumer goods), and those not radically. Wholesale prices remain centrally fixed, the Gossnab, the administrative mechanism for distributing supplies, remains untouched.[22] But, in Hungary, the Gossnab is abolished, most wholesale prices are free and there is an interenterprise market. The list of extended enterprise powers and duties is very small beer: an increased role in planning; increased responsibility for saleability; may use the portion of amortization quotas set aside for central repairs to buy different equipment; have more access to credit; may set higher wage rates if wage-fund underspent; bonuses still a function of output, but preconditions are contract fulfillment, sales plan fulfillment, rising labor productivity, falling material use, and so on.

This is all less than what Kosygin did in 1965 (Kosygin's reform was later quietly reversed by Brezhnev). Andropov did not put his name to this experiment. Indeed no one did, and it has not been firmly associated with any senior official. It came out quite anonymously as a decree of the Central Committee and Council of Ministers. There was no great meeting and no speech. Clearly, it was a compromise document, threatening to some, disappointing to others. It was in no sense a *new* experiment, but merely a rehash.

Andropov does not come well out of this. He did not even go so far as Poland, which must have been nearer the top of his mind than Hungary. The Soviet government has been much more amateurish than the Polish government, while facing very similar problems. No doubt, however, the very notion of imitating Poland is laughable in the USSR.

Chernenko, on the other hand, openly favored more decentralization while in power: 'The work on this has only just begun. It includes a broadly based economic experiment in the extension of the rights and increase of the responsibility of the enterprises.'[23] Under him, too, the experiment spread to nearly the whole economy. This is one of the many facts that leads me to reject the cliché of Chernenko, the stick-in-the-mud.

6   Gorbachev and the Normless Link

Much more important, but very similar, is the decision (not law) taken by the Politburo to support the group contract on *sovkhozy* and *kolkhozy* (11 March 1983). This is the pet policy of Gorbachev.[24]

The small normless links (*beznaryadnie zvenya*) in agriculture have a long history behind them: the pre-World War II link, and its perpetuation and extension under German occupation; the late-1940s link under A. A. Andreyev; its abolition in 1950 by Khrushchev; its revival in the 1960s; the martyrdom of I. N. Khudenko, the supporter of links in Kursk and Kazakhstan, in about 1965; the revival under Brezhnev in about 1980; and now the crowning mercy of Gorbachev, bringing about the Politburo's decision (*poruchenie*) of 11 March 1983.

The normless link hands over to a small group some agricultural function, by means of a contract with the farm. The link members divide the proceeds among themselves, and are not subject to (much) planning—they are 'normless.' This distinguishes them very sharply from the contract brigades in building and industry, whose contracts stipulate all the outputs and only decentralize the actual work decisions. The normless link thus takes production decisions according to profit. This is an internal decentralization of agricultural enterprises of great promise, amounting almost to capitalist tenant-farming. The Politburo's *poruchenie* gave strong support to a nominally voluntary movement. The announcement was entirely anonymous, however, and in itself a most unusual way of dealing with an important nonemergency matter.[25] There was no Central Committee meeting and not even an *ad hoc* top-level conference at the time, and it is not upon this incident that the evidence of Gorbachev's involvement rests.[26] Moreover, Andropov was even more than usually coy about it. In a long speech of stupefying dullness, clearly written for him by bureaucrats, at a subsequent high-level agricultural confernce[27] he appears not to have mentioned it at all. It is Gorbachev who has publicly identified himself with this measure. His speech on that occasion seems to have been the main one, but was not published. The group contract affair may well be a historic decision. But it seems not to have been Andropov's. In part, it pre-dates his rule and it did not involve his initiative.

We have every reason to attribute the normless links in agriculture to Gorbachev. First, there are the two speeches referred to above. Secondly, there is the story of the leaked Zaslavskaya memorandum.[28] This important document, writted by a distinguished female agricultural economist from Novosibirsk and delivered at a conference in Moscow in April 1983, is of a distinctly revisionist tone but, refreshingly, does not touch on industrial planning—which so many people instantly and only call to mind when economic reform is mentioned. It is about the work relation of the individual to the whole system, and demands more economic independence for him/her. Normless links, not mentioned *totidem verbis*, are right up Zaslavskaya's alley.

What interests us here, however, is the Hungarian 'codicil': Gorbachev was in the chair at the Moscow meeting. When Zaslavskaya had finished her presentation all eyes turned to him, and he said: 'But what can I do alone?' I have this story from two Hungarian sources—which may well, of course, be a mere duplication of a single original Hungarian source. Unlike the Hungarian stories about Andropov, this one sounds crisp and precise: a *chose vue* not a wish-fulfilling rumor. Similar rumors were also picked up in Moscow by Robert Kaiser.[29]

This, then, as Kremlinology goes, is a sure attribution of a particular policy to a particular important man. We must instantly qualify it twice. First, we repeat the standard warning against the idea that politicians in any country present easily identifiable syndromes of policy or ideology. It is a far cry from normless links in agriculture to East–West détente or friendly overtures to China. It is true that Gorbachev is very young (born 1931) for a Politburo member. He never went through the Great Purge (1936–8); he has not been 'frightened for ever' as even Romanov (born 1923) has been. It is true that he has an engaging and open personality, and an educated and very pretty wife—such a woman being almost miraculous among Politburo wives in recent decades. His wife is *salonfähig*, internationally presentable. Can the unpresentability of Politburo wives after—shall we say?—Mrs Lenin and Mrs Trotsky help to account for Soviet cultural isolationism? All this makes an attractive, but not a persuasive, case for the all-round liberal Gorbachev. Too little, for a start, is known of his military and foreign policy views.[30]

Our second qualification is that the normless links are not as attractive as they seem.[31] They must keep very close records and the farm authorities constantly interfere. One-year contracts are usual—which makes them remote in practice from capitalist long-term or Chinese and Hungarian medium-term leases. Often officials choose the members and set up the teams, so that the family solidarity that marked Andreyev's links is absent. The incentive effect of the bonus is undermined by its smallness and by the supply interruptions (tools, fertilizer, etc. are not delivered on time) that characterize the Soviet economy. Moreover, the bonuses are subject to official maxima—here, as elsewhere, the authorities will not let go of income distribution. Small wonder, then, that the links often dissolve themselves. It will need considerable changes in the whole *spirit* of Soviet administration to put an end to all this chicanery. It is possible that Gorbachev sees in the link only the advantage to him of installing mutual, well-motivated, *disciplinary supervision at the grassroots and the milk pails*: the link members make each other work.

7 Andropov, Chernenko and Contradictions under Socialism

Peripheral to economic policy, but shedding much light on it, is the latest and most fashionable ideological rift: can *antagonstic contradictions* occur under socialism? I place this issue here because of its connection with Zaslavskaya. The old view, blessed by Stalin himself, was no: socialism is irreversible,[32] the dialectic operates harmlessly, if at all, after the Revolution; there are no longer any revolutionary leaps. The new view is that Hungary (1956) and Poland (1980–date) show, on the contrary, antagonistic contradictions at work after the 'Revolution.' The protagonist is A. P. Butenko[33] of the Institute for the Economy of the World Socialist System.

Under Brezhnev, Chernenko initiated this debate but, in a typically anodyne article, took no personal stance.[34] The new view is the natural view for someone urgently interested in internal change, and seeking an ideological excuse for pushing it: 'Look, comrades, contradictions can be antagonistic under socialism, our own situation is very serious, the economy can grind to a halt, there may even be riots.' The Zaslavskaya memorandum fits perfectly into that way of thinking. It even recalls the very phraseology of Marx in *Das Kapital* (I, 23) when he predicts the downfall of capitalism:

> The present system of production relations has substantially fallen behind the level of development of the productive forces. Instead of enabling their accelerated development, it is becoming more and more of a brake on their progressive advancement. One outcome of this is the inability of production relations to provide modes of conduct for workers in the socio-economic sphere that are needed by society.[35]

Given the plausible rumor that he presided over Zaslavskaya's presentation and spoke in its favor, Gorbachev is also of this view; but he has published little.[35a]

Some time before, as the man in the Central Committee apparat in charge of socialist countries, Andropov was in charge of Butenko's institute. Nevertheless, he came down against this line, at least as far as satellite countries are concerned, in 1983,[36] holding that all contradictions under socialism are nonantagonistic, though they might, indeed, cause 'serious collisions.' To such ridiculous shifts is ideology perverted, when it is being used not on its own account but as a means of esoteric communication. The inference is weak but persuasive: Andropov would not have taken this standpat attitude had he had any sense of urgency or need for radical reform.

Chernenko heeded this message while Andropov lived and, indeed, seems not to have tried to cancel it when he had the power. Perhaps, after all, it does not matter. Between averting serious collisions and solving antagonistic contradictions, Alec Nove once asked, is there really a noticeable policy difference? Must we not already be shooting people, or abolishing the Gossnab and freeing wholesale prices, in the former case?

Before we leave ideology, it is important to settle who *is* the top ideologist. Under Lenin and Stalin this function was reserved to Lenin and even Stalin. Khrushchev seems to have been more modest as to his own abilities, and his power was anyhow circumscribed. Suslov took over the function, using it *against* him.[37] It is thus Suslov that created the tradition of a high priest operating out of the Secretariat like a Benedictine abbot, thundering at the mere bishop in the valley below distracted by his quotidian pastoral cares. He retained this function under Brezhnev, to whom he was more friendly.

Suslov died on 25 January 1982, before Brezhnev, and his self-created position has quite naturally never been filled. It may perhaps be that Chernenko *thought* he had stepped into Suslov's ideological shoes when he became Second secretary, and did indeed wear them in Brezhnev's last months. But Andropov disillusioned him, and broke the new tradition, as is evident in many places here, reverting to Lenin's position. This he was personally able to fill, being, of course, a KGB intellectual.

It is not clear what Chernenko, less capable but now able to choose, did about this when in power. In general, his concerns were more with education and 'agitation' than with 'propaganda.' But we must beware of thinking that Gorbachev, the new second secretary, had the same ideology portfolio that Suslov had.[38] Surely no one so blatantly pragmatic should be entrusted with it. Suslov seems in retrospect to have been unique.

8 Workers' Contracts in Industry and Construction

The law on labor (as opposed to farmers') collectives (12 April 1983) is less important in practice, though ideologically, of course, it is a remarkable figure of 8 on thin ice. Andropov did not openly support it, leaving the matter to Aliev (18 June 1983).

The fact that Aliev, another KGB man in Andropov's Politburo, supported it sheds a flood of light on this decree. It fits perfectly into Andropov's discipline campaign. The idea behind these contracts, between the enterprise management and the small brigade of workers, is to get the latter to supervise each other, demand of each other performance adequate to ensure the collective bonus and, if necessary, complain about each other. The 'brigade contract' is not to be seen, said a very official Soviet economist to the author, as decentralization, it is all 'controlled by the government' and its object is to 'get people to work harder.' It is imitative of, and chronologically later than, the normless links in agriculture. These nonagricultural brigades are, of course, heavily 'normed,' since the tight central plan applies to them.

9 Military Economics

There were, of course, other economic issues during Andropov's rule, that while highly important did not separate the Politburo in any discernible way. Thus *military economics* presents two issues at least: what shall be the total defence burden; and what organization of industry is best for that part of the burden that is weapons production?

It is a fair assumption, at all times, that the military-industrial complex wants more money. This means Ustinov (the first purely civilian Minister of Defence since Trotsky, with a purely weapons-producing background), and, of course, the generals and admirals themselves. This assumption is a worldwide constant, irrespective of the polity concerned. But it also means Romanov, the supervisor of military affairs from the Secretariat. Romanov is a true hawk and also a cultural Stalinist. Only two senior politicians can be definitely identified as their opponents: Chernenko, clearly, and probably Gorbachev! But the identification is doubtful, and falls outside our period (see Appendix I).

While little of great certainty emerges from Appendix I, this much can be said:

  (i) It is certainly not disproved that Gorbachev is a dawk.
 (ii) But Chernenko *was* a dawk. It was his initiative that brought the extremism of Gromyko to heel. Moreover, he spoke openly this way under Brezhnev.[39]
(iii) Andropov, however, was probably a hawk, to judge by his attitudes to the introduction of cruise missiles and the shooting down of the Korean passenger aircraft.
 (iv) It is not yet known whether defense expenditures were *really* increased in the 1985 budget, nor whether the *overt* rise was Gorbachev's victory or his defeat.
  (v) Quite generally, anyone who supports normless links and is open-minded on most other subjects *should* be a dawk! But one thing is surely excluded: that anyone could rise under Khrushchev and Brezhnev to Politburo status while being a true dove.
 (vi) Probably Romanov more or less agreed with Ustinov, but the usual Party–State quarrels divided them, especially in the case of Ogarkov's dismissal.

What is the military attitude to the way the economy is run? It is customarily assumed that the whole Soviet military establishment, from gun-makers to artillery generals, prefer a centralized command economy. For, in such an economy, a powerful man can take what he likes since he can write, or cause to be written (and rewritten), his own and everyone else's plan. He can also keep down his apparent cost to society by manipulating the prices of his inputs—while of course ordering suppliers to continue to supply, at whatever loss.

Thus the Soviet-type economy as we know it is very tempting to those who have to procure weapons. They will always get the same amount they have ordered, but at two very high costs. Innovation will be slow and quality low, and the burden on the even more inefficient civilian sector will be felt to be intolerably high.

However, the system is particularly useful in emergencies. Raw materials that unexpectedly become short within the duration of the operative one-year plan can be simply diverted from the legal, planned use of enterprises with lower priority. Strictly, this is the duty of the Gossnab, or of one's own *tolkach* in Moscow, but military industry can call on the much more powerful support of the local *obkom* secretary. The latter can even make inter*oblast'* level exchanges, thus substituting the *obkom* secretary network for the Gossnab.[40]

There can be little doubt that Ustinov, old, conservative and probably Stalinist, saw things this way. He had certainly protected the defense industry against Khrushchev's *sovnarkhozy*. These were local organs, exercising within each small region the same powers over all commodity branches that previously the Moscow ministries had expected within one commodity branch over all regions. The *sovnarkhozy* did nothing to enhance the market or enterprise independence or optimal allocation; they did not reduce the number of plan indicators or rationalize prices; they just shifted to 100 territorial authorities the same set of powers over enterprises as twenty ministries in Moscow had previously exercised. They therefore threatened to bring military industry, previously concentrated into about five ministries, under civilian control.

The way in which Ustinov at that time (1958–64) defeated the First Secretary and preserved central control over military industry are technical[41] and do not concern us here. Our point is that this experience threw him on to the same side in the struggle as the semi-Stalinists Suslov and Brezhnev. Nothing links him to mild genuine reform either, such as Kosygin brought in in 1965, after Khrushchev had been thrown out, the *sovnarkhozy* disbanded and the commodity branch ministries re-created.

Ogarkov, on the other hand, is the Soviet Admiral Rickover.[42] Like Rickover, he is very far from Politburo membership but very influential. He seeks quality not quantity, even to the extent of substituting new and extremely complicated 'conventional' weapons for more missiles—the latter are basic but we have enough—and demanding that the 'Star Wars' latest technology be developed. Now Rickover merely called for higher standards and made a nuisance of himself. It may be that Ogarkov did little more, but since he had to deal with Soviet, not the American, economy it is very tempting to suppose that he ranged himself on the side of economic change (see Appendix II). It is even more tempting to place Romanov here, since he *has* been, if not reforming, then reorganizing, Leningrad industry (Leningrad is a big arms-manufacturing city and Romanov was its *obkom* secretary.[43]

How far such people go along with normless links in agriculture we can only guess, having repeated our warning that nowhere do all politicians think in syndromes. But, in general, Romanov is a *centralizing modernizer*; an attitude natural to the progressive mind in military and heavy industry. Such people favor '*that kind of* centralism which reflects the latest achievements in the theory of management.'[44] They would doubtless welcome the retirement of the old and corrupt, and the shamefaced acquisition of relevant capitalist technology. They might even demand a wholesale price reform, but only to plan better with. They would oppose freedom for managers, and utterly reject worker participation.

10   Centralizing Modernizers

When we look at the hesitancy of Andropov, and even Gorbachev, on this issue, we must say that outside agriculture, where Zaslavskaya's type of reasoning is generally accepted, the centralizing modernizers are in the overwhelming majority among high officials. Few indeed, since Kosygin, have been decentralizers—perhaps only Chernenko? Here, from the academic world, is another tone-setting quotation:

> The growing socialization of production and the high level of the technical base achieved in the course of the scientific-technological revolution demand a corresponding development in the material base of planning and management, and in the improvement of their forms and methods. The advantages of the planned socialist system, the possibility for the conscious management of economic and social processes throughout the entire society, allow for the much broader and more effective application than under capitalism of economic-mathematical methods (such as optimal planning, economic-mathematical modeling, balancing, program/goal setting, etc.) and automatic cybernetic technology.[45]

Below the Politburo level there are, of course, many schemes of economic reform. We pass them by as irrelevant to our theme, except that we should linger on the scheme of B. P. Kurashvili.[46] Though often quoted, it is surely very eccentric. For, in general, no one who wishes to resuscitate the *sovnarkhozy*[47] can be taken seriously; nor does he mention the fate of the Gossnab or of wholesale prices in his scheme of things. He is, however, a brave and open-minded man, and he has at least thought hard about the military sector. He specifically reserves for them a traditional centralized administration, and keeps the revived *sovnarkhozy* civilian. Thus his proposals are extremely reminiscent of what Ustinov actually did under Khrushchev (see above): a hybrid system perhaps only acceptable to Romanov. Even at the top, his defense sector is altogether independent, outside his new single ministry, the Minnarkhoz. This is itself reminiscent of Khrushchev's Supreme Sovnarkhoz, but still more of Hungary today, which has such a single ministry, and weapons factories 'enjoy' a special, centralized, nonmarket administration.

It is extremely important that in this, at least, Kurashvili's economics is as realistic as his politics. It is perfectly sensible to decentralize a sector of output while the others remain centralized, and vice versa: this involves no self-contradiction. There is always an interface between the command plan and the market, except under Full Communism and total laissez-faire, when one or other of the opposing systems is absent. There must always be friction at that interface, best mollified by flexible prices and taxes but anyway capable of being mastered, say, by queues.[48] Subject to this general disadvantage, moving the interface around makes little difference.

Thus most of Soviet agriculture and much of house-building have always been far more decentralized than the rest of the economy without ill effect (the failures of agriculture, of course, arise from policies and institutions, not from friction at a market/planning interface). Hungarian exports to CMEA remain successfully under command of the government. Soviet exports to capitalist countries remain awkwardly responsive to the market. It is the inconsistent treatment of *functions not sectors* that involves self-contradiction. Thus the *sovnarkhozy* were incapable of coordinating R and D, which is in its very nature a commodity-branch matter. Again, the Kosygin reforms decentralized investment finance but left bricks and machines to the Gossnab or the Gosplan: so how could the free investment money be spent? An independent and centralized defense sector would not only keep Ogarkov, Romanov and Ustinov quiet (or at least quarrelling among themselves only), it would also present reasonably frictionless interfaces with the decentralized supply of their basic inputs. To these suppliers, these deliveries would be a sort of export.

Apart from Kurashvili, these issues only surfaced into publication under Chernenko but they were, of course, very much present under Andropov; the present always illuminates the immediate past. In particular, Reagan first made his Star Wars proposals in March 1983, and this is directly relevant. For he would not have made them if the USA has not been ahead in laser technology, and the USSR, by showing itself acutely nervous on this issue, is admitting its backwardness. Any sane Soviet soldier, therefore, viewing the general stagnation of the economy, feeling its technical backwardness in space, conventional weapons and now lasers, and listening to the flood of civilian controversy on the causes of civilian failure, might well question the long-run military benefits of the present set-up.

What was the reaction of the Andropov leadership as a whole? It seems to have been unconstructive, and political rather than economic. This is understandable, since before Star Wars there was Gromyko's orchestrated anti-American campaign against the Cruise missile (which failed); and hard on the heels of Star Wars came KAL 007 (September 1983), and Reagan's orchestrated anti-Soviet propaganda campaign on that event. It seems as if Andropov considered all these things to be merely foreign policy matters, and gave Gromyko his head. Gromyko was incensed, clearly on a personal level, against Reagan, and carried on a very tough foreign policy indeed until, finally properly established, Chernenko called him to heel (26 September 1984: see Appendix I). The first, or at least the most important, person to draw attention to the economic side of Star Wars was Ogarkov (see Appendix II).

Underneath the surface, however, economic reform of a very mild kind has been going on in the military sphere. Thus defense factories also produce consumer goods—a natural state of affairs under capitalism, where an enterprise that concentrates solely on arms risks bankruptcy from political vicissitudes. In the USSR, too, this is, surprisingly, a very old practice. It has the advantage of providing that key element in military supply, 'surge capacity': the possibility of switching a factory or part of it immediately to the production of arms. Julian Cooper of Birmingham (seminar at London School of Economics, December 1984) points out that in the last few years this practice has been upgraded. Instead of being an undignified and resented chore, as under Malenkov (1953), it has become an equal road to promotion within this or that weapons-producing ministry, and a source of foreign technology for the ministry (since foreign technology is, unless stolen, only civilian).

11   The Second Economy and Suppressed Inflation

It is of extreme importance to realize that the latter is only one part of the former. The plan, as well as suppressed inflation, creates shortages and so queues. Again, queues form for appendectomies: things that in most countries have no price and so are queued for everywhere. Moreover, there are political queues, as for exit visas, for example. Again taxes are very heavy indeed, under all systems, and will be evaded whatever the excess money supply. Bribery arises from all three of these phenomena just as easily as from suppressed inflation.

Bribery, and corruption at the top, *were* objects of Andropov's policy, as we have already seen. His cry for labor discipline did encompass all society, and he did dismiss certain very senior officials for unstated reasons that must have been corruption. But he achieved, and even seems to have attempted, very little against petty corruption. The idea was to make people not better but more hardworking.

This is as much as to say that the problems posed by the second economy are very deep. Suppressed inflation not being their sole cause, no monetary sleight of hand will abolish them, though it would reduce them. The detailed planning system is itself responsible for much, and its liquidation *à la hongroise* would deal the queues a big blow. The legal recognition of petty capitalism, again *à la hongroise*, would, at the very least, change the name of part of the second economy by putting it on the right side of the law. But things depend above all on the morals of the people. Andropov was therefore right to fire and prosecute senior people; he was right, if the death penalty is used at all, to use it on Georgia, too, and so on. They must indeed 'begin discipline with the Minister.' Moral questions, like military morale, depend on fairness and a good example at the top.

A word, as usual, of warning about the data. Crime data are very bad everywhere. In the USSR, in addition, they are not published. There seems to be universal agreement about the increase since 1960 in corruption in towns, though on *kolkhozy* it can hardly have increased since 1929. But it is sobering that all this mountain of Soviet and Sovietological print, all these draconian new laws, and indeed now a few corpses, rest on no scientific data.

We come now to suppressed inflation. It is the USSR's proud boast, very often dogmatically trumpeted abroad, even in specialist journals, that socialism is incompatible with inflation. There is not a word of truth in this boast. Andropov seemed to know he must do something about it. He threatened the workers of Sergo Ordzhonikidze with uncompensated retail-price rises, and complained of wages outstripping consumer-goods production.[49] It certainly is a key destroyer of discipline, since:

(i) Queues in shops mean absenteeism—if you do not go in the lunch hour or on the way home you may possibly get in.
(ii) Unusable, indeed virtually unwanted, cash easily becomes a bribe, including a bribe within the planned socialist sector. In this sector, cash payments are forbidden, but there is nothing to prevent plan violation for a bribe financed by the cash sector.

If discipline continues to be the watch-word, then, suppressed inflation has to go. Just possibly there will be a Stalin-type currency reform. But as the inflationary gap is not *very* large—a small and persistent one will do all the damage you want—uncompensated retail-price rises are more likely. Nevertheless, they have not occurred on a large-enough scale, and wages and social incomes continue to catch up with them. It seems more likely that nothing will be done. The queues, I learn in December 1983, are longer than ever, while the police predictably returned to their normal duties in the summer of that year, after Andropov had absurdly diverted them to the shops.

Suppressed inflation is not only one of the many causes of the second economy, but an evil of a different sort. As the prime cause of queues, rather than theft or bribery, it lowers real income more than public morality. For, if we stand longer to buy the same quality of goods, we have effectively worked longer for them, so we are less well off. It is even possible that we might become a little more productive, and so make more goods for the population to consume in the same official hours; we are still worse off if the queues lengthen enough. The vast discontent of the Soviet people, their conviction that they are actually worse off, may well be due to financial mismanagement not falling productivity. In 1984 the female urban adult probably spent some ten hours in queues a week; the male half as many.[50] Rural 'queuing' is greater, since it includes the bus ride into town—in order to join the urban queues. Rural shops are notoriously negligible.

To some extent, the inflation is already not suppressed. Price rises, open but not reported, or concealed by giving products a new name, are the order of the day. New measures of economic performance result which consist simply in estimating a true rate of rise of the prices the state actually charges, and using it to deflate the nominal monetary volume of the goods it produces. The resulting real volumes fall rather below the CIA's performance indicators.

It is important to understand the reasons for the existence of a large monetary overhang. One is Keynesian: the perpetual tendency for wages (both the rates and the total bill) to rise as enterprise costs go up and up. What Janos Kornai has taught us to call the enterprise's 'soft budget constraint,' a typical feature of communist and capitalist public sectors, means that the bank will always lend money 'just to tide you over'—with a term that is not enforced. So the rising costs are not sternly fought, nor financed by higher prices (that would be inflation, a very bad thing!), but by more money (which is said not to occur—a lie). The new money is basically issued to pay higher wage rates in violation of the wage plan, or wages due to people who have been employed to make goods not yet sold, in violation of the sales plan.

This explanation is very Keynesian, in that it concerns flows not stocks. Nay more, it is post-Keynesian since it concerns cost-push. It is true—but not more true than the only recently appreciated 'monetarist' explanation, which concerns the stock of money treated as a portfolio asset. There is by now an enormous accumulation of liquid savings in the pockets and savings accounts of the population. In a way, this is a Soviet success story: the people are rich enough to save.

Naturally, the sum of all savings accumulates to vast proportions over the years unless the hoarded cash is dissaved or unless the state or society offers illiquid assets, satisfactory in the long run to savers, which they will want to stick to for a long time. What might these be? All candidates are capitalistic! There simply does not exist a socialist illiquid asset. By far the biggest is the tolerated but blatantly nonsocialist private dacha, of which one may only own one, and of limited size. Then there are antiques and collectors' items, which border on the second economy—and that, within the law, is all. There are not even private pension schemes. So the substantial savings, genuinely creditable to the system, pile up in liquid form, ready at any moment to finance a queue for a desirable new consumer good, or merely one thought to be going short soon.

Andropov, as we saw, threatened price rises uncompensated by wage increases. Since no one can consume what is not there, this would not have reduced the nation's real wage, indeed by abolishing queues it would have increased it. But each individual would have felt a reduction, and there would have been price riots, as in Poland.[51]

Andropov never did raise prices, however. The next candidate is a monetary reform: a forced exchange of notes at, say, two old for one new, and a somewhat less penal exchange of savings accounts. But monetary reforms also cause riots (for example, Pilsen, 1952), and the loss of international prestige would be tremendous.

Is there a third way out of the queues? Yes: sell more consumer goods at current prices—that is, produce fewer arms and more clothes. There is even a fourth: sell off the gold stock for foreign textiles. These would be to substitute for a monetary change real changes, and ones almost totally unacceptable to the Kremlin.

Fifthly, however, there is a way, much used by Stalin until his currency reform and tentatively resuscitated in Poland, that is surely the least of all evils: 'commercial' shops. These sell, not for foreign currency—such shops exist already—but for rubles at black market prices, that is, the state enters the black market and soaks up the money. Of course, it must not divert too much from the state shops and the low prices, or once again the population will riot. And, as with other price rises, the super-profits of these shops must again go into a genuine budget surplus, that is, the notes must be burned.

It seems unthinkable that so weak a General Secretary as Chernenko could have been strong here where Andropov was weak. Moreover, it is not in the nature of populists to take unpopular measures, such as all deflationary measures always are. So it is no surprise that Chernenko followed his predecessor in failing to grasp the nettle. Meanwhile, of course, the nettle will grow since people continue to save. It seems that one day neglected inflation will impose a terrible reckoning.

12 How Do Our Heroes Compare?

At the end of the term the headmaster must write a report. Let us do so now for Yuri Vladimirovich and, greatly daring, attach a rather hurried one on Konstantin Ustinovich, his successor as head boy.

Andropov performed worse, and Chernenko better, than expected. The fabled intelligence, flexibility and sophistication of the USSR's elderly Fouché, the patron of the promising Hungarian experiment, the drinker of Scotch, the listener to jazz, did not carry over into economics. But the equally elderly sufferer from emphysema, who could not even find the place in his own speech, the pale copy of the corrupt, pompous, stick-in-the-mud Brezhnev, the provincial Agitprop official whose military record was confined to the frontier troops, the mere distributor of medals and greeter of ambassadors, has mildly surprised us.[52] Thus:

(i) In foreign policy—which is not our subject, but touches us very nearly—Andropov was an unimaginative hawk. He did not take charge of the KAL 007 incident, and while clearly not responsible for it must remain absolutely responsible for the diplomatic disaster it became. He gave Gromyko his head when Gromyko was clearly no longer motivated by Soviet interest but by personal resentment. He withdrew from the Olympic Games without plausible cause. He failed again in the attempt to prevent Cruise missiles—just because of these three mistakes. Chernenko, on the contrary, dismissed Ogarkov, called Gromyko to heel, and did apologize for the Cruise missile that went astray in Finland (30 December 1984). His exact role in these events, except the all-important second one, is of course uncertain.

(ii) Andropov did not properly take into account the military-economic cost of the end of détente (it had been, of course, Brezhnev's act to end détente, by invading Afghanistan). Chernenko's attitude is not clear.

(iii) Andropov merely tinkered with the reform of industrial planning, and this despite his Hungarian connections. He had no ideas of his own. Chernenko gets no more credit, though the reform did become under him the 'large-scale experiment.' It is possible, however, that Chernenko's sense of the urgency of reforms tempted him to revise ideology: lack of reform could be serious for Soviet rule. Their (by itself ridiculous) verbal difference on 'contradictions under socialism' shows Andropov's lack of *sérieux*.

(iv) Correctly perceiving the importance of work discipline, Andropov had the courage to approach the workers personally, as man to man—or, at any rate, as General Secretary to man. But he chose a cure that could not be applied consistently, or for long enough: the police went back to normal duties. Chernenko, however, a true Brezhnevite at least in this, simply relaxed. On the other hand, for all his generally populist stance, he succeeded no better in talking to anyone as man to man.

(v) Apart from a single vague threat of price rises, Andropov did nothing at all about queues and suppressed inflation. Yet in any list of ten separate social and economic problems this would surely figure next to alcoholism as number two: way ahead of industrial planning reform. So the problem continued to fester on down, growing all the time, to his successor—who also did nothing at all.

(vi) Andropov attacked corruption at the very top, always the right place to begin. Chernenko, the alleged Brezhnevite, did not stop these attacks, but merely relaxed them.

(vii) Andropov did something to restrict the second economy at popular level. But he did not do the main things: legalize some of it, as in Hungary, and attack suppressed inflation. No doubt the policeman in him preferred to enforce the law, not change it. It would have been in keeping with Chernenko's populist style if he had legalized some activities in private construction and agriculture, but this did not happen.[53] The normless links could have lent themselves to this purpose, but were not used in this way.

It is not suggested that Andropov was not an able man. But his genius was not adapted to economics; he had never come up against it before. Moreover, with a narrow Party base he had no powerful clientele. So he had to rely on the elderly, hawkish, conservative politicians who had helped him to power: Gromyko and Ustinov. Also he was old and ill. His successor was also old and ill, and less intelligent. But as a long-time provincial Party official he knew something of Soviet society, and had had to develop at least some feel for economics. Again as the heir to Brezhnev's clientele, everyone was beholden to him. The weaker man was thus in the stronger position, but he did not use it very well.

If a man with so few definite ideas can be type-cast at all, Andropov was a centralizing modernizer, though with more emphasis on the latter. He comes somewhere between Romanov and Deng Hsiaoping. Like the latter he was the old man who will break the gerontocracy and get us moving again. Very many promising people in their thirties looked up to him with hope.[54] But, unlike Deng, he had few serious economic ideas, and so did not know *whom* to promote or back. He had no *Gesamtkonzept*, no vision. With such a weapon, his action against the old and the corrupt would have been far more successful.[55] East and West, he was overrated.

But history will be kinder to Chernenko than his contemporaries have been. He had little intellect but much common sense, and he differed unexpectedly from his master, Brezhnev, on many points. He was serious on industrial planning reform and on peace. He liked the common people—though not to the extent of talking to them! He even innovated ideologically: a curious step in a total nonintellectual. His quiet but complex personality would reward a deeper study.[55a]

Appendix I: Is Gorbachev a Dawk?

Though not friendly to each other, both Chernenko and Gorbachev are, or were, 'dawks.' Our evidence for, and against, this debatable point must take the form of a strict, dull, chronological narrative.

On 9 May 1984 Marshall Ogarkov, then Chief of Staff and Deputy Minister of Defense, asked for an economic effort to parallel Star Wars (see Appendix II). On 6 September 1984 he was dismissed—surely by Ustinov, with whom he has twice publicly disagreed: once on the possibility of a victory in nuclear war and once on the military economy and its functioning. Romanov was in Addis Ababa. He might well have voted the other way (see below). This was, then, quite possibly an affair that divided the military establishment—Marshal Ogarkov is a divisive character. We may be sure that Gromyko, whose opposition to Star Wars was very personal, voted against Ogarkov.

Then, and quite possibly by chance, came the great turn toward mildness in foreign policy, with Chernenko's speech on 26 September. This announced a shift just when Gromyko was in New York taking a very strong line against Star Wars and US policy generally—which he immediately altered. At this point, Gorbachev was riding high, and shortly afterward Ustinov fell ill, to die on 21 December.

But in mid-October Gorbachev seems to have fallen under a cloud. Thus on 14 October, Romanov (freer to act in military affairs now that Ustinov was ill?) announced an important new military planning appointment for Ogarkov, who was then permitted to publish (nothing important!) in the journal *Communist of the Armed Forces*; allowing for the printing period this decision was finalized on about 10 December. Then, on 19 October, Gorbachev lost one place in the Politburo pecking order (to Romanov). He did not address the Central Committee plenum on agriculture on 23 October 1984 (Chernenko did, avoiding all mention of normless links and propounding a foolish and expensive land amelioration scheme, quite in the old Brezhnevian style. The difference between the two men had already been made explicit on 26–28 March, at the All-Union conference on agriculture).[56] But Gorbachev bounced back into second place on 5 November (in preparation for the 7 November parade).

On 15 November, however, there was an enlarged Politburo meeting instead of the usual Central Committee meeting before the Supreme Soviet. Gorbachev was not even present (on holiday!); he also cancelled an appointment with Neil Kinnock.

On 27 November 1984 he was again no. 2 in the pecking order at the Supreme Soviet. At this session, the overt defense budget was raised for the first time since 1969. Was this a victory for him? It can have been: he may have prevented a larger rise than the one actually voted. Of course, the overt budget allocation bears hardly any relation to the sum actually spent. Indeed, Gorbachev may even have won only a small victory: to raise the revealed budget for statistical honesty—perhaps on an unchanged real vote!

Finally, in Appendix IV we give good reason to believe Gromyko is no friend of Gorbachev, and himself a hawk. We also note, perhaps the most significant matter of all, that when in power Gorbachev ended the custom that the military leaders should stand on Lenin's tomb for the burial of a general secretary, during the parade (March 1985). Perhaps, however, their pain was lessened by memories of Chernenko's hostility to them? Or did *they* take the initiative in refusing to stand? We know that Fidel Castro found Chernenko altogether too dovish, and refused to come.

We take this opportunity to mention that Gorbachev never came out flatly for decentralization in the economy outside agriculture until several months into his leadership (*Pravda*, 12 June 1985); notably, he was silent on it in a long and wide-ranging election speech in Stavropol during Andropov's rule (*Izvestiya*, 1 March 1983). Nor is the speech of 11 June 1985 'Hungarian' by a long chalk. It is rather 'East German,' in Ulbricht's own style: moderated but still effectual centralization plus science, modernity and (Gorbachev's own contribution) energy. He is indeed a Janus figure, exceptionally hard to interpret or predict.

Appendix II: Ogarkov and the Economy

It would make sense for a senior officer, or a military procurement expert, to go further than Romanov's 'modernizing centralism' (Appendix III) and opt for out and out decentralization. He has only to believe that the economy would be more productive that way, so that defense could take more while leaving more to consumption as well. Of course he would need to pay honest prices, and procurement procedures would have more of a voluntary character. But one can accustom oneself to that—and to being less unpopular. Also quality would improve.

Some such thoughts must have inspired 'T. Bul'ba, Ph.D in Economics,' who wrote an economic reform in the serious Party journal of the armed forces in 1973.[57] Behind a hedge of careful words he laments the recent demise (in about 1971) of Kosygin's reforms, from a military point of view. This was a bold thing for a writer to write, or for a publisher to publish, in 1973. The pseudonym fits the action.

The late Thorold Rafto, of Norges Handelshøgskole Bergen, used to say, producing evidence from a visitor to his own seminar, that Marshal Ogarkov was of this mind. But the evidence was indirect and did not really separate his views from those of Romanov.

When we turn, however, from institutions to policy we are on firmer ground. Ogarkov published an interview in the Army daily *Krasnaya zvezda* on 9 May 1984.[58] Considering the controversial nature of his personality it is surprising how anodyne this interview is. Surely, it was but one factor in his dismissal. The three points on which this supposition rests are, as he numbers them:

(i) 'On the one side, one might think, there is the uninterrupted growth of the capability of a nuclear power to annihilate its opponent, and on the other there is an uninterrupted and, I would say, still quicker fall in the aggressor's capability to deal a so called "disarming blow." . . . (because the defending power will always have enough nuclear weapons left over to deal a crushing counter-blow) . . .'

(ii) (Conventional weapons are very much improved and have greatly changed the character of war) 'but this in its turn is conditional on the capability to wage war with conventional weapons that are qualitatively new and incomparably more destructive than before . . .'

(iii) The very rapid development of science and technology in the last years creates real pre-conditions for the appearance quite soon of yet more destructive but previously unknown weapons, based on new physical principles. Work on these new kinds of weapon is already in progress in a number of countries, e.g. the USA. Their development is a reality of the very near future, and to take no account of this would be a serious mistake . . .'

Point (i) is old and well known. It hardly constitutes criticism of current policy, and indeed in the sixth column nuclear weapons are called the 'basic factor in halting an aggressor.'

Point (ii) is a fairly conventional demand for more money, and to that extent indeed a criticism of the civilian government. But the Politburo has heard all that before.

Point (iii), however, refers to the super-sensitive subject of Star Wars, and is a fairly direct attack on Ustinov, who was behind in lasers, and on Gromyko, who was trying, like King Canute, to halt the tide of military invention.

Both points (ii) and (iii) are developed and sharpened versions of what Ogarkov had said a year before (*Izvestiya*, 9 May 1983). This issue was, then, alive already under Andropov.

But all this concerns only Ogarkov's demands upon the economy: not his views on how it should be run. We are not privy to these views. It is, for instance, not at all obvious that in 1981 he demanded, however discreetly, a reform of economic planning.[59]

Appendix III: Romanov and the Economy

Romanov is a modernizer: he used sociologists and town planners very freely while he was in charge of Leningrad.[60] Here, however, are his strictly economic views when he had the great honor of delivering the revolutionary anniversary speech, in 1983 when he had become a Politburo member resident in Moscow (*Pravda*, 6 November 1983).

First, he spoke a great deal on new technology and R and D. This is not surprising, since he had pioneered the shift from Brezhnev's 'production associations' to the new 'science and production associations' of enterprises. Then he said:

> These purposes will also be served by the improvement of the entire mechanism of economic management. The Party has defined the basic areas of work. What is involved here is the *improvement of centralized planning*,[61] the strengthening of plan discipline and Khozraschet, and the development of the initiative of labour collectives. The economic experiments under way in the country to expand the rights of the productions and enterprises and the design and technological organizations of a number of ministries will *help us to find new forms of incentives and of enhancing responsibility*[62] for the final results to work.
>
> Knowing how to take accurately into account the requirements of various

social groups, striving for an optimal combination of personal and local interests with nationwide interests and using them as the motive force of economic growth—this is one of the most important tasks in the improvement of our economic mechanism. In accomplishing this task, a great deal depends on improving the activity of the managerial apparatus.[63] As is known, unjustifiably inflated staffs in some institutions impede the fulfillment of their assigned functions and engender irresponsibility. Therefore, simplifying the administrative apparatus, cutting its cost, reinforcing it with competent personnel capable of operating at peak efficiency in the conditions of the scientific and technological revolution, and raising the level of work of the entire management system remain urgent tasks.

Romanov was later fired by Gorbachev, probably in May 1985, when he went walkabout in Leningrad, Romanov's home base, and denounced alcoholism. This event tells us little we did not already know, unlike the Gromyko case in Appendix IV. Even if we discount the scandalous personal rumors that so often attend the falls of hated direct rivals, it seems unlikely that the two men's slightly divergent attitudes over economics counted for much. There were surely foreign policy clashes, but the basic clashes were over power and sheer life style or personality.

Appendix IV: Gromyko's Actual Views

Gromyko began, of course, as young men must, as a mere executant of top-level policy. His promotion was due to his being supremely competent, conscientious and adaptable. He kept telling foreigners, 'my views do not matter; I am the executant.' However, it seems plain that under Chernenko he ran foreign policy until 26 September 1984 (Appendix I). These, then, were his actual views: hawkish and isolationist.

It is true that he made the speech nominating Gorbachev to the Central Committee, but the speech is remarkably candid, by Soviet standards, for its reference to past disagreements. Moreover, Gromyko appears to have tried to prevent this appointment for some months before[64]—perhaps precisely since that crucial date, 26 September 1984, referred to in Appendix I. Bialer gives no evidence for his statement, but it is certainly rendered plausible by the manner of his departure from Foreign Affairs. On this we note the following:

(i) The presidency, to which Gromyko was raised in July 1985, is a great honor, but Gromyko's words were not warm on that occasion.

(ii) In breaking with custom by not taking it himself, the new General Secretary showed modesty; a characteristic the Soviet people surely admire but very seldom observe in their rulers. But if he had lost an ally at the Ministry of Foreign Affairs this gain would have been quite outweighed. Therefore he was losing no ally: he kicked Gromyko upstairs.

(iii) Further evidence that Gromyko is no ally lies in the appointment of Shevardnadze as his successor. It is inconceivable that the old professional should have approved a total ignoramus, hardly speaking Russian let alone English, however distinguished in other fields, as his successor. But the General Secretary needs somebody pliable in that post (and perhaps, too, appreciates the necessity of having more nonRussian diplomats).

(iv) Shevardnadze's public manner is like that of Gorbachev: open, approachable, nonparanoid. It marks a return to Litvinov after the long ice age of Molotov and Gromyko. The substance is unchanged, but if the manner really takes root it will be difficult not to change the substance. It is not fanciful to relate the new style in foreign ministers to the new style in Politburo wives. If these stylistic changes are considered to be an essential part of modernization they will eventually influence policy.

(v) The International department of the Central Committee apparatus has gained largely from these changes, becoming the official host to many foreign non-communist visitors. But Gromyko always fought for his ministry, and cannot but see in this protocol change a slight to his own senior officials.

All this reasoning lends support to, but does not confirm, our feeling that Gorbachev is a dawk.

As for Gromyko's domestic views, referred to in Section 1 of this chapter, we must affirm that the question is not an absurd one, since he has a Politburo vote. But he has lived many years now isolated from the people, on the seventh floor of his ministry, and knows very little about them. As his daughter Emilia said: 'My father lives in the skies. For twenty-five years he has not set foot in the streets of Moscow. All he sees is the view from the car window.'[65] Perhaps the safest line to take on this is that he is a moderate Stalinist, ignorant of all the latest, and most of the earlier, developments in economic theory and life.[66]

Notes: Chapter 10

For the convenience of the reader, I have translated the titles of all Russian and German articles into English.

1 *Ekonomika i organizatsiya promyshlennogo proizvodstva.*
2 In Jiri Valenta and William Potter (eds), *Soviet Decisionmaking for National Security* (London: Allen & Unwin, 1984), pp. 165–8. Similar thinking is now standard in political science quite outside Sovietology.

3 Permanent, or at least durable, subunits in *sovkhozy* and *kolkhozy*, which operate for their own profit subject to constraints imposed by the farm management. They thus resemble tenant farmers on short leases.

4 Except the *Ekonomika i organizatsiya promyshlennogo proizvodstva* which comes right out with 'reforma.'

5 Archie Brown, 'Andropov, discipline *and* reform?' *Problems of Communism* (January 1983).

6 As in note 33.

7 art. cit. at note 5.

8 Private information.

9 'Brotherhood, warmth and complete mutual understanding' (*Pravda*, 21 December 1982). Ceauşescu, on the contrary, rated only a 'frank, comradely atmosphere' *Pravda*, 21 December 1982). See Brown, art. cit. at note 5. Moreover, the Hungarian Party was the only one to welcome his appointment by a message to the Soviet Central Committee '*led by* Yu. V. Andropov' (*Pravda*, December 1982, my emphasis). There are even stories coming from Budapest of a modern Maria Walewska (Napoleon's Polish mistress)—a Hungarian lady influencing the great despot in her little country's favor in return for her own (past?) favors. But rumors about another Maria Walewska are two a kopek in dictatorships. Similar ones ran about Brezhnev in Moldavia, a republic that has indeed been singularly favored. Incidentally, Maria Walewska did not succeed in freeing Poland.

10 It cannot be too often insisted that a monopoly in a market is very much more responsive than a Soviet producer following a plan. The monopolist does, indeed, restrict output to raise price, but he or she gives consumers the qualities and the innovations that they want. Most Hungarian enterprises, in so small a country, are monopolists.

11 Incidentally, it becomes then possible for a republic to cancel the freedom of its enterprises. This has happened to some extent in Bosnia, where both political and economic Stalinism are more complete than in Hungary.

12 This position is developed at length by Gregory Grossman in Padma Desai (ed.), *Marxism, Central Planning and the Soviet Economy*, Festschrift for Alexander Ehrlich (Cambridge, Mass.: MIT Press, 1983). It is so historically conditioned that economists much underrate its importance. In a word the USSR has, like Australia and Saudi Arabia, been a long-time sufferer from the 'Dutch disease': easy material exports remove the incentive to improve industrial quality.

13 They are not quite the same. In my British experience, young and junior bureaucrats are by far the most inert; junior bureaucrats stay inert, but promotion makes people flexible, until they become more inert again as they pass 60.

14 Tatyana Zaslavskaya's untitled memorandum can be found in *Survey* (London, 1984).

15 Undated document of about 1977. I have been 'privileged' with many such!

16 Alexander Yanov, *Détente after Brezhnev* (Berkeley, Calif.: University of California, Institute of International Studies, 1977), pp. 3–5.

17 The militia were withdrawn to normal duties within about two months, as he must have expected, and things reverted to normal.

18 *Ekonomicheskaya gazeta*, no. 48 (1982), p. 3, col. 1.

19 This is Brown's (art. cit. at note 5) brilliant question. I disagree with his answer. I also avoid the word 'reform' as loaded, since it means good change. I am discussing 'change.'

20 Some countries have patchy data on absenteeism and 'sickness,' especially on Mondays. For the USSR, cf. Kontorovich, 'Discipline and growth in the Soviet economy,' in *Problems of Communism* (December 1985), an excellent, but

inconclusive study of the reaction of Soviet railway performance to Andropov's drive.

21 *Ekonomicheskaya gazeta*, no. 6 (1983), p. 3, col. 4 and p. 4, col. 5; my emphasis.

22 But new consumer goods may be given their prices by the enterprise without consulting the State Committee on Prices (*Pravda*, 23 November 1983, p. 3).

23 *Pravda*, 14 February 1984.

24 As is evident from his speeches in *Pravda*, 10 and 19 February 1983; and his much earlier article, 'The village working collective: ways of socialist development,' *Kommunist*, no. 2 (1976), when he was a mere *obkom* secretary in Stavropol.

25 It should be recalled that one of Andropov's innovations was to publicize in the daily press every meeting of the Politburo and even (?some of) its agenda. The item of 11 March was one such.

26 See note 24.

27 Summarized in *Pravda*, 19 April 1983.

28 See note 14 above.

29 *International Herald Tribune*, 26 September 1984.

30 I leave this paragraph, for honesty's sake, just as it was written in late 1984.

31 This paragraph owes very much to a seminar address by Michael Ellman at the London School of Economics in November 1984.

32 This is a side-issue for us here, but an important one. It has particular reference to satellites and, in fact, this whole debate was launched by recent Polish events. Cf. my article 'Irreversibility: theory and practice,' *Washington Quarterly* (Winter 1984/5).

33 Cf. his 'Contradictions of the development of socialism as a social system,' and his 'Once again on the contradictions of socialism,' in *Voprosy filosofii*, no. 10 (1982) and no. 2 (1984). I owe these references and most of the ideas in the text to Helmut Dahm of the Bundesinstitut für Ostwissenschaftliche Studien, Cologne. Also good is Ernst Kux, 'Contradictions in Soviet socialism,' *Problems of Communism* (November–December 1984).

34 'The avantgarde role of the Communist Party, an important condition of its development,' *Kommunist*, no. 6 (1982).

35 Zaslavskaya, op. cit. at note 14, p. 92.

35a Cf. his speech of 10 September 1984, in his *Izbrannye Rechi*.

36 Cf. his article 'The teaching of Karl Marx and central questions of socialist construction in USSR,' *Kommunist*, no. 3 (1983).

37 Cf. Anatol Dolberg and Peter Wiles, 'The true power position of Khrushchev,' *Osteuropa*, no. 8–9 (1962); and Peter Wiles 'On the export of Revolution,' *Detente* (Birmingham University, Winter 1986).

38 When Khrushchev promoted himself to one capital letter ('First secretary') in 1961 he gave Frol Kozlov the same graphical bonus ('Second secretary'). Suslov took over this capital letter, when in 1976, having long been the chief ideologue, he took over *also* as Second secretary, from the dismissed Kozlov. Thus the Second secretaryship has only connoted the ideology portfolio since 1976. Gorbachev was merely second secretary. Cf. Boris Meissner, 'Soviet policy from Andropov to Chernenko,' *Aussenpolitik*, no. 3 (1984). It is evident as we go to print that Ligachev sees himself as filling Suslov's shoes.

39 Marc D. Zlotnik, 'Chernenko succeeds,' *Problems of Communism* (March–April 1984), p. 27.

40 Cf. Yanov, op. cit. at note 16, ch. 2. It is important that Yanov's celebrated incident of arbitrary supply diversion took place in Romanov's Leningrad.

41 Cf. my *Economic Institutions Compared* (Oxford: Blackwell, 1977), pp. 506–7. It is probably this impressive use of military power that inspired B. P. Kurashvili to exempt the military explicitly; cf. Section 10.

42 Reference is to Hyman Rickover, the US advocate of nuclear submarines and critic of sloppy weapons engineering and undemanding technical education.

43 Cf. Blair A. Ruble, 'Romanov's Leningrad,' *Problems of Communism* (November–December 1983), esp. pp. 46–8.

44 S. S. Il'in, in F. M. Volkov and S. S. Il'in (eds), *Soedinenie dostizhenii NTR s preimushchestvami sotsializma* [Combining the achievements of the scientific-technical revolution with the advantages of socialism] (Moscow, 1977), p. 50; original emphasis.

45 B. N. Topornin, in B. N. Topornin (ed.), *Sotsialisticheskoye gosudarstvo, pravo i NTR* [The socialist state, Law and the Scientific-Technical Revolution] (Moscow, 1975), p. 32. This and the previous quotation were gathered by Erik P. Hoffman and Robbin F. Laird, *The Politics of Economic Modernization in the Soviet Union* (Ithaca, Ill.: Cornell University Press, 1982), p. 95.

46 'State administration of the national economy: perspectives of development,' *Sovetskoye gosudarstvo i pravo*, no. 6 (1982); 'The fate of commodity-branch administration,' *Ekonomika i organizatsiya promyshlennogo proizvodstva*, no. 10 (1982). Cf. Ronald Amann, 'The writings of B. P. Kurashvili,' *Detente* (University of Birmingham, Winter 1987).

47 For all the things that were wrong with the *sovnarkhozy*, cf. my *Political Economy of Communism* (Oxford: Blackwell, 1962), ch. 8.

48 It is better to avoid 'sandwich' sectors with two interfaces, that is, with respect to their inputs and to their outputs. The Soviet *kolkhoz* has, with the passage of time, become such a 'sandwich,' receiving many of its inputs from, and delivering many of its outputs to, enterprises subject to command plan.

49 *Ekonomicheskaya gezeta*, no. 6 (1983), p. 3, col. 4.

50 Two hours a day (? 12 hours a week) total shopping time: Hedrick Smith, *The Russians* (London: Sphere, 1976), p. 87. This is double the ordinary estimate of 35 billion hours a year for the whole urban population. This seems to rest on research by the Ministry of Retail Trade conducted *inside* shops. Leading to 5 hours per woman per week, the estimate is absurdly small. I am now confirmed by V. D. Patrushev, of the Institute of Sociological Research, who makes it 65 billion hours, and evidently includes time spent physically outside shops (*Izvestiya*, January–February, 1985: source, Serge Schmemann, *New York Times*, 6 February 1985; but extensive reading does not reveal the exact date in *Izvestiya*!) Even Patrushev does not include time spent searching for the appropriate shop (e.g. which one has coffee today?). He probably excludes restaurants and public offices, at that. We have applied to these national totals the estimate that women queue 2.25 times as long as men (*Pravda*, 9 June 1984).

51 Before the first Polish price riot in December 1970 there were price riots in Novocherkassk in July 1962. Forgotten by us, this incident, when about 200 people died, is not forgotten in the Kremlin. Note that such price rises would not be successful unless the resulting budget surplus was hoarded, that is, the notes were burned.

52 Including the author, who certainly fell for the standard view of Chernenko at his inception.

53 On this, cf. Meissner, art. cit. at note 38.

54 Private information from one such person. Gorbachev was, and is, of their party, of course. He has even taken pains to insert himself sympathetically into the filmed life of Andropov (*Daily Telegraph*, 13 June 1985).

55 I owe this point to Fabio Bettanin, in *Rinascita*, 17 February 1984. Cf. *Osteuropa*, no. 6 (1984), p. 300.

55a Cf. Dusko Doder, *Shadows and Whispers* (Random House, 1986).

56 Kux, art. cit. at note 33, p. 3.

57 'The root question in the economic policy of the CPSU,' *Kommunist vooruzhennykh sil,* no. 18 (1973). Taras Bul'ba was a Ukrainian Cossack insurgent of the seventeenth century who appears to have been invented by Gogol. Nevertheless, he was a 'historically progressive phenomenon' who has become a favourite subject for historical kitsch painters.

58 I quote p. 3, cols 4 and 5.

59 'Defending peaceful labor,' *Kommunist,* no. 10 (1981), pp. 85–6. He quotes indeed Brezhnev to this effect, but only in order to draw the conclusion that military administration must also be reformed.

60 Ruble, art. cit. at note 43.

61 My emphasis. There is nothing about free choice, profit as a criterion, etc.

62 Note 61 applies here too. 'Responsibility' was something Stalin also demanded; it is not at all the same as power. Indeed, under Stalin they were opposed.

63 This is a little puff for his own management of Leningrad.

64 Seweryn Bialer, *New York Times,* 14 July 1985, p. E27. The speech itself is printed in *Kommunist,* no. 5 (1985).

65 Cf. Arkady Shevchenko, *Breaking with Moscow* (London: Cape, 1985), p. 155. Many senior civil servants in the West are, of course, equally remote; but all politicians must at least face the hustings.

66 Incidentally he has published two books on the US economy! No-one reads them.

Index

251